The Australian economy in the long run

The Australian Economy in the Long Run is the first attempt in over a decade to provide a comprehensive account of the Australian economy of the twentieth century. At the same time, the book makes a contribution to the current debate on the alleged poor growth performance of Australia and the need for fundamental structural changes in the economy, by placing these topics in historical perspective.

The eleven economists and economic historians who have contributed to the book adopt the position that Australia, as a small and open economy, has a limited ability to set the terms on which it interacts with the international economy. Thus in the long run, living standards of Australians are primarily determined by international economic conditions and the responsiveness of the community to changes in them. The long-held strategy of industrialising through the protection of import-competing manufacturing, and through associated heavy labour market regulation, is brought under serious question. This strategy is seen as a major cause of the structural problems that emerged in Australia even before the oil-price shocks of the 1970s.

This book should prove to be of considerable value to students of twentieth century Australian economic history as well as economists and others concerned with the country's serious long-term economic problems and strategies for their solutions.

The Australian economy in the long run

Edited by

RODNEY MADDOCK
Universidad de Antioquia
(*formerly at Australian National University*)
and
IAN W. McLEAN
University of Adelaide

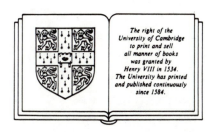

The right of the
University of Cambridge
to print and sell
all manner of books
was granted by
Henry VIII in 1534.
The University has printed
and published continuously
since 1584.

CAMBRIDGE UNIVERSITY PRESS
Cambridge
New York   New Rochelle   Melbourne   Sydney

Published by the Press Syndicate of the University of Cambridge
The Pitt Building, Trumpington Street, Cambridge CB2 1RP
32 East 57th Street, New York, NY 10022, USA
10 Stamford Road, Oakleigh, Melbourne 3166, Australia

First published 1987

Printed in the United States of America

Library of Congress Cataloging-in-Publication Data
The Australian economy in the long run.
Bibliography: p.
1. Australia – Economic conditions – 1945–
I. Maddock, Rodney. II. McLean, Ian W.
HC605.A7767 1987   330.994   86–26345

ISBN 0 521 32674 5 hard covers
ISBN 0 521 33933 2 paperback

British Library Cataloguing-in-Publication Data applied for

TP

Contents

v

viii   **Contents**

Acknowledgements

The contributors to this volume met at the Australian National University on four occasions to discuss progress on their work, a strategy made possible through the support of the Financial and Economic Research Fund of the Reserve Bank of Australia and the Department of Economic History in the Research School of Social Sciences at the Australian National University. At the final meeting of contributors in June 1984, helpful comments on drafts of the chapters were received from the following invited discussants: Alan Barnard, Neville Cain, Selwyn Cornish, Bob Gregory, Fred Gruen, Bryan Haig, Alan Hall, Stuart Harris, Helen Hughes, Neil Johnston, Frank Jones, Michael Keating, and Boris Schedvin.

We are grateful to the anonymous referees for constructive suggestions, and to Colin Day of Cambridge University Press in New York both for his general encouragement and for his detailed comments and suggestions.

Kerry Clift, Cherie Cromwell, Nilss Olekalns, and Yvonne Sheard provided valuable assistance with the production and editing of the manuscript. We are especially indebted to Noel Butlin. He supported the initiation of this project; his ideas and writings have been central to our investigations; and the enterprise would have been made more difficult without the generous access provided to the research facilities of his department.

Contributors

Kym Anderson, University of Adelaide

Matthew W. Butlin, Department of Prime Minister and Cabinet

Michael Carter, University of Canterbury

John W. Freebairn, Monash University

Rodney Maddock, Universidad de Antioquia

Ian W. McLean, University of Adelaide

Adrian Pagan, University of Rochester

Jonathan J. Pincus, Flinders University

David Pope, University of New South Wales

Tom Valentine, Macquarie University

Glenn Withers, La Trobe University

Editors' note

Australian financial years end on June 30, and are indicated throughout this book by the following convention: 1900/1 refers to the year ended June 30, 1901. A clear indication is given where this convention has been departed from.

It is usual practice in Australia to regard gross domestic product (GDP) rather than gross national product (GNP) as the appropriate measure of the performance of the economy. This convention is adopted here.

Introduction

This book provides an overview of the evolution of the Australian economy since federation. The analyses and interpretations offered necessarily rest heavily on the research of others, but we discovered few attempts to integrate this material into a general account of the course of the economy in the twentieth century. Boehm (1979) comes closest, and his summaries of evidence were of great assistance to this project. N. G. Butlin, Barnard, and Pincus (1982) consider the same period but are preoccupied with the changing relationship between government and the private sector; the collection of essays in Forster (1970) offers an uneven coverage of the subject and is now somewhat dated. Australian economists' understandable concern with contemporary events has tended to limit their perspective to the very recent past. For their part, economic historians over the past two or three decades have paid greater attention to the nineteenth century than to the twentieth.

This study emphasises long-run trends in the economy and focuses attention on the major issues of the period rather than offering a detailed account of short-run fluctuations in the economy, the operation of major economic institutions, or the history of specific economic policies. The two principal objectives of the contributions to this volume are thus to account for the long-run performance of the economy and to assess the contribution of economic policies to that performance.

In pursuit of these objectives we have relied mainly though not exclusively on the methods employed and questions posed by economists. This approach in part reflects the skills and orientation of the contributors, but has also been taken in the belief that it complements existing approaches to the same historical terrain. Those aspects of the economy's performance thought to be vital by one generation of Australians (including economists) need not be those that receive most attention from the next. Similarly, changes occur in the prominence given particular economic policies, and not least because of shifts in the intellectual climate in general and in economic theory in particular. To view the experience of earlier decades from the perspective of the 1980s is to some degree unavoidable. However, it is important to attempt also to understand the past in its historical context, and the studies of eco-

1

nomic policies and performance included in this book recognise the essential complementarity that exists between these approaches.

The contributors approached this study of the Australian economy in the long run taking as an initial point of reference the small open economy model. That is, Australia's economy was viewed as having been shaped fundamentally by its international economic relations. Australia has generally been a price taker in world product markets, unable significantly to influence to its advantage the terms under which it traded internationally, booms and slumps in the traded sector being transmitted to the nontraded sector by movements in domestic relative product and factor prices. The importance of foreign investment and of immigration in augmenting, respectively, domestic savings and labour force expansion increased the integration of the world and domestic economies. Thus we see Australia's long-run economic performance as determined heavily by the terms of trade and the country's relative attractiveness to foreign labour and capital. Similarly, we view economic policy as having been formulated within the same exogenously determined constraints.

Of course, as with any stylised perspective, the small open economy model is not meant fully to describe reality. There have been variations in the degree to which external economic influences determined domestic economic performance and conditioned domestic economic policy making. The trade ratio has declined since 1900 and foreign capital and immigration have been variously discouraged and encouraged. During some periods strenuous efforts were made to reduce the economy's vulnerability to external shocks, and short-run domestic policy formation sometimes proceeded apparently little constrained by external factors beyond the policy makers' control. However, the international economic environment remains the fundamental influence on long-run economic performance and the principal consideration in the pursuit of long-run policy goals. Thus, as a shared perspective within which to begin our individual inquiries, the small open economy model appeared the most relevant and powerful.

It was our hope that each chapter would present a coherent view of some aspect of the economy, yet tell a story within the shared framework. Each chapter would be expected to treat the notable events or phenomena of its subject and to place in context at least some of the relevant literature. The approach and views adopted should stimulate debate and research on the twentieth-century Australian economy. In addition, a valuable perspective should be provided to current economic policy questions and to our understanding of the structure and performance of the economy.

Chapter 1 provides an introduction to, and overview of, the long-run growth of the Australian economy, highlighting the nineteenth-century background and indicating some of the principal characteristics of the twentieth-century economy. Chapters 2 through 5 provide a chronological sequence of studies of macroeconomic performance and policies from 1901 to the early 1980s. The two decades of depression (the 1930s) and stagflation (the 1970s) are accorded separate treatment; the three decades following federation and again following 1940 are each viewed as having an internal coherence with respect to broad economic objectives, policies, and (in the case of the latter period) outcomes. Hence Chapters 2 and 4 are much longer than Chapters 3 and 5. Following this survey of the overall experience of the economy, Chapters 6, 7, and 8 treat the major productive sectors, the natural resource, manufacturing, and services industries respectively, each tracing the pattern of sectoral development over the full eighty-year period. The sectoral analysis is followed by chapters on the twentieth-century evolution of the capital and labour markets. The two subsequent chapters stand back a little from the development process to consider some broader implications. Chapter 11 explores the influence of government on the nature of Australian economic development, and Chapter 12 considers the impact of economic growth, structural change, and policies on the level and distribution of wellbeing of the Australian population.

A certain variation among the chapters in style, level of exposition, and breadth of focus remains, as does a small degree of overlap. However, these characteristics are not only inevitable in a collaborative enterprise, but are to some extent desirable. It is extremely difficult when charting the economic landscape of Australia since 1900 not to cross one's path from time to time. Furthermore, the tastes of those with an interest in the development of the Australian economy vary. Particularly with Chapters 5 and 11 we have encouraged a divergence from the general design. With respect to Chapter 5 (the economy in the 1970s), this seemed justified given the comparatively extensive and accessible literature on the subject, including general surveys. It was important that the story told in this volume be brought up to date, but a fresh interpretation was preferred to another telling of a relatively familiar tale about the recent past. Regarding Chapter 11 (on the role of government in the economy), an interpretive essay was also warranted, since many pieces of the subject had to be covered in other chapters. A survey of the topic would have involved excessive repetition, yet its significance in the Australian experience deserved separate consideration.

A word of caution is necessary concerning the limited availability and uneven quality of aggregate economic time series for the period before the second world war. Official estimates of the national accounts begin from 1938/9. All our analyses for earlier years depend directly or indirectly on the series constructed by Noel Butlin (1962). These have been subjected to a variety of criticisms (for example, Boehm 1965, Clark 1963, McLean and Pincus 1982) but little development. All recent interpretations of the evolution of the economy thus rest on a slender statistical base. A small number of the key time series have been reproduced in an appendix to this book, drawn from the unpublished work of Matthew Butlin (1977). To maximise consistency between chapters, this source has been adopted as the standard statistical reference in the volume.

We have tried to minimise the employment of formal techniques and technical terms from economics; however, we have assumed that readers do have some knowledge of economics. For this we make no apologies. To have done otherwise would have severely constrained the exploration of most issues canvassed in the book. It is difficult to discuss almost any substantive issue in economic history without recourse to theoretical economics. Any reader with a principles course behind him or her, or concurrently studying intermediate macro- and microeconomic theory, should have little difficulty coping with the level of exposition adopted.

References

Boehm, E. A. 1965. "Measuring Australian economic growth, 1861 to 1938–39". *Economic Record* 41: 207–39.

  1979. *Twentieth Century Economic Development in Australia*. 2d ed. Melbourne: Longman Cheshire.

Butlin, M. W. 1977. *A Preliminary Annual Database 1900/01 to 1973/74*. Research Discussion Paper 7701. Sydney: Reserve Bank of Australia.

Butlin, N. G. 1962. *Australian Domestic Product, Investment and Foreign Borrowing, 1861–1938/39*. Cambridge: Cambridge University Press.

Butlin, N. G., A. Barnard, and J. J. Pincus. 1982. *Government and Capitalism: Public and Private Choice in Twentieth Century Australia*. Sydney: Allen & Unwin.

Clark, C. 1963. Review of N. G. Butlin, (1962). *Economic History Review* 16: 198–200.

Forster, C. (ed.). 1970. *Australian Economic Development in the Twentieth Century*. Sydney: Allen & Unwin.

McLean, I. W., and J. J. Pincus. 1982. *Living Standards in Australia 1890–1940: Evidence and Conjectures*. Working Papers in Economic History No. 6. Australian National University.

CHAPTER 1

The Australian economy in the very long run

RODNEY MADDOCK AND IAN W. McLEAN

This chapter offers a historical perspective on the Australian economy at the beginning of the twentieth century; an overview of broad trends in economic activity during the period from the gold rushes in the mid nineteenth century to the 1970s; and a succinct introduction to some of the main developments in the twentieth-century economy. It thus provides a context within which the eleven chapters that follow may be located and integrated, especially for readers unfamiliar with the story of the long-run evolution of the economy.

1.1   The historical context

In the early fifteenth century there began a period of overseas expansion by European societies that was to last for five centuries. The Portuguese and Spanish were the first to establish maritime empires, with the Dutch, the English, and French also early participants in the process. The complex impulses behind this outward movement encompassed in addition to intellectual curiosity and sheer adventure the search for profits either from trade or plunder and the equally avid search for souls to save. The process also reflected an international extension of the rivalries existing among the fledgling nation states of Europe. By the eighteenth century the principal rivalry was that between France and England, with contested territorial claims in the West Indies, India, and North America. At the close of that century the first British empire was dealt a serious blow with the successful revolt of the thirteen American colonies.

It was at this time, between the American war of independence and the outbreak of war with France in Europe, that Britain reinforced its claim to Australia and in 1788 created the first settlement there, albeit one of unusual social composition. The decision to establish a colony at Botany Bay makes sense only in the wider context of eighteenth-century imperial competition and, specifically, the recent loss of the thirteen colonies. The motives underlying that decision are the subject of debate among Australian historians. Reflecting the larger mosaic of European overseas expansion, possible reasons for the settlement at

5

Botany Bay include strategic moves to counter possible French designs in the South Pacific, prospects for trade in naval supplies, and the desire to find a new location for the convicts previously transported to the American colonies.

In the century after 1815 the expansion of European influence and economic power continued; it probably reached its peak at the outbreak of the first world war. An international economy emerged that integrated the industrialising societies in Western Europe in a complex pattern of relationships with widely scattered regions of the globe. Trade between Europe and distant parts had, of course, existed before. What emerged in the nineteenth century, however, was different both in kind and in the degree of its importance to Britain and other European nations. The volume of trade rose faster than that of domestic output, making the participating economies increasingly open to international influence. An international payments system emerged in the form of the gold standard, which functioned satisfactorily until the first world war. Investments on a historically unprecedented scale were made by Europe in the United States, Latin America, India, Britain's white colonies, and even Russia. Immigration from Europe to the "new world" and beyond occurred at rates far above those of earlier centuries.[1]

This newly formed international economy is sometimes described in terms of two sets of actors: the countries of the "centre" and those of the "periphery". Britain is in the leading role among the former. The share of her workforce engaged in manufacturing was rising while that in agriculture fell. Real per capita incomes increased over the century as a whole despite the growth in population, which itself was becoming increasingly urbanised. In this context, economic growth and prosperity came to depend more heavily on two conditions: the availability of raw material supplies for industry and food for the urban population on the one hand, and on the other a continuing growth in demand for the new industrial products. By the 1820s it was demonstrated that it was profitable to ship Australian wool to the English textile mills, later to ship Kansan or Californian wheat to Liverpool, and by the end of the century to land Argentine chilled beef or New Zealand refrigerated butter on the London market. These countries of recent settlement in the periphery possessed an abundance of farmland and were developing more efficient techniques of agricultural production than prevailed in Britain. As a consequence, considerable adjustment was required in British agriculture, but the reallocation of the workforce towards industry raised

---

[1] Surveys of the international economy during the nineteenth century are contained in Foreman-Peck (1983) and Kenwood and Lougheed (1983).

average productivity and hence incomes. In turn this contributed to the growth in domestic demand for manufactured goods, to which was added the growing foreign demand. The latter arose initially because industrialisation elsewhere lagged behind that in Britain. Hence the demand for manufactured goods by countries in the periphery was paid for out of their receipts from exporting the food and raw materials demanded in the industrialising centre.

Economic interaction between centre and periphery was not confined to mutually beneficial trade based on the exploitation of comparative advantage. European savings were invested abroad, and the best returns were found frequently in those countries with which the closest trade ties existed. The result was the gradual creation and integration of an international capital market, with its centre in London. As well, the centre became a large exporter of labour to the periphery. The tendency was for flows of both labour and capital to fluctuate together and, with some exceptions, to exhibit a similar geographical distribution. This flow of factors served to increase the markets abroad for European industrial products. The system was therefore mutually reinforcing and produced a virtuous circle of growth and trade down to 1914. Not until the period between 1945 and the early 1970s do we observe again a similarly favourable conjunction of events in the world economy.

This centre/periphery characterisation of the nineteenth century is a useful simplifying device, but not all the historical evidence fits neatly into it. For example, the British invested in India and the French in Russia, but in neither case were there accompanying flows of migrants. The Australian case fits rather well, however, in the close relationship that existed between the six colonies and Britain in trade, investment, and migration, and, more fundamentally, in that Australia at the time of federation in 1901 was very largely a creation of the international economy.

Australia thus shares with a number of countries and regions a common development experience through its integration with the emerging and vigorous world economy of the nineteenth century. It is also one of several countries outside Europe in the temperate zones that at the beginning of the nineteenth century were sparsely inhabited by non-Europeans, and had either no or only limited numbers of European settlers. By 1900 the populations of these countries had grown rapidly as a result of the infusions of European immigrants; they had occupied their respective frontiers; and they had created for their transplanted inhabitants and their descendants standards of living that were in most cases the equivalent of or better than those enjoyed in the regions of northwestern Europe where the industrial revolution had first matured.

These regions of recent European settlement included Argentina, Uruguay, New Zealand, Australia, South Africa, and all of Canada and the United States west of the Mississippi and the Great Lakes.[2] Between 1821 and 1915 more than forty million Europeans emigrated, primarily to these countries. In the process the last major areas of the globe that were easily settled were occupied, and the outward movement of Europeans that began five centuries earlier with the Portuguese exploration of the northwest coast of Africa had reached its limits.

1.2   Australian economic growth before 1900

In 1815 the Napoleonic wars ended and a century of remarkable economic progress in Western Europe and North America was ushered in. In Australia in that same year the European population numbered a mere fifteen thousand – a very small community tentatively occupying a land mass having almost the same area as the continental United States. In the quarter century since the first of their number had arrived, however, the settlements of whites had attained some measure of economic self-sufficiency, and even prosperity, relative to the hardships that had attended their initial years. The principal economic activities were small-scale farming and a variety of "public sector" functions associated with the operations of the penal institutions. The latter gave a peculiar character to early white Australian society, but that society should not be thought of as simply a prison, nor its economy as that of a jail and hence based solely on command rather than market allocative mechanisms. Small numbers of immigrants were joining the emancipists and the native born in the free population. Nonetheless, in 1815 the prospects for the European presence in Australia – its geographic spread, its growth in numbers, its political evolution, and its economic base – must have seemed very uncertain to the colonists.

By the end of the century the fifteen thousand had become four million, and a highly urbanised society and diversified, open economy delivered to the greatly expanded population an average standard of living that may have been the equal of that enjoyed anywhere. This was a notable achievement, considering especially the distance from Britain, the dominant trading partner and source of foreign capital and immigrants, and considering too the unfavourable initial conditions. For the Australian economy in the nineteenth century was essentially built from scratch. In North America westward expansion in the nineteenth century, which shares many of the characteristics of Australian history,

---

[2] The study by Denoon (1983) compares the southern hemisphere members of the group.

proceeded from a contiguous area along the Atlantic coast that had been settled for nearly two centuries, and within which industrial development was occurring in a manner similar to that observed in northwestern Europe. But Australia at the beginning of the nineteenth century possessed no comparable regions, and the subsequent economic development effort was thereby more total. How was it achieved?

It may be helpful to characterise Australian economic development during the nineteenth century as having been shaped essentially by the interaction of two very broad sets of forces. From the supply side, the important influences were the progressive expansion of the natural resource base as a result of the discovery of land suitable for farming and of mineral deposits; the expansion of the workforce as a result not only of the natural rate of increase in the initially small resident population but also by immigration; and the augmentation of domestic savings and investment through foreign borrowing. Other things being equal, the growth of the economy was closely and positively related to the rate at which these factors of production were accumulated. From the demand side, a high rate of population growth stimulated certain types of production, especially the provision of foodstuffs, building and construction activity, and the supply of other nontradable goods and services. In addition, Australia exported large (in per capita terms) quantities of natural resource–intensive commodities in strong international demand, exploiting a comparative advantage, and importing those commodities that either could not be produced domestically or could be produced only at very great cost. The level of aggregate demand in the economy was therefore subject to both domestic and foreign influences.

These demand and supply forces interacted to produce periods of faster or slower growth during the century, to influence the rate and the geographic spread of settlement, and to shape also the structure of the domestic economy as well as the volume and commodity composition of foreign trade. If we adopt a more chronological perspective, four broad phases in the development of the economy between about 1820 and the end of the century can be discerned.[3]

During the 1820s and 1830s there occurred the first pastoral boom based on the raising of merino wools on natural grassland for export in an unprocessed state to British woollen manufacturers. Australia had discovered an export staple that was ideally suited to a land-abundant but labour-scarce economy, that required little physical investment (be-

---

[3] Introductions to the economic history of the Australian economy in the nineteenth century are offered by Jackson (1977) and Sinclair (1976). For an excellent survey of writings on the history of the economy covering the entire period of European settlement see Schedvin (1979).

yond the building up of sheep numbers), and that was sufficiently valuable relative to its weight that no great obstacles were posed either by the extremely primitive state of inland transport or by the long sea journey to Britain. Despite a sharp recession in the early 1840s, the initial occupation for grazing purposes of a large land area running from southern Queensland to coastal South Australia was under way. Although wool was the staple export, agriculture more broadly defined flourished near population centres and where soil and climatic conditions permitted. Especially in South Australia and during the 1840s, more specialised wheat growing for intercolonial markets using primitive mechanical harvesting technology began on coastal plains close to ports. In the same colony and decade, copper was discovered, mined, and exported. By 1851 the total European population had reached 400,000. Sydney had 54,000 residents and Melbourne 29,000, early evidence of a high degree of concentration of the population in a few urban areas that has continued to this day. In 1851 the towns contained a range of manufacturing establishments, but there was no industrial activity of any complexity; food processing, brewing, brick works, and sawmills dominated. Nonetheless, by mid century, with the transportation of convicts all but ended, the Australian colonies were firmly established, the European occupation secure, the domestic economy exhibiting some modest diversification, and one major export commodity underpinning economic prosperity.[4]

In the 1850s the Australian economy experienced a boom of which the relative magnitude has not since been equalled. Gold was discovered in 1851, first in New South Wales, then in Victoria. The production of gold in the peak years was of the same magnitude as in California, where the rush had begun three years earlier. Wool was displaced by gold as the principal export for almost the next two decades. The population jumped from 400,000 to 1.1 million in ten years. Fortuitously, the deposits initially discovered were alluvial, thus attracting large numbers of immigrant fortune seekers. Furthermore, the discoveries were made in areas that, although at the time occupied by pastoralists for grazing sheep, were, as a consequence of the regional demands of the goldfields population for food, soon found to be capable of more intensive agriculture and thus closer settlement. Hence agriculture, building, and construction all received a major stimulus from the economic boom. There was considerable leakage to imports from the surge in domestic

---

[4] N. G. Butlin (1984) reports the first attempt to devise national product measures for Australia for 1788–1860.

incomes, and wool growing languished, though the increased demand for meat helped cushion the sheep owners from the massive adjustments that occurred in the economy.[5]

The boom was not followed by bust. With the exception of a few years in the early 1860s during the New Zealand gold rushes, net immigration remained positive. Whatever their initial motivations, the great majority of people attracted directly or indirectly by gold in the 1850s stayed on as permanent settlers in occupations other than goldmining. The 1850s also mark the separation of both Victoria and Queensland from New South Wales and the granting of "responsible" self-government by Britain. The whole complexion of Australia – demographic, social, political, and economic – had been greatly changed during this tumultuous decade at mid century.

From the 1860s to 1890 the expansion of the wool industry resumed, but the second pastoral boom is less dominant as an engine of growth than in the pregold era. In the first place, gold production declined only slowly, thus making a continuing contribution to the balance of payments and also to the attractiveness of Australia to British investors. Second, farming for purposes other than specialist wool production replaced pastoral activity in some areas in southeastern Australia. Wheat, meat, dairy products, and beef were produced, often on "mixed" farms also producing some wool. The sheep station producing only (or mainly) wool may have been the typical enterprise type in the drier, marginal inland areas into which the graziers drove their flocks during these decades, but wool was also produced on smaller and more diversified selectors' holdings. Third, in the period after the gold rush, colonial governments became deeply involved with what might be labelled a "development strategy". They issued bonds on the London market, sold public lands, and collected modest sums from revenue tariffs. From these sources they financed the construction of railways, roads, ports, and urban utilities; they continued the practice of subsidising immigration; and they funded higher education and agricultural research and set up postal, telegraph, and later telephone systems. Public enterprise was the prevalent form of many utilities, enhancing their scope as agencies of state-directed economic development. But by the end of the 1880s there were signs of stress in the colonial economies, of which the continuing prosperity was dependent on the expansion of wool and other exports on the one hand and, on the other, a concomitant willingness on the part of the London capital market to continue lending to Aus-

[5] A recent study is by Maddock and McLean (1984).

tralian governments to finance imports and agricultural, transport, and urban development.[6]

The 1890s saw the first major recession in the economy since that of the 1840s, and significant shifts occurred in the composition of economic activity. The causes of the downturn included the serious overextension of the wool industry into areas that were found through bitter experience to have low and very unreliable rainfall; heavy investment by governments in development infrastructure having at best low returns in the long run; a speculative property boom mainly centred in Melbourne; and changed perceptions in the capital market in London concerning the wisdom of continued lending to Australia. Whatever the balance of contributing causes, the early 1890s saw a very sharp reduction of the sheep population, a major shakeout in the financial sector, a cessation of immigration, and increased unemployment. There was no general economic collapse, however. Economic activity was supported by a strong and timely revival in the gold industry and by a diversification of agricultural exports. Gold production during the 1890s, particularly from new discoveries in Western Australia, exceeded the peak levels attained during the 1850s. The diversification of farm exports occurred as a consequence not simply of the steep decline in wool production, but also of the growth of mixed and nonpastoral farming, especially wheat, meat, and dairy farming. In addition, the successful introduction of refrigeration to long-distance shipping in the 1880s opened the British market to Australian meat and dairy producers.[7]

Recovery from the recession began in the second half of the 1890s. However, a severe drought at the turn of the century delayed for several years any sustained upturn. Thus federation in 1901 occurred at the end of a decade that had seen no general economic prosperity. The regional and structural shifts that had occurred during the decade had nonetheless laid the basis for the further development of the new export industries, and the reconstruction of the pastoral industry would be to its long-run benefit, however painful the short-run adjustment. The 1890s also witnessed important developments in the capital and labour markets that were to have implications for twentieth-century economic history. The shakeout among financial institutions, particularly in Victoria, cast a long shadow over banking practices and regulations. In the labour market, a decade of unaccustomed lack of employment opportunities and particularly bitter industrial disputes lay behind growing pressure for

---

[6] The late nineteenth century has been extensively researched by Noel Butlin; most relevant to the present discussion are (1959) and (1964).

[7] A major study of the 1890s is reported in Boehm (1971).

extensive regulation, culminating in the establishment in the early years of federation of the commonwealth arbitration court.

Economic development in the nineteenth century was, therefore, based largely on the importation of labour (immigrants) and capital (British savings) to exploit the natural resource endowment (agricultural and mineral) for the production of a number of resource-intensive commodities in which Australia had a comparative advantage. The symbiotic economic relationship with Britain was completed by strong British demand for these commodities and British ability to supply Australia's import requirements.

1.3   Long-run economic performance 1861–1981

The federation of Britain's six Australian colonies occurred on January 1, 1901, but the immediate economic impact of this dramatic political event was slight. Indeed, the progress of the economy during the period up to 1914 does not appear to have been greatly affected, directly or indirectly, by the act of federation. That cruel arbiter of Australia's agricultural prosperity, drought, had a far greater impact on economic conditions at the turn of the century. Why, then, begin our inquiry into the evolution of the modern Australian economy at federation? One reason is that the new federal government acquired constitutional powers that led eventually to its dominance over the state governments in such important areas as regulation, macromanagement, and economic development. The constitution also provided for a free trade area between regions where tariffs had previously existed. Federation therefore marks a step in the gradual integration of the colonial economies into a single market, a process that had received a considerable fillip from the gold rushes of the 1850s and from such transport innovations as the river boats and railways. For the student of the history of the Australian economy there is also a practical convenience in selecting 1901 as a benchmark date. Source material, particularly official statistical collections, not only becomes more abundant from that time but is more likely to be available on a consistent national basis. Reconstructing "Australian" aggregates from information available for the six colonies is frequently complex and sometimes impossible.

The few long-run aggregate series that exist permit only the broadest comparisons of the pre- and postfederation performance of the economy. However, they do provide some quantitative evidence to support the earlier discussion of late-nineteenth-century economic growth. Annual estimates of gross domestic product are available from 1861. In this section we shall use these and related series to offer a first impression

Table 1.1. *Economic performance indicators, 1861 to 1981/2 (cols. A to D: annual growth rates, percentages; col. E: average annual rate, percentages)*

Years	Real GDP (A)	Population (B)	Real GDP per capita (C)	GDP deflator (D)	Unemployment (E)
1861 to 1889	4.8	3.5	1.3	−0.4	N.A.
1889 to 1904/5	0.8	1.7	−0.8	−0.1	N.A.
1904/5 to 1913/14	5.2	2.3	2.9	2.2	3.9
1913/14 to 1919/20	−1.6	1.3	−2.6	8.2	3.9
1919/20 to 1929/30	3.2	1.9	1.1	−0.8	6.0
1929/30 to 1938/9	1.6	0.8	0.6	0.1	13.5
1938/9 to 1945/6	3.4	1.0	2.4	3.7	3.0
1945/6 to 1973/4	4.8	2.2	2.5	5.8	1.9
1973/4 to 1981/2	2.4	1.3	1.1	9.0	5.6

Note: All series except unemployment are expressed as annual average growth rates (percentages). Unemployment is the average rate, in percentages, for the year following the beginning year to the end year of each subperiod.
Sources: 1861 to 1973/4: cols. A, C, and D: McLean and Pincus 1982: 29–31; col. B: Australian Bureau of Statistics, *Demography Bulletin*; col. E: M. W. Butlin 1977: 90–92.
    1973/4 to 1981/2: cols. A, C, and D: Australian Bureau of Statistics, *Australian National Accounts, National Income and Expenditure, 1981–82* (Canberra, March 1983); col. E: *Reserve Bank Bulletin*, December 1981 and July 1982.

of the changing performance of the economy in this century. Thus in Table 1.1 is shown for nine subperiods between 1861 and 1981/2 the rates of real growth in the economy, of population increase, of the improvement in living standards, and of inflation, and the average level of unemployment.[8]

We have described previously how the long period of growth and prosperity that followed the gold rushes of the 1850s gave way in the 1890s to over a decade of recession and drought-induced stagnation in the economy. The first two rows in Table 1.1 starkly summarise the contrast between these two periods: The rate of population increase was halved; real output growth fell from a vigorous 4.8 percent before 1890 to under 1 percent per year over the next fifteen years; and living standards (real GDP per person) declined slightly after 1890 following the steady rise recorded across the three previous decades. The now formally

---

[8] The data on the GDP and GDP deflator are basically derived from N. G. Butlin (1962), though amended by subsequent scholars.

integrated economy that entered the new century did so against a background of poor recent performance.

After the ending of the droughts at the turn of the century economic activity recovered strongly, and in the decade to the first world war there was a return to growth in living standards and a resumption of immigration (Table 1.1). In part this represented a rebound from the depressed conditions of the 1890s, but the economic growth recorded between 1904/5 and 1913/14 was sustained beyond the recovery phase. The international economy grew strongly from the mid 1890s to 1914, and Australia participated in these last years of the era of general prosperity.

During the first world war the economy experienced some contraction – at least according to the estimates reported in Table 1.1. Temporarily cut off from traditional sources of imports, with export markets disturbed by the demands of the war economy in Britain, and with trade restricted by curtailed shipping capacity, Australia was sharply reminded of its dependence on international trade for its economic prosperity and specifically of its vulnerability to changes in Britain's economic circumstances. The first world war did, however, stimulate some import substitution, a development that was to lead to demands for tariff protection in the 1920s when peacetime trading returned.

The 1920s marked, as in other high-income countries, the appearance in significant numbers of the new symbols of private affluence and status – automobiles, telephones, and radios, for example. Assisted immigration was resumed, and there was also renewed government encouragement for the expansion or intensification of rural production and settlement. Despite the diffusion of consumer durables and the stimulus to further rural development, unemployment remained higher than before the war even before the economic slowdown began. Declining world prices for primary products, together with the failure of the migration and closer settlement schemes, indicated that economic prosperity was not any longer to be found in the development strategy that had been successful before 1914. Some economic indicators started turning down two years or more before the crash on Wall Street in late 1929 heralded the beginning of the depression in the United States. Overall, as revealed in Table 1.1, the decade before 1929 did not represent a return to "normalcy", if by that term is meant the economic performance attained before 1890 and again in the ten years prior to World War I. There were serious problems in the Australian economy well before the world depression made its full impact.[9]

The depression of the 1930s was severely felt, though the fall in real

---

[9] Chapter 2 focuses on the history of the economy between 1900 and 1930.

output in Australia was less than that which occurred in the United States. The peak unemployment rate may have reached 30 percent among trade union members; at the census in the middle of 1933, when recovery was just beginning, the rate of unemployment among all workers was closer to 20 percent. Recovery was slow. The level of economic activity by the late 1930s had only marginally exceeded the levels that were recorded in the 1920s, and unemployment remained sticky, averaging over 13 percent across the 1930s – more than twice the twenties average rate of 6 percent. In Australia as elsewhere there was some experimentation with policies to assist recovery, including inducements to grain growers to expand wheat production, devaluation, increases in tariff protection, a general wage reduction, and public relief schemes.[10] However, the climb out of the depression was completed only under the stimulus of war. For the impact of the second world war on the economy stood in sharp contrast to that of the first. The period between 1939 and 1945 was one of vigorous growth in output and living standards and, by historical standards, relatively full employment of resources (Table 1.1).

The long economic boom in the world economy that followed the end of the second world war was fully shared by Australia. International demand for agricultural and mineral products was generally buoyant: Wool, meats, sugar, wheat, beef, iron ore, and bauxite/alumina were major export earners at one time or other. During this period the economy grew at the same average rate (4.8 percent) as it had in the long boom of the late nineteenth century, there was a similar prolonged surge in immigration, and there was a return to substantial inflows of foreign capital. Living standards rose steadily, and the economy operated throughout the period at levels closer to full employment than at any time since at least 1890. The population almost doubled from seven to thirteen million. It was also a period of rapid industrial development, with immigrants forming an important component of the manufacturing workforce, and of the return of mineral industries to prominence as export earners.[11] When the world economic boom sputtered out in the early 1970s with a crisis in the international monetary system and the major hikes in the world oil price, Australia did not escape contagion.

The contrast between the economic experience of the 1970s and the preceding two and a half decades is clearly evident in Table 1.1. Lower levels of immigration were the principal cause of a reduction in the rate

---

[10] The depression was the subject of a major study by Schedvin (1970) and is the topic of Chapter 3 in this volume.

[11] Chapter 4 contains an analysis of developments in the economy between 1939 and the end of the postwar boom.

of population increase; the underlying growth rate of the economy was halved, while in per capita terms the decline was even greater; and there were significant and simultaneous increases in inflation and unemployment. The averages in the table for the period 1973/4 to 1981/2 mask considerable annual variation in levels of activity – an additional point of contrast to the pre-1973 era of relative economic stability. Economic policy debates focused on the eradication of stagflation, and structural problems in highly protected segments of the manufacturing sector also attracted increasing attention.[12] Some observers drew parallels with the experience of the 1930s, especially regarding the levels of unemployment, which were the highest since the depression, but the comparison was an ill-fitting one. Unemployment, though serious by postwar standards, was less than half the level of the 1930s; the price level rose rapidly during the 1970s, whereas in the early 1930s it had declined; and although aggregate growth and living standards rose sluggishly, there were no marked declines in absolute levels as had occurred in the early 1930s. After nearly three postwar decades of economic growth and prosperity, which most Australians had probably come to regard as the normal state of economic affairs, it was perhaps understandable that there should emerge a fear of a 1930s-type economic collapse. If the 1970s experience is to be compared with an earlier episode of Australia's economic history, a stronger case might be made for the similarities with the 1920s (though the price level behaved quite differently). It is perhaps salutary to note that during the 1970s the economy grew at a rate close to the average for the entire span of years between 1861 and 1981, a reminder that what is normal and what exceptional in economic performance may be very much a question of perspective.

If we step back from this chronological account of the economy's fortunes it is possible to make some broader observations about very long-run trends. One is that the Australian economy since the 1860s has moved, with few exceptions, in sympathy with the state of the international economy, sharing the depressions or recessions (in the 1890s, 1930s, and 1970s) and the intervening periods of greater or less prosperity. The Australian recovery from the 1890s recession was delayed by climatic and perhaps other domestic causes, but the broad conformity to the generalisation seems clear. A second observation is that only a slight increase is recorded in per capita GDP over the half century between 1890 and 1940 considered as a whole. On the basis of available

---

[12] Chapter 5 examines the recent record of the economy. An inquiry by a group of North American economists into many aspects of the Australian economy in the 1970s and early 1980s is in Caves and Krause (1984).

statistics, rises during these decades were almost totally offset by falls, implying virtual stagnation in living standards as conventionally measured. A major issue for economic historians is why two periods of relative success (before 1890 and after 1945) were separated by such a long period of apparent failure.[13] A final observation is that Australia has experienced much higher rates of population growth than most other advanced economies this century. This reflects in large part the social consensus that existed until recently on the desirability of rapid population increases through immigration whenever conditions in the labour market were bouyant. Although the long-run economic consequences of immigration have not been fully articulated, a number of important links have been identified.[14]

This quick sketch of the performance of the economy in the very long run has drawn attention to only the boldest features of the historical landscape. To emphasise the principal changes and the conventional chronology, however, does offer a basis from which thematic or period-specific issues in twentieth-century economic history may be examined in more detail. And that, of course, is the purpose of the eleven chapters that follow.

1.4   Salient features of the economy since 1900

Economic growth in the twentieth century has not taken the form simply of replicating on a larger scale the 1900 methods of production, mix of occupations, or commodity composition of output, all within a static institutional framework.[15] In this sense, the figures in Table 1.1 that formed the basis of the discussion in the last section are unhelpful, even misleading. In the following paragraphs we indicate some of the more important changes in the economy since 1900. These include shifts in the relative importance of primary, secondary, and tertiary economic activities, in the size and functions of the public sector, and in the nature and significance of Australia's international economic relationships. Also of particular interest to the student of this economy is the process of factor accumulation. This selection is based in part on their relevance to the analysis of any modern economy over the long run, partly because

---

[13] McLean and Pincus (1983) evaluate the evidence suggesting slow growth in living standards. This topic is further examined in Chapter 12.

[14] The economic–demographic links are considered especially in Chapters 2 and 10 below. Important studies that include nineteenth-century experience are those of Hall (1963) and Kelley (1965).

[15] Useful sources of statistical information on the economy since 1900 are Boehm (1979) and M. W. Butlin (1977).

Table 1.2. *Changing structure of the economy (as percentage of* GDP *at factor cost)*

Year	Farming	Mining	Manufacturing	Other
1900/1	19.3	10.3	12.1	58.3
1913/14	23.5	5.1	13.4	58.0
1919/20	23.5	3.0	13.5	60.0
1928/9	21.2	1.8	16.7	60.3
1938/9	19.5	3.3	18.5	58.7
1948/9	21.3	2.5	26.2	50.0
1955/6	15.9	2.3	28.0	53.8
1962/3	12.6	1.7	26.8	58.9
1968/9	9.6	2.4	26.1	61.9
1973/4	9.6	4.0	23.2	63.2
1980/1	5.4	6.5	20.6	67.5

Note: The adoption in 1971 of a standard industrial classification means that the series from 1962/3 on are not entirely consistent with the previous years.
Sources: Boehm 1979: Table 1.1; Australian Bureau of Statistics, *Australian National Accounts, National Income and Expenditure, 1981/82.*

of their special place throughout Australia's economic history, and partly because of the perspective on that history adopted in this book.

Structural change

By 1900 the Australian economy had already acquired many of the structural characteristics of modern urban industrial societies. For example, the "primary" sector (agriculture and mining) accounted for less than a third of economic activity, and the most important broad group of industries were in the "services" sector (building and construction, government administration, transport, financial services, retailing, etc.). Australia was therefoe well removed from the image it sometimes has that at this time its population comprised mainly pastoralists grazing sheep on large outback properties. In one important respect, however, the economy was not yet "modern" – the manufacturing sector was relatively small (Table 1.2), and industrial activities in the main consisted of simple processing of primary products and raw materials. Thus Australia did not pass in linear fashion through a sequence of stages that can neatly be labelled agricultural, industrial, and service sector–dominated. At least from the 1860s, when sectoral output estimates become available, the service sector has been of considerable importance. Australia's highly efficient and largely export-oriented agricultural and mineral industries underwrote a high standard of living for its residents that generated a strong demand for services. Being essentially nontraded activities, these were met from within Australia, while the demands for capital goods and for many manufactured consumer products were satisfied by imports.[16]

Subsequent changes in the sectoral composition of the economy are readily summarised (Table 1.2). The importance of farming (ignoring the short-run fluctuations to which Australian agriculture is particularly prone) was unchanged until after the second world war, since when its contribution to GDP has declined to around 5 percent, compared with over 20 percent for most of the first half of the century. The relative importance of mining at federation was temporarily boosted by the surge in gold production at the end of the nineteenth century. As this subsided, so did the economic significance of the mineral industry within the economy. Only in the 1960s and 1970s did a succession of mineral discoveries and major mining projects modestly lift the share of the industry in total production – though not back to its 1900 level of importance, despite the impression that may have been given by the frequent use in recent years of the term "minerals boom". If the agricultural and mining industries are jointly considered as the natural resource sector, then its importance has declined from just below 30 percent of production at the beginning of the century to about 12 percent in 1981.[17]

The relative importance of manufacturing in the economy increased little until the 1920s, when a number of new industries were established and a protective tariff was raised. However, the industrialisation process (at least viewed as a share of output) received its greatest push during the second world war, with the urgent demands for equipment and munitions not just from the Australian military but also from American armed forces in the southwest Pacific theatre. The 1950s and 1960s are, however, usually thought of as a period in which manufacturing truly flourished in Australia, and a great expansion in the iron and steel, automobile, consumer durables, and other major industries did occur during the postwar boom. The growth of the industrial sector was, however, only in step with that of the whole economy, thus leaving its share approximately the same in 1948/9 and 1968/9, as the figures in Table 1.2 indicate.

From the late 1960s the relative importance of manufacturing has declined, as it has in many Western economies, suggesting that the causes

---

[16] Further analysis of the changes in the structure of the economy, and in particular of the place of services therein, is given in Chapter 8.
[17] See Chapter 6 for a study of agriculture and mining since 1900.

are not specific to Australia. In one respect, however, both the rise and decline of manufacturing in Australia are associated with a special feature, namely, the importance of tariff policy. Taking the broadest view, it is clear that much of Australia's twentieth-century industrialisation was induced by government policies, with the tariff being the principal though not the only policy instrument. There was in the early decades an expectation that with initial encouragement industry would eventually become cost competitive through reaping scale economies, for example, and survive with less protection. The policy succeeded in encouraging the domestic production of import-competing goods; it failed to produce a viable manufacturing base. The shakeout in the automobile, shipbuilding, apparel, iron and steel, and other industries in recent years is a sign of this failure, and the figures in Table 1.2 indicate its magnitude – from above 26 percent of GDP at factor cost in 1968/9 the share of manufacturing had fallen by 1980/1 to under 21 percent.[18]

Government and the economy

Around the turn of the century, social experimentation and reforms in Australia attracted international attention. One aspect frequently commented on was the propensity of Australians to seek solutions to social and economic problems through government rather than through private sector action. We have noted previously the prominent role of government in the economic development of the colonies and the spate of labour market and social welfare legislation in the 1890s and 1900s. Australia thus entered the twentieth century with a tradition of greater government intervention in economic life than was true of either Britain or the United States.

The changing role of the government in the economy is notoriously difficult to quantify, and only proxy indicators are available. One is the share of public sector employment in total employment; this rose between federation and the first world war, during the second world war, and in the 1970s (Table 1.3). By 1981 almost a quarter of the workforce were employed in government and its agencies, more than twice the 1900 figure. It should be emphasised that these workers were not all public service bureaucrats – they include employees of the many publicly owned trading enterprises (such as airlines, railways, telecommunications, and electricity supply authorities) operated by the federal or state governments, and of the publicly funded schools, hospitals, universities,

---

[18] Chapter 7 takes up the examination of the manufacturing sector and of government policies towards it.

Table 1.3. *Government shares of investment and employment (percentages)*

Year	(A)[a]	(B)[b]
1900/1	51.8	8.7
1913/14	48.3	11.9
1919/20	51.5	13.3
1928/9	52.6	14.5
1938/9	54.8	13.7
1948/9	37.2	18.7
1950/1	39.6	19.1
1955/6	36.1	19.3
1962/3	35.8	18.8
1968/9	34.8	19.3
1973/4	32.7	19.7
1980/1	31.7	23.1

[a](A): Public sector investment as a percentage of gross domestic capital formation.
[b](B): Public sector employment as a share of total employment.
Sources: M. W. Butlin 1977; N. G. Butlin, Barnard, and Pincus 1982; Australian Bureau of Statistics, *Labour Statistics* and *Quarterly Estimates of National Income and Expenditure.*

and research organisations, as well as those employed in government administration. By contrast, the share of public sector investment in aggregate gross domestic investment has substantially declined since federation (Table 1.3). Before the second world war governments and their agencies accounted for approximately half of all capital formation. This ratio was much lower after the war, and has trended further downward during the past three decades to less than one-third. The increased importance of private foreign investment, especially in mining and manufacturing in the postwar years, and the end of major rural development schemes based on publicly provided infrastructure are two factors contributing to the change.

There is, of course, much more to the story of the economic role and influence of governments than is reflected in the movement in these ratios. However, they point to the importance that must be accorded this topic in any survey of the Australian economy this century.[19]

---

[19] The relationship between government policy and economic performance is a theme in

Table 1.4. *Components of population growth (average annual rate of growth, in percentages)*

Period	Natural increase (1)	Net migration (2)	Total (3)	(2) ÷ (3) × 100 (4)
1901–10	1.53	0.10	1.63	6.13
1911–20	1.60	0.43	2.03	21.18
1921–30	1.32	0.53	1.85	28.65
1931–40	0.79	0.05	0.85	5.88
1941–50	1.13	0.47	1.61	29.19
1951–60	1.39	0.89	2.27	39.21
1961–70	1.19	0.83	1.96	42.35
1971–5	1.08	0.49	1.59	30.82
1976–80	0.82	0.40	1.22	32.79

Note: Discrepancies between the sum of the rate of growth due to natural increase and net migration and the rate of total growth are the result of intercensal adjustments.
Source: Australian Bureau of Statistics, *Year Book Australia, 1982,* p. 87.

Population growth

The goal of rapid growth of the (European) population was perhaps the primary objective during the early years of colonial settlement, and, as previously discussed, it retained its importance throughout the nineteenth century. The justifications offered included the need to exploit the abundant natural resources and the defence (from Asians, it was made clear) of the sparsely settled continent. In the decade before the first world war, in the 1920s, and again in the quarter century after 1945, the rate of population growth was boosted by immigration, much of it assisted by government subsidies. The relative contribution of immigration to the increase in the population is shown in Table 1.4, with the 1950s and 1960s the decades when immigrants made the greatest demographic impact. One contrast with the nineteenth-century role immigrants were expected to play in the economy is that instead of being added to the rural workforce – and thus literally helping to settle and secure the country – it was accepted that they would form additions to the urban populations. Indeed, emphasis was placed on the role of (primarily unskilled) immigrant labour in the expanding manufacturing sector. The nexus among immigration, protection, and manufacturing

most chapters of this book, with Chapter 11 providing an interpretive essay. A recent collaborative work on the subject is N. G. Butlin, Barnard, and Pincus (1982).

development is most clearly evident in the post-1945 period, but its origins lie in the first decades of the century.[20]

Immigration has done more than just increase the rate of growth of Australia's population. In the period since 1945 its ethnic composition has diversified away from the previous Anglo-Celtic concentration with the arrival of large numbers of Italians, Greeks, Germans, and East Europeans together with smaller numbers from many other countries. But the economic impact of immigration has also been important through its specific contributions to the labour force. The age structure and workforce participation rates of immigrants compared with those of others lowers the ratio of dependants to workers in the community. The easier allocation of new arrivals than of the native born to available jobs increases job mobility where structural and regional adjustments in the labour market are required. Further, Australia has imported skilled labour it has not had to train, enterpreneurs it might not have produced, and unskilled workers it did not have to provide for prior to their entry into the labour force. There have been disadvantages in this reliance on imported human capital, however, and Australia has comparatively low education retention rates at secondary and tertiary levels, with particularly low participation in formal technical education.[21]

Investment

As with labour supply, the augmentation of domestic savings by foreign borrowing has been a key characteristic of Australian investment (Table 1.5). Before the second world war the public sector was the principal borrower and the London capital market the principal source of funds. The high and rising cost of servicing these foreign debts as export prices declined was one of the principal mechanisms triggering the onset of the interwar depression. In the postwar period foreign investment was more typically private and direct or portfolio in nature, and thus associated with the establishment in Australia of foreign (especially American) corporations. These in turn became an important vehicle for the introduction of foreign technology and management practices.[22]

Investment in physical assets is regarded by economic historians as an important determinant of Australian economic growth during the boom in the late nineteenth century.[23] It was also associated with the long economic boom that followed the second world war. Part of the

[20] See Chapter 2.
[21] These issues are addressed in Chapter 10.
[22] See Chapter 9.
[23] This view is primarily associated with a major study by Noel Butlin (1964).

Table 1.5. *Foreign investment (net apparent capital inflow as a percentage of total gross fixed capital expenditure)*

Period	Capital inflow
1901–14	1.8
1920–30	19.6
1931–9	7.7
1950–5	9.4
1956–60	9.6
1961–5	9.6
1966–70	13.2
1971–5	3.8
1976–81	12.2

Sources: Boehm 1979: 136; Australian Bureau of Statistics, *Balance of Payments*.

sharp postwar rise in the ratio of investment to aggregate output was due to the need to house and provide the related urban infrastructure for the rapidly expanding population during those decades. However, it is clear from Table 1.6 that most investment occurred in nondwellings in the private sector rather than in housing or as a result of the activities of governments and state-owned enterprises.

Land augmentation

We have emphasised the importance for Australian economic development before 1914 of the exploitation of additional land for rural production and of mineral resources (especially gold). However, it must not be thought that the cessation of *extensive* rural settlement by the early twentieth century meant that farm output also ceased to grow. Table 1.7 indicates that major changes in rural land use patterns have occurred in Australia this century, with the result that the volume of agricultural output has risen markedly. This growth in rural production reflects the substitution of additional capital and intermediate inputs, new technology, and improved management for additional quantities of rural labour and (unimproved) land.[24] Indeed, the post-1945 long boom in the economy, though frequently associated with the expansion of manufacturing, partly reflected a return to a nineteenth-century pattern

[24] Elaboration of these points may be found in Chapter 6.

Table 1.6. *Investment ratios (fixed capital formation as a percentage of GDP*

Period	Private sector	Public sector	Housing component	Total
1901–10	7.3	5.8	2.8	13.2
1911–20	6.9	7.3	2.8	14.2
1921–30	8.7	9.2	4.1	17.9
1931–40	7.1	6.6	2.7	13.7
1941–50	7.9	4.9	2.4	12.8
1951–60	15.3	9.0	4.9	24.3
1961–70	17.0	9.4	4.8	26.4
1971–80	15.0	8.5	4.5	23.5

Sources: 1901–70: M. W. Butlin 1977: Table IV.1; 1971–81: *Australian National Accounts*, various issues.

of development. The rapid expansion of exports of both traditional and new rural products and of the new mineral deposits underpinned the ambitious immigration and industrialisation programmes of the period. Throughout the twentieth century Australia has thus remained largely dependent for its economic prosperity on the vagaries of world market demand for natural resource–intensive products and on the ability to expand the supply or improve the quality of the natural resource base.

Foreign trade

The story of nineteenth-century Australian development told earlier in this chapter had as its focus the importance of links with the international economy. This perspective also offers useful insights into the changing structure and performance of the economy since 1900.

The economy remains small in the economists' sense that international economic conditions are largely beyond Australia's capacity to influence. A desire to reduce the resulting vulnerability of exporters' incomes and hence of aggregate activity to wide fluctuations partly motivated protectionist policies aimed at diversifying the economic base of the country. These policies led to a more closed economy, the decline in the share of trade in economic activity, and the diversion of resources to the production of high-cost import-competing activities.[25] Table 1.8 reveals the fall in the trade ratio that occurred after the first world war; the

---

[25] This is the focus of Chapter 7.

Table 1.7. *"Improved" rural land*

Year	Fallow (%)	Crop (%)	Sown grasses (%)	Total (mill. hectares)
1901/2	14.9	76.0	9.1	4.5
1910/11	18.6	66.3	15.1	7.3
1920/1	19.7	63.4	16.9	9.6
1930/1	23.2	63.4	13.4	14.1
1938/9	24.8	52.8	22.4	18.0
1949/50	17.9	43.8	38.3	19.2
1960/1	10.1	40.4	49.5	29.7
1970/1	7.8	32.2	60.0	46.7
1980/1	9.3	39.6	51.1	48.7

Note and Sources: The area of "improved" rural land is defined as the sum of the area in fallow, the area under crops of all types, and the area planted in sown or "artificial" pastures and grasses (variously described in the sources). The data were obtained from Australian Bureau of Statistics, *Production* bulletins, *Rural Industries* bulletins, and *Rural Land Use and Crop Production* bulletins.

ratio of exports to GDP has continued to show a declining trend. A further means of reducing the vulnerability of a small open economy to external trading shocks is through the diversification of export markets and commodities. As indicated in Table 1.8, this also has occurred, but significantly so only in the period following the second world war: Australia had previously remained heavily dependent on the United Kingdom market and on rural exports, especially wool.

Conclusion

Since 1900 Australian society and the economy have undergone a major transformation. The population has grown from less than four to fifteen million and become more ethnically diverse. It has also become more urbanised in what was already a highly urbanised society. The importance of agriculture and mining as employers of labour has shrunk dramatically, while that of manufacturing and especially of services has increased. Australian exports are more diversified in their markets and commodity composition, though their natural resource content remains high, reflecting a continuing comparative advantage. Living standards have greatly increased, though Australia's turn-of-the-century position as approximately equal to the best in the world has not been maintained. Located in an area with the greatest proximity to southeast Asia, Australia (together with New Zealand) remains today as in 1900 an outpost

Table 1.8. *Foreign trade measures*

Year	Trade ratio (%)	Wool share of exports (%)	UK share of exports (%)
1901	44.9	31.9	57.0
1911	43.1	34.2	44.0
1921	42.8	35.0	51.1
1929	36.9	47.6	36.6
1931	27.3	29.8	44.0
1939	32.7	30.6	54.5
1946	31.1	32.6	27.3
1951	56.7	51.5	32.7
1961	32.8	41.7	23.9
1971	31.0	18.1	11.3
1975	32.6	17.3	5.5
1981	35.7	8.6	3.7

Notes: Trade ratio = exports plus imports as a proportion of GDP. Years are financial years except for the wool share of exports in 1901 and 1911, which relates to calendar years.
Sources: M. W. Butlin 1977; Australian Bureau of Statistics, *Year Book* and *Australian National Accounts, National Income and Expenditure.*

of predominantly European settlement, and with economic, social, and political systems similar in most fundamental respects to those of North America and Western Europe.

References

Boehm, E. A. 1971. *Prosperity and Depression in Australia 1887–1897.* Oxford: Oxford University Press (Clarendon Press).
    1979. *Twentieth Century Economic Development in Australia.* 2d ed. Melbourne: Longman Cheshire.
Butlin, M. W. 1977. *A Preliminary Annual Database 1900/01 to 1973/74.* Research Discussion Paper 7701. Sydney: Reserve Bank of Australia.
Butlin, N. G. 1959. "Colonial socialism in Australia, 1860–1900", in H. G. J. Aitken (ed.), *The State and Economic Growth,* pp. 26–78. New York: Social Science Research Council.
    1962. *Australian Domestic Product, Investment and Foreign Borrowing, 1861–1938/39.* Cambridge: Cambridge University Press.
    1964. *Investment in Australian Economic Development 1861–1900.* Cambridge: Cambridge University Press.

1984. *Contours of the Australian Economy 1788–1860.* Working Papers in Economic History No. 21. Australian National University.

Butlin, N. G., A. Barnard, and J. J. Pincus. 1982. *Government and Capitalism: Public and Private Choice in Twentieth Century Australia.* Sydney: Allen & Unwin.

Caves, R. E., and L. B. Krause (eds.). 1984. *The Australian Economy: A View from the North.* Washington, D.C.: Brookings Institution.

Denoon, D. 1983. *Settler Capitalism: The Dynamics of Dependent Development in the Southern Hemisphere.* Oxford: Oxford University Press (Clarendon Press).

Foreman-Peck, J. 1983. *A History of the World Economy: International Economic Relations since 1850.* Brighton: Wheatsheaf Books.

Hall, A. R. 1963. "Some long period effects of the kinked age distribution of the population of Australia, 1861–1961". *Economic Record* 39 (March): 43–52.

Jackson, R. V. 1977. *Australian Economic Development in the Nineteenth Century.* Canberra: Australian National University Press.

Kelley, A. C. 1965. "International migration and economic growth, Australia: 1865–1935". *Journal of Economic History* 25(3) (September): 333–54.

Kenwood, A. G., and A. L. Lougheed. 1983. *The Growth of the International Economy 1820–1980.* London: Allen & Unwin.

McLean, I. W., and J. J. Pincus. 1982. *Living Standards in Australia 1890–1940: Evidence and Conjectures.* Working Papers in Economic History No. 6. Australian National University.

1983. "Did Australian living standards stagnate between 1890 and 1940?" *Journal of Economic History* 43(1) (March): 193–202.

Maddock, R., and I. W. McLean. 1984. "Supply-side shocks: the case of Australian gold". *Journal of Economic History* 44(4) (December): 1047–67.

Schedvin, C. B. 1970. *Australia and the Great Depression: A Study of Economic Development and Policy in the 1920s and 1930s.* Sydney: Sydney University Press.

1979. "Midas and the merino: a perspective on Australian economic historiography". *Economic History Review* 32(4) (November): 542–56.

Sinclair, W. A. 1976. *The Process of Economic Development in Australia.* Melbourne: Longman Cheshire.

PART I

The macroeconomy

CHAPTER 2

Population and Australian economic
development 1900–1930

DAVID POPE

Through much of Australia's history one theme perhaps shines above all others, the desire of Australians to see their continent more speedily populated. The comparatively high unemployment rates of recent years; the march of military technology, which has greatly reduced the need for human battalions to secure a nation's defence; and the awakening of social scientists to the diseconomies and disamenities of urban population growth obscure to the student of today the power and conviction with which such views were held. But in earlier times, population growth – and here immigration of the *right* sort was seen as the means of rapidly accelerating its rate – was treated as a kind of cure-all, a panacea, for problems of defence and development in all but the years of deepest recession. W. H. Hughes, Australia's prime minister at the opening of the 1920s, put it simply: "Population is the golden key which will unlock all doors, sweep aside all obstacles."

If smallness of numbers was Australia's original sin, then population growth and selective immigration could correct it. The vision of those policy makers into whose hands this task fell in the late nineteenth and early twentieth centuries was one of building a white prosperous oasis in the south that would draw breath primarily from the British economy. Central to this view were the transfer of labour and capital from Britain and the furthering of overseas trade, exporting those goods for which Australia's climate and estate – that is to say, natural resources – afforded a comparative advantage. Yet the story of population and development is far more complex than this. The wool industry, Australia's premier export sector, while yielding high real returns per worker, did not require a large workforce for its operation; it therefore could not underpin a rapidly expanding population. Increasingly the population objective was supported by policies of closer settlement (breaking up land into small farms and diversifying the range of rural output) and industrialisation (manufacturing with import replacement behind a high protective wall). Both of these policies, and especially the latter, might

I am grateful to Lucia Carozzi for research assistance. Co-authors and the editors are also thanked for their comments on earlier versions of this chapter.

33

absorb population but involved an important trade-off. Population absorption meant an increasing share of Australian resources going into lower productivity activities and, in consequence, downward pressure on growth in real output per capita.

There was another difficulty. The white oasis was an economy open to factor transfers and overseas trade, with exports paying for the servicing of foreign loans. But to assure high living standards for white Australians, it was thought certain protective walls must be built. These reduced the degree of "openness" of the economy and impaired the international competitiveness of Australia's exports and import-competing industries, thus reducing both trade and allocative efficiency. Nor was the exchange rate used as an instrument to affect Australia's competitiveness.

Yet measured in terms of the goal of peopling Australia, the years 1900–30 were not without achievement, for Australia in these years attained one of the highest population growth rates in the West. How it did this and the interrelation among demographic expansion, economic growth, trade, and structural change in the economy are the subjects of this chapter. The chapter falls into two parts. The first part (sections 2.1 and 2.2) looks at the shape of the economy over the years of interest to us. The second (sections 2.3 and 2.4) investigates the policy objectives of these times – our focus being on population growth – and the consistency and efficacy of the instruments used by governments to achieve this and other goals.

2.1   Growth and structural change

In this section I am concerned with the rate at which the Australian economy expanded and diversified; in the following section we shall look at Australia's external transactions in trade and factor flows.

Just how fast did the economy grow?

Boehm (1979) suggests that during the long upswing from 1860 to 1890 real GDP rose along a path that bore the imprint of a trade cycle of two to four years' duration. This pattern continued during the years before the first world war; in the 1920s it varied between two and three years, with peaks in the last quarters of 1920, 1924, and 1927 and in the second quarter of 1929. It is also apparent that the performance of the economy was patchy. The pace of real GDP growth was most rapid in the years before the first world war and in the first half of the 1920s – the so-called Roaring Twenties. The second half of that decade, however, certainly did not roar (Table 2.1).

Table 2.1. *Australian output and population growth 1901–30 (average annual percentage change)*

Period	Real GDP	Population	Real GDP per head
1901–14	4.0	2.0	2.0
1901–9	3.6	1.5	2.1
1909–14	4.8	3.0	1.8
1920–30	3.3	1.9	1.3
1920–5	6.5	2.0	4.4
1925–30	0.0	1.8	−1.8
1901–30	2.7	1.9	0.8

Sources: M. W. Butlin 1977; Commonwealth Bureau of Census and Statistics, *Demography Bulletin*, various issues.

Most of the growth in aggregate demand both before the war and in the first half of the 1920s came from private investment demand for dwellings and public investment in structures other than housing (Table 2.2). The end of a protracted drought (which between 1894 and 1902 reduced sheep flocks by half) coupled with rising export prices led to an intense export boom between 1902/3 and 1906/7. This helped renew and quicken the pace of economic activity. But thereafter and until the outbreak of war, public investment and (from 1908/9) private housing demand were the principal vehicles of the expansion.

In the early 1920s private investment in dwellings grew at a staggering 17.4 percent per annum. This compared with 13 percent between 1908/9 and the outbreak of war, and −5.0 percent in the second half of the 1920s. This housing boom reflected a complex of stimuli. Backlogs in demand caused by the war and returning servicemen, demands triggered by new styles and standards in housing, immigration, and the drift of population to the cities all played a role. Most of those causes had worked themselves through, or were less expansive, by the mid 1920s. The boom before the war, especially in the years immediately before it, reflected autonomous demand engendered by the echo effects of past population growth (the children of the 1880s now entered the housing market) and the return to heavy migration after 1909.

Turning to the public sector, the growth of public investment expenditure in nondwellings ran at some 6 percent per annum before the war (more speedily at 10 percent between 1908/9 and 1913/14) and then at nearly 12 percent in the first half of the 1920s. In the second half of

Table 2.2. *Growth rate indicators (constant prices; average annual percentage)*

Indicator	1901–14	1920–5	1925–30
Demand side			
Private consumption	3.5	7.7	1.5
Private investment			
(a) Dwelling	11.4	17.4	−5.0
(b) Nondwelling	6.0	5.1	−8.9
Public investment			
(a) Nondwelling	6.3	11.6	1.2
Exports	2.2	.1	2.7
Imports	3.8	17.3	1.7
Liquidity (real M3 balances)	3.3	3.3	4.1
International competitiveness	1.0	−1.9	−2.3
Supply side			
Labour input	2.5	2.1	−1.0
Capital input	2.5	3.3	3.0
Total factor productivity	1.6	4.1	−1.2

Note: International competitiveness is measured by an index of the exchange rate trade-weighted ratio of real labour costs per unit of real output of employed workers overseas compared with Australia. Falls imply a deterioration in competitiveness.
Sources: M. W. Butlin 1977; Kaspura and Weldon 1980.

that decade the rate fell to 1.2 percent per annum. In particular, it sagged after 1926/7 and became negative in 1928/9 and 1929/30.

On the supply side, growth was sustained in the early 1920s by the quite rapid rise in factor inputs and in total factor productivity, although the latter partly reflects the effects of clement weather and the bountiful harvest of 1920/1. Arithmetic reveals a slower rate of technical progress generally before the war, but the biggest contrast with the early 1920s is with the collapse of total factor productivity growth in the second half of the decade. Labour inputs also fell. By this logic, what prevented the total collapse of the economy in the second half of the 1920s was the continuing injection of capital. However, a sizeable proportion of the new capital had been borrowed from abroad and repayments would have to be made.

The speed of economic activity produced by the supply and demand conditions just discussed in turn affected the demand for labour and the unemployment rate. Although the correlation was not perfect, the latter generally fell as output accelerated. Unemployment receded from about the middle of the first decade to what approximated full employment

Figure 2.1. Inflation and unemployment. *Source:* M. W. Butlin 1977.

in 1911/12 (Figure 2.1). Unemployment rates were generally higher after the war than just before it, rising rapidly as the decade closed. Figure 2.1 also hints at the inverse movement of prices (the GDP deflator is shown) and unemployment. Was there a Phillips curve trade-off between the two? Econometric estimation of an augmented Phillips curve relation (augmented by foreign prices, indirect tax rates, wage awards, and price expectations) suggests that there was in fact a short-term trade-off between the growth of prices and unemployment (Pope 1982b). Interestingly, *negative* price expectations followed price rises – Australians in these earlier decades appear to have thought in terms of some normal level of prices, so the expectation following price rises was for some lowering of prices. In short, price expectations were not the fuel for further inflation they are today. Inflation as a consequence was a good deal less persistent.

Although at times, as we have seen, economic activity in Australia grew briskly and there was more to spread, arithmetically (among the increasing population) the first three decades were overall not a period

Table 2.3 *Comparative output and population growth rates (average annual percentage change)*

Country	1901–14	1920–5	1925–30
United States			
Real output	3.2	5.5	0.6
Population	1.9	1.7	1.2
Real output per capita	1.3	3.7	− .6
Australia			
Real output	4.0	6.5	0.0
Population	2.0	2.0	1.8
Real output per capita	2.0	4.4	− 1.8
United Kingdom			
Real output	1.3	1.7	1.3
Population	0.8	0.6	0.4
Real output per capita	0.5	1.1	0.9

Sources: Table 2.1; Feinstein 1976; *Historical Statistics of the United States* 1975.

of substantial per capita growth. As can be seen from the bottom line of Table 2.1, Australians' real output per capita crawled along at an average rate of under 1 percent per annum. By contrast, the long boom that followed the second world war witnessed a per capita growth rate three times this. A question that arises from this is whether Australia's long-run per capita growth performance in the early twentieth century was worse than the track records of other Western economies. The answer is that the Australian economy did no worse, indeed a good deal better, than the British and United States economies before 1914 (Table 2.3). However, the economic setbacks of the 1890s had been more severe in Australia than in either of these countries; thus Australian growth advanced from a lower base. As for the 1920s, Australia's per capita growth rate was higher in the first half of the decade but compares quite unfavourably with other economies in the second half. Taking the years 1900/1–1929/30 as a whole, Australian per capita output grew more sluggishly at 0.8 percent per annum than that of the United States (1.3) though considerably faster than that of the United Kingdom (under 0.5 percent).

Yet it would be wrong to conclude that the Australian economy was little different on the eve of the depression from what it had been at federation. A good deal of structural change and diversification had occurred by 1930 in terms of the mix of output and in the sectoral distribution of inputs employed. Such changes helped set the style if not the pace of future growth.

Diversification of output

The 1890s depression induced some restructuring of the Australian economy. Goldmining, notably in Western Australia, enjoyed a recovery. This can be linked to depressed commodity prices relative to the fixed price of gold and to the rising number of prospectors from among the unemployed in the cities and on the farms. Also, depressed wool prices hastened diversification of rural land use. Interest in refrigerated meat exports quickened in the 1890s and led to the establishment of new export industries centred on meat and dairy products. From 1896 wheat growing also expanded greatly though erratically, a fact related to the twist of the natural elements and relative prices. Acreage under wheat for grain rose from five and a half million acres in 1900 to fifteen million in 1930. This expansion was facilitated by technical advances, both biological (new wheat strains) and mechanical, which permitted wheat farming to spread into arid lands. The expansion, however, was to cause concern in the second half of the 1920s, for by this time some observers believed that the exploitation of less productive lands was bringing diminishing returns to producers in its train. Most economists of the day took the view that the limits to closer settlement had been reached and that secondary industry, not agriculture, should provide – indeed already had provided – the job openings needed to employ Australia's increasing population.

Governments played an important role in promoting rural diversification and closer settlement. The expansion of grain production depended on relatively heavy government expenditure on branch railways that criss-crossed the old nineteenth-century rail trunk lines in the wheat belts. But there was also a new element in government intervention, perhaps because of the economic instability of the 1890s. Governments began to develop detailed policies to support and stabilise rural expansion. In the wheat industry, for instance, this took the form of the establishment of government agricultural banks and the diffusion of technical knowledge to the farmer. Great irrigation schemes were pursued, including easy finance for the pioneer settlers. Governments also paid bounties on the export of meat, wine, and dried and canned fruit and on the production of cotton. Butter and sugar production benefited from home consumption price support schemes through which local consumers subsidised growers.

It was also in the 1920s that economic policy increasingly turned to support urban-based manufacturing and services. (And it was in the cities in such activity that the new migrants were overwhelmingly to settle.) Growth in manufacturing output showed no sign of faltering before the second half of the 1920s, and then its rate of increase declined, though the level did not fall. The share of manufacturing in GDP expanded over the first three decades from 13 to 16 percent, while the rural sector's share sagged from 28 to 25 percent. Over the same time manufacturing increased its share in the workforce from 15 to about 20 percent, while the rural sector's fell slightly from 25 to 24 percent (N. G. Butlin 1970; N. G. Butlin and Dowie 1969). Thus manufacturing was not only expanding, but also, of greater significance to our story, its growth was labour-intensive.

Up to the war, manufacturing largely centred on the traditional and basic industries of food and drink, clothing (but not textiles), and machinery and engineering.[1] The greater part of industrial activity involved comparatively small-scale simple operations, many being associated with the processing of primary products and the maintenance of transport, especially railways.

The wartime rupturing of trade significantly speeded up the diversification of output as the economy was revealed to be hopelessly inadequate to meet emergency demands. The troops could perhaps be clothed, but they could not be armed and equipped. Construction had already begun under an American consulting engineer, David Baker, of the BHP pig iron and steel works at Newcastle. Baker's plans for the scope of the plant had been fairly modest, concentrating on the production of rails on a limited scale, though some diversification was envisaged in later years. The plant was completed in 1915. But the war transformed market prospects for the company, and output soared and quickly diversified beyond original expectations. Expansion of aggregate manufacturing capacity was, however, constrained during the war by the shortage of capital equipment, although by the end of it many new forms of heavy and light engineering, textiles, and basic chemical manufacture had been established. Substantial substitution of domestically produced goods for imports had taken place.

Not all industries benefited from the war. Indeed, estimates of real output in the private nonfarm sector of the economy reveal contractions in the growth rate in every year between 1914/15 and 1917/18. Construction activity slumped because of the cutback in demand and on account of labour shortages, and allied manufacturing industries suffered. Decline in consumption and employment was also experienced in the tobacco and brewing industries. The shortage of shipping had adverse ramifications for activity levels in processed rural outputs, especially timber. The basically "unprocessed" rural outputs of wool and

---

[1] The largest single sector in 1911 was food (about 22 percent), followed by machinery and engineering (11.2 percent) and clothing (8.8 percent).

wheat were largely insulated from this last problem by government arrangements for the bulk purchase and storage of produce. The British government was the principal purchaser at fixed prices of both commodities, as it was also of very large quantities of Australian beef and mutton. This wartime experience led to a number of postwar schemes for the regulated marketing of primary produce.[2]

We have already noted that manufacturing expanded rapidly in the first half of the 1920s. This was related to the relative ease of securing capital, to new avenues of consumer hire-purchase credit (excluded, of course, from M3 in Table 2.2), to the rise of new consumer durables and taste changes (the auto, new chemical and electrical goods, and housing styles), and to the growth of income and population. It was in the early 1920s too that Australia grasped the principle of high protection with both hands: Higher taxes (by way of the tariff) were imposed on imports.

The more rapid expansion of job opportunities in the cities than in the country reflected not only developments in manufacturing and the lower labour intensity of agriculture. The provision of services, both public and private, also had a strong urban bias, the natural outcome of already established trends in the distribution of Australia's population. Construction activity also came to focus more on the cities. Residential construction boomed in the years before the war, especially just before it, and shortly again in the first half of the 1920s, as we saw above. And public construction increasingly complemented urbanisation. Though the return of high levels of public capital formation before the war and in the 1920s assisted the diversification of rural production and closer settlement, there was a swing in the emphasis of public investment away from the rural sector. Whereas only four-tenths of public investment had been in the cities in the 1880s, the ratio was more like six-tenths in the 1920s: in water supply and sewerage, street improvements, roads, public buildings, the telephone, electricity, and the electrification of urban transport services.

2.2   Australia's external transactions

International transactions were of great importance to the Australian economy between 1900 and 1930. To begin with, around 20 percent of Australia's GDP was exported. Half of these exports were destined for the United Kingdom market, and France took an additional 10 percent. Wool accounted for half of the goods shipped from Australia, the balance

---

[2] For a full discussion of the economic effects of the war see Forster (1953) and Scott (1936).

being made up principally of wheat and flour, hides, dairy products, and meats, in that order. Manufactured exports other than processed primary products were negligible. In most years imports exceeded exports. The biggest source of the former was again the United Kingdom, which supplied at least half of the total; next in importance was the United States, supplying around 20 percent. What was it that Australians imported? Metal manufactures including machinery were the largest single component, followed closely by clothing, textiles, and footwear. On some counts, producers' materials and capital equipment together made up 65–70 percent of Australia's import trade (Cain 1970; Lundberg and Hill 1956).

For all but a comparatively short span of time Australia ran a sizeable deficit. Yet this was not a problem so long as British investors were prepared to lend their savings to Australians. Indeed the deficit on current account reflected the fact that they were. By permitting lower exports or higher imports, capital inflow enabled Australians to enjoy higher levels of domestic expenditure or absorption.

Unlike today, when nearly all capital inflow takes the form of private portfolio and direct investment, in the early years of this century much of it was fixed interest loans to governments, especially the states. The loan market centred on the London stock exchange; prior to the late 1920s U.S. foreign investment in Australia was negligible. The demand for capital by state governments related primarily to the provision of "social equipment" (namely, water, sewerage, electricity) in the burgeoning cities and towns of Australia (N. G. Butlin 1959). As this construction activity involved largely pick-and-shovel work, a high proportion of the borrowed outlays went directly on local wages.

In 1901, when the six colonies federated to become the Commonwealth of Australia, their combined population numbered 3.8 million. By 1930 Australia's population had grown to 6.5 million, with net migration being responsible for about 30 percent of the expansion (Figure 2.2). Three-quarters of the net arrivals came from the United Kingdom, largely from the most populated and industrial counties of England (Pope 1981a). The rate of net migration can be seen in the middle panel of the figure (the rate excludes troops and nurses). By way of comparison with our more recent demographic history, the peak attained just before the first world war equalled in size the peak years 1949–51. The 1920s saw a return to high migration, though the prewar rates of 1910–14 were not matched (Pope 1984).

As with capital inflow, Australian governments actively sought to promote population and labour flows, the most direct way of doing this being to reduce and defray the cost of transport. The government contribution cut the average assisted fare to between one-half and one-third

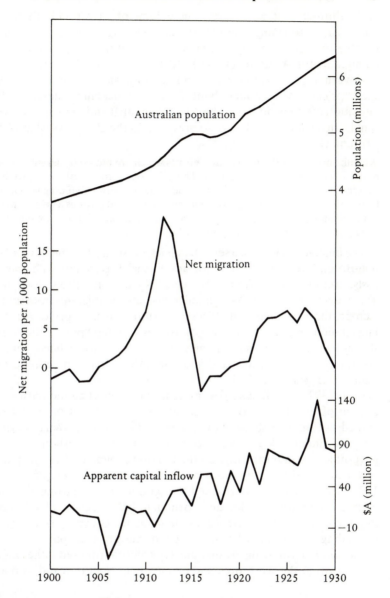

Figure 2.2. Factor migration. *Sources:* M. W. Butlin 1977; Pope 1976;
Australian Bureau of Statistics, *Demography Bulletin*, various issues.

of the third-class steamer fare.[3] The volume of migration in these years was sensitive to changes in the cost of transport; hence it is not unreasonable to suggest that government subsidy of fares secured additional immigrants for Australia (Pope 1981b).

Government effort to increase immigration was not limited to altering such "prices". More roundabout means of quickening the pace of immigration are to be found in the Australian tariff and in the public works (public investment) that were so prevalent in the 1920s. As Bland (1930: 74) remarked:

We must not forget the many other efforts which are indirectly serving the same purpose [of increasing population]. There are our [protected] secondary industries into which the war projected us headlong; our railway building which yearly throws the line of steel rails across our open spaces and gives us a greater mileage per head of population than any other country in the world; there are our storage dams, irrigation projects [and] our harbour works.

The immigrants were in a sense handpicked. With a few minor exceptions non-Britons were not eligible for any financial assistance with transport costs, and immigrants from many countries were positively discouraged. This was not only true of Asian immigrants but of immigrants from southern Europe, the group that in the 1950s was to form the backbone of Australia's immigration programme. Again governments altered "prices", this time by steeply increasing the landing money requirement – cash in hand – of southern Europeans to between £50 and £200. This compared with the £3 required of arrivals from the United Kingdom.

In the 1920s the British government lent support to the outward migration of its citizens. By the Empire Settlement Act of 1922 Britain agreed not only to share with Australia the cost of passage assistance but also undertook to share interest payments on certain Australian government loan borrowings on the London capital market, the purpose of which would be to promote land settlement and development (Pope 1976). The war had strengthened the sentiment for a strong and united empire. The economic climate in Britain in 1920–1, especially its mounting unemployment, and the possible gains to its export trade through expanding overseas markets made good sense of such policies.

The migrants arriving in Australia typically contributed rather more to the growth in the workforce and employment than they did to popula-

[3] This certainly would not have been a trivial saving. The cheapest contract rate for an adult in 1924 was £36. Average weekly money earnings were 94s. 4d. in Australia and 60s. in the United Kingdom. With a marginal propensity to save of .10, the difference between the assisted rate and no government assistance amounted to nine months' savings at UK wages. And migrant household heads needed not one fare but probably enough for two adult passages plus fares for three or more children.

tion. Before the war UK migrant workers on average accounted for 34 percent of the incremental rise in Australian employment and over the years 1921–7, 40 percent. Such an increase in labour certainly expanded economic activity (real GDP) in Australia beyond what it would have otherwise been, though whether real GDP per capita was advanced by this migration is a more complex issue that I leave to the section on policy.

The history of Australia's external dealings during the period would be incomplete without reference to two sets of relative prices, the terms of trade and the exchange rate. A rise in the ratio of export to import prices generates an increase in a country's real income (if nothing else changes). With an improvement in the terms of trade through to 1905, real income rose to a higher level than that shown by real GDP. Thereafter until the middle of the first world war the terms-of-trade effect was insignificant. Australians again gained from relative price movements from the early to mid 1920s. The magnitude of the greatest gain was 6–7 percent of real GDP; equivalent losses had been incurred earlier. These shifts in the terms of trade probably reflected conditions of demand and supply external to Australia (Wilson 1931).

Before 1914 most major countries were on the gold standard, which fixed exchange rates within narrow limits. As for maintaining the gold standard, Australia effectively had no central bank until 1924, nor did this bank (the Commonwealth Bank) subsequently attempt the defence of the gold standard by manipulating credit, as did the Bank of England. Yet between federation in 1901 and the end of 1929 the exchange rate was remarkably stable: £100 sterling never cost less than £97.50 nor more than £101.63 Australian. Moreover, both Australia and Britain were off the gold standard during the war and until 1925, yet the margins never went outside those quoted above. How was this accomplished?

The answer is that the private Australian trading banks pegged the pound as close as possible to sterling. They did this simply by exchanging in virtually unlimited quantities Australian pounds for sterling at a rate equal to or close to parity. Now we might expect such a policy to have at times left the banks with unnecessarily large London balances of sterling and at other times embarrassingly meagre ones. But generally this was not so. For when the banks sold Australian pounds to a buyer in Britain, the buyer took delivery in the form of a bank deposit in Australia. As Australian bankers attached importance to the ratio of credit advances to bank deposits in Australia, trading banks tended to lend more liberally at home as their London funds (and hence domestic deposits) rose. An expansion in credit, however, stimulated Australians to buy imports from Britain (and hence increased the demand for sterling), which in consequence diminished London balances. Conversely, a reduction of London funds occasioned a credit contraction in Australia. This reduced import demand, which then tended to restore London funds. The upshot was that the trading banks met the strains imposed on the stability of the exchange rate (by varying London balances and Australian credit) and that the Australian currency continued to sail along roughly at parity with the English currency. But this very fact robbed Australia of an important adjustment mechanism.

2.3   Economic policy: goals and instruments

When discussing government policies towards the economy and the effects that these had upon economic aspects of the lives of Australians, it is useful to draw a distinction between policy *goals* and policy *instruments*. The former represent the objectives of government economic policy, the latter the means of obtaining them. Even with the aid of this distinction, policy is still a very nebulous and difficult thing to identify. Let me make two points. First, the stated *intentions* of governments about economic policy regularly diverge from their subsequent *actions*. Political and economic events can intervene and cause divergence. Second, economic policy today is mostly associated with the federal government. By contrast, seventy and eighty years ago the states were far more powerful, so one cannot afford to lose sight of differences in the goals, instruments, intent, and actions of the separate governments. This makes the description and analysis of policy more complex.

When the century opened, the economy was suffering from perhaps the worst drought in Australia's white history and was still feeling the effects of a deep depression that had largely stopped capital inflow and halted immigration.[4] High unemployment relative to what had been known in the 1880s soured talk of immigration, and most of the states abandoned the system of offering immigrants assisted passage. As recovery flowed through the veins of the economy this situation changed. New South Wales and Victoria, the states that were to attract between them two-thirds of the immigrants, resurrected their assisted passage schemes in 1906 and 1907, their expenditures multiplying greatly in the years just before the war. The other states acted similarly. The new federal government also started to advertise the opportunities for immigration in Britain in 1907 – and after the war footed the bill (with Britain) of the passage schemes as well as participating in settlement schemes.

What was the purpose of increasing Australia's population? Defence

---

[4] Not all states suffered, or suffered equally. The discovery of gold in Western Australia at the tail end of the nineteenth century led to a boom and population growth.

and development were the key elements. Coghlan, chairman of the 1905 Agents-General Committee on the need for immigration, recorded succinctly: "... firstly as an insurance against aggression" (1905: 1179). Most Australians feared an "eastern overflow" from Japan and China. The term "yellow peril" was in vogue. Nor did the Great War dissolve Australia's basic and deepest fear, Japan continuing to be thought of as the potential and probable enemy. As for "development", in the Australian context this fundamentally meant quantitative increase in output and activities. In the early years of European occupation it involved geographic spread. Between 1860 and 1930 it meant closer settlement. But development was not restricted to rural pursuits. Though not using the word, Coghlan's report captured much of its flavour when he wrote of the reasons for promoting immigration: "... and secondly, as a way of adding to the country more producers, more consumers, more taxpayers" (1905: 1182).

Relatedly, policy aimed at the quantitative expansion of job opportunities. Job expansion was needed to absorb the immigrants who would add to population, but – and here the plight of the unemployed in the 1890s exercised an influence – quantitative expansion implied jobs for everyone, residents and migrants alike. The outward shift in the demand for labour along with wage fixing (a policy instrument) would help support Australians' living standards, or so it was thought (in this period living standards were usually perceived in terms of workers' real wages but occasionally as something approaching the concept of per capita real income). Domestic budget deficit financing, however, was not as yet viewed as a means of creating employment during depressions.

Were particular sectors of the economy favoured in the objectives of population growth and quantitative increase in output and jobs? Judged in terms of actions and outcomes, policy had an increasing urban-cum-industrial bias: Nearly all the migrants settled in the urban industrial regions of New South Wales and Victoria; public investment (a policy instrument) was increasingly directed into the cities and towns; the sectoral share of nonfarm GDP, including that of manufacturing, in total GDP was rising; and it was in the 1920s that the tariff – an instrument that stood to damage the rural sector – was stepped up.

Whether this drift was intentional on the part of governments is difficult to say. The answer may not only differ among the states but in the case of federal government even among prime ministers. Whereas all states believed in closer settlement and in the expansion of rural exports, some states' economies (notably Queensland's and Western Australia's) were more rural-oriented in terms of output and in the comparative abundance and cheapness of land. By comparison the populous states of Victoria and New South Wales were more industrialised and "land scarce". In Victoria manufacturing had had a long history of deliberate nurturing by protection dating from the 1860s, which had been very largely justified on the basis of the tariff's ability to promote resource utilisation (jobs for labour and capital) and to support population. As immigration climbed towards record levels in the years just before the war, Victoria and especially New South Wales intentionally aimed at providing a faster expansion in the industrial labour force to ease the growing constraint on manufacturing development. Commissions were dispatched to the cities of Britain to recruit artisans, and the nomination system was geared to introduce those "classes, and those alone who can be readily assimilated in the industrial life" (NSWPP, II, 1913: 187). With the end of the war in 1918 the premiers of both states briefly jumped on the bandwagon of migrant land settlement. But their commitment was remarkably weak. The shortage and high cost of suitable land, accentuated after the war by the promise to settle returned soldiers, was the principal explanation as to why migrant land settlement under the Empire Settlement Act was of minor importance in these states.[5] So far as immigration is concerned, if in these states the intent in 1922 was to settle large numbers of Britons on the land, then this plan was soon consciously revised, although the "vision", or less politely the "babble", lingered on. This was not the denial of closer settlement; rather, Australia's native sons and daughters qualified first for scarce land.

In the federal sphere the prime minister of the day, Hughes, was sorely disappointed at what he saw as the slow progress of migrant land settlement.[6] (The states, not the commonwealth, controlled crown lands and had the right to repurchase land in private hands.) Bruce, who replaced him in 1923, seemed more flexible on the issue. The same year the federal treasurer, Earle Page (1923: 1657), reported in the budget that

migration *was* confined to land settlement. It is the desire of the Commonwealth Government that migration projects should be extended to cover developmental

---

[5] In pursuance of that act Western Australia had negotiated to settle 6,000 migrant families, New South Wales and Victoria 2,000 each. After almost a decade Victoria had placed just 361 on the land. In New South Wales the scheme was barely launched. Thirty-eight migrants were settled in the course of the 1920s and not even all of these by dint of the programme.

[6] Certainly the inseparable relation between land settlement and immigration that Hughes was espousing in the early 1920s was his longstanding and passionately held view. It was part of the 1912 Labor platform, of which Hughes was the architect, and his attitude on the question can be traced further back to a series of newspaper articles, "The Case for Labor", written in 1909 for *The Daily Telegraph*.

works and power undertakings, so as to produce *a reciprocal and proportionate development of primary and secondary industries* [emphasis added].

Whereas "development" certainly meant rural development and closer settlement, for states such as Victoria and New South Wales and for the commonwealth from the early 1920s it also meant the intentional fostering of secondary industry (Pope 1985). The leitmotif was "more jobs for more people". Nor was there any major contradiction in attempting to do both, at least before 1914. A large part of manufacturing involved the simple processing of primary outputs; hence government support for one was seen as indirect support for the other.

2.4   Problems with economic policy

We have seen that the goals of policy were population growth and the quantitative increase of output and jobs; population growth was to be maximised subject to the constraint that living standards were maintained. The means or instruments to be used in achieving these objectives were several: assisted passages (to increase immigration); public investment supported by capital inflow (acknowledged as increasing jobs as well as living standards broadly defined); wage fixing (to ensure minimum living standards); tariffs (to increase jobs and in secondary industries maintain workers' living standards); and rural props including export bounties, subsidies, price support schemes and rural investment (to increase rural output and exports). Those instruments that increased jobs and supported living standards also increased population by increasing immigration. To complete the picture, the note issue was in the hands of the Treasury from 1911 to 1920, thereafter with the Commonwealth Bank, though the latter saw itself as a body above governments (the fiduciary issue could not be changed by government decree), nor was treasury bill finance used much before the 1930s. The exchange rate, as we have seen, was fixed by the private banks to sterling and hence unassigned as a government instrument. Below we look at the problems with "policy".

Population growth, immigration, and per capita income

It is my view that in the absence of assisted passage schemes a significant proportion of migrants who came to Australia would not have done so. In turn migrants increased Australia's employment base and, as a result, real GDP. This probably did not mean, however, that real GDP per capita rose. Whether it did or not depends critically on the migrants' contributions to the growth in the productive capital stock and on technical change. For if their only contribution was to increase labour and population, then unless the favourable age distribution effect of the UK inflow on the total Australian workforce participation rate (migrants were young and proportionately more were in the working age bracket than Australian residents) outweighed the effects of diminishing returns to labour as the workforce rose, income per capita had to fall. Research suggests that the former effect did not outweigh the latter (Pope 1977).

Now, a reduction in income per head could be avoided if migrants increased Australian productivity (output per worker). A major route to increased productivity is by a rise in the level of productive capital per worker. How did migrants affect this ratio? Migrants' demand for "unproductive" investment in housing and social infrastructure must have drawn resources away from productive investment and thus worked to lower, not increase, the productive capital–labour ratio.

Migrants, on the other hand, could have transferred savings that might have been used to increase productive capital. Moreover, their savings behaviour might have raised the average Australian gross savings ratio. But neither of these possibilities seems very likely. Growth in the capital stock from the first source was negligible. Wilson (1931) estimates that only 1.5 percent of Australian gross savings can be attributed to migrants. Given the size of the base capital stock, little of its growth can be attributed to savings transferred by migrants. The second point is less clear. Once having arrived, migrants might have been more frugal than resident Australians, thus raising the average savings ratio. However, as migrants represented such a small addition to the total number of Australian savers, it is difficult to see how they could have had any great influence.

Another dimension is that the supply of foreign capital to Australia might not have been so large in the absence of population flows. In per capita terms the importance of this effect is difficult to estimate. A substantial part of the borrowed funds went into "unproductive" ventures in town as well as country, and not into efficient investment that raised the average product of capital.

Finally, migrants could have promoted growth, outside their contributions to capital and labour, through improvements in "efficiency": they may have brought with them special skills and, as consumers, permitted industries to obtain scale economies. About one-third of the adult inflow before and after the war was skilled workers. Because of classification difficulties it is extremely difficult to compare this proportion with the proportion of skilled workers in the Australian workforce. There were some instances where migrant skills were crucial for the development of particular industries, two cases being British migrant instructors in the Australian textile industry in the 1920s and, in the same decade, American blast furnacemen in the Australian iron and steel industry. But in terms of aggregative effects it remains unlikely that new arrivals could have greatly influenced the *average* quality of the Australian workforce. On the second point, it is possible to find instances of scale economies in individual industries, one of the best known being the steel industry. Yet some early econometric work by Douglas (1948) on production relations in Victoria (1907–27) and New South Wales (1901–27) suggests the absence of increasing returns to scale, the implication being that simply having more bodies in the population to feed and clothe, and thus a bigger market, did not guarantee a fall in unit costs of production. Work by Forster (1970) also suggests that constant returns applied among the range of simple industries existing in the early part of the century. As the century progressed, some of the new industries – steel and autos, for instance – were probably established with below optimal plant size. However, over the whole sector, Douglas's results suggest the absence of increasing returns, a finding not inconsistent with Forster's.

Thus whereas migration clearly expanded economic activity or real GDP, my assessment is that it probably did not advance real income per capita.

Public investment

Taking the period as a whole, the level of public investment can be seen to have matched private investment in volume (Figure 2.3). In the 1920s it tended to be more stable than the former and to sustain total real investment longer. Whether the contours of total investment would have looked very different without public investment depends of course on the extent to which public sector initiatives in capital markets crowded out or choked off private investment. The main government borrowing instrument was inscribed stock. Specialist financial intermediaries in the City of London were used to manage issues and under British law (Colonial Stock Acts) dominion government issues could feed on trustee portfolio investment in a fashion that private borrowers could not. Under the existing institutional arrangements, governments drank from a different pond from Australian private borrowers of longer-term British funds. But this does not prove that private investors did not suffer, as government activity in one pond, even one with different risk premiums, could still affect interest rates or borrowing costs in another, causing some cutback in private borrowing. On the other hand, it is unlikely that Australian governments were such large borrowers in London as

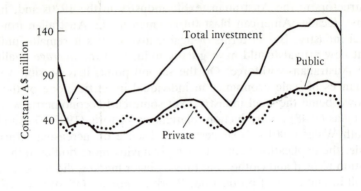

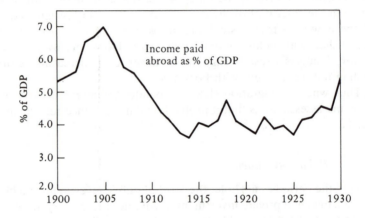

Figure 2.3. Real investment and income paid abroad. *Source:* M. W. Butlin 1977.

to cause a significant movement in British money rates facing private Australian borrowers, especially as financial intermediaries carefully coordinated the public issues (Gilbert 1971).

Did public investment effectively bar private ventures, for example in the construction of railways and sewerage systems? My assessment is that the bulk of public investment was not simply choking off private investment. As such it augmented total investment, though not by its full or total volume.

Nor was it a cure-all. There were three problems. First, interest payments had to be made, and net property income paid abroad (Figure 2.3) rose sharply from the mid 1920s as a consequence of this. The extremely high rates in the years prior to 1905 reflect exactly the same process initiated by record capital inflow in the decade or two before the 1890s depression. Interest and dividend payments as a percent of exports rose from 15 to 30 in the course of the 1920s. Income transfers put noticeable pressure on the current account by the late 1920s and drove a wedge between Australian real GDP and real income, the latter sagging 5 percent below real GDP. This was of no great moment so long as the returns were high and capital inflow continued.

The second problem was that the returns from investment in infra-structure and rural development were low and delayed in coming. At least part of the explanation for low returns was that there was no thorough economic planning or careful choice among projects.[7] The rate of return was of little importance, whereas employment was. As early as 1927, British financial circles had began to question Australia's public borrowing.

The third problem arose out of the second. British investors and money men started to react. But curtailment of loan expenditure meant pressure on the capital account of the balance of payments, and on the domestic front deflation and rising unemployment. Many believed that "artificial prosperity" bought by the loans programme brought its own inevitable nemesis. Certainly it would have been difficult for Australia to escape some contraction.

Protection all round

Protection was also something that made good political sense but received scant economic analysis, at least before the 1929 tariff inquiry. Protecting local manufacturers by imposing a tariff had been used in Victoria from the 1860s. The policies of other colonies ranged from free trade to moderately protectionist. At federation a single tariff was introduced for all states, which served to raise revenue for the new commonwealth government but also was set at a level that ensured that existing Victorian industries would not be damaged by overseas competition. Subsequent changes to the tariff schedules were more overtly protectionist in intent, the most protectionist being the Greene tariff of 1920 (Pope and Manger 1984).

In tabling the bill, the minister for trade and customs, Greene (1920: 700), said that it would "protect industries born during the war, ... encourage others that are desirable, and diversify and extend existing ones". It would keep money in Australia and create jobs. He also felt

---

[7] The only rudimentary economic analysis was by a commonwealth government body (Development and Migration Commission). This body rejected half the proposals brought before it by the states.

that wage rates could be higher (1920: 700): "We shall protect established Australian industries, and develop and foster new enterprises. Whilst giving adequate Protection by means of an effective Customs Tariff, we shall arrange that the workers in all industries will get their full share of the benefits of protection."

In earlier years Prime Minister Deakin's "New Protection" policy had linked wages to protection. The commonwealth's first truly protectionist tariff, the Lyne tariff of 1907, was supposed to permit employers to pay "fair and reasonable" wages. Excise duties could only be avoided by employers if in fact they complied. The Sunshine Harvester Works, an agricultural machinery maker, applied for such an exemption, and the case heard by Justice Higgins in the commonwealth court of conciliation and arbitration in 1907 set the commonwealth's first basic wage, seven shillings per day for a man with a wife and about three children to enable them to live in "frugal comfort". The New Protection was subsequently ruled unconstitutional, but the basic wage remained and the general idea of a tariff/wage package continued.

Something of a deal involving labour and capital had long been apparent in some quarters. In Victoria, the home of protection, it was not by coincidence that moves towards wage and factory regulation in the 1890s were accepted by employers at times when the Labor party's support was needed to win higher protective duties (Macarthy 1967: 324–5). High unemployment in the 1890s and later the fear of a postwar slump turned the urban labour movement increasingly towards support for protection of the manufacturing sector. It became less a matter of extracting concessions than of labour genuinely seeing its interests as married with those of the manufacturers. The costs of protection in the form of higher prices to workers as *consumers* were too thinly spread to be seen by the individual worker, certainly relative to the honeypot of a job and high wages. The employers also saw themselves as clear gainers, so an alliance or compact was struck between capital and labour that for the most part still stands.

So far as real wages are concerned, the authors of the tariff inquiry (Brigden et al. 1929)[8] at the end of the 1920s correctly assessed the direction of the income redistributional effects of the tariff – that real wages would be higher.[9]

---

[8] J. B. Brigden, D. P. Copland, E. C. Dyason, L. F. Giblin, and C. H. Wickens.

[9] However, it is unclear whether the authors anticipated the Stolper-Samuelson theorem of 1941, or rather finished up with the same result by upending Ricardian economics of labour in a corn-importing economy to produce a view of labour in a grain-exporting economy (Samuelson 1981; Manger 1981). Ironically, both arguments are premised on zero international labour and capital movements, so it is puzzling how such practical

One group, the rural producers, were highly articulate concerning the rise in production costs imposed on them by the growth of the tariff and wage fixing. The government's response was a second-best type of policy: compensating the rural sector for the harm done to it by these policies, especially the tariff. It then became a matter of protection all round. The rural sector had always been supported by public investment and other props, but with the formation of the Country party (and the tariff was the principal factor behind the party's birth) more was done. Even whole states received compensatory grants. As Maclaurin (1937: 5) observed, "Having failed to check the steady advance of the tariff, the party leaders apparently decided that the only way to defeat the vicious circle of mounting tariffs [and wages] was to get into the circle themselves."

Whereas the tariff and rural props were in keeping with the Australian gospel of development, there were problems. Allocative efficiency suffered. As the economy moved further away from market prices, the costs of misallocation rose, which meant a smaller national cake in terms of real GDP. If labour's wage rate and slice of the cake rose on account of the tariff, the brunt was borne by the exporters in the less sheltered parts of the economy in the form of higher costs. Although it is true that many of these received assistance, compensation to rural producers could not have neatly neutralised the initial misallocative effects.

Wage fixing

Wage-fixing bodies and tribunals found their way onto the statute books in most states at the end of the last century or the beginning of this one. The days before the 1890s depression had been golden for the unskilled worker. This was partly a consequence of the scale of government capital projects in the 1880s, which were labour-intensive. But it was also the case in mining and the pastoral industry that it was the unskilled workers who were the most sought after. Unskilled wage rates were bid up to the point where wage differentials narrowed to the barest margin. The depression of the 1890s radically changed these circumstances. Capital inflow all but dried up and unemployment soared. Worst affected were the unskilled, and it was their plight that lay at the centre of the twentieth-century government experiments in fixing minimum wages.

The Harvester judgment set the first commonwealth basic wage at a

men as Australia's early economists could have adopted either. Some recent work suggests that if international capital mobility is allowed, labour probably neither wins nor loses (Sjaastad and Clements 1981). See also Chapter 7.

level equal to the predepression rate for unskilled labour, seven shillings per day. In practice the award did not have an instantaneous effect, for it applied only to workers whose wages were fixed by the commonwealth court (that is, those industries in which there had been disputes extending beyond state boundaries); even as late as 1921, the court's share in total wage prescription was only about 20 percent. Higgins's award, however, set a standard. After the judgment there was a rush of requests for new tribunals, increasing numbers of trades and occupations being brought under some system of wage fixing. Gradually the state tribunals and courts came to follow the lead of the commonwealth court. This process was fairly well established by the 1920s, by which time most of Australia's unskilled city workers were receiving the 1907 Harvester award in real terms. Secondary wages or margins for skill assumed considerably less prominence in the business of wage regulation.

Strange as it may seem today, the whole system was erected without any attention to how employment levels might be affected. Would employers shed labour, especially the unskilled, and refuse to take on new hands? The basic thoughts were not these, but rather that social justice had been done and that Australian living standards were as solid as the rock of Gibraltar. Yet the rock was to cast a shade.

The general pattern of real wages in Australia in the 1920s differed from that in countries like Britain and the United States. Australian nominal wages grew briskly at 5.25 percent per annum in 1921 and contracted at only a modest rate (3 percent) in 1922, whereas in Britain money wages fell by almost 5 percent in 1921 and by 22.5 percent in 1922. Neither in Britain nor the United States do we observe a conjunction of wage inflation and price deflation in 1921 as we do in Australia (Figure 2.4). Indeed, this occasioned a turnaround in Australia's international competitiveness, shown in Table 2.2, and worked to dilute the effects of the Greene tariff.

The major jump in real wages in 1921 coincided with courts and tribunals clearing the backlog of cases brought before them by inflation, and with a deliberate effort by state tribunals to implement the 1907 federal award in real terms. Both these developments occurred in a period of falling prices. Also assisting the jump were the rise in the commonwealth's share in total wage prescription in 1921 (for its basic award was higher than the states') and, towards the end of 1921, Justice Power's three shillings' loading onto the basic wage. The decision to adopt indexation sealed in much of these gains. And coexisting with higher wage costs during the 1920s were higher rates of unemployment. Nor is it fatuous to link the two. Econometric estimation of the private sector's demand for workers reveals that changes in the real cost of

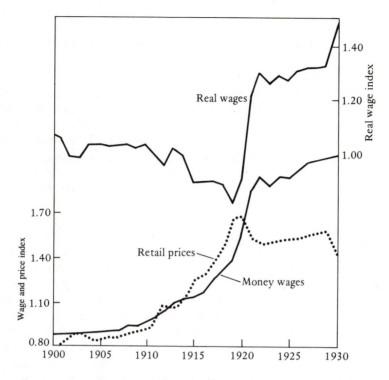

Figure 2.4. Wages and prices (1911 = 1.0). *Sources:* M. W. Butlin 1977; Bambrick 1970.

labour were a significant determinant of changes in the level of private employment and hence, by deduction, of unemployment (Pope 1982a). Thus government efforts to protect workers' real wages could have reduced living standards by reducing employment.

2.5   Conclusions

There were many inadequacies in Australian policy in the first three decades of this century. Gross interference with the price mechanism – not just the tariff but wages policy and ad hoc countervailing assistance to rural producers along with overcapitalization using foreign funds and the lack of any tight criteria in public investment – stood to cause problems in the end. To the economists watching in the wings as the 1920s came to a close, serious imbalances were already apparent on both internal and external fronts: Unemployment was thought abnormally high and domestic and foreign cost structures alarmingly divergent, and external debt commitments were eating dangerously into Australia's sterling balances. An economic crisis was taking shape in Australia well before Wall Street announced hers to the world in the closing months of 1929. On the eve of the great depression Australia was already in need of a basic overhaul.

But we must also acknowledge the considerable success of key aspects of policy. Australians in these times felt isolated and vulnerable. Though we may find it amusing or sad today, Australians' perception of the "yellow peril" was real and very frightening to them. When asked by Deakin in 1905 about the functions of a larger population, Coghlan, it will be recalled, replied, "Firstly, as an insurance against aggression". In the absence of immigration between federation and the first world war, Australia's population would have been about 5 percent smaller; in the 1920s without it, similarly smaller again. With the exception of a handful of years, Australia's population growth rates exceeded those of Europe and matched or bettered those of North America. Governments can take a good share of the credit for this; six in every ten arrivals were assisted. The net effect of such other instruments as public investment (partly assigned to "job creation") and the tariff (long acknowledged as a way of creating jobs) also helped by boosting the demand for labour.

If the small-country assumption is applied to Australia in its trade (that is, it was a price taker not a price setter), then the tariff could not have helped Australia's export sector by (in reducing its relative size) making it behave like a profit-maximising monopolist.[10] Reduced trade implied lower per capita real income. And immigrants via their likely adverse effects on the productive capital–labour ratio most probably forestalled rises in average real income. These things partly explain Australia's poor long-term per capita growth performance discussed at the beginning of this chapter. But in terms of history these considerations partly miss the mark. Historically Australians thought less in terms of maximising per capita standards of a small population than of increasing population without loss in existing per capita standards. Among Aus-

---

[10] Any shrinkage of the Australian export sector most likely would not have caused export prices to rise, and hence overseas buyers to bear the cost of higher Australian wages. However, this is a little contentious. The Brigden committee did appear to think that in the absence of the tariff exporters' revenue might be squeezed, which opens the possibility of the optimum tariff argument: The tariff on imports could have made the Australian export sector act like a profit-maximising monopsonist/monopolist. Empirical work is needed, though for the moment I stick with Wilson's small country assumption. Finally, one economist, E. R. Walker, thought that the tariff was not an unqualified bonus to urban labour. For by encouraging many small establishments to pop up like mushrooms after rain, only to die back with competition, it "reduced the probability of permanent employment for the average worker" (Walker 1932).

tralians generally this distinction was not so crisply articulated, but it was similar to the common sentiment that smallness was Australia's original sin and that more people and expansion in the scale on which things were done would bring salvation while permitting a handpicked white population the rich standards already established. Judged in these terms, policy met with a measure of success.

References

Bambrick, S. 1970. "Australian price indexes". Ph.D. thesis, Australian National University.

Bland, F. A. 1930. "Development and migration", in Persia Campbell (ed.), *Studies in Australian Affairs,* no. 3, pp. 49–77. Melbourne: Institute of Pacific Relations.

Boehm, E. A. 1979. *Twentieth Century Economic Development in Australia.* 2d ed. Melbourne: Longman Cheshire.

Brigden, J. B., D. P. Copland, E. C. Dyason, L. F. Giblin, and C. H. Wickens. 1929. *The Australian Tariff.* Melbourne: Melbourne University Press.

Butlin, M. W. 1977. *A Preliminary Annual Database 1900/01 to 1973/74.* Research Discussion Paper 7701. Sydney: Reserve Bank of Australia.

Butlin, N. G. 1959. "Some structural features of Australian capital formation, 1861 to 1938/39". *Economic Record* 25: 389–415.

  1970. "Some perspectives of Australian economic development 1890–1965", in Colin Forster (ed.), *Australian Economic Development in the Twentieth Century,* pp. 266–327. Sydney: Australasian Publishing Company.

Butlin, N. G., and J. A. Dowie. 1969. "Estimates of Australian workforce and employment, 1861–1961". *Australian Economic History Review* 9: 138–55.

Cain, N. 1970. "Trade and economic structure at the periphery: the Australian balance of payments, 1890–1965", in Colin Forster (ed.), *Australian Economic Development in the Twentieth Century,* pp. 66–122. Sydney: Australasian Publishing Company.

Coghlan, Timothy. 1905. "Memorandum by the Agents-General on the question of immigration". *Commonwealth Parliament Papers,* v2.

Douglas, P. 1948. "Are there laws of production?" *American Economic Review* 38: 1–41.

Earle Page, Dr. 1923. *Commonwealth Parliamentary Debates,* CIV.

Feinstein, C. H. 1976. *Statistical Tables of National Income, Expenditure and Output of the U.K., 1855–1965.* Cambridge: Cambridge University Press.

Forster, Colin. 1953. "Australian manufacturing and the war of 1914–18". *Economic Record* 29: 211–30.

  1970. "Economies of scale and manufacturing", in Forster (ed.), *Australian Economic Development in the Twentieth Century,* pp. 123–68. Sydney: Australasian Publishing Company.

Gilbert, R. C. 1971. "London financial intermediaries and Australian overseas borrowing, 1900–29". *Australian Economic History Review* 11: 39–47.

Greene, W. 1920. *Commonwealth Parliamentary Debates*, XCI.

Historical Statistics of the United States: Colonial Times to 1970. Part 1, 1975. U.S. Department of Commerce, Bureau of the Census. Washington, D.C.

Kaspura, A., and G. Weldon. 1980. *Productivity Trends in the Australian Economy: 1900–01 to 1978–79*. Working Paper 9. Canberra: Department of Productivity. August.

Lundberg, E., and M. Hill. 1956. "Australia's long term balance of payments problem". *Economic Record* 32: 28–49.

Macarthy, P. 1967. "The Harvester judgment: an historical assessment". Ph.D. thesis, Australian National University.

Maclaurin, W. R. 1937. *Economic Planning in Australia, 1929–1936*. London: P. S. King & Son.

Manger, G. J. 1981. "Summing up on the Australian case for protection: comment". *Quarterly Journal of Economics* 96: 161–7.

NSWPP *(New South Wales Parliamentary Papers)*. 1913. II.

Pope, David. 1976. "The peopling of Australia". Ph.D. thesis, Australian National University.

1977. "The contribution of United Kingdom migrants to Australia's population and economic growth: federation to the Great Depression". *Australian Economic Papers* 16: 194–211.

1981a. "Contours of Australian immigration: 1901–30". *Australian Economic History Review* 21: 29–52.

1981b. "Modelling the peopling of Australia: 1900–1930". *Australian Economic Papers* 20: 258–82.

1982a. "Wage regulation and unemployment in Australia: 1900–1930". *Australian Economic History Review* 22: 103–26.

1982b. "Price expectations and the Australian price level: 1901–1930". *Economic Record* 58: 328–38.

1984. "Some factors inhibiting immigration in the 1920s". *Australian Economic History Review* 24: 34–52.

1985. "Australia's development strategy in the early twentieth century: semantics and politics". *Australian Journal of Politics and History* 31: 218–29.

Pope, David, and Gary Manger. 1984. "The tariff and Australian manufacturers' international competitiveness". University of New South Wales. Mimeograph.

Samuelson, P. A. 1981. "Summing up on the Australian case for protection". *Quarterly Journal of Economics* 96: 147–60.

Scott, E. 1936. *Australia during the War*. Sydney: Angus & Robertson.

Sjaastad, L., and K. Clements. 1981. *The Incidence of Protection: Theory and Measurement*. Economics Discussion Paper. University of Western Australia. June.

Walker, E. R. 1932. "The unemployment problem in Australia". *Journal of Political Economy* 40: 210–26.

Wilson, R. 1931. *Capital Imports and the Terms of Trade*. Melbourne: Melbourne University Press.

CHAPTER 3

The depression of the 1930s

Australia
1313
0480

TOM VALENTINE

The depression of the 1930s (the Great Depression) was the dominating economic event in Australia in this century. It was an economic catastrophe of the first order that left a permanent imprint on the personalities not only of those directly involved, but also of the following generation. Similarly, community attitudes that were strongly conditioned by the depression experience had an important later influence on economic policy. Most prominently, achievement of "full employment" became the major objective of economic policy after World War II and continued to occupy that position until the 1970s.

The 1970s have often been compared in popular discussion with the 1930s, but the resemblance is only superficial. Unemployment was much greater in the depression years. Moreover, whereas unemployment was combined with deflation in the earlier period, it was coincident with a high level of inflation in the 1970s.[1] The latter fact led to a shift of emphasis in the objectives of macroeconomic policy; the authorities became much more concerned with dealing with inflation. These questions are discussed in detail in Chapter 5.

The great depression produced considerable social disruption and personal suffering, which have been documented by, amongst others, Fox (1977) and Mackinolty (1981). Another way in which the situation of the thirties differed from that of the seventies was that there was no social security net in the earlier period. As Snooks (1985) tells us, the unemployed initially received relief from private charitable organisations; government action was tardy and, when it emerged, uncoordinated and incomplete. For example, Davidson (1985) suggests that farmers were induced to stay on the farm because the income they could obtain there was higher than what they would have received from un-

I am particularly indebted to Boris Schedvin for detailed comments on this chapter. I am also grateful to Peter Jonson, Stephen Grenville, Glenn Stevens, an anonymous referee, and the authors of the other chapters (especially the editors) for their assistance, and to Russell Agnew for research assistance and for a number of suggestions on the topics discussed.

[1] A detailed statistical comparison of the two periods is provided by Jonson and Stevens (1983).

employment relief. Relief consisted of sustenance support (food relief) and relief work. Snooks argues that the latter was expanded largely at the expense of normal public works.

It is not the purpose of the present chapter to dwell once again on this human misery. Our objectives are rather the more prosaic ones of charting the course of the depression as reflected in economic variables, examining the causes of the contraction, explaining why it was so protracted, and indicating the source of the partial recovery that occurred in the early to mid thirties.[2]

3.1 The course of the depression

The major variable to be used to trace out the path of the depression is the series on trade union unemployment collected for the months of February, May, August, and November over the period 1913 to 1942 (see Figure 3.1). There are some difficulties with this series (see Forster 1965). For example, the data for Queensland tend to underestimate unemployment. Nevertheless, the series appears to be accurate enough to be used as an indicator of the depth and path of the depression.

The unemployment rate is the measure most frequently cited in discussions of the depression, but there are alternative indicators that deserve some attention. One of them is gross national product. However, Schedvin (1970b) argues that national product is a poor indicator of the depth of the depression because it includes farm output, a large part of which is exported. Schedvin uses national expenditure as an indicator to describe the depression, but agrees that it also has weaknesses. An important advantage the trade union unemployment series has over these alternative measures is that it is available on a quarterly basis and thus will allow something to be said about the timing of the events of the depression.

It is clear that unemployment fluctuated in the 1920s. It peaked at 12.5 percent in 1921 and at 10.3 in 1924, but by the March quarter of 1927 it had fallen to 5.9 percent. From the June quarter of 1929 it jumped sharply, and we can regard this as the beginning of the depression.[3] The

---

[2] Schedvin (1970a) provides the most comprehensive modern discussion of the depression, and this reference is required reading for anyone studying the subject. Boehm's review of Schedvin's book (Boehm 1973) is also of interest. Briefer discussions of the depression are given in Boehm (1980) and Sinclair (1976).

[3] This corresponds to the business cycle dating given by Boehm (1979), which is based on a number of series in addition to the trade union unemployment rate. It was not necessary to correct the unemployment series for seasonal variation because there were no obvious seasonal fluctuations in it. This is probably a result of the heavy emphasis on manufacturing in the unions contributing to the series.

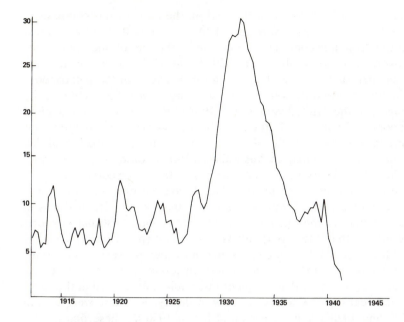

Figure 3.1. Australian unemployment rate (percentages). *Source:* Australian Bureau of Statistics, *Labour Report* (cat. no. 61010), various issues.

unemployment rate continued to increase until it peaked at 30.0 percent in the June quarter of 1932; thereafter it fell steadily until the June quarter of 1938. Even then it had not reached levels thought to be acceptable in the post–World War II environment or, indeed, the levels that prevailed in at least some of the years of the 1920s.[4]

The commonwealth figures hide some variation amongst the individual states in terms of their unemployment experience. The downturn came in the same quarter (June 1929) in all the states except Queensland and Western Australia, where it occurred in the December quarter of 1929. The trough of the contraction occurred in the June quarter of 1932 in all the states except South Australia (September 1932) and Tasmania (December 1931). The unemployment rate was higher in South Australia and New South Wales than in other states.

Schedvin (1970b) examines the effect of the depression on real national product, real national expenditure, industrial production, and

---

[4] It should be noted that Schedvin (1970a: chap. 12) points out that the unemployment figures might underestimate the extent of the recovery; if it is viewed in terms of aggregate expenditure it appears to be more substantial.

unemployment in seven countries and on the basis of this comparison concludes that Australia was one of the countries that suffered most from the economic contraction. In terms of the rate of unemployment, the average for Australia over 1930–4 was 23.4 percent, which was greater than that for five of the countries included in the comparison. Germany was the only country with a worse record. For example, the average for the United States was 19.0 percent and for the United Kingdom 19.2 percent. On the other hand, Twomey (1985) argues that Australia was not as badly affected as two countries, Canada and Argentina, that were similar to Australia in a number of ways. For example, the share of industry in GDP and the percentage of exports to GDP for the three countries were similar and all three countries were substantial importers of capital. Twomey points out that output declined less in Australia than in the other two countries and that Australia's exports suffered less than the exports of Argentina and (particularly) Canada.

Tables 3.1 and 3.2 include series on some other measures of economic performance over the interwar period. In terms of the rate of growth of real GDP, it is clear that the record was quite mixed even in the 1920s and that real GDP continued to grow in the 1930s. There were falls in 1927/8 and 1928/9 and a substantial fall in 1930/1. These figures also suggest that the economy began to recover in 1931/2 and that the recovery became a fairly strong one in 1932/3.

The figures on the percentage increase in private nondwelling fixed capital expenditure (Table 3.2) indicate that this variable was strongly affected by the depression and in turn contributed significantly to its depth. It fell over the years 1929/30 to 1932/3 and increased, although very sharply, only in 1933/4 and 1934/5. Public expenditure fell in 1929/30, fell sharply in 1930/1, and fell again in 1931/2. These falls were largely due to a contraction in public capital formation (see Table 3.2). The level of public consumption expenditure remained fairly steady throughout this period. A major cause of the contraction in public capital formation was the closing of British capital markets to Australian official borrowers.

The share price index constructed by Lamberton (1958a and b) is given in the final column of Table 3.1. It shows that share prices increased over the 1920s and did not fall until 1930. This indicates that falls in share prices did not have the same role in initiating the Australian depression that they had in the case of the United States. The table also shows that they began to increase again in 1932. This is consistent with the more detailed information supplied by the unemployment rate.

The interwar period was on average a period of deflation. At the end of 1938/9 prices were at a lower level than they had been at the end of 1920/1. The largest falls occurred in 1929/30 and 1930/1. The long-term bond yield

Table 3.1. *Various Australian economic indicators 1927–39 (percentages)*

Year ending June	Increase in GDP (constant prices)	Increase in exports (constant prices)	Increase in exports (current prices)	Ratio of exports to GDP	Ratio of gross private capital formation to GDP	Increase in public expenditure (constant prices)	Rate of inflation (GDP deflator)	Long-term bond yield	Share price index (avg. of 3 years ended June 1939 = 100)
1927	4.2	−2.2	−5.3	16.5	9.0	5.4	0.0	5.34	64.4
1928	−0.9	−4.4	2.4	16.8	8.8	2.2	1.5	5.43	70.0
1929	−1.9	13.9	5.1	18.0	8.5	0	0.4	5.26	74.0
1930	1.4	−9.2	−29.9	13.8	6.3	−4.6	−9.8	5.57	51.5
1931	−9.4	22.9	−6.9	15.6	5.6	−19.3	−9.3	6.51	43.9
1932	1.7	10.2	9.0	18.1	4.1	−8.8	−7.6	4.68	52.6
1933	6.0	4.6	2.7	17.1	4.7	5.3	−1.4	3.92	64.5
1934	3.7	−9.4	15.1	19.1	5.7	10.5	3.4	3.61	75.4
1935	2.2	12.4	−5.8	17.0	7.2	17.1	3.3	3.31	84.9
1936	5.1	−6.6	17.6	18.2	7.4	4.5	4.6	3.74	93.8
1937	3.2	2.9	24.0	20.7	7.5	2.4	5.7	4.02	105.0
1938	6.4	10.7	−1.7	18.8	8.7	6.3	1.7	3.68	98.6
1939	−4.0	10.0	10.3	17.3	8.9	2.4	2.0	3.90	96.4

Sources: The share price data are averages for the calendar year. They were obtained from Lamberton 1958a and b. The other series are from Butlin 1977.

Table 3.2. *Investment expenditure 1927 to 1939 (percentages)*

Year ending June	Increase in public fixed capital expenditure (constant prices)	Increase in private nondwelling fixed capital expenditure (constant prices)	Increase in private fixed capital expenditure on dwellings (constant prices)
1927	8.2	−4.8	8.8
1928	1.7	−4.8	3.0
1929	−4.8	2.3	−13.1
1930	1.0	−32.7	−27.5
1931	−29.7	−4.0	−46.8
1932	−26.9	−23.5	−36.5
1933	11.7	−0.8	71.2
1934	4.7	41.9	13.6
1935	26.6	38.3	26.8
1936	5.0	6.3	26.1
1937	11.5	2.6	9.3
1938	10.9	30.1	10.5
1939	−7.5	15.3	1.1

Source: Butlin 1977.

is shown in Table 3.1; comparison of this series with the rate of inflation indicates that the latter variable appears to have had very little influence on interest rates. This meant that real interest rates were large and positive whenever prices fell substantially, i.e. in 1929/30 to 1931/2.

The recovery that commenced in 1932 continued through the thirties, as is shown by Tables 3.1, 3.2, 3.4, and 3.5. The real wage fell from 1932 on, while productivity in manufacturing was increasing (Haig 1975). The rate of profit increased substantially in 1933/4 and share prices increased from 1932 on; these factors probably contributed to the upturn in business investment in 1933/4. Dwelling investment picked up in 1932/3. Public capital formation increased in 1932/3 and 1933/4 and expanded sharply in 1934/5. Table 3.1 shows that public expenditure increased through the thirties from 1932/3 on, with marked increases in 1933/4 and 1934/5.

3.2   The causes of the depression

It will be useful to adopt a simple saving–investment framework to allow discussion of the causes of the depression and the reasons for its depth.[5] The equality of income and expenditure requires that

---

[5] This approach was suggested by Gordon and Wilcox (1981).

$$S = I + DF - CF + DFX \qquad (3.1)$$

where I is (private and public) investment, S is domestic saving, CF is capital inflow in the balance of payments, DF is the budget (cash) deficit, and DFX is the change in foreign exchange reserves. Equation (3.1) can be rewritten by assuming that $S = sY$, where Y is income, and dividing through by Y^*, the full-employment level of income. Then

$$\frac{sY}{Y^*} = \frac{I}{Y^*} + \frac{DF}{Y^*} - \frac{CF}{Y^*} + \frac{DFX}{Y^*} \qquad (3.2)$$

Assume that there is a fall in investment relative to full-employment income. If there is no offsetting change in the other factors on the right-hand side of (3.2) (a corresponding increase in the cash deficit, fall in capital inflow, or increase in foreign exchange reserves relative to full-employment income), and if it is assumed that s is constant, income must fall below the full-employment level to maintain the equality.

There are, of course, some interactions amongst the terms in equation (3.2), and these played an important role in the events that precipitated the onset of depression in Australia. The initial event was a fall in export prices, which produced a fall in export income and created a balance-of-trade deficit. Export prices fell by 7.7 percent in 1928/9 and by 22.7 percent in 1929/30, largely because of the contraction in the world economy. The fall in export income reduced domestic expenditure and, therefore, aggregate income.

This reduction in income requires a fall in one of the elements on the right-hand side of the identity (3.2). The obvious adjustment would have been an increase in capital inflow, which would also have offset the balance-of-trade deficit created by the falls in the prices and volume of exports. Table 3.1 shows that the ratio of exports to GDP fell off markedly in 1929/30. Unfortunately, as shown in Table 3.3, the sources of foreign lending dried up at the same time (see Schedvin 1970a: chap. 5). Initially the authorities filled the gap by supplying foreign currency to the foreign exchange market, but this support could not be maintained and they were forced to devalue the Australian pound in January 1931 (see ibid.: chap. 8) after some attempts to ration foreign currency that had produced a black market. The devaluation of the pound was, therefore, more a passive reaction to balance-of-payments pressures than a deliberate policy measure aimed at improving matters.

The cessation of capital inflow also reduced the first term in (3.2), i.e. the ratio of investment to full-employment income. The lack of overseas funds had an effect on public investment expenditure, as is shown in the first column of Table 3.2. This effect is discussed in detail by Schedvin (1970b). The net effect on the right-hand side of (3.2) was

Table 3.3. *Australia's overseas debt position 1926/7 to 1938/9 (in million dollars)*

Year ending June	Australian government securities domiciled abroad	Interest on securities overseas	Public borrowing overseas
1927	977	49	3
1928	1,089	55	73
1929	1,094	57	5
1930	1,197	53	3
1931	1,153	59	56
1932	1,160	59	7
1933	1,151	66	−9
1934	1,142	58	−9
1935	1,140	57	−2
1936	1,136	55	−4
1937	1,132	55	−4
1938	1,134	55	2
1939	1,139	55	5

Source: Butlin 1977.

negative, and this meant that income had to remain below the full-employment level to maintain the equality.

There has been a continuing discussion of the causes of the depression in Australia. In its recent form, this discussion arose out of the work of Schedvin (see Schedvin 1970a and b; Boehm 1973). The issues that form the basis of this discussion are briefly but well summarised by Clark (1981).

Clark refers to this discussion as a debate, but in fact it is sometimes difficult to distinguish amongst the positions of the participants in it. As Clark points out, there is general agreement that the depression was precipitated by overseas factors – falls in export income and a cessation of capital inflow. There also appears to be agreement that domestic factors interacted with these external pressures to deepen the Australian depression.

The only disagreement appears to be over the significance of the domestic factors. Boehm (1973) argues that Schedvin tends to attach too much importance to them. He argues that the depression was an unusual economic contraction that was imposed on Australia's natural business cycle from outside. Unfortunately, Boehm argues, the external pressures impinged on Australia at a time when it had not fully recovered from its most recent cyclical contraction, and this magnified the impact of the external factors.

A number of domestic factors have been identified as having influenced the depth of the depression. It has also been argued in some cases that they would eventually have caused difficulties for the Australian economy even if the international economy had remained prosperous. It will be useful to survey these problems briefly at this point.

First, it has been suggested that the Australian economy had developed structural problems largely arising from a tariff structure that protected an increasingly uncompetitive manufacturing industry.

The second argument advanced in support of the view that Australia was headed for economic difficulties at the end of the twenties is illustrated by Table 3.2, which suggests that the rate of growth of public investment was faltering by the end of the twenties (Sinclair 1975). This also appears to be the case with housing investment (third column of Table 3.2). It is likely therefore that the level of investment would have fallen in any case. According to equation (3.2), this fall would have required a reduction in income to maintain the equality of saving and investment.

A third argument is that wage levels were too high in Australia and that this was bound to cause difficulties sooner or later. Wages increased by more than prices during the 1920s, i.e. the real wage increased over that period. This increase in real wages would probably have led to increased unemployment even if other factors had remained the same. Results reported by Valentine (1978) and Pope (1982) support the view that in the interwar period the unemployment rate increased as real wages increased.

Jonson and Stevens (1983) point out that the increase in Australian wages in the 1920s reduced competitiveness relative to the United Kingdom. This suggests that difficulties would have arisen in the balance of payments even if export prices had not collapsed. The relationship used to explain imports in the econometric model reported by Valentine (1978) includes a significant term in relative prices, indicating that the loss of competitiveness probably did increase imports in the 1920s. The argument that there was a basic weakness in the Australian balance of payments is reinforced by the fact that a debt-servicing problem was created over the twenties by continued borrowing overseas. The interest payable on securities held overseas rose from $ 33m in 1920/1 to $ 57m in 1928/9. As a standard of comparison, exports in 1928/9 were $ 308m. As Schedvin (1970b) points out, the debt-servicing problem would have become critical whenever export proceeds fell for any reason.

Australia's vulnerability to a fall in export prices was increased by the

Table 3.4. *Nominal and real wages 1927 to 1939*

Year ending June	Increase in average weekly earnings (%)	Real wages (1966/7 = 1,000)
1927	2.7	0.562
1928	1.5	0.562
1929	− 1.9	0.549
1930	1.3	0.610
1931	− 8.3	0.616
1932	− 9.7	0.602
1933	− 3.0	0.593
1934	− 1.4	0.565
1935	0.9	0.552
1936	2.9	0.543
1937	3.5	0.532
1938	6.3	0.557
1939	2.6	0.546

Source: The measure of real wages was calculated from the series for average weekly earnings and the implicit deflator for GDP given in Butlin 1977.

undiversified nature of its exports. In 1928/9 37.5 percent of Australian exports went to the United Kingdom and another 14.1 percent went to British possessions. In the same year wheat, flour, and wool constituted 62.1 percent of exports.[6] In addition − and this is another reason for thinking that Australia would have experienced difficulties even if a contraction had not occurred in the international economy − export prices were affected by some long-term structural problems, e.g. there was an oversupply of some of the agricultural products exported by Australia (Schedvin (1970a: chap. 11).

This discussion highlights the fact that in the 1930s Australia was faced with a balance-of-payments constraint. It was necessary to meet interest and repayment commitments; Table 3.3 shows that these obligations remained at a constant level throughout the thirties. Until the onset of the depression, obligations could be met from new capital inflow, so that it was unnecessary to run a balance-of-trade surplus. However, when the overseas sources of funds dried up, as they did at the beginning of the depression, it became necessary to produce a balance-of-trade surplus to meet the commitments. This process was complicated by the

---

[6] These figures are taken from the *Year Book of the Commonwealth of Australia for 1930*. For a detailed analysis of the Australian balance of payments over a longer period see Cain (1970).

collapse of export markets that occurred at the same time. The only solutions to this problem were to deflate the economy to reduce imports or to devalue the currency.[7]

Some evidence on the relative importance of these factors has been obtained by simulations of a modified version of the model described in Valentine (1978). A counterfactual simulation in which exports grew steadily over the 1930s and export prices were held constant at the average level achieved in the 1920s was carried out (Valentine 1984). In this simulation, the depression disappeared. This result supports Boehm's view that the depression was largely imported and that the importance of the domestic factors mentioned in the previous paragraphs has been somewhat exaggerated.

As mentioned above, the writers who suggested these arguments did not put them forward as alternative explanations of the depression. They are best regarded as explanations of the fact that the contraction that started in 1929 was unusually deep and protracted. In terms of equation (3.2), the Australian economy by 1930 had reached a situation in which saving was equal to investment at a low level of income. The only way in which it could be moved out of this position of stagnation was to increase investment in some way. This would have been extremely difficult given the internal problems outlined above.

One explanation for the severity of the depression in the United States is that it was aggravated by a collapse of the money supply arising partly from bank failures. This view is identified with Friedman and Schwartz (1963). It is still being hotly debated – see, for example, Temin (1976) and Brunner (1981). It does not, however, appear to be relevant to the Australian case. Schedvin (1970a: 203–10) notes that the Australian money supply did not contract during the depression to anywhere near the same extent as the U.S. money supply, because the banks took a flexible attitude to their reserve ratios. M3 fell by 4.5 percent in 1929/30 and by 3.5 percent in 1930/1 but increased by 6.6 percent in 1931/2. Comparison of these figures with the figures for growth in GDP and inflation for the years in question suggests that monetary growth had little effect on the latter variables. It is also important to note that real M3 (M3 divided by the implicit deflator for GDP) actually increased over the period 1929/30 to 1933/4. If anything, monetary forces would have lessened the severity of the depression in Australia. For example, the 15.3 percent increase in real M3 in 1931/2 may have contributed to the upturn in 1932. However, it is more likely that the money supply was demand-determined and reacted passively to changes in income. Indeed,

---

[7] The issues discussed in this paragraph are further considered in Chapters 2 and 9.

all writers on this period treat interest rates as exogenously determined policy variables; and if this is correct, the volume of money could not have been controlled by the authorities.

3.3   The recovery

Governments could not remain impassive in the face of such a macroeconomic collapse. A variety of policy actions were taken in 1930, 1931, and early 1932. They included

> the tariff increases introduced by the Scullin government in 1930 and 1931 (see Chapter 7);
>
> the wage reduction of 10 percent ordered by the arbitration court in January 1931;
>
> the devaluation of the Australian pound of about 20 percent relative to sterling;[8] and
>
> the adoption of the "premiers' plan".

The premiers' plan was developed out of public discussion and political negotiations that are detailed by Schedvin (1970a: chap. 10). It required a reduction (relative to 1930 levels) of 20 percent in all adjustable government expenditure; a reduction of the interest rates on outstanding government debt by 22.5 percent; an equivalent reduction in bank lending and borrowing rates; and increases in taxation.[9] The net effect of all these policies was to produce the improvement in 1932 shown in Figure 3.1. It will be instructive, however, to consider their relative importance in producing this outcome.

First, Schedvin (1970a) argues that the premiers' plan was deflationary because of the cuts in government expenditure; this view receives strong support from the econometric simulations reported in Valentine (1978). Schedvin (1970a) does, however, suggest that the interest rate cuts included in the plan might have had a stimulating effect on the economy. Simulations of the econometric model reported in Valentine (1978) suggest that the effect of this policy was marginal. Indeed, given the fact, mentioned above, that real interest rates were very high (around 15 percent) in the early 1930s, it would have been surprising if the small reductions in nominal interest rates had had any effect on economic activity.

Second, the simulations reported by Valentine (1978) indicate that wage reductions did contribute to reducing unemployment. It is not entirely clear, however, through what channels the wage reductions

---

[8] See Butlin (1977: 68) for details.
[9] See *Year Book of the Commonwealth of Australia for 1932*, pp. 847–8.

Table 3.5. *Rates of profit 1930–7 (percentages)*

Year ending June	Manufacturing profit/ total capital	Retailing profit/ total capital	Aggregate profit/ total capital
1930	6.4	5.6	8.1
1931	3.8	−0.6	4.4
1932	4.6	−0.3	4.7
1933	5.2	1.1	5.2
1934	6.4	3.4	7.2
1935	5.2	4.8	7.4
1936	7.6	6.2	8.5
1937	10.1	6.8	10.0

Note and sources: The figures in the first and third columns are for companies reporting on June 30 of each year. They were obtained from various issues of *Jobson's Investment Digest*. The data for retail profits were obtained from *Jobson's Investment Digest* for January 1939 and include profits of all companies reporting during the year.

worked. In the econometric model in question, there is a direct relationship between wages and investment. However, the evidence for this link is not strong, and Table 3.2 shows that private fixed capital (non-dwelling) expenditure did not begin to increase until 1933/4, i.e. after the upturn. It is unlikely, therefore, that this channel was an important contributor to any economic improvement generated by the wage reductions.

It has already been noted that there is evidence that in the interwar period employment depended directly on the real wage rate. Table 3.4 shows that there was in fact a fall in the real wage in 1931/2. It should be noted, however, that the real wage remained high, compared with historical levels, until the second half of the thirties. This is one explanation for the persistence of high unemployment rates throughout the thirties.

The real wage was particularly high in 1930/1 and the productivity of workers in manufacturing fell in that year (Haig 1975). As a result, the share of profits in national income fell to a low level in 1930/1, recovering in 1931/2 (Walker 1953). Table 3.5 shows that these movements were reflected to some extent in the rate of profit. Since, however, investment did not pick up until 1933/4, these fluctuations must be regarded as reflecting what was happening in the economy rather than as causing it.

Apart from any direct effect they may have had, the wage reductions contributed to an improvement in the competitiveness of Australian industry, which was also increased by the devaluation of the Australian pound. The index of the Australian real effective exchange rate (based on the wholesale price index and using trade weights) constructed by McKenzie (1982) fell by 15 percent between 1930 and 1932. The measure of competitiveness calculated by Jonson and Stevens (1983) also shows that a substantial improvement occurred over this period. It remains to be established, however, how this factor led to improved economic conditions. It is true that from 1930/1 on, the balance of trade was in surplus, but these surpluses arose largely because of the fall in imports caused by the contraction of the economy and less from an increase in exports. They were necessary to meet the interest payments set out in Table 3.3. Schedvin (1970a: 292) notes that the value of exports was kept up in the early thirties by farmers expanding their production to make up for the lower prices (see Table 3.1). In the case of wheat there was actually a government programme to encourage increased production – the "grow more wheat" campaign–which was reinforced by a price guarantee (Schedvin 1970b: 145ff.). Increased output also resulted from a series of good seasons. Additional exports generated in this fashion did not increase income or domestic expenditure and therefore had little influence on unemployment. It seems, therefore, that the major stimulatory effect of the improvement in competitiveness arose largely from an improvement in the profitability of import-competing industries. Some industries received additional tariff protection as well as benefiting from the improvement in competitiveness.

It has been suggested[10] that the recovery in the Australian economy (as well as its downturn) can be attributed to the movement in exports. Table 3.1 shows that the ratio of exports to GDP increased markedly in 1931/2. The table also suggests that this ratio is correlated with the ratio of gross private capital formation to GDP[11] and that this relationship provides one mechanism whereby exports affect domestic economic activity. It must be noted, however, that

> the ratio of private investment to GDP actually fell in 1931/2; and
>
> the increase in the ratio of exports to GDP in 1931/2 was partly caused by a fall in the latter.

Schedvin (1970: chap. 12) attributes the recovery to an increase in activity in manufacturing industry. Schedvin's view that the recovery began in the manufacturing sector has been questioned by Boehm (1973) on the grounds that employment declined to a greater extent in this sector than elsewhere in the economy and that it had therefore to recover

[10] By a referee of an earlier draft of this book.
[11] This statement is supported by econometric work I have recently carried out.

Table 3.6. *Unemployment amongst trade union members in various industries: quarterly, 1929–32 (in percentages)*

Quarter	Wood Furniture, etc.	Engineering, metal works	Food	Clothing, etc.	Books, printing	Other manuf.	Total
1929: 4	15.5	15.4	12.8	10.0	3.3	22.1	13.1
1930: 1	20.6	16.7	9.3	12.5	3.8	25.5	14.6
2	25.2	20.5	14.2	16.7	6.8	31.0	18.5
3	21.3	21.9	15.4	21.0	8.4	32.8	20.5
4	29.4	25.2	16.8	22.5	10.1	38.7	23.4
1931: 1	31.1	27.7	17.4	25.9	12.6	42.3	25.8
2	33.3	30.2	20.7	26.7	14.4	44.8	27.6
3	34.0	31.2	20.5	27.4	15.0	45.0	28.3
4	34.8	31.2	20.4	23.7	15.0	42.5	28.0
1932: 1	36.6	31.1	17.1	22.8	15.4	42.5	28.3
2	39.6	33.9	19.4	22.6	16.8	43.0	30.0
3	39.4	32.9	20.7	21.3	16.7	41.3	29.6
4	38.4	31.6	18.4	17.8	15.6	39.8	28.1

Source: Year Book of the Commonwealth of Australia, various issues.

further in order to regain its previous position. This is certainly true, but it does not contradict Schedvin's basic proposition that the recovery began in the manufacturing sector.

Some support for this view is provided by Table 3.5, which indicates that the rate of profit increased in manufacturing before it increased in retailing and at about the same time as it increased for business as a whole. Schedvin (1970a: chap. 12) also notes that it was the textile industry that turned up first, and this is borne out by Table 3.6. Unemployment in the clothing industry began to fall in the fourth quarter of 1931.

It is likely, therefore, that the improvement in economic activity from 1932 on was due largely to the improved competitive position of manufacturing industry. This in turn can be attributed to the wage reduction, the devaluation of the pound, and the Scullin tariff. It is, however, impossible to disentangle the separate effects of these policy initiatives, because they were introduced at more or less the same time. For example, the index of tariff levels makes no important contribution to economic activity in the econometric model reported in Valentine (1978), but this is only because of its correlation with the exchange rate and wages. In particular, some of its effect could have been attributed to the exchange rate. Also, the increase in competitiveness helped in restricting imports and allowing Australia to meet its overseas interest commitments without further deflation.

Is there any other policy the authorities could have followed that would have produced a more substantial improvement? The obvious possibility is an increase in government investment. This would have increased the ratio of investment to full-employment income and, according to equation (3.2), forced an increase in income in order to produce the additional saving required. The simulations reported in Valentine (1978) suggest that this policy would have produced a substantial reduction in the unemployment rate. It would, however, have created balance-of-payments difficulties that might have necessitated a further depreciation of the currency. The success of such a policy would depend on the reaction of other countries, i.e. on the extent to which they would have engaged in competitive devaluations. It should be noted, however, that the simulation of the effect of increases in public expenditure in Valentine (1978) does not combine them with wage cuts. If wages had been cut, the balance-of-payments problems would have been reduced. This suggests that a successful policy would have combined increases in public expenditure with a depreciation of the Australian pound and wage cuts.

3.4   Conclusion

In this chapter I have discussed an experience unique in Australia's economic history. The depth of the depression, particularly the high rates of unemployment suffered, has given it a prominent role in Australian political and economic discussion.

The evidence suggests that the depression was almost completely imported. It was initiated by the collapse of the world economy, which produced a dramatic fall in export income. This loss of income led to a deep contraction that may have been reinforced by domestic factors. There were signs that both dwelling and public investment were slowing down at the end of the 1920s. And wage increases in the 1920s had undermined the competitiveness of Australian industry. Finally, the high interest bill incurred overseas meant that any contraction in export income would create difficulties for economic management. A surplus in the balance of payments was necessary to meet this, and when it could not be obtained from high export income, an alternative method of producing it had to be found, e.g. maintaining the economy at a low level of economic activity.

The upturn that occurred in 1932 can be attributed to the policies adopted by the Australian authorities: a reduction in wages, the devaluation of the Australian pound, and the Scullin tariff. These led to an increase in competitiveness and appear to have had a stimulating effect on import-competing industries in particular. A tantalising question remains. Could the authorities have done even better?

References

Boehm, E. A. 1973. "Australia's economic depression of the 1930s". *Economic Record* 49 (December): 606–23.
  1979. *Twentieth Century Economic Development in Australia.* 2nd ed. Melbourne: Longman Cheshire.
Brunner, K. (ed.). 1981. *The Great Depression Revisited.* Boston: Martinus Nijhoff.
Butlin, M. W. 1977. *A Preliminary Annual Database 1900/01 to 1973/74.* Research Discussion Paper 7701. Sydney: Reserve Bank of Australia.
Cain, N. 1970. "Trade and economic structure at the periphery: the Australian balance of payments, 1890–1965", in Forster 1970, pp. 66–122.
Clark, D. 1981. "A closed book? The debate on causes", in Mackinolty 1981, pp. 10–26.
Davidson, B. R. 1985. *Australian Agriculture in the Great Depression.* Working Paper, No. 37. Department of Economic History, Research School of Social Sciences, Australian National University.
Forster, C. 1965. "Australian unemployment, 1900–1940". *Economic Record* 41 (September): 426–50.
Forster, C. (ed.). 1970. *Australian Economic Development in the Twentieth Century.* London: Allen & Unwin.
Fox, L. (ed.). 1977. *Depression Down Under.* Potts Point: Len Fox.
Friedman, M., and A. J. Schwartz. 1963. *A Monetary History of the United States 1867–1960.* Princeton, N.J.: Princeton University Press.
Gordon, R. J., and J. A. Wilcox. 1981. "Monetarist interpretations of the great depression: an evaluation and critique", in Brunner 1981, pp. 165–73.
Haig, B. D. 1975. "Manufacturing output and productivity 1910 to 1948/9". *Australian Economic History Review* 15(2) (September): 131–61.
Jonson, P. D., and G. R. Stevens. 1983. *The 1930's and the 1980's: Some Facts.* Research Discussion Paper 8303. Sydney: Reserve Bank of Australia.
Lamberton, D. McL. 1958a. "Some statistics of security prices and yields in the Sydney market, 1875–1955". *Economic Record* 34 (August): 253–9.
  1958b. *Share Price Indices in Australia.* Sydney: Law Book Company.
McKenzie, I. M. 1982. "Essays on the real exchange rate investment and the current account". Ph.D. thesis, MIT.
Mackinolty, J. (ed.). 1981. *The Wasted Years?* Sydney: Allen & Unwin.
Pope, D. 1982. "Wage regulation and unemployment in Australia: 1900–30". *Australian Economic History Review* 22(2) (September): 103–26.
Schedvin, C. B. 1970a. *Australia and the Great Depression.* Sydney: Sydney University Press.

78   Tom Valentine

1970b. "The long and the short of depression origins", in R. Cooksey (ed.), *The Great Depression in Australia*, pp. 1–13. *Labour History*, no. 17.

Sinclair, W. A. 1975. "Economic development and fluctuation in Australia in the 1920s". *Economic Record* 51 (September): 409–13.

1976. *The Process of Economic Development in Australia*. Melbourne: Longman Cheshire.

Snooks, G. D. 1985. *Robbing Peter to Pay Paul: Australian Unemployment Relief in the Thirties*. Working Paper No. 41. Department of Economic History, Research School of Social Sciences, Australian National University.

Temin, P. 1976. *Did Monetary Forces Cause the Great Depression?* New York: Norton.

Twomey, M. J. 1985. "Economic fluctuations in Argentina, Australia and Canada during the depression of the 1930s", in D. C. M. Platt and G. di Tella (eds.), *Argentina, Australia and Canada: Studies in Comparative Development 1870–1965*, pp. 179–93. New York: St. Martin's.

Valentine, T. J. 1978. "The battle of the plans: an econometric analysis". Paper presented to the Seventh Conference of Economists, Sydney.

1984. "The causes of the depression". Paper presented to the 13th Conference of Economists, Perth.

Walker, K. E. 1953. "The size and performance of Australian firms with special reference to 1920/21–1938/39". M.Ec. thesis, Sydney University.

CHAPTER 4

The long boom 1940–1970

RODNEY MADDOCK

Per capita consumption in Australia in 1970 was double what it had been in 1940. By contrast, the 1940 level was almost exactly the same as it had been thirty years earlier and only 10 percent higher than it had been sixty years earlier, in 1880. The period of the "long boom" was clearly one of the outstanding epochs in the history of the country. Not only were the people richer as a result, but there were a lot more people. Seven million Australians had become twelve and a half. The economy thus had operated to provide 80 percent more people double the standard of living that had been enjoyed thirty years earlier. This experience is the subject matter of the chapter.[1]

Simplifying, one can say that economic policy in Australia for the first thirty years of this century was focused on expanding the scale of the economy. Population growth was pursued to expand the potential output of the country, the aggregate supply of goods and services that could be provided. In Chapter 2 David Pope argued that this policy was successful. Real GDP grew at 2.8 percent per year over the period. However, demand was often inadequate and this caused the economy to operate below capacity: Unemployment of labour fluctuated between 2 and 9 percent. This failure of demand became chronic in the thirties with unemployment reaching a peak of over 20 percent and maintaining a level of over 10 percent for six consecutive years.

By contrast, the period from 1940 to 1970 was extremely successful by both criteria. The growth rate of GDP averaged 3.9 percent per year and for only two years was unemployment over 3 percent. Policy, how-

Doug Whaite, Wayne Naughton, and Vanessa Nikias provided valuable assistance during the preparation of this chapter. I would also like to thank the many commentators who have been generous with their assistance.
[1] Amongst the literature that complements this chapter the Vernon report (1965), which tried to assess trends and suggest policies for Australian development, provides the most complete analysis. Waterman (1972) provides a chronicle of the macroeconomic cycles. Unfortunately neither of these works makes any significant comparisons with the prewar period. Boehm (1979), N. G. Butlin, Barnard, and Pincus (1982), and Sinclair (1976) do provide a greater historical perspective, as does Cain (1970). The basic data source is M. W. Butlin (1977); unsourced data quoted in the text come from that source.

ever, was more complex. Migration of labour and foreign capital were pursued to encourage high growth rates, monetary and fiscal policy was directed towards the maintenance of stability and full employment, and direct controls on imports were used to maintain external balance.

The key features of the economy in the period are thus that economic growth accelerated, that the economy operated near its potential, and that the performance was remarkably stable. Figure 4.1 presents the high, stable growth performance of GDP, the long period of near full employment, and the strong tendency for prices to rise through the period.

This boom in the economy in the middle of the twentieth century was not simply an Australian phenomenon. Analysing the economies of Western Europe, Japan, Canada, the USA, and Australia, Maddison (1982) finds that, on average, GDP per head of population grew by 3.8 percent a year from 1950 to 1973 compared with just 1.3 percent from 1870 to 1950. Quite clearly any explanation of the improvement in Australia's economic performance should be made in the context of the global trend.

This chapter is written in three main sections. The first asks the question What caused the boom? It sketches the relation of the Australian experience to the global prosperity while highlighting the particularly high rates of factor accumulation that prevailed in the Australian economy. The section that follows lays bare the anatomy of the boom. It traces the forces underlying shifts in the aggregate supply and demand curves and their consequences for inflation and unemployment. The third section, "Economic Incidents", places these analytical elements in a more historical context. Here, for example, the war economy is discussed as a whole rather than through its supply and demand components. This is followed by a short conclusion.

4.1   What caused the boom?

The causes of the accelerated growth of the world economy since 1945 are poorly understood. The greater stability of economies can probably be explained by the application of policies for the management of demand and the successful stabilisation of world currencies under the Bretton Woods agreement, but the higher growth rates remain something of a mystery.[2] The suppression of investment demand during the

---

[2] Abramovitz (1979), after discussing the absence of a widely accepted explanation, suggests that it was a period of catch-up as the best technology and capital were exported from the most advanced economies to countries whose industry was more backward.

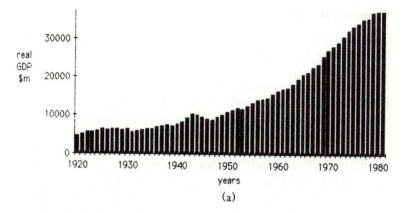

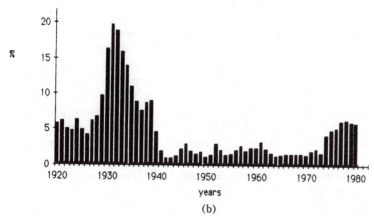

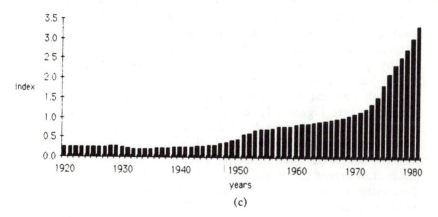

Figure 4.1. Main indicators of the long boom in Australia: (a) Real
GDP (1966/7 = 100). (b) Unemployment rate. (c) GDP deflator of prices
(base 1966/7). *Source:* M. W. Butlin 1977.

depression and war, and the physical destruction of capital in the latter, provided the basis for a worldwide investment boom in the late forties and early fifties.

This alone would have produced a classic investment-led upturn of the business cycle and probably explains much of global expansion through to the mid fifties. The extension of the long boom for a further fifteen or twenty years seems to have more to do with the effects of the greater international mobility of capital and technology in search of profit opportunities, and with the rapid growth of world trade as impediments were removed and peace, together with relatively stable currency values, became accepted. To these one might add some bunching of technological innovations leading to heightened demands for motor vehicles, domestic appliances, and perhaps the arms race.

If the postwar boom was shared by many countries, was it inevitable that Australia would be involved? To the extent that the boom was a cyclical response to high levels of income and depreciated capital stocks, the answer is clearly yes. As elsewhere, investment within Australia had been postponed during the thirties and the war so that there was considerable scope for expansion. By the mid fifties such catch-up investment was probably completed and a continuation of the boom depended on other forces. The extension of buoyant economic conditions until the early seventies then seems to result from demand conditions. High levels of household formation, demand for domestic appliances and motor cars, the expansion of exports to meet demand, and the need for investment goods in those industries fulfilled this condition. Wage growth at rates not very different from productivity trends did nothing to upset the strong growth pattern. Australia was unlike many other countries in that this was not a period of rapid growth of the public sector, so that the extension of the boom after the war period is explained best by the development of private industry, although such public policies as high immigration targets were important.

Overall it is clear that Australia entered the boom phase at the start of the war (see Figure 4.1), not in 1945. This difference from many European economies is simply a reflection of the fact that they suffered from extensive destruction and dislocation of physical resources until at least the late forties. The broad pattern of the Australian experience, however, mirrored the global pattern: The long boom in Australia had three distinct phases – the war economy, the investment boom, and the demand expansion.

A major idiosyncrasy of the Australian growth experience, however, has been the accumulation of labour. As discussed below, local additions to the labour force were much greater in the sixties than in the fifties, but immigration has played a more important role in the postwar period than have domestic increases. Economists working in the area of immigration tend to talk about the factors that "push" people out of their own countries and those that "pull" them here. Because Australia has had higher living standards than most other countries, it has generally had an excess supply of migrants on offer and has rationed access. The white Australia policy, quotas, and strict language tests have all been used to restrict immigration. At the same time assistance has often been available to migrants from Britain and Ireland to induce them to shift. Postwar policy was designed to tap this excess supply. The consensus discussed in Chapter 2 that Australia was underpopulated was reinforced by the threatened invasion of World War II.

However, despite these variations, the growth of the labour supply still did not parallel the dramatic increase in the capital stock. The growth in capital was driven basically by a sharp rise in the marginal propensity to invest and augmented by *private* capital inflows that more than offset lower levels of overseas borrowing by the *public* sector. In the immediate postwar period household liquidity and savings were high as a result of war financing, expenditures were controlled by rationing and import controls, and generous depreciation allowances were available, so that high levels of investment were to be expected. These effects were enhanced by the long period through depression and war in which investment had been at low levels. Household saving declined as a source of funds for investment, to be replaced in the late fifties and early sixties by corporate savings accumulated especially through depreciation allowances.

A second major idiosyncrasy of Australia's economic development in the postwar era was the sluggish growth of trade. Figure 4.2 charts exports plus imports as a percentage of GDP. The stimulus provided to the economy by the traded sector in the period immediately after the war is apparent, but the level sustained through the sixties is well below the level of the twenties; in earlier periods the rates had been even higher. In the postwar period world trade grew considerably faster than world production (Maizels 1963).

In summary, the Australian economy grew faster in the postwar period than before the war. The global boom was probably a cyclical phenomenon associated with low levels of investment during the period 1930–45 (Matthews 1968). It continued for longer than earlier booms because the high levels of demand were sustained without substantial inflation, because trade liberalisation allowed specialisation, and perhaps because of product booms based on the motor vehicle, electronics, and petrochemical industries. Australia shared the investment boom and then

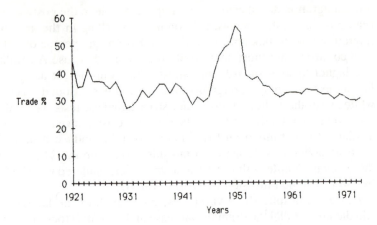

Figure 4.2. Ratio of trade to GDP. *Source:* M. W. Butlin 1977.

sustained high levels of activity mainly through population growth and the import of capital. Foreign direct investment, induced to Australia by protective barriers, was an important conduit for the inflow of capital and technology. Although one might think that the expansion of the public sector might have been important, and that trade could have stimulated the growth rates, neither seems to have played a major role.

4.2   Anatomy of the long boom

The easiest way to understand the nature of the long boom is to consider its supply and demand aspects. The major features of supply that will be considered are the growth of labour inputs, the growth of capital inputs, and technological change. On the demand side the major categories are the money supply, investment demand, housing, public sector demand, and exports.

Supply

Two main studies have attempted to explain differences between the economy's ability to supply goods during the long boom and earlier periods. Both rely on a technique – growth accounting – used extensively by Denison for a variety of countries.[3]

---

[3] It assumes that the aggregate output of the economy is produced by the joint application of given proportions of labour and capital, and that new technology simply increases the amount of output produced with fixed quantities of inputs. The proportions used are the shares of labour and capital in national output.

Table 4.1. *The role of the factors in the long boom (annual cumulative percentage increases)*

Period	Output	Inputs		
		Labour	Capital	Residual
Haig and Cain (manufacturing)				
1919/20–1928/9	4.0	1.9	4.9	0.9
1948/9–1960/1	5.9	2.4	4.8	3.0
Kaspura and Weldon (private economy)				
1900/1–1978/9	2.9	1.1	2.7	1.1
1946/7–1978/9	4.5	1.7	5.2	1.4

Sources: Haig and Cain 1983: 187; Kaspura and Weldon 1980: 13. The rates quoted in the text come from Kaspura and Weldon's appendix tables.

These studies suggest that the important change in the economy after the depression lay in the role of capital and technology. Whereas the major policy drive in the first thirty years of the century had been a population expansion and hence has fallen on the labour side of production, capital played the major role in the long boom. From Table 4.1 this is quite obvious. Haig and Cain (1983) find a small increase in labour inputs, more in capital, and a large role for technological change (the residual). Kaspura and Weldon (1980) again see labour as a minor contributor. By contrast, however, they see increases in capital inputs as playing a much larger role than technology. The fact that one study points to technology and the other to capital as providing the major stimulus does not seem especially significant, since most of the new technologies introduced have been embodied in new capital equipment. Since the studies are based on different industries and different time periods and make different adjustments for qualitative changes, the divergence in results is not particularly substantial. From a supply point of view the long boom was based on capital, not on labour.

Growth of labour inputs: While appreciating that capital played a more important role than labour in expanding national production during the long boom, it is important to recognise that the quantities of both increased significantly. Labour inputs grew by 1.2 percent per year from 1900/1 to 1938/9 but by 1.7 percent from 1946/7 to 1978/9.

The bulk of the explanation of this increase is to be found in the labour market chapter by Glenn Withers, but some brief comment can be offered here. Labour inputs to production are basically hours of work contributed by members of the labour force. The total pool of persons able to work is determined by birth rates, death rates, and net migration rates. Of that potential workforce, a percentage choose, or are forced, to work in the market and they select, or are required to work, certain numbers of hours. Thus one can select the key variables in determining the growth of labour inputs – hours of work, rates of labour force participation, rates of natural increase of population, and migration.

Because hours of work fell by over 10 percent, the explanation of the increase in growth of labour inputs must lie in either participation rates or growth of the potential labour force. Average labour force participation rates for males were about 5 percent lower in the postwar period, but this was compensated for by a slightly larger rise in female participation rates (based on all ages). Participation rate changes thus make little contribution to the higher growth of labour inputs. Birth rates, too, have been in historical decline. Rates of over seventy per thousand population prevailed for most of the period up to the thirties and sixty has been the more usual level in the postwar years. To make matters worse, the birth rate fell to around fifty during the depression, far lower than rates (such as ninety) recorded in the 1890s, so that the rate of natural addition to the labour force after the war was far lower than for any period for perhaps a hundred years. This leaves migration as far and away the greatest source of labour force addition and as the principal agent behind the more rapid labour force growth after 1945. Net migration in the first four decades of the century had contributed 0.1, 0.4, 0.5, and 0.1 percentage points to population growth rates compared with 0.5, 0.9, and 0.8 for the decades from 1940 to 1970.

The international flow of factors of production such as migrant labour is hardly surprising. Australia has maintained controls on migration for many types of immigrant for many years. In such a situation of excess supply, changes in immigration policy have been the major determinants of the levels of migrant inflow.

Growth of capital inputs: As we saw above, the change in the rate of growth of inputs to the economy was even greater for capital than it was for labour. Growing at just 2 percent per year in the four decades to 1940, capital inputs expanded at 4 percent per year from 1940 to 1970. If we ignore the war years the rate jumps to 5.2 percent per year for the period 1946/7 to 1969/70. The measurement of capital inputs is particularly difficult, but it is clear that only the twenties of the prewar years come close to the rates sustained for most of the postwar period, a result that seems quite robust to definitional changes. (This explains

Table 4.2. *Private fixed capital investment by industry (millions of 1966/7 dollars)*

Year	Primary	Mining	Manuf.	Commerce	Finance	Other	Total
1918/19	67	13	74	38	N.A.	7	199
1928/9	69	20	71	96	N.A.	8	264
1938/9	106	43	166	84	N.A.	17	416
1948/9	309	20	272	104	7	106	818
1958/9	363	46	513	296	73	266	1,557
1968/9	546	419	908	403	311	603	3,190

Sources: N. G. Butlin 1964 for figures prior to 1940; *Australian National Accounts*, various years, after that.

some of the differences between Haig and Cain and Kaspura and Weldon.)

Whereas public nondwelling investment had dominated the earlier period, it in turn was dominated by private nondwelling investment after 1950. There was some increase in residential investment, but hardly on a scale to match the other categories. Contrasting the 1950s with the 1920s, we find that in real terms investment in nondwellings absorbed a larger share of the investment funds. Investment in real terms rose some 40 percent from 1950/1 to 1959/60, and 55 percent of that went to private nondwelling investment. By contrast, for the next decade the latter absorbed just 47 percent of the gain of 72 percent. Overall investment grew more rapidly in the sixties than in the fifties with less of the addition going to private nondwellings and more to private housing and the public sector.

Looking more closely at the industrial composition of private nondwelling investment (see Table 4.2) reveals that the initial increase was mainly investment in equipment in the rural sector, although manufacturing was also important. Then in the fifties commerce and manufacturing dominated investment; in the following decade mining and finance joined manufacturing as the major investing sectors. Thus we saw an export and an import-competing industry dominate the forties and an import-competing industry and a service industry rule the fifties, and then all three sectors expand dramatically in the sixties. Investment in equipment in the rural sectors in the late forties may have been promoted by the high rates of return implicit in historically high world prices. Since little of it went into fixed improvements, this period may just have been one of substitution of capital for labour. The rapid expansion of manufacturing was associated with substantial capital inflows and associated

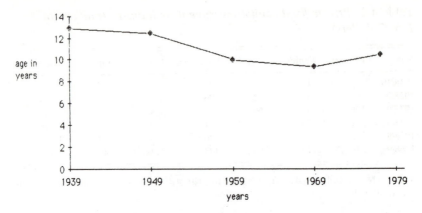

Figure 4.3. Average age (in years) of capital stock. *Source:* Haig 1980: data for manufacturing.

with the global growth of multinationals as well as the incentives provided by the Australian system of tariffs. The growth of mining investment was part of the round of resource discoveries that characterised the decade of the sixties.

The rates of return earned by foreign investors were high, especially in the 1950s. Studies by Brash (1966) and Johns (1967) found earnings rates of well over 10 percent for U.S. investors in the fifties, falling to around 6 percent in the sixties, and for British investors falling from 8 to 6 percent. This capital inflow was probably an important device by which Australia shared the productivity rises enjoyed in the postwar period. Foreign firms especially brought with them "best practice" techniques and technology and increased the productiveness of Australian inputs. Survey findings suggest that import controls and tariffs were important considerations for investing firms. The removal of controls in 1960 increased the level of competition and removed many of the rents being earned. Thus Johns (1967) found that the profitability of American direct investment in Australia had dropped by the mid sixties to much the same levels as prevailed elsewhere in Australian industry, and for British firms to below the level earned by the parent company in Britain. Opening up the Australian economy in the 1960s to more international competition may thus have retarded private sector investment in manufacturing and redirected at least some of it towards resource-based industries as well as to the nontraded sector.

These investment trends had a marked impact on the nature of the stock of capital used in production. Figure 4.3 gives some indication. Forgone investment during the depression and war caused an aging of the capital stock that was soon reversed after 1945. Gregory and James (1973), Haig (1975), and Salter (1962) have argued over whether or not new factories built in the mid fifties in Australia were more productive than existing factories, but it is difficult to believe that such a dramatic reduction in the average age of the capital stock was not at least partly responsible for the high rates of growth recorded in the fifties – although it was in part a consequence of the higher growth rate.[4]

The sources used to fund investment also changed over the course of the boom period. For most of the postwar years, domestic saving provided some 90 percent of the savings required to finance investment. Household savings played a gradually decreasing role, as did the government surplus on current account, while depreciation allowances and undistributed profits became progressively more important. Household saving fell while corporate saving increased, although postwar household saving was probably high by historical standards. These topics will be considered in the chapter on capital markets.

Demand

If one thinks of aggregate domestic demand as the final sales of goods and services in current dollars, then it is closely proxied by nominal GDP. By this measure, demand grew by 3 percent per year from 1920 to 1940, by 6 percent to 1947, and then by 9 percent from 1947 to 1967. This acceleration of the growth of aggregate demand is a notable feature of the long boom, and the 11 percent rate for 1967–74 suggests that excessive demand pressures may have played a role in the ending of the boom.

Table 4.3 presents the evidence. Monetary growth is an obvious candidate explanation of the six-percentage-point acceleration in demand growth during the boom relative to the twenties and thirties. M3 growth jumped five percentage points, from 3 to 8 percent per year, and thus offers a likely explanation. The table does not reveal, however, that most of the monetary growth actually took place between 1940 and 1947 (up 14 percent per year when demand grew by just 6 percent, compared with 6 percent annual growth from 1947 to 1967 as demand accelerated by 9 percent). The rates of monetary growth thus move in the wrong direction to explain adequately the growth of demand, so that one must look to the interaction of monetary and nonmonetary forces.

From Table 4.3 it seems that the initial expansion of demand between

---

[4] Matthew Butlin suggests in Chapter 9 that part of the fall is a result of a decline in the share of capital in (long-lived) buildings relative to plant and equipment.

Table 4.3. *Rates of growth of some elements of demand (growth rates as percentage per year in real terms)*

Element	1921–40	1937–47	1947–57	1957–67
GDP	−1.4	3.2	4.5	4.7
Private consumption	1.1	−0.2	4.1	4.2
Residential investment	−1.5	−15.6	8.1	5.8
Other private investment	0.4	1.5	8.8	6.9
Other public investment	0.2	−9.0	8.9	6.1
Public expenditure	1.5	9.3	5.9	5.4
Real M3	2.5	5.9	7.2	6.8

Source: All data from M. W. Butlin 1977; all rates calculated by regression of the log of variable concerned against time. Some of the rates cited were not statistically significant.

1937 and 1947 was largely accounted for by the growth of public expenditure associated with the war. At its peak, war-related expenditure by government had made up nearly 40 percent of total national expenditure, part of which was a direct contribution to demand and part a displacement of other expenditure and consumption categories. As the economy emerged from the war, other categories of investment grew rapidly, displacing public expenditure from its leading role. Although the pace slowed after the initial burst of postdepression, postwar investment was put in place, investment did retain its leading role through the boom.

Analysts of the U.S. economy (such as Okun in commenting on Gordon 1980) have suggested that the growth of government was an important factor in explaining the more stable economic performance of that country in the postwar period, but it seems to have had a less pronounced impact here. However, Auld (1967) does find that the adjustments to public expenditures during the postwar period were generally in the right direction to offset incipient cyclical tendencies.

The contribution of exports to the maintenance of high levels of demand was variable. Export revenue grew strongly through the late forties, peaking with the Korean war. After a sharp fall in 1951/2, it tended to grow at much the same pace as national income, though with a slight tendency to lag. This relatively steady performance masks some dramatic changes in the composition and direction of trade. Wool's share rose from around 40 to over 50 percent of export receipts in the early fifties, only to fall to around 20 percent by the end of the sixties. In volume terms, wool exports grew strongly but reductions in price from the postwar highs, in part due to competition from synthetic fibres, lessened

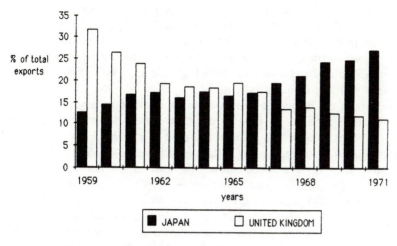

Figure 4.4. Direction of trade: Japan versus Britain. *Source: Year Book Australia*, various years.

its contribution to export receipts. The shares of manufactured goods and mine products are those that showed the greatest increases. Figure 4.4 dramatically depicts the decline of the UK and rise of Japan as markets for Australian exports. Whereas Australia had been tied into a system of British Commonwealth preference since 1932, which protected trade with Britain, Japan had been prevented from buying iron ore since 1938. The signing of an agreement on trade with Japan in 1957, the lifting of the iron embargo, and the entry of Britain into the *EEC* were all instrumental in the dramatic change in the direction of trade. Hitching Australia to Japan's rising "sun" boosted the demand for Australian products in the decade of the sixties.

Matching supply and demand

Unemployment had dropped from a peak of around 20 percent in 1931/2 to 7.5 percent in 1937/8; it then rose slightly to nearly 9 percent in 1939/40 before falling to 1 percent in the face of the high wartime demand for labour. The small rise in unemployment just before the war seems to have been associated with a contraction of the U.S. and other economies (the unemployment rate in the USA was at a new peak of 19 percent in 1938 compared with 25 percent in the depths of the depression). The sharp increase in output from around 1940 as the economy responded to rapidly rising demand caused a remarkable reduction in unemployment. It effectively closed the gap between potential and actual output. And from 1941/2 until the mid seventies Australian unemployment exceeded 3 percent only once, in 1961/2. This long period of operation of the economy at close to its capacity level suggests that aggregate demand was maintained at a high enough level to fully employ the rapidly growing output potential.

For part of the period there was either open or suppressed inflation. Price controls moderated inflation during the war, but as the controls were lifted an annual rate of price increase of around 10 percent per year prevailed through the late forties (see Figure 4.1). The years immediately after the war were characterised by high commodity prices flowing into the economy, producing a peak in 1950/1 (during the Korean war) when general prices rose nearly 26 percent. Part of this inflation was probably also the result of an undervaluation of the pound, since Australia had devalued relative to the U.S. dollar twice in the decade by retaining a fixed value in relation to the pound sterling. The collapse of export prices in the early fifties and the expansion of supply to meet shortages and bottlenecks moderated the inflationary pressures and ushered in a new era of price stability. Though prices never fell, as they had for example in four years of the twenties and in three of the thirties, the annual inflation rate from 1953/4 to 1970/1 never exceeded 4 percent for two consecutive years.

This balance between demand for goods and services, in the face of their ever expanding supply, is one of the remarkable characteristics of the long boom. Again, it is a characteristic shared by many countries and for which no specifically Australian explanation need be sought. Broadly it seems that the competition for income shares was less dramatic in many countries in this period than it was to be later or even than it was in Latin America during the boom (Maier 1978). If the natural rate of unemployment of the economy is defined as the minimum level of unemployment compatible with stable prices, then it was around 2 percent in the late fifties and sixties. This contrasts sharply with conjectures that the natural rate of unemployment is now around 6 to 8 percent. Explaining this difference is a major challenge to contemporary commentators on the economy.

4.3   Economic incidents

Despite the earlier suggestion that the postwar era can be characterised as one of steady economic growth, a number of important economic episodes deserve a unified treatment.

Depression legacies

Perhaps the most important effect of the depression was the psychic impact on those who lived through it. There had been partial recovery by 1938/9, but unemployment was still above the 1920s average of about 6 percent. Memories of the dark days of 1931 and 1932 when nearly one worker in five had been out of work were strong in the minds of policy makers, and much of the forties and fifties was dominated by the concern not to allow a recurrence of mass unemployment. There was far greater sensitivity to economic suffering than had been the case before.

It was widely accepted that the financial sector either had been responsible for the depression or had at least acted so as to worsen its consequences. The banking system was thus specifically targeted for reform. In 1935 the Lyons (conservative) government set up a royal commission into banking, amongst the members of which was future Labor prime minister Chifley. The commission is notable mainly in two ways: It recommended a system that required private banks to keep a proportion of their reserves on deposit with the central bank; and much of the discussion took place in the context of Keynes's *The General Theory of Employment, Interest and Money* (1936), to which members of the commission had access. Implementation of the reserves recommendation allowed government a greater control over monetary policy than had previously been the case, and Keynesian analysis came to dominate economic policy making for the next thirty or forty years.

The long depression decade had a marked effect on the accumulation of factors of production. Birth rates fell, as did migration, and formation of both public and private capital was put off. Marriages were postponed, the crude birth rate dropped by a third, and immigration stopped. Investment slowed. Public capital formation by the end of the thirties was back at its late twenties level, while for the private sector the figure stood just 10 percent higher. Machines aged as investment was postponed. In summary one can say that the depression caused a backlog of demand for children and for investment, setting the scene for the postwar boom in each.

War economy

The economic management problem posed by war was that of restricting the resources used for civilian purposes in order to redirect them to war use. Policy during World War II was designed by a core of economists – Giblin, Wilson, Copland, Melville, and Coombs – whose names were to become associated with the Keynesian thrust of postwar policy. They preferred to restrict the private use of resources by a series of direct controls (such as rationing), by borrowing heavily from the public, and by increasing taxation, though monetary expansion was also important.[5]

The redirection of the economy was substantial. Private consumption and investment fell from 86 percent of gross national expenditure in 1938/9 to just 56 percent four years later, a decline in real terms of over 20 percent. War-oriented expenditure grew from 10 to 36 percent in that same period. The armed services grew from virtually zero to roughly a quarter of the male workforce.

Constructing this war economy and then reconstructing the civilian economy were planned by a group of economists employing explicitly Keynesian models (Maddock and Penny 1983). Planning the war economy had commenced well before the outbreak of hostilities, and planning for peace was under way even before the Japanese had been turned back in New Guinea. With the memories of the depression in mind, the planners were much impressed with their successful wartime experience in manipulating aggregate demand by the coordination of monetary and fiscal policies supplemented by direct controls. The monetary policies of the central bank and the taxation and expenditure policies of the Treasury had been used to steer the macro economy for the first time. The redirection of the labour force needed to recruit so many males to military duties was achieved by three main methods: growth of the labour force (natural growth augmented by retirees and young workers), elimination of unemployment, and a reduction of the number of civilian jobs held by males. The loss of males to the civilian labour force was partly made up by females. The female labour force participation rate jumped from 29 percent in 1938/9 to 35 percent in 1943/4 – a 20 percent increase in five years, but not to a level that seems unusual by present standards.[6]

---

[5] The story of the war economy is told in S. J. Butlin (1955) and S. J. Butlin and Schedvin (1977).

[6] The need to recruit females to the labour force had important repercussions for pay relativities. Females had traditionally been paid just 55 percent of male pay rates, the difference being justified by the assumption that females were dependants, and made easier by the division of jobs into "male" and "female". This neat discrimination was upset by the war. Male bodies were needed as sacrifices to the god of war – that being another traditional male role – and female bodies were needed to maintain production. The movement of females into "male" jobs was handled for wage purposes by creation of a Women's Employment Board. For a probationary period of between six months and two years women were paid about 66 percent of the male rate, after which they usually moved to 90 percent. These devices served to attract many women to what had previously been male industries, although the failure to award, in general, the full male rate was widely criticised. The 1949/50 basic wage inquiry led to the general assessment

Although the wartime increases in taxation applied to both direct and indirect taxation, the income taxation story had the greater significance for the future. Prior to 1942 both the states and the commonwealth had taxed incomes. The Australian constitution allows the commonwealth government the right in times of war to impose extensive controls over private activity. Price controls, for example, were put in place under these provisions. Rather than use these defence powers to gain control of income taxation, the Curtin (Labor) government devised a scheme that would allow it to monopolise income taxation for the commonwealth even after the war. Amongst the motives were equity concerns (state taxation had been very uneven), the need to increase taxation takes in order to reduce private demand pressures, and the preference for more centralised control of financial administration (Maddock 1983). One consequence has been that in the postwar period the states have found it difficult to finance their programmes, while the commonwealth has not; fiscally Australia has become more centralised. The High Court has limited the states' use of indirect taxation, and the commonwealth legislation on direct taxation has made them reluctant to impose income tax surcharges.

War also distorted the foreign influences on the economy. The war itself meant that trade patterns and factor flows were altered. At first glance it appears strange that the volume of imports rose during the war years, but after imports of aeroplanes, ammunition, etc. are netted out the ratio of nonmilitary imports to nonmilitary gross national expenditure was quite stable during the war years at around 13 percent. This suggests that there was little scope during the war years for import replacement. Nevertheless the demand for war materials did cause a dramatic increase in industrial production. Though total factory output increased by only a quarter in real terms, the greater part of this was in war-oriented industries. The category "metals, machinery, etc." more than doubled and accounted for nearly half the total increase. The big changes were understandably in aeroplane and arms production, but sizeable gains were made in metals processing and engineering. The industrial pattern established during these war years persisted through the fifties and sixties. The metals, machines, and engineering industries retained their expanded roles, with motor vehicles and metal fabrication expanding as the war production in that category slowed.

In several ways the war intensified certain effects of the depression.

of the female basic wage at 75 percent of the male rate. Since that time female participation in the labour force has steadily increased, although the female pay rate stayed at that level until the late sixties and early seventies.

The most obvious concerned investment. Private capital formation in terms of the replacement of obsolete production lines, the construction of new premises, and the maintenance and upgrading of the housing stock had been further postponed. The real level of capital formation in the private sector in 1945/6 was at the level of 1928/9 but was to double in the next three years. Public capital formation stood at less than half its earlier level. The squeeze on investment other than in war production during the war years clearly provided a sizeable backlog of desired investment. It was also in the war period that Australians learned to look to the USA rather than to the UK.

Demographic trends were likewise affected. There was an element of pessimism during the war about Australian population trends: "It seems reasonably clear that marriage-fertility has declined continuously over the past twenty years, despite great changes in economic conditions. There is no sign that this trend has been halted by war conditions" (Karmel 1944: 80). But the war itself, and especially the direct threat of invasion from Asia, had reinforced a preference for an expanded population. The land area occupied was seen as too large for a population of just over seven million to defend. With a greater population desired, and doubts held about the rate of natural increase, large-scale immigration was seen as the only solution.

Postwar reconstruction

As the military effort wound down and the moral support for controls lessened, how would the economy respond? How does one add 700,000 persons to the civilian workforce without having an addition of 700,000 unemployed? What happens to aeroplane and armament factories? These problems had concerned economists in government from as early as 1941, and a series of plans for postwar reconstruction developed. The economic effort for war had been planned and so too was that for peace.[7]

The central fear of the planners and most economic analysts was that after a brief flurry the economy would relapse into a depressed state, as it had done after the first world war. If the economy had gone from 8 percent unemployment to under 1 percent under the strong demand stimulus of government wartime expenditure, it was widely accepted that the end of the war could see a return to a high rate once again. The desire to avoid this was widespread, but how was it to be avoided? The reconstruction planners saw three main mechanisms. The first was

---

[7] This topic is also discussed in some detail in Chapter 11 and is probably best surveyed in the Postwar Reconstruction Seminar (1981).

the need for a commitment by other countries to the maintenance of full employment; the second was the use of aggregate demand policies to achieve full employment within Australia; and the third was the need to maintain price controls during the postwar adjustment period while the excessive private sector savings were released. Considerable effort towards the achievement of the first objective was exerted in international conferences and forums. In the event, both Great Britain and the USA committed themselves to full employment policies in the postwar era. The allied countries had feared a relapse to restrictive trade and currency practices and came to agreement at Bretton Woods in 1944 on a variety of principles concerning trade and exchange rates.

The goal of maintaining full employment was enshrined in the white paper *Full Employment in Australia* tabled in parliament in 1945.[8] Its basic proposition was that private expenditure is volatile and that "the essential condition of full employment is that public expenditure should be high enough to stimulate private spending, to the point where the two together will provide a demand for the total production of which the economy is capable when it is fully employed" (p. 5). Public expenditure was thus to underwrite full employment. Whereas the head of the Treasury Department could argue in 1939 that unemployment was a state rather than a federal concern, by 1945 full employment became the central plank of federal economic policy.

The third aspect of the reconstruction package concerned the need to retain price and other controls in the short run. Whereas the USA and Canada chose to remove controls quickly, allowing rapid adjustment to the new situation, Australia and Britain chose a more cautious route. Inflation peaked in the USA by 1949, but Australian prices kept rising until they were caught up in the Korean boom, though the trends in unemployment were not very different. One important consequence of the inflation was that it reduced the value of fixed-interest government debt held by the private sector. In a sense it reduced the cost to the government of the war.

Australian postwar reconstruction policy was heavily concerned with unemployment policy and with the growth of the public sector but only superficially concerned with manufacturing.[9] The desire to take advan-

---

[8] See Cornish (1981) for a full discussion of the genesis.
[9] Another major initiative concerned the disposal of war materials. About 100,000 vehicles were sold off as war surplus. Priority was given to purchasers in the rural industries, and some 70 percent of vehicles went there. Some army vehicles had no obvious alternative use, but with fewer than 60,000 tractors in use at the end of the war this policy gave a big boost to rural production and clearly was important to the postwar agricultural expansion (Martin and Penny 1983).

tage of changes in the nature and scale of production during the war was mainly contained in tariff policies and import controls. The motor vehicle industry alone attracted very specific planning concern. S. J. Butlin and Schedvin (1977) tell an interesting story of the process of negotiating with General Motors. The policy makers' desire to have a high employment industry such as cars in place in the postwar period overcame Labor party opposition to foreign ownership and control of key industries. Believing Australia was unlikely to be a base for such an industry, the government accepted General Motors' terms with scarcely a quibble.

Labour also sought its postwar quid pro quo. The jump in female relative wages from 54 to 70 percent, the general acceptance of two weeks' annual leave, and the reduction of standard hours from forty-four to forty are three obvious cases. The labour movement had sought a number of these changes before the war. During the war years it had accepted high levels of production and deteriorating working conditions as part of the war effort, but with the peace, and with a Labor government in power federally, it expected some gains. Chifley, the prime minister, clearly felt his postwar reconstruction programme could be threatened if wages and conditions improved too rapidly in the first few years after the war, when a major recession was considered likely. As the economic position improved, the unions became more emphatic and won their way to both a wage increase and an hours reduction.

Investment incentives were also offered to encourage postwar development. All industries were offered accelerated depreciation allowances from 1945 to 1951, though after that the rural sector alone maintained this privilege.

Korean episode

The Australian economy flourished in the immediate postwar years. Unemployment peaked at under 3 percent in 1946/7, when half the armed forces were demobilised in one year. Real GDP grew strongly, as did the number of civilian jobs; and although prices also increased sharply, the much feared postwar recession failed to materialise. The inflation was quite predictable, since the real value of the stock of money had doubled over the war years as a result of expansionary monetary policy and price controls while real production had only increased by a quarter. In December 1949 a conservative coalition government was elected to office on a policy of dismantling many of the controls the continuation of which was seen as necessary by the Labor party. The leader of the new government, Menzies, was fortunate in that he came to power at the start of a long period of strong growth. His name is now inextricably linked in Australian history with the long boom.

Having handled the postwar adjustment easily, the economy was about to be shocked by a huge increase in export revenues with the advent of the Korean war. A combination of buoyant export prices, foreign capital inflow, and continuing licensing of imports had led to big gains in international reserves. Britain devalued by 30 per cent with respect to the U.S. dollar in September 1949, and despite a strong balance-of-payments situation Australia followed suit. Australia had also devalued by 14 percent, along with Britain, at the start of the war. With buoyant exports, the government chose a policy of further easing import restrictions rather than revalue.

The Korean war gave a new upward thrust to export revenues. By mid 1950 wool prices (wool earned about 45 percent of export revenues in the late forties) had started to rise rapidly – up 50 percent on the previous season. Led by wool, and with metals and other prices also high, Australian exports, which had already been at a historically high proportion of GDP, jumped to over 30 percent in 1950/1. Imports could not adjust as rapidly, and the consequent buildup in reserves and the increase in the money supply caused a large jump in prices, around 25 percent, the largest increase this century on a year-to-year basis. The government chose to ease the import restrictions further, and this caused a large growth in imports the following year just as export prices and revenues fell sharply. Fearing a balance-of-payments crisis, the Menzies government imposed direct controls on virtually all imports. They were relaxed slightly several times but not finally removed until the sixties.

The contraction of the economy was so sharp that real GDP growth was negative in 1952/3 and male unemployment reached 4 percent for some months. The import spree of 1951/2 had important consequences for an economy that had suffered restrictions for so long. The composition of imports changed hardly at all, but the volume of imports in 1951/2 reached double its 1947/8 level, which in turn had been equal to the prewar peak.

Steady growth

From 1953/4 to the mid 1970s the Australian economy experienced a long period of steady growth with few shocks.[10] Recessions occurred in 1957/8, 1961/2, and 1965/6, but these were much milder than most of the others this century. Throughout, the annual unemployment rates

---

[10] Waterman (1972) provides probably the best chronicle of these years.

were low and the economy grew strongly in terms of scale and wellbeing. The major challenges were the removal of import restrictions in 1960 and the arrival to the labour force of the baby boom cohort.

At the exchange rates that prevailed during the fifties and the early sixties, Australian imports had a tendency to exceed exports, and much of the policy discussion of the period concerned potential crises with the balance of payments. Australia's capacity to import had been enhanced by several factors. Capital inflows exceeded remittances abroad for virtually the whole period, so that none of the export revenues were committed to meet those claims, and by the late sixties the net capital inflow was strongly positive. The terms of trade were also favourable (though gradually deteriorating), so that a certain volume of exports allowed an increased quantity of imports. Despite this, strong demand for imports tended to threaten the balance of payments. This was used to justify the maintenance of direct import controls until 1960 and also the occasional use of contractionary monetary and fiscal policy.

By 1959, however, a resolution to remove the direct controls had been achieved. Export prices rose and the restrictions on imports were first relaxed and then virtually abandoned in early 1960 (Moffatt 1970). Imports surged as a consequence. This tendency was exacerbated by an increase in GDP growth, by a cut in income taxes, and by faster wage growth. These actions coincided with a fall in export receipts. The signs of a balance-of-payments crisis were thus "obvious". Waterman (1972) argues, however, that import competition had slowed domestic production by mid 1960 and that the import surplus had a contractionary effect on financial markets. The consequent decline in domestic activity may have reestablished equilibrium in the balance of payments without policy action. Misreading the signs, the Menzies government provoked a credit squeeze with a supplementary budget in November 1960 wherein both borrowing and lending were made more difficult. A sharp contraction of the economy resulted, with unemployment peaking at just over 3 per cent. It was enough to choke off the high levels of import demand but almost unseated the government.

Whereas the dominant policy concern of the 1950s had been the fear of balance-of-payments deficits, it ceased to be a major issue in the sixties. Diversification of exports, especially into minerals, and sustained high levels of capital inflow rendered revaluation of the Australian dollar possible in the early 1970s, whereas devaluation had seemed more appropriate in the 1950s. The 1960s saw the fastest growth rate of any decade this century, and also the fastest per capita growth rate. This was achieved despite the decline of the principal export, wool, and the demise of Britain as the principal trading partner.

These changes were in part natural and in part the result of policy. Agricultural diversification had been pursued since the 1880s with the extension of transport facilities and subsidies, subsidised research, irrigation schemes, and extensive price supports. The elimination of the rabbit problem in the 1950s, however, had made pasture improvement worth while and had produced increased payoffs to investment, which in turn led to the flowering of the agricultural sector starting in the sixties. This and the provision of an improved road network seem to have aided meat exports as well. The expansion of mineral exports is somewhat harder to explain. The traditional mineral export, gold, was in decline, but iron and coal grew rapidly, and booms in nickel, aluminium, and other metals occurred in the seventies. Exports of iron had been embargoed since 1938. The relaxation of this prohibition in the sixties resulted in a rapid growth in trade in iron and also coal with Japan (ironically the earlier embargo had been designed to stop trade with Japan in materials for war). The use of open-cut techniques and bulk handling at ports made Australia a competitive supplier of these types of minerals at the ruling exchange rates.

The major success of the economy in the sixties was probably the expansion of the volume of exports. Taking the average of the 1920s as a base of 100, average export quantum in the thirties was 128, the forties 140, the fifties 187, and the sixties 334. Even with import prices rising faster than export prices, this expansion allowed the demand for imports to be met with little pressure on the balance of payments. The major contributors to this were minerals and manufactures, which are discussed further in Chapters 6 and 7 by John Freebairn and Kym Anderson respectively.

The postwar period is well known as one of great immigration, but the effect was unequally spread over the period. Migrants made up 70 percent of the workforce growth in the fifties but just 40 percent in the sixties. In numbers, the average annual intake of migrants was almost the same in the two decades, so that the decline in their contribution to the workforce in the latter period is almost wholly due to a rapid increase in nonimmigrant additions. During the great depression birth rates had been low. Consequently in 1947 the fifteen- to nineteen-year-old cohort was small – just over 10 percent of the potential workforce. As a result of the postwar baby boom, that cohort represented 16 percent by 1961. Such an addition to the workforce required a considerable expansion in the number of jobs available as well as providing a fillip to demand. The economy had added an extra 1 percent of jobs per year during the late fifties; this jumped for the mid sixties to nearly 3 percent, with only the short period of unemployment associated with the credit squeeze. The growth of the housing sector and of durables production in the late sixties was at least in part a result of home formations by the baby boom children. One can speculate that the decline in these sectors by 1980 was a result of the passing of this kink in the age distribution through the age group when households are formed.

The emergence of inflation

The price level as measured by the GDP deflator rose 78.6 percent over the course of the fifties compared with 32.5 percent in the following decade. The Korean war inflation and the relaxation of price controls account for most of the early rise, and the period from about 1953/4 through 1968/9 is one of slow upward movement in prices. Considering the very low levels of unemployment, this must be considered surprising. If the economy was operating so near full employment, why were not different groups taking advantage of the shortages of their skills? Why was there so little inflation?

Some tentative explanations can be put forward. Excess demand pressures were able to be met by the relaxation of import quotas while they remained in place so that a government determined to resist inflation had a ready tool. The willingness of adversely affected groups to accept this may have been born in the experiences of the 1930s. Such groups were unwilling to rock the boat or to undermine the social consensus that underlay full employment. Claims on social resources were muted. By the late sixties, after the long period of prosperity and full employment, after the unions had shaken off their internal wranglings over communism, and after the economy had been in both external and internal balance for such a long period, it hardly seems surprising that the quickening of the per capita growth rate should have produced competition for shares. The fact that the upsurge in inflation occurred globally suggests the working of an external force Australia could not resist or the working here of conditions that also applied elsewhere in much the same way. Inflation, in part caused by competition for income shares, became a central focus of policy in the seventies. The next chapter develops this theme.

4.4   Conclusion

Australia's postwar economic performance paralleled that of many other economies. A small trading economy could hardly avoid it. The unusual characteristics of the period were limited: The sustained growth spurt started earlier, the expansion of scale was greater, and the per capita performance a little worse than average. The share of trade in GDP tended to fall.

In the global boom the expansion of world trade is usually thought to have played an important role through allowing countries to reap the benefits of increased specialisation. Australia eschewed such a strategy. It encouraged diversification through protection, inducing producers to look to domestic expansion for their growth while shielding them from foreign competition. The immigration policy in turn provided the basis of an expanding local market. Thus rather than exploit the advantages of trade Australia diverted resources into servicing the domestic economy, with obvious costs to growth. The economy has become considerably more diversified and in many ways more resistant to global economic downturns, but this has not been achieved without cost.

References

Abramovitz, M. 1979. "Rapid growth potential and its realisation: the experience of capitalist economies in the postwar period", in E. Malinvaud (ed.), *Economic Growth and Resources,* vol. 6: *The Major Issues,* pp. 1–30. London: Macmillan.

Auld, D. A. 1967. "A measure of Australian fiscal policy performance, 1948–49 to 1963–64". *Economic Record* 43: 333–53.

Boehm, E. A. 1979. *Twentieth Century Economic Development in Australia.* 2d ed. Melbourne: Longman Cheshire.

Brash, D. T. 1966. *American Investment in Australian Industry.* Canberra: Australian National University Press.

Butlin, M. W. 1977. *A preliminary annual database 1900/01 to 1973/74.* Research Discussion Paper 7701. Sydney: Reserve Bank of Australia.

Butlin, N. G. 1964. *Australian Domestic Product, Investment and Foreign Borrowing, 1861–1938/39.* Cambridge: Cambridge University Press.

Butlin, N. G., A. Barnard, and J. J. Pincus. 1982. *Government and Capitalism.* Sydney: Allen & Unwin.

Butlin, S. J. 1955. *War Economy 1939–42.* Canberra: Australian War Memorial.

Butlin, S. J., and C. B. Schedvin. 1977. *War Economy 1942–45.* Canberra: Australian War Memorial.

Cain, N. 1970. "Trade and economic structure at the periphery: the Australian balance of payments, 1890–1965", in C. Forster (ed.), *Australian Economic Development in the Twentieth Century,* pp. 66–122. London: Allen & Unwin.

Cornish, S. 1981. *Full employment in Australia: the genesis of a white paper.* Research Paper in Economic History No. 1. Australian National University.

Denison, E. F. 1967. *Why Growth Rates Differ.* Washington, D.C.: Brookings Institution.

Gordon, R. J. 1980. "Postwar macroeconomics: the evolution of events and ideas", in M. Feldstein (ed.), *The American Economy in Transition,* pp. 101–62. Chicago: University of Chicago Press.

Gregory, R. G., and D. W. James. 1973. "Do new factories embody best practice technology?" *Economic Journal* 83: 1133–55.

Haig, B. D. 1975. "Do new factories embody best practice technology? – a comment". *Economic Journal* 85: 378–82.

1980. *Capital Stock in Australian Manufacturing.* Canberra: Department of Economics, Research School of Social Sciences, Australian National University.

Haig, B. D., and N. G. Cain. 1983. "Industrialization and productivity: Australian manufacturing in the 1920's and 1950's". *Explorations in Economic History* 20: 183–98.

Johns, B. L. 1967. "Private overseas investment in Australia: profitability and motivation". *Economic Record* 43: 233–61.

Karmel, P. 1944. "Fertility and marriages – Australia 1933–42". *Economic Record* 38: 74–80.

Kaspura, A., and G. Weldon. 1980. *Productivity Trends in the Australian Economy 1900–01 to 1978–79.* Research Branch Working Paper No. 9. Canberra: Department of Productivity.

Keynes, J. M. 1936. *The General Theory of Employment, Interest and Money.* London: Macmillan.

Maddison, A. 1982. *Phases of Capitalist Development.* Oxford: Oxford University Press.

Maddock, R. 1983. "Unification of income taxes in Australia". *Australian Journal of Politics and History* 28: 354–66.

Maddock, R., and J. Penny. 1983. "Economists at war: the Financial and Economic Committee 1939–44". *Australian Economic History Review* 23: 28–49.

Maier, C. S. 1978. "The politics of inflation in the twentieth century", in F. Hirsch and J. H. Goldthorpe (eds.), *The Political Economy of Inflation.* London: Martin Robertson.

Maizels, A. 1963. *Industrial Growth and World Trade.* Cambridge: Cambridge University Press.

Martin, A. W., and J. Penny. 1983. "The Rural Reconstruction Commission, 1943–47". *Australian Journal of Politics and History* 29: 218–36.

Matthews, R. C. O. 1968. "Why has Britain had full employment since the war?" *Economic Journal* 78: 555–69.

Moffatt, G. G. 1970. *Import Control and Industrialisation.* Melbourne: Melbourne University Press.

Postwar Reconstruction Seminar. 1981. Held at Australian National University. Collected papers and transcript of discussion are amongst the Oral History Holdings of the National Library of Australia.

Salter, W. E. G. 1962. "Marginal labour and investment coefficients of Australian manufacturing industry". *Economic Record* 38: 137–56.

Sinclair, W. A. 1976. *The Process of Economic Development in Australia.* Melbourne: Longman Cheshire.

Vernon, J. 1965. *Report of Committee of Economic Enquiry.* 2 vols. Canberra: Commonwealth of Australia.

Waterman, A. M. C. 1972. *Economic Fluctuations in Australia, 1948 to 1964.* Canberra: Australian National University Press.

CHAPTER 5

The end of the long boom   *Australia*

ADRIAN PAGAN

1227
1313

There was a mood of optimism in 1966/7 concerning the economic future of Australia. The foreword to the Treasury's *The Australian Economy, 1966* captures this perfectly: "Nevertheless, the outlook as a whole seems reasonably propitious both abroad and at home, and there is certainly a strong urge for expansion within the economy and a wealth of opportunities for it. The scope for it is bounded only by the limitations of our resources of capital and labour." Such an attitude had good historical support. From 1947/8 to 1967/8 the Australian economy grew at an average rate of 5.1 percent as measured by GDP at constant prices. Moreover, as Figure 5.1 shows, after the early 1950s growth was uniformly high, with only occasional deviations induced by episodes such as the 1961 credit squeeze. But, as this graph also illustrates, the conjunction of events that resulted in such growth seemingly came to an end in the 1970s. Table 5.1 charts the way in which the rosy outlook of 1966/7 faded.

A number of distinctive features are revealed by an examination of this table. The long boom continued until 1973/4, but in its closing years inflation began to emerge as a serious problem for policy makers. Growth in the years to 1973/4 rarely declined from the average for more than a single year, but between 1970 and 1973 inflation jumped from around 3 percent to 7 percent per annum. After the end of the long boom in 1973/4, Australia experienced a period of very sluggish growth, averaging only 2 percent per annum in the period 1974/5–1977/8. With an increasing labour force and productivity, this inevitably meant a rise in the rate of unemployment, and the 1970s witnessed a number of increases in that rate. By the end of the decade it stood at 5.8 percent, in comparison with the 1.4 percent it had been at the beginning. Despite this, inflation remained stubborn. After a burst of 19.6 percent in 1974/5, the minimum yearly rate of increase in the gross national expenditure (GNE) deflator achieved in the 1970s was 7.7 percent, and the decade closed with inflation rising again to 10.4 percent per annum.

I am grateful to Bruce Chapman, Alan Hall, and Neil Johnston for their comments on previous versions of this chapter.

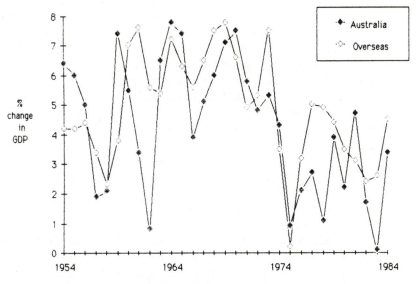

Figure 5.1. Percentage change in GDP 1953/4 to 1983/4. Key: ——— UK, USA, and Japan growth rate in GDP weighted by shares in Australian exports. . . .Australian nonfarm GDP growth (prior to 1960/1 GDP growth). *Sources:* Up to 1981/2: Norton and Garmston 1984: Tables S.18, 1.4, 5.2. Thereafter: OECD, Economic Outlook, June 1985, with export weights for 1982/3.

The 1980s opened with much the same optimism as had been evident in 1966. Another of the periodic mining booms that have characterised Australian history led to euphoria over Australia's future, and the average yearly growth rate of 3.6 percent in nonfarm GDP over the years 1978/9–1980/1 seemed to support that outlook. Unemployment registered its first decline since 1973/4, and it was only the stability of the inflation rate that constituted a cloud on the horizon. Perhaps the last was not surprising given the correspondence of actual and potential growth rates in Table 5.1 during 1978/9–1980/1. In retrospect, this was just the ride to the top of the roller coaster; the drop in 1982 was precipitous, with the level of GDP actually declining in 1982/3, unemployment jumping to a record 11.4 percent, and inflation almost halving in response to the depressed conditions. As with all roller-coaster rides, however, the plunge down was followed by an upsurge, and the yearly growth rates in GDP seen in Australia in the years 1983/4 and 1984/5 of 4.9 percent and 4.6 percent were quite remarkable. Not since 1970 had there been sequential years of such good economic performance.

Figure 5.1 is striking evidence of another feature; the end of the long boom signalled a break in Australia's relations with the rest of the world. Until 1973/4 Australia's economic growth experience largely mirrored that elsewhere. Thereafter Australia failed to share in the strong recovery evident internationally in the mid seventies, ending the decade with growth at the same pace as overseas economies purely because they were exhibiting a strong downward trend. For a period in the 1980s Australia even resisted the world recession, but when it finally succumbed the effect was dramatic, ushering in the worst recession of the postwar years.

The facts of recent economic experience to be explained in this chapter are therefore the ending of the long boom around 1974; the extraordinarily weak growth in the economy over the mid 1970s relative to that occurring in the developed world; the recovery at the end of this decade; and the strong recession in 1982. Because of the space devoted in Chapter 4 to the factors sustaining the long boom, most of this chapter is concerned with the elements bringing about its end. But, as the evolution of any economy is conditioned by its past states, reviewing the terminal phase of the boom is an essential ingredient in any analysis of the subsequent downturn. Recognition of this relationship largely determines the structure of the chapter. It begins with a brief résumé of the theoretical apparatus underpinning the investigations, proceeds to an account of the period 1966/7 to 1972/3, provides a description of developments during the seven years following the end of the long boom in 1973/4, and culminates with an analysis of the 1982/3 recession. Some of the major themes are then drawn together in a conclusion.

The two great commandments for journalists "What happened?" and "Why did it happen?" constitute alternative approaches to the subject of this chapter. Much has been written in the first vein. Norton (1982) collects a series of interpretive articles he has written about the era, and Jolley (1978) gives an account of events until 1977. Publications such as the *Australian Economic Review* and the Statement No. 2 accompanying the commonwealth budget speech furnish readily accessible and thorough histories of the events that this chapter is concerned with. However, very few of these documents aim to interpret this experience with the tools supplied by macroeconomic theory.[1] Such a deficiency motivates the approach taken in this chapter. Inevitably this decision means that what is offered is only incidentally an economic history per se. It is the interpretation of the economic history that is paramount.

---

[1] Hewson and Nevile (1983) and Pitchford (1983) are notable exceptions.

Table 5.1. *Growth, unemployment, and inflation in Australia 1966/7–1983/4 (percentages)*

Period	Phase	Nonfarm GDP[a]	Potential nonfarm GDP[b]	Unem-ployment[c]	Inflation[d]
1966/7–1969/70	Upswing	6.3	6.0	1.6	3.5
1970/1–1973/4	Downswing and strong recovery	5.0	5.0	2.1	8.4
1974/5–1977/8	Recession with aborted recovery	2.3	4.0	5.3	14.2
1978/9–1980/1	Upswing	3.6	3.6	5.8	9.4
1981/2–1983/4	Downswing and strong recovery	1.8	3.6	8.3	9.5

Sources: [a]Nonfarm GDP at 1979/80 prices: Treasury/Australian Bureau of Statistics NIF–10S model data base (year-on-year growth).

[b]Potential nonfarm GDP at 1979/80 prices: NIF–10S model data base (year-on-year growth). Constructed by the peak-to-peak method.

[c]Rate of unemployment (survey unemployed as a percentage of civilian labour force averaged for each August); taken from Norton and Garmston 1984: Table 4.3.

[d]Average rate of inflation in implicit GNE deflator (year-on-year growth); taken from Norton and Garmston 1984: Table 5.15b. For the first period, average 1966/7 prices are used; for the next two, 1974/5; and for the last, 1979/80.

5.1   Some theory

No consistent account of the developments of the 1970s is really possible without some model of the economic process to guide the analysis. The basic analytical tools of this chapter are the aggregate demand and supply curve for *domestic* output that formed the core of Keynes's great contribution. Because of the centrality of inflation, the curves are expressed in terms of rates of change rather than in levels, and Figure 5.2 illustrates how the two schedules interact to determine the *growth rate* in output and the *inflation rate* of domestic prices.[2]

Each of the curves in Figure 5.2 is drawn under the assumption that certain factors are held constant. For the demand curve, these can be placed into one of three categories corresponding to effects originating from (i) the international economy, (ii) the stance of monetary and fiscal

[2] The emphasis on domestic output and prices arises from the need to place the theory in the context of an open economy. Dornbusch and Fischer (1984) contains a good account of the theory outlined here.

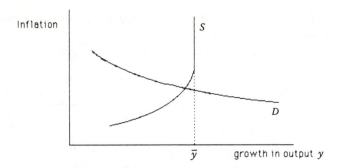

Figure 5.2. Determination of output growth and inflation.

policies, and (iii) the state of expectations. Under (i) the rate of growth in demand for domestic output will depend upon movements in foreign economic activity and changes in the competitiveness of export and import-competing industries. Changes in the domestic policy stance have an obvious influence upon aggregate demand, although measuring such variations is not an easy task. Finally, the state of expectations is important for certain items of expenditure making up demand; uncertainty associated with variable income streams is particularly likely to be a cause of sustained shifts in demand growth.

The most important characteristic of the supply curve in Figure 5.2 is the growth rate in output, $\bar{y}$, at which it becomes vertical. This barrier will be referred to as the *sustainable* rate of growth, as attempts to make the economy expand faster for any appreciable period merely create inflation. Because the growth rate in output and the rate of unemployment are connected, an alternative way of expressing this constraint is to refer to a natural rate of unemployment, rather than to sustainable growth. By definition this unemployment rate becomes that which is consistent with constant unit labour costs. Whenever unemployment is lowered below this rate, pressures on labour costs are such as to make extra production unprofitable.[3]

Looking at capacity problems from this labour market perspective is helpful in identifying factors influencing the sustainable growth rate. Suppose that the natural rate of unemployment is a constant. Then the sustainable growth rate is that which keeps the actual unemployment

---

[3] In symbols, unit labour costs (ULC) depend upon deviations of unemployment (u) from its natural rate $(\bar{u})$, while Okun's Law connects actual (y) and sustainable $(\bar{y})$ growth to the same factors. The two equations expressing these relationships are ULC $= b (u - \bar{u})$ and $u - \bar{u} = a (y - \bar{y})$.

rate constant at that level. As such, its limits are set by the growth rates in productivity and in the labour force. If the rate of natural increase in the population or of technical change slows, the ability to import labour skills is the key ingredient in determining sustainable growth rates. Later in this chapter this feature is identified as basic to any understanding of the long boom. Policy during that period concentrated upon facilitating strong demand expansion and keeping a rapid growth in supply available by a vigorous immigration programme.

Shifts in the supply curve cannot be wholly ignored, as unit costs may rise independently of the state of demand. Sometimes this may reflect legislation raising unit labour costs directly, or indirectly through on-costs such as annual leave loadings and a shortening of the work week. At other times the influence of droughts or price rises in strategic raw materials may be important. Not all of these effects lead to permanent shifts in the supply curve, but the period of dislocation may nevertheless be substantial. Over the period this chapter covers, examples of almost every kind can be found.

5.2   The terminal phase of the long boom: 1966/7–1972/3

The years from 1966/7 to 1972/3 were good ones for the Australian economy, although performance was no better than that attained in the rest of the world. Real nonfarm GDP growth never dropped below 4.2 percent and even reached 7.1 percent in 1969/70. There were supply-side shocks from the farm sector in 1967/8 and 1972/3, but the picture is one of fairly uniform growth with low rates of unemployment. Table 5.2 shows the main features of this transitional epoch.

Rapid growth in the years 1966/7–1969/70 reflected strong demand and a conscious effort to overcome any supply problems. On the demand side these years witnessed expansionary fiscal policies with budget deficits for the commonwealth government averaging 1.17 percent of GDP, although there was a conscious anticyclical pattern with the largest deficit of $643 million in 1967/8 and the lowest of $191 million in 1969/70. Much of the stimulus to economic activity did not originate in the government sector, however, with growth being particularly strong in exports and various components of private investment. Measured in constant 1966/7 prices, private dwelling investment, exports, and private nondwelling construction rose by an average of 9.5 percent, 10.9 percent, and 6.2 percent per annum respectively from 1966/7 to 1969/70.

Dwelling investment was boosted by the high rate of household formation in the mid 1960s, achieved through echo effects from the postwar baby boom and through a high migrant inflow. Both of these factors

Table 5.2. *Economic performance indicators 1966/7–1972/3*

Year	Nonfarm GDP[a] (%)	GDP[a] (%)	Unem-ployment rate[b] (%)	Inflation[c] (%)	Index of real unit la-bour costs[d]
1966/7	5.1	6.6	1.6	3.4	100
1967/8	6.0	3.6	1.7	3.5	98.8
1968/9	7.1	9.6	1.6	2.7	97.5
1969/70	7.1	5.6	1.5	4.7	96.8
1970/1	5.5	5.0	1.4	7.0	100
1971/2	4.4	4.7	1.7	7.1	100
1972/3	5.3	3.7	2.5	6.9	100

Sources: [a]Norton and Garmston 1984: Table 5.2. Year-on-year growth rates at constant 1974/5 prices except for 1966/7, which is at constant 1966/7 prices.
[b]Ibid., Table 4.3.
[c]Year-on-year growth in the deflator for GNE: ibid., Table 5.15b. Base as for note *a*.
[d]Treasury, *Round-Up of Economic Statistics*, September 1978, p. 25.

imparted an "autonomous" element to investment. Export growth reflected the export phase of a mining boom. Of the 44.6 percent increase in the value of exports from 1966/7 to 1970/1, some 27.9 percent was due to coal or metal-related exports (Norton and Garmston 1984: Table 1.3a). This was a notable shift, since mineral exports were only 16.9 percent of total exports in 1966/7. Gray and Gruen (1982: Table 4) attribute some 54 percent of the growth of GDP in the years 1966 to 1970 to the growth in exports. Import replacement was also extensive owing to the development of domestic oil fields. A large part of the private nondwelling investment in these years was also related to the development of the mining sector.

Both factors created a strong tendency to an external surplus, giving rise to the structural concerns of growth expressed in the Gregory thesis (1976). The central implication was that, ceteris paribus, the real exchange rate would appreciate and the traditional export industries would be forced to contract. An extensive debate was spawned concerning this proposition. Agriculture's share in GDP certainly declined over these years in parallel with mining growth, but the decline in this sector had been apparent for most of the century. The share of manufacturing in GDP (at 1968/9 prices) in fact rose slightly from 27.1 percent in 1966/7 to 27.7 percent in 1969/70.

Thus this phase of the long boom can be viewed as externally generated growth allied with a strong autonomous movement in investment. For policy, it was the level of sustainable growth rather than demand stimulation that became the central issue in the closing years of the sixties, a fact emphasised in *The Australian Economy, 1971* in its review of the period (p. 11).

To build the larger economy now thought possible would require very large amounts of additional capital and much more labour. Some of the additional capital would be accumulated locally and some would doubtless come from abroad. Similarly as to labour – we would be looking partly to local increase and partly to immigration. Strong though the impetus to growth might be, the rate at which it could be achieved in real terms would be limited by these factors.

The flexibility available in labour supply is seen in the expansion of the labour force at an average of 2.88 percent per annum from August 1966 to August 1970, giving a total increase of 571,000. The ability to import labour must have been an essential element in allowing a high sustainable growth rate. Participation rates of married females continued their steady increase, rising from 26 percent in August 1965 to 35.2 percent in August 1970. Productivity grew at much the same rate as in the 1950s and 1960s, averaging 3.1 percent growth per annum. Thus both the quantity and quality of the labour force during the 1960s were adjusted through a number of mechanisms, many of which might be expected to moderate any wage pressures built up by fast growth – an expectation borne out by the statistics on labour costs in Table 5.2.

Many of the factors responsible for the strong growth of 1966–70 continued into the early 1970s, but a new phenomenon began to claim attention. For most of the latter half of the 1960s the Australian economy appeared to defy the conventional wisdom and to puzzle policy makers by its ability to deliver growth with low inflation. But that concordance was to end with the new decade and, although growth would continue strong for some years thereafter, policy would become increasingly preoccupied with the issue of inflation; ultimately so much so as to make it the sole macroeconomic policy objective. In retrospect, the inflation rates experienced during 1970–2 seem modest, and it is sometimes difficult to comprehend the level of concern over them. However, it needs to be remembered that the institutions of the economy were ill adapted to an inflationary environment, and that the previous episodes of inflation, such as the Korean war, had been sharply terminated by resolute and immediate action.

What disturbed policy makers most about the developments of 1969/70 to 1971/2 was the rapid rise in unit labour costs – shown in Table 5.2 – without a great deal of change in unemployment. One possible interpretation was that the natural rate of unemployment had risen, making it necessary to restrain demand to allow unemployment to rise to this new level. Such a stance can be justified, since the main source of wage movements in these years was the changes made to awards occasioned by two major decisions of the Commonwealth Conciliation and Arbitration Commission. The first, the national wage case of December 1970, resulted in a 6 percent increase in all awards under its jurisdiction. The second was the metal industries award of July 1971, which added 9 percent to award wages through 1971 as a consequence of flow-on decisions. There seem strong grounds to believe that the national wage case decision shifted the natural rate of unemployment. It had been justified by the need to eliminate the wage drift that had occurred as a result of demand pressures and therefore raised nominal wages for a group of employees above what they would have been otherwise. The situation is not so clear for the metal industries award, as investment in metal-related activities had risen very strongly during 1969/70 to 1970/ 1. Of course such sectoral claims do not justify flow-ons.

Policy reacted to these events with the anti-inflationary budget of 1971. When combined with the effects of a monetary contraction begun in mid 1970, the effect was to produce a pause in growth in 1971/2 and a rise in unemployment between 1970/1 and 1972/3. But this early attempt to stamp out inflation was short lived. Monetary policy was relaxed in October 1971 and the 1971 budget strategy was reversed just four months after it had been set out. Fiscal policy continued on its expansionary way with the 1972 budget, framed largely with the 1972 election in mind.

More than just a weakening of resolve occurred, however. Domestic political considerations had meant a small 1.75 percent devaluation when major currencies were realigned in December 1971. In the light of the strong export performance in the late 1970s it was generally considered that the Australian dollar was undervalued at the new rate. Figure 5.3 indicates that a real exchange rate depreciation did occur after 1969, although of only a few percentage points. More important, reserves had increased from a historically high level of $2.7 billion (American billion) in December of 1971 to $4.4 billion in September of 1972. Part of this accumulation was undoubtedly the consequence of a speculative inflow in anticipation of an appreciation. With an election due at the end of 1972, there was a strong bias against sterilising the monetary consequences of such reserve changes, and throughout 1972 monetary expansion was continued at an increasing rate. Where the December-on-December growth in real M3 for 1971 had been 1.29 percent, by December of 1972 it was an enormous 13.13 percent. The long boom was about to end with a burst of inflation not seen since the Korean war years.

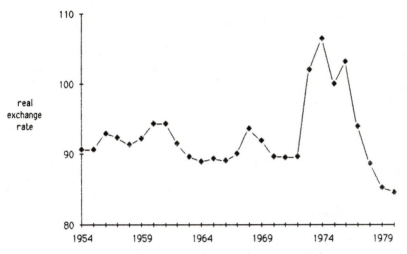

Figure 5.3. Real exchange rate index – Australia (1975 = 100). *Source:* McKenzie 1982. The real exchange rate is based upon consumer price indexes with import shares as weights.

5.3   The aftermath of the long boom: 1973/4–1980/1

The long boom actually ended in the June quarter of 1974, but its demise was presaged by a rapid decline in activity after the September quarter of 1973. Whereas yearly growth in the latter quarter had been 6.93 percent, by the first quarter of 1974 it had slumped to less than half that amount. Pessimism about the future of the economy developed correspondingly. The Australian Chamber of Manufactures/Bank of New South Wales survey for the last quarter of 1973 reported that some 73 percent of firms were expecting a slowdown, and a majority were convinced that it had already begun. Not that everybody felt the same way. The commonwealth treasurer, Mr. Crean, for instance, expressed doubts over the possibility of a recession emerging, stating in the *Adelaide Advertiser* (June 5, 1974): "Anyone who can read the present economic signs should be an optimist not a pessimist. Nineteen seventy four would be a more prosperous year then ever before for Australia."

Not only was this wrong, it was badly wrong. What few probably realised, however, was that this deterioration in economic performance was not transient but the precursor to a long period of relative stagnation for the economy. Nonfarm GDP growth, which had averaged over 5

Table 5.3. *Economic performance indicators 1973/4–1980/1 (percentages)*

Year	Nonfarm GDP[a]	Unemployment[b]	GNE deflator[c]
1973/4	4.3	1.8	13.2
1974/5	0.9	2.4	19.6
1975/6	2.1	4.6	16.0
1976/7	2.7	4.7	11.6
1977/8	1.1	5.7	9.5
1978/9	3.9	6.2	7.7
1979/80	2.2	5.8	10.4
1980/1	4.7	5.9	10.1

Sources: [a]Norton and Garmston 1984: Table 5.2, at 1979/80 prices.
      [b]Ibid., Table 4.3.
      [c]Ibid., Table 5.15b. Base as for note *a*.

percent a year for the six years prior to 1973/4, reached only 3 percent for the six that followed (Table 5.3).

Table 5.3 creates the impression of a steady recovery from a low point in 1974/5, interrupted by a very sharp downward shock in 1977/8. Such a description in fact conceals a considerably more variable performance: Boehm and Moore (1984) determine a classical cycle peak in June 1974 and a trough in October 1977. The growth cycle tends to be much the same, except that the peak is in February 1974. To emphasise the variable performance, it is interesting to note that the growth in nonfarm GDP over the year 1976 (December-on-December) was 4.2 percent when measured in 1979/80 prices. Although relatively small when compared with some of the rates recorded in 1973, it was not unimpressive.

Demand – the international influences

The world economy had turned down in 1974 following the first oil price shock and it was inevitable that Australia could not remain totally insulated from such a decline. But, although some deterioration in performance could not be avoided, the rapidity with which the downturn emerged in 1974 suggests that other factors were also involved. One candidate for this role from the demand side is a loss of international competitiveness, operating to shift the demand curve to the left. To assess the importance of this factor, Table 5.4 presents the real exchange rate from 1971/2 to 1979/80.

The strong real exchange rate appreciation experienced in Australia

Table 5.4. *Real exchange rate, structural deficit, and real M3 growth 1971/2 to 1980/1*

Year	Real exchange rate[a]	Structural deficit[b]	Real M3 growth[c]
1971/2	97.8	0.2	3.6
1972/3	104.7	1.2	15.7
1973/4	113.8	0.6	−2.0
1974/5	112.7	2.8	−3.1
1975/6	110.9	2.3	−1.3
1976/7	107.6	1.0	0.5
1977/8	99.6	0.3	−0.2
1978/9	94.9	0.1	2.8
1979/80	92.6	−2.5	0.9
1980/1	N.A.	−3.6	3.2

Sources: [a]Averages of calendar year results in McKenzie 1982: Table 1, Appendix C. CPI-based; 1975 = 100.

[b]Hewson and Nevile 1983: Table 5.1. This is the deficit adjusted for the influence of cyclical factors expressed as a percentage of GDP.

[c]June-on-June growth rates are used. M3 is taken from Norton and Garmston 1984: Table 3.3. The GNE deflator is at June of each year and is from *Quarterly Estimates of National Income and Expenditure*, December 1983, Table 42.

during the 1970s stands out in this table. Historically, there have been only two previous episodes in Australian history showing such strong appreciation (during the years 1921/3 and 1950/3), but in both of these cases the appreciation can be considered a reaction to an earlier depreciation. This was not so for 1972/3 to 1976/7. During the period of the long boom following the Korean war there was no discernible trend in the real exchange rate, making the appreciation begun in 1973 an unusual event.

What is of greater import is that the loss of competitiveness was largely a consequence of an appreciation of the nominal exchange rate rather than of relative price changes. From the last quarter of 1972 to the fourth quarter of 1974 there was an 18 percent real appreciation, of which 16 percent can be attributed to a nominal appreciation in the trade-weighted index.[4] Policy was therefore actively engaged in switching expenditure from domestic to foreign sources. In doing so it placed the import-competing (and export) sectors under severe competitive

---

[4] This represents a decomposition of the index of competitiveness based on consumer prices described in Table 7.5, National Economic Summit Conference, *Information Paper on the Economy*. Data supplied by the commonwealth Treasury.

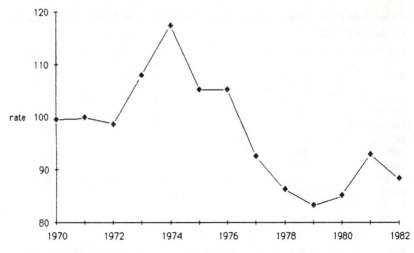

Figure 5.4. Trade-weighted rate of the Australian dollar. *Source:* Norton and Garmston 1984: Table 1.20.

pressure.[5] This pressure resulted in a yearly growth in nonfarm GDP for each of the three quarters after September 1973 of less than half the growth in gross national expenditure, while the yearly growth of imports was over 25 percent for the full year 1973/4.

A reversal of exchange rate policy occurred in September of 1974 with a devaluation of 12 percent against the American dollar. But, as Figure 5.4 shows, it was not until the 17.5 percent devaluation of November 1976 that the trade-weighted index returned to its level at the beginning of the decade. This is reflected in the real exchange rate; it is only in 1978/9 that the same state of competitiveness is attained as characterised most of the period of the long boom. Accordingly, there seems little doubt that the recession, although probably inescapable, was intensified by a policy that opted for an overvalued exchange rate.[6]

---

[5] The 25 percent tariff cut of June 1973 added to this; its effect was estimated in *The Australian Economy, 1973* to be equivalent to a 5 percent revaluation.

[6] An Australian Industry Development Association (AIDA) survey in 1977 (AIDA 1978) found that 26 percent of respondents gave import penetration as the primary cause of unemployment from 1974 onwards, with some 33 percent ranking it as second in importance. A question posed by the developments recorded in Table 5.4 is whether a real appreciation would have been observed if exchange rates had been more flexible. Private foreign exchange transactions for the 1973/4 year show a small surplus, perhaps indicating that the market was satisfied with the rate set. It is difficult, however, to infer very much from such a statistic, owing to the problems of separating portfolio from short-term speculative investments. As well, expectations regarding exchange rate

Demand – the domestic influences

Economic policy was extremely variable over the 1970s. As Table 5.4 shows, monetary policy swung from being very lax in the years leading up to 1973 to very tight in 1974, when record interest rates were observed, a peak of 22 percent in the ninety-day commercial bill rate occurring in May 1974. Barry (1978) cites the monetary actions of 1974/5 as the most severe over the whole sixteen-year period from 1961 to 1976. Thereafter, monetary constraints were relaxed for a short time, at least until the advent of the Fraser government in 1976. From the third quarter of 1976 to the second quarter of 1978 real growth in M3 was negative – see Pitchford (1983: Table 2) – and monetary "targets", first announced in 1976, were achieved until 1978/9. Thereafter, targets were exceeded, with real growth in M3 between 2 and 3 percent per annum. Monetary settings in the 1970s were therefore selected to restrain demand, with some very severe impacts at times.

Table 5.4 also contains evidence on fiscal policy variation, as measured by the ratio of the structural component of the commonwealth budget deficit to GDP. One interesting feature is the way in which monetary and fiscal policies were frequently in competition, the most prominent examples being in 1974/5 and 1979/80. Moreover, because it is *changes* in the structural deficit that cause shifts in the aggregate demand curve of Figure 5.1, Table 5.3 shows that fiscal policy was not designed to stimulate growth after 1974/5, and must have been a major contributing factor to the poor growth in 1979/80. Thus, during almost all of the 1970s either monetary or fiscal policy was actively seeking to depress growth in aggregate demand.

A belief that tight fiscal and monetary policies severely constrained economic performance in the epoch under study is by no means original; see for example the analysis by Pitchford (1983). Indeed, at several times during these years, official documents made explicit laudatory mention of the "restrictive fiscal/monetary settings". Perhaps the best summary of the attitudes of policy makers at that time comes from Statement No. 2 of the 1978/9 budget (p. 30):

Economic policy in recent years has been based on the premise that sustained economic growth can be achieved only through a revival in the private sector; within the constraints operating upon the policy framework, policy instruments

---

movements cannot be divorced from the rate-setting mechanism in force. It is hard to see why a speculator in 1973 would have been anticipating a devaluation in the short term when a newly elected government was clearly determined to force an appreciation and had both the resources and powers to control capital movements that would enable it to do so.

have therefore been set so as to achieve the pre-conditions for a sustained recovery in private activity. Central to this has been the endeavour to control and reduce inflation.

In popular discussion this strategy became known as "inflation first", owing to its predicate that growth would resume only after inflation had been controlled. Table 5.3 throws considerable doubt upon the validity of that proposition, the correlation between inflation and growth looking remarkably weak. The theoretical case for an exclusive concentration of policy upon inflation was equally weak, relying primarily upon a postulated relation between inflation and aggregate demand. Research on the links between inflation and demand, both here and overseas, suggests that the major effects are associated with the existence of regulated interest rates and the taxation of nominal rather than real quantities.[7] Inflation certainly reduces private demand in that it redistributes income between the private and public sectors through the capital losses of the former being balanced by capital gains of the latter, but aggregate demand would fall only if policy fails to offset such redistributive effects. A failure to compensate for these losses does appear to have occurred in the Australian context during the 1970s.[8] Anstie, Gray, and Pagan (1983) and Ouliaris (1981) attribute most of the reduction in the household consumption ratio to the capital losses sustained on financial assets held by the household sector when interest rates failed to rise with inflation. Pagan and Gray (1983) determine that a proportion of the decline in the after-tax rate of return to capital during the 1970s stemmed from the higher effective corporate tax rate induced by the interaction of inflation and the tax system. This reduction in profitability acted to depress private investment to some extent.

Demand – the influence of expectations

Possibly the major explanation for the increasingly restrictive policies of the Fraser government lies in the advent of wage indexation in July of 1975. Although complete indexation was rare, with most decisions providing indexation of wages only up to a "plateau" amount, its introduction meant that unit labour costs would fall only very slowly from

---

[7] See Pagan and Trivedi (1983) for a summary of this research.

[8] In fact, inflation also distorts the picture of the fiscal stance presented by Table 5.4, in that it is only real interest payments in budget expenditure that have a multiplier effect. Increased interest receipts by households that only compensate for inflation fail to provide any stimulation. Some rough computations in Pagan and Trivedi (1983: Table 23) show that the level of the deficits is changed quite markedly with this adjustment, although the movements are much the same from 1974/5 to 1978/9.

the level prevailing in mid 1975. As these had registered a sharp rise in 1973/4 and 1974/5, their mirror image, the rate of return to capital, would therefore only slowly return to levels characteristic of the long boom. Such depressed profitability had a direct effect on investment (Pagan and Gray 1983) and may also have had a strong dampening effect on the "animal spirits" of businessmen. A slack labour market was therefore seen as the best way of offsetting these effects and bolstering the case for partial indexation. In this perspective it is not inflation per se that is the policy objective but the restoration of business confidence.

There can be little doubt that the degree of uncertainty surrounding business decisions was heightened by the events of 1973 to 1975. Inflation rates were not only high but extremely variable. Monetary policies ran from being strongly expansionist to strongly contractionary; and developments involving taxation and protection were very unpredictable. In such an environment, there was a clear case for a stable set of policies, particularly those designed to encourage "faith in the future". Whether the policies actually adopted were right, however, is a different question. Initially, they probably were, but it is hard to escape the impression that the policies of restraint were continued far too long.

A major disadvantage of attempting to modify expectations through aggregate demand constraint is that it is very easy for the low level of demand to become the norm. Capacity decisions are then made relative to it, and it becomes increasingly difficult to depart from these anticipations without placing strains upon wages and prices. Cast in terms of Figure 5.2, the sustainable growth rate declines. There is some evidence that this occurred in the 1970s. The proportion of respondents reporting satisfactory capacity utilisation in the Confederation of Australian Industry/WESTPAC Survey of Manufacturing Activity fell from 55.2 percent in 1973/4 to a low of 29.0 percent in 1974/5 before a strong recovery to 42.25 percent in 1979/80. As seen in Table 5.3, the sharp rise in utilisation came from only moderate increases in output, suggesting that capacity had adjusted to the lower growth rates of the mid 1970s. This feature provides that prop for the dramatic increase in real wages that was to characterise the breakdown of wage idexation in 1980/1.

The supply side

From the preceding discussion it appears that a sustained leftward shift in the aggregate demand curve was a major factor in bringing the long boom to an end and in preventing any subsequent recovery. But shifts in the supply curve were also of some importance. With a constant natural rate of unemployment, sustainable growth is limited to the sum-

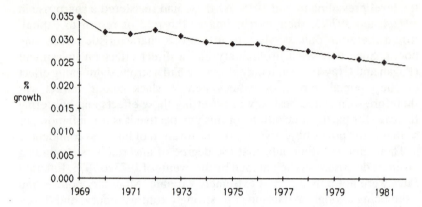

Figure 5.5. Growth rates in productivity 1968/9 to 1981/2 (percentages). *Source:* Data underlying National Economic Summit Conference (1983), *Information Paper on the Economy*, Table 5.10.

mation of workforce and productivity growth. Both of these components slowed markedly in the latter half of the 1970s. Population aged fifteen and over grew at 2.26 percent, 2.24 percent, and 1.78 percent for each of the three half decades covering 1966 to 1980 (Norton and Garmston 1984: Table 4.3), with a substantial part of this decline coming from less immigration.

Productivity growth also fell. Figure 5.5 plots growth rates of nonfarm GDP per hour from 1968/9 onward, illustrating the declining growth after 1973/4.[9] A comparison of productivity pre- and post-1973/4 indicates that a drop of one percentage point in the average growth rate occurred.

The combination of a lower potential labour force growth with reduced productivity performance could have lowered sustainable growth by some 1.5 percent per annum in the seventies compared with the sixties, giving growth of the order of 4 percent a year as an upper limit after 1973/4. But this would still yield growth well in excess of that which occurred, pointing to the importance of restrictive demand policy as an explanation of weak growth over most of the 1970s. Only if the natural rate were continually increasing could supply considerations be taken as solely determining growth. Some theories of macroeconomic performance do envisage such a scenario; for example, Hargreaves Heap

[9] Each growth rate at a point in time is computed from a regression of productivity against a constant and a time trend from 1966/7 to the relevant point. Data correspond to those in Table 4.1, National Economic Summit Conference, *Information Paper on the Economy* (1983).

(1980) argues that the natural rate of unemployment tends to converge with the actual rate through increasing mismatch in the labour market as new entrants fail to accumulate the requisite skills.[10]

What is at issue here is the initial origin of the unemployment. It could be that low levels of demand for some years ratify a new unemployment rate, as discussed earlier in the context of capacity. Alternatively, the unemployment may arise through factor substitution. Undoubtedly, some of the unemployment emerging in the 1970s reflected the latter, particularly during years such as 1974/5 that witnessed very rapid rises in unit labour costs for the nonfarm sector, the index for the latter increasing from 105.3 in 1973/4 to 110.5 in 1974/5 before declining to 105.3 in 1980/1.[11]

5.4   A false dawn: the mining boom of the early 1980s

The opening year of the 1980s saw the best growth in Australia since the opening years of the 1970s. At first sight such a result is surprising, as the rest of the world was rapidly heading into recession (Figure 5.1) and fiscal policy became even more contractionary (Table 5.4). Nevertheless, there was a major offset in the form of autonomous movements in investment. Dwelling investment had begun to recover in 1979, recording year-on-year growth (at 1979/80 prices) of 11.7 percent and 12.5 percent in the years 1979/80 and 1980/1 (Norton and Garmston 1984: Table 5.11). Undoubtedly, a facet influential in this surge was the looser monetary policy followed over the period from 1978.

The most striking features of 1980/1, though, are the very large growth rates in real business investment recorded, with plant and equipment expanding at 17 percent and nondwelling construction rising at an amazing 27.4 percent. This reflected a new mining boom. Very little of the response can be attributed to variations in the average rate of return to capital, as this had risen only slightly since 1977/8.[12] But the marginal returns to mineral-related investments were clearly viewed by the market as substantial. To better appreciate this point, Table 5.5 decomposes aggregate business investment for the period 1966/7 to 1981/2 into those components originating in the nonbase metal manufacturing, the base-

---

[10] Many other factors might account for year-to-year movements in the supply curve. One important candidate is the movement to import parity pricing of crude oil after 1978. This gave Australia a somewhat delayed oil price shock. Vincent et al. (1979) suggest this could have reduced GDP by 0.52 percent.

[11] Treasury, *Round-Up of Economic Statistics*, October 1983, Table 5.

[12] Pagan and Gray (1983) have the gross average after-tax real rate of return to capital in 1969/70, 1977/8, and 1980/1 as 15.77 percent, 11.87 percent, and 11.06 percent respectively.

Table 5.5. *Constant price (1979/80) business investment 1966/7–1981/2 (in million dollars)*

Year	Manufacturing		Mining[a]	Total[b]
	Nonbase metals[a]	Base metals[a]		
1966/7	2,495	682	949	N.A.
1967/8	2,532	605	1,286	N.A.
1968/9	2,634	519	1,661	N.A.
1969/70	2,798	642	1,942	10,197
1970/1	2,759	1,009	2,696	11,310
1971/2	2,515	969	2,839	11,205
1972/3	2,552	551	1,396	10,713
1973/4	2,650	516	1,349	11,246
1974/5	2,351	726	1,336	10,601
1975/6	2,247	619	1,145	10,746
1976/7	2,630	474	781	10,543
1977/8	2,998	417	1,158	10,666
1978/9	3,204	500	1,585	12,090
1979/80	2,919	767	1,402	11,787
1980/1	3,241	1,494	2,057	14,145
1981/2	3,072	2,036	2,717	14,129

Sources: [a]Hall 1984.

[b]Sum of private nondwelling construction and equipment investment, *Quarterly Estimates of National Income and Expenditure*, June 1983, Table 40.

metal manufacturing, and the mining sectors. Two mining booms stand out in the series. During the period of the second boom, 1980/1 to 1981/2, the total increase in business investment was $2,342 million (in 1979/80 prices) while that in mining plus base-metal manufacturing was $2,584 million. In contrast, investment in the nonbase metal manufacturing sector was stagnant, emphasising the importance of the autonomous element supplied by the mining booms of 1969/70 to 1970/1 and 1980/1 to 1981/2 as generators of growth.

5.5   Recession and recovery: 1981/2–1983/4

The resource boom ended as abruptly as it had begun. While it lasted it delivered very strong growth, with the calendar years 1980 and 1981 displaying yearly growth rates in nonfarm GDP of 3.5 percent and 3.4 percent respectively. But, as Boehm and Moore (1984) observe, activity actually reached a peak in June of 1981, with growth in nonfarm GDP during the last half of 1981 being a miserable 0.47 percent, in contrast

Table 5.6. *Economic performance indicators, 1981/2–1983/4 (percentages)*

Year	Nonfarm GDP[a]	GDP[b]	Unemployment[c]	GNE deflator[d]
1981/2	2.0	2.8	6.2	10.2
1982/3	0.1	−0.6	9.0	11.0
1983/4	3.4	4.9	9.6	7.0

Sources: [a]As for Table 5.3 but taken from *Quarterly Estimates of National Income and Expenditure*, June 1985.
   [b]As for Table 5.3; source as in note *a*.
   [c]Average rate of unemployment over the year. Taken from Statement No. 2, *1985/86 Budget Papers*.
   [d]As for Table 5.3; source as in note *a*.

to the 2.3 percent growth rates of the two previous half years. Worse was to come, and Table 5.6 outlines the dramatic effects upon both inflation and unemployment of the slowdown in growth.

Nineteen eighty-one saw a global recession that sent resource prices tumbling and caused reassessment of the value of many resource projects. Almost immediately investment prospects faded, with plant and equipment investment, growing at 8.5 percent and 19.5 percent in the half years of 1980/II and 1981/I, declining dramatically to register a 7.5 percent contraction in the last half of 1981. The worldwide recession that Australia had previously managed to avoid could no longer be ignored, but the developments of 1982 were affected to some extent by the settings of policy instruments. Table 5.7 looks at some of these.

Substantial expenditure switching occurred in the years 1980 and 1981 as Australia experienced the loss of international competitiveness seen in Table 5.7. At its peak in August 1981, the nominal exchange rate had appreciated by 13.5 percent, and this had been translated into a rise of 12 percent in the real exchange rate. After that time the trade-weighted index "floated" downward, but it was not until December 1982 that it returned to its level prior to the resource boom. During that boom an appreciation was an appropriate response to the record levels of capital inflow and the expectation of a strong current account in future years. But just as in 1973/4, the appreciation was sustained for far too long in the face of a downturn, and it meant only very slow output growth in the second half of 1981 despite the 3 percent growth in gross national expenditure. Imports rose 6.4 percent in the last half of 1981 and another 5.7 percent in the first half of 1982, and it was not until the second half of 1982 that they began to decline.

Table 5.7. *Real exchange rate, structural deficit, and real base money growth, 1981/2–1983/4*

Year	Real exchange rate[a]	Structural deficit[b]	Real base money[c]
1981/2	106.6	−4.5	2.0
1982/3	103.3	−4.0	−3.2
1983/4	105.6	−1.6	4.5

Sources: [a]Morgan Guaranty Index of Competitiveness; base: 1979/80 = 100.
[b]As for Table 5.4; source Nevile 1984.
[c]As for Table 5.4; sources are the *Reserve Bank Financial Bulletin*, August 1984 (base money), and GNE deflator in Table 5.6.

By 1982 there was another serious legacy from the resource boom for the real exchange rate. Wage indexation was formally abandoned in June of 1981, and collective bargaining was encouraged by the federal government. In a milieu of heightened expectations about future rises in living standards, some unions needed little encouragement to extract current real wage gains, and their task was facilitated by a substantial rise in capacity utilisation in the economy. Accordingly, the index of real unit labour costs for the private nonfarm sector jumped from 102.1 in 1980/1 to 105.7 in 1981/2, and this kept the real exchange rate high even in the face of a nominal depreciation.

Nineteen eighty-two was the worst year for Australian economic performance since the great depression, with the 1982/3 financial year exhibiting a reduction in the level of GDP and only a small expansion in nonfarm GDP. All of the factors described above as shifting the aggregate demand curve to the left coalesced with a tight monetary stance. Real base money shows a contraction in 1982/3 (Table 5.7), and interest rates were the highest since the second quarter of 1974, with the Australian Merchant Bankers Association ninety-day bill rate being 22.5 percent in April 1982. Not all of this movement can be attributed to tight monetary policy. Some must have been a delayed reaction to a phenomenon seen in overseas economies somewhat earlier – the reemergence of positive real interest rates on financial assets. Accounting for this development is not possible here, but it most likely reflects the substantial deregulation of financial markets occurring in the 1980s, particularly the removal of interest rate ceilings on bank deposits in December 1980 and the introduction of a tender system for treasury bond sales in July 1982. Whatever the cause, interest-sensitive components of demand such as dwelling investment registered large declines, that particular series fall-ing 24.7 percent in 1982/3.

So demand suffered a severe contraction in 1982. Policy did little to counteract it. That there was some recognition of the need for stimulus is apparent from Table 5.7; for the first time since 1978/9 the stance of fiscal policy ceased to be contractionary. In retrospect, though, the stimulus appears to be much too small, and it is only possible to un-derstand the inaction by noting the treasurer's remarks when presenting the 1982/3 budget: "However, we have not ignored the compelling ne-cessity to maintain an anti-inflationary economic strategy. To abandon that strategy would be to condemn the Australian economy to much greater travail than it presently experiences."

Attitudes such as this explain why the principal response of the com-monwealth government was not through the monetary or fiscal policy instruments, but through wages policy. A six-month wages freeze for public sector employees was agreed to at a premier's conference in December 1982. Subsequently it was extended to all private sector work-ers covered by federal awards, and there can be little doubt that, allied with the new Labor government's Statement of Accord on wages with the Australian Council of Trade Unions entered into in February 1983, these developments did much to restore competitiveness. The index of real unit labour costs fell from 106.2 in 1982/3 to 99.4 in 1983/4, actually falling below what it had been in 1966/7–1972/3.

If it was only aggregate demand that had declined after July of 1981, Australia would probably have experienced a recession anyway. But the worst drought in the eastern states since settlement generated a major supply-side shock, with gross farm product declining by 17.4 percent between 1981/2 and 1982/3. To understand the recession therefore re-quires both the demand and supply side of the scissors. But one should not overestimate the importance of the drought. O'Mara (1985) suggests that it made a negative contribution of 0.29 percentage points to nonfarm output in 1982/3 and concludes (p. 27): "However, it would seem highly improbable that the recession can be explained entirely in terms of the farm sector shock."

May of 1983 saw the bottom of the recession. Little needs to be said about the recovery, as its causes are almost the mirror image of those creating the recession. Figure 5.1 shows that, internationally, growth was strong. A change in the commonwealth government meant an em-phasis upon the reduction of unemployment, with fiscal policy playing a major role. As Table 5.7 records, the federal budget of that year was very expansionary, with a stimulus exceeding that of 1974/5. Finally, aided by good rainfall in the autumn and spring of 1983, farm output rebounded to its highest level ever. All of these features combined to initiate the strong expansion that still had not peaked some thirty months later in November of 1985.

5.6   Conclusion

Many factors go to make up a boom. But for a small trading country operating under a regime of fixed exchange rates, by far the most important one is the level of activity in its trading partners. If growth elsewhere is strong, domestic policy can be assigned to the task of retaining competitiveness, the principal instruments being directed at the promotion of productivity and the lessening of strains on labour markets. This scenario seems most applicable to the long boom. What departures there were from the pattern of growth elsewhere were largely transient. Sometimes these arose as a consequence of deliberate action, as in the 1961 credit squeeze; sometimes from climatic shocks, as in the various droughts of the postwar period; and sometimes from a reevaluation of the extent of natural resources. Although different in nature, all these shocks had the shared characteristic of impermanence and, when viewed in a longer time perspective, seem small disturbances around a smooth path.

It is the expectation that this was the normal state of affairs that characterised Australia in the mid 1960s. At that time there was a rapid improvement in the balance of trade, making the external position of less concern to policy makers than it had been for many years. Growth therefore accelerated, and most attention was devoted to avoiding supply bottlenecks.

Of course externally generated growth is a two-edged sword. The monetary consequences can easily lead to externally generated inflation, and demands are placed upon the authorities to manage the exchange rate wisely. For a number of reasons this requirement was ignored in the early 1970s, and such a failure ultimately proved to be the seed for the rapid inflation observed in the remainder of that decade. By the time action was taken it was too late. What was worse, it went too far in the opposite direction. Rather than adjust the exchange rate to offset existing (and projected) inflation differentials, policy aggressively appreciated the nominal exchange rate. The resulting real exchange rate appreciation was disastrous. Coming at a time when the rest of the world was about to move into a downturn induced by the first oil price shock, the policy quickly brought the long boom to an end.

It is remarkable how long the real exchange rate was overvalued in the 1970s. This feature cannot be ignored as a major contributing factor to the poor growth performance of this decade, particularly given the much better results achieved elsewhere. But it cannot be the sole reason. Sustainable and potential economic growth rates had both almost certainly declined as a consequence of the reduced productivity growth and a slower expansion of the labour force. However, both were substantially above recorded growth rates. This gap draws attention to the role of the demand side, and here it is noteworthy that either one of fiscal or monetary policy was always in a contractionary phase after the mid 1970s as attempts were made to eradicate inflation in Australia and to restore business confidence from the low point of 1974.

Initially such a policy met with success, although after 1978 it was imposed in the face of lower world inflation and in retrospect seems misguided. But, as in the long boom, external events eventually conspired to make the domestic stance largely irrelevant. The second oil price shock of 1979 began a recession in most of the world. In contrast, it brought to Australia an investment boom that more than offset the restrictive domestic policies being practised, and gave Australia its best growth for more than a decade. Such a stimulus could not be sustained permanently in the face of the return of a worldwide recession, and eventually Australia shared in the latter. A loss of international competitiveness, tight monetary policies, and severe falls in aggregate demand brought to Australia the worst recession since the disaster of the 1930s.

References

Anstie, R. K., M. R. Gray, and A. R. Pagan. 1983. "Inflation and the consumption ratio", in A. R. Pagan and P. K. Trivedi (eds.), *The Effects of Inflation: Theoretical Issues and Australian Evidence*, pp. 321–49. Canberra: Centre for Economic Policy Research, Australian National University.

Australian Industry Development Association. 1978. *Understanding Unemployment*. Melbourne: AIDA Research Centre.

Barry, P. 1978. "An indicator of central bank policy in an open economy", in M. Porter (ed.), *The Australian Monetary System in the 1970s*, pp. 171–86. Clayton, Victoria: Faculty of Economics and Politics, Monash University.

Boehm, E. A., and G. H. Moore. 1984. "New economic indicators for Australia, 1949–84". *Australian Economic Review* 4/84: 34–56.

Dornbusch, R., and S. Fischer. 1984. *Macro-Economics*. 3d ed. New York: McGraw-Hill.

Gray, M. R., and F. H. Gruen. 1982. "Inflation and unemployment in Australia", in R. L. Mathews (ed.), *Public Policies in Two Federal Countries: Canada and Australia*, pp. 97–114. Canberra: Centre for Research on Federal Financial Relations, Australian National University.

Gregory, R. G. 1976. "Some implications of the growth of the mineral sector". *Australian Journal of Agricultural Economics* 20: 71–91.

Hall, A. R. 1984. "Leasing finance and the industry composition of investment". Australian National University. Mimeograph.

Hargreaves Heap, S. P. 1980. "Choosing the wrong 'natural' rate: accelerating inflation or decelerating employment and growth". *Economic Journal* 90: 611–20.

Hewson, J. R., and J. W. Nevile. 1983. "Monetary and fiscal policy in Australia". Paper presented to the Conference on Government Policies towards Inflation and Unemployment in Developed Economies, Macquarie University.

Jolley, A. 1978. *Macro-Economic Policy in Australia, 1972–1976*. London: Croom Helm.

McKenzie, I. M. 1982. "Essays on the real exchange rate, investment and the current account". Doctoral thesis, MIT.

Nevile, J. W. 1984. *Budget Deficits and Fiscal Policy in Australia*. Working Paper No. 68. Centre for Applied Economic Research, University of New South Wales.

Norton, W. E. 1982. *The Deterioration in Economic Performance: A Study of the 1970's with Particular Reference to Australia*. Occasional Paper No. 9. Sydney: Reserve Bank of Australia.

Norton, W. E., and P. M. Garmston. 1984. *Australian Economic Statistics 1949–50 to 1982–83*. Occasional Paper No. 8A. Sydney: Reserve Bank of Australia.

O'Mara, L. P. 1985. *The Contributions of the Farm Sector to Annual Variations in GDP: Some Results from a Simple Empirical Model*. Discussion Paper No. 122. Canberra: Centre for Economic Policy Research, Australian National University.

Ouliaris, S. 1981. "Household saving and the rate of interest". *Economic Record* 57: 205–14.

Pagan, A. R., and M. R. Gray. 1983. "Inflation and investment: an historical overview", in A. R. Pagan and P. K. Trivedi (eds.), *The Effects of Inflation: Theoretical Issues and Australian Evidence*, pp. 261–81. Canberra: Centre for Economic Policy Research, Australian National University.

Pagan, A. R., and P. K. Trivedi. 1983. "The effects of inflation: a review with special reference to Australia", in A. R. Pagan and P. K. Trivedi (eds.), *The Effects of Inflation: Theoretical Issues and Australian Evidence*, pp. 10–100. Canberra: Centre for Economic Policy Research, Australian National University.

Pitchford, J. D. 1983. "Problems of Australian macroeconomic policy in the seventies". *Economic Papers* 2(1): 1–15.

Vincent, D. P., P. B. Dixon, B. R. Parmenter, and D. C. Sams. 1979. "The short term effect of oil price increases on the Australian economy with special reference to the agricultural sector". *Australian Journal of Agricultural Economics* 23(2): 79–101.

PART II

Sectors and product markets

CHAPTER 6

Natural resource industries

JOHN W. FREEBAIRN

Development of the Australian economy throughout the twentieth century has been closely linked to and dependent upon expansion of the primary sector. Over 80 percent of export receipts have been based on agriculture and mining products. The export income and wealth generated in the sector have provided an underpinning for the ambitious immigration and industrialisation policy programmes. The aggregate level of real output and productivity growth have trended upwards throughout the century in the case of agriculture. Large-scale capital-intensive mining projects and oil discoveries from the 1960s onwards have provided a major source of stimulus to employment, net exports, and real income growth. Diversification of the primary sector over the century has resulted in a more broadly based and stable contribution from the sector in the post–World War II economy as compared with the earlier decades of the century.

Australia's endowment of natural resources has given it a comparative advantage in the production and export of agricultural and mineral products. But, tapping the natural resources of the "Lucky Country" required considerable research, substantial investment, and much hard work in trying conditions. At the same time, fluctuations in seasonal conditions and dependence on the vagaries of world markets made it necessary to continually adjust the output mix and to develop and adopt more efficient production methods. Rising living standards, a decline in the relative cost of capital to labour inputs, and developments elsewhere in the economy were other forces for change.

Government policies directly and indirectly influenced the course of development of the natural resource industries. Sometimes these were negative, as for example in banning exports of iron ore between 1938 and the early 1960s and in affording a relatively high level of protection to the manufacturing sector. Other policies were positive influences: for example, government-funded research and extension and the provision of infrastructure.

I would like to thank Roy Powell, Stuart Harris, Alan Hall, Fred Gruen, and other contributors to this volume for their comments on earlier drafts.

This chapter falls into three sections. The first sketches the evolution of the agricultural and mining industries over the twentieth century in terms of output levels, markets and prices, use of inputs, methods of production, and contribution to national output and foreign trade. The following section discusses some of the key forces behind the observed changes. A supply and demand model framework is used to assess the effects of both autonomous and sectoral-induced shift influences, including government policy. Some of the interactions between the natural resource industries and the rest of the economy over the century are highlighted in a final section.

6.1   The stylised facts[1]

Around 1900

Both the agricultural and mining industries were more important parts of the national economy in 1900 than they are today. Agriculture provided about 20 percent of national income. In turn the pastoral sector was responsible for half of agricultural output and the wheat industry for a third; dairying, sugar, and fruit also were important. The mining sector contributed about 10 percent of national income, of which one-half came from gold, 20 percent from coal, and important components from copper, silver, lead, and tin. Over 95 percent of Australia's exports, some 20 percent of national income, was earned by the natural resource industries. Minerals provided 35 percent of export receipts, wool 35 percent, and other agricultural products (principally wheat, meat, and dairy products) about 25 percent. Most exports in the first instance went to Britain.

Organisation of the agricultural industries around the turn of the century reflected Australia's comparative advantage in land-intensive products and production techniques. Following the gold boom of the 1850s and the associated scarcity and high cost of labour, pastoralists developed methods of running large numbers of sheep with little labour except for shearing. Contract labour was employed for shearing and

---

[1] This section draws on a large number of sources of information. Basic statistical material comes from M. W. Butlin (1977), N. G. Butlin (1962), Haig (1966), Keating (1967), Bureau of Agricultural Economics (various publications), and Australian Bureau of Statistics (various publications). General references on Australian economic growth over the twentieth century include Boehm (1979), Forster (1970), and Shaw (1980). References more specific to the agricultural sector include Davidson (1981), Dunsdorfs (1956), Edwards and Watson (1978), and D. B. Williams (1982). References more specific to the mining sector include Bambrick (1979), Barnett (1979), Blainey (1978), Cook and Porter (1984), Raggart (1968), and B. Smith (1983).

hand shears were the dominant method. Developments in cultivation and harvesting machinery in the last half of the nineteenth century, together with inexpensive land, enabled Australian farmers to grow wheat profitably on larger areas and with substantially lower yields than European farmers. Horses and men provided most of the power and all grain was handled in bags. Transport costs had been reduced significantly with the arrival of railways and steamers. Refrigeration made possible the development of export outlets for meat and dairy products, principally butter, from the late nineteenth century, and these activities developed in the higher-rainfall coastal areas. Milking machines were a rarity in 1900. A labour-intensive sugar industry had developed with cheap indentured Kanaka (Melanesian) labour; however, federation ended this advantage.

Family farms were the dominant form of farm organisation in 1900, as is the case today. The farmer and his or her family provided most of the labour and capital. In those days the farmer also contributed a large part of capital development within the farm, particularly in land clearing, construction of water storage facilities, fencing, and building. Farm equipment and materials and domestic household needs were purchased from the rest of the economy. Generally the farmer depended on others for the transport and processing of farm production. Share farming was of some importance in the wheat industry. Government influences were directed primarily to the cost and availability of land and to the provision of infrastructure. The provision of railway, road, and port facilities was essentially in the hands of state governments. A large part of the development of irrigation schemes was initiated and financed by government. By 1900 the six states had departments of agriculture responsible for improving agricultural technology, and some of the agricultural colleges and university schools of agriculture had been established. But the contribution of publicly funded research, extension, and education to increased productivity was small at the time of federation.

The Australian farm sector differed in important ways from its counterparts in Europe and the longer settled eastern regions of North America. From the beginning Australian farmers were commercial rather than subsistence operators. Australian farmers were dependent primarily on market sales, principally export markets, for most of their income. Most of their household consumption needs, including some food, was purchased rather than farm-produced. Unlike the European, the Australian decision environment has not included fragmentation of farm plots and restrictive intergenerational transfer regulations. A harsher physical environment together with the high level of dependence on fluctuating world markets on the other side of the globe resulted in greater fluctuations of farm incomes in Australia than in Europe and in most of North America. On average, the typical Australian farm family received an income comparable with its urban counterpart, a characteristic not shared by the majority of northern hemisphere farm families. There were, however, many similarities between the Australian farm sector around 1900 and that of the midwest and great plains regions of the United States and of the Canadian prairie provinces.

Most of the mining industry of 1900 involved corporate enterprises, many assisted with overseas and particularly British funds, working underground mines. Examples are the gold mines of Coolgardie–Kalgoorlie, the lead, silver, and zinc (although most of the zinc was yet to be recovered from tailings dumps) mines of Broken Hill, and the coal mines providing fuel for trains and ships. About a third of coal output was exported. Although the miners had developed expertise in quarrying the ore, compared with developments to come the techniques of acquiring the precious metals from that ore and refining it were primitive and little different from techniques used in preceding centuries. Much energy was provided by people and horses together with steam power. The sophistication and scale of equipment were small relative to current methods.

Both the mining and agricultural industries of 1900 were subject to marked fluctuations and uncertainty. Market prices, which were heavily tied to export prices set in the European markets, were volatile. Seasonal conditions influenced agriculture as much then as now, and miners faced the uncertainties of size and mineral content of ore bodies.

1900 to 1930

Agriculture and mining followed different paths during the period 1900 to 1930. After a short spurt in growth to 1904/5, real output and employment in the goldmining industry declined through to the mid 1930s. Prices remained static or fell. The emergence of a steel industry after 1915 signalled the beginning of iron ore mining, but only for domestic use, and it stimulated the demand for coking coal. Coal exports to North, South, and Central America steadily increased up to 1924/5 and then declined with the shift to oil-fired ships and a loss of Australian coal industry competitiveness. By 1930 the share of the mining industry in national output had fallen from 10 percent in 1900 to under 2 percent, and the contribution of mineral exports in total exports was less than 5 percent.

Output from the agricultural sector trended upward throughout the period 1900 to 1930, particularly during the first decade, when it more than doubled; in part this reflects the low base caused by the severe droughts of the late nineteenth century. Most of the increased output was in wheat and to a lesser extent dairy products, with wool output remaining fairly constant. The increased wheat came from both more land and higher yields. Employment in farming rose throughout the period and reached 500,000 in 1929/30. A large part of the additional output was exported, principally to Britain, with small amounts to other European countries. The share of agriculture in national income fluctuated around a steady 20 percent, and the sector provided nearly 80 percent of export receipts in the 1920s.

During the early decades of the twentieth century agricultural production methods underwent significant changes, more so with crops than with livestock. New varieties attuned to the Australian rather than the European environment were released. The application of fertilisers, mainly superphosphate, became routine. There was a switch from continuous cropping to rotations with phases of fallowing, and mixed crop and livestock farming developed.

Government policy towards the agricultural sector had a strong growth orientation, particularly after the first world war. Also, there was a wish to diversify the economy, including the agricultural sector, to achieve greater stability. Agricultural development was seen to be important for population expansion and for generating export receipts. To some extent the decline of mining also exerted a positive push on governments. The early decades of the century witnessed further development of the railway system, increased investment in roads, additional irrigation schemes (including the Murrumbidgee Irrigation Area Scheme), and active involvement in closer settlement schemes. Government intervention in marketing became important after the period of extensive regulations during the war and the collapse of commodity prices in the late 1920s. Often the protection afforded manufacturing was used as a supporting argument. The policy of home consumption price schemes began in this period with sugar and soon was applied to butter, dried vine fruits, and wine grapes. Marketing boards were given official status and encouragement under specific state legislation.

In the mining industry considerable technological advances were successfully introduced to increase the retrieval rate of minerals and to expand the types of ores that could be mined profitably. New developments included the cyanide processes for goldmining. Flotation processes nearly doubled the recovery rates of lead and silver at Broken Hill and enabled the recovery of zinc. In addition, developments in mining machinery increased the rate at which ore and coal could be quarried.

1930s and 1940s

Agricultural output increased rapidly in the early 1930s and then sta-
bilised in the late 1930s and 1940s. The increase in the early 1930s,
despite the collapse of commodity prices from 1929/30 to the mid 1930s,
reflected the lagged response to extensive investment in the 1920s, favourable seasonal conditions, and a positive response by farmers to the
plea of government to "grow more wheat". The depressed market outlook was revealed in static investment, a decline in employment, and
lower output during the late 1930s and 1940s. Employment was fairly
constant over the 1930s, fell during the second world war, and partly
recovered after the war. Although the share of agriculture in national
income fell by a few percentage points, agricultural products continued
to be the principal source of export receipts.

The depression years brought a short revival in mining activity. Employment rose from 47,000 in 1930/1 to a peak of 65,000 in 1937/8 and
then steadily declined to 56,000 in 1949/50. The devaluation of 1932 and
increases in gold prices, together with readily available labour, contributed to a revival of both alluvial and underground goldmining. This
period included the discovery of deposits at Tennant Creek and re-
opening of the mines at Mount Morgan. By 1949/50 mining's share in
national income had fallen to 2 percent and its contribution to export
receipts was about 7 percent.

Increased intervention by government was an important characteristic
of the 1930s both overseas and in Australia. Efforts by European governments to protect their domestic agricultures from falling world prices
and from the volatility of world prices aggravated the fall in world prices
and subsequently also their volatility. The fall in farm incomes and the
high incidence of cases of bankruptcy during the depression provided
the impetus for a marked increase in Australian government support of
commodity prices, in the provision of finance at concessional rates of
interest, and in the provision of subsidies on fertilisers and fodders.[2]
Assistance by means of two-price schemes whereby domestic prices were
supported above world prices, with consumers rather than explicit government outlays footing the bill, was the favoured method. The schemes
also aimed to provide greater stability of prices both to producers and
domestic consumers. These schemes required complementary federal
and state legislation and proved a bonanza for lawyers in disputes over
interpretation of section 92 of the constitution, which specified free trade
between the states. Even with the government assistance, farm prices

---

[2] For details see Australian Rural Reconstruction Commission report (1946).

were at historically low levels during the first part of the 1930s. The fortunes of the wool and meat industries were still left to market forces.

Government intervention was pervasive during the second world war and subsequent years. Regulations supported a policy of cheap food prices. A trading arrangement with the United Kingdom and the two-price schemes kept the prices of many farm products to farmers below world market levels. At the same time the government became the principal purchaser of wheat and wool. Large stocks accumulated during the war period were not disposed of until the late 1940s.

Although major advances in machinery design and in the mechanisation of particular farm activities had been made during the period, only the beginnings of the massive investment programme necessary for the widespread adoption of this new technology were in place by the end of the 1940s. Though the storage, transport, and export of grain off-farm was by bulk, most farmers still employed labour-intensive bag systems. At the beginning of the depression horses provided most of the energy for cropping; by 1941/2 this figure had fallen to about a half; and by 1949/50 tractors were used for over 80 percent of the land cropped. Hand milking remained the dominant method in dairies, and gangs of men cut sugar cane with little help from machines. Reasons for the slow spread of mechanisation include depressed returns, the ready availability of labour until the war, physical restrictions on the availability of machinery during the war and the immediate postwar period, and a somewhat pessimistic belief that prices would fall after the second world war as they had after the first. The growth of mechanisation increased the share of farm output spent on nonfarm inputs and the dependence of the rural sector on the rest of the economy.

1950s and 1960s

Substantial changes were experienced by the agricultural sector in the 1950s and 1960s. Output rose by an average of 2 percent per annum in the 1950s, largely from the sheep industry in response to the Korean war boom, the adoption of improved pastures, and the control of rabbits. Growth in real farm output of about 3 percent per annum in the 1960s was dominated by wheat expansion and to a lesser extent by a renewed interest in summer grain crops and cotton; dairy and fruit production actually fell. Despite the growth in agricultural output, the sector's relative share in the economy declined sharply from 25 percent of national income in 1949/50 to 8 percent in 1969/70, a period in which first manufacturing and then the tertiary sector expanded dramatically. Export markets increased in relative importance, but the geographical location of these markets changed. From a heavy dependence on Britain and Europe in the 1950s new markets were developed, particularly in Japan and the USA. Formation of the European Economic Community in 1957 and Britain's entry into that body in 1973 effectively blocked an expansion of agricultural exports to Europe except for wool and feed grains.

The adoption of new technology, much of which had been available previously, contributed to the output expansion. Important developments included improved pastures based on introduced legumes (particularly subterranean clovers) and fertilisers (mainly superphosphate and in some areas trace elements), the control of rabbits (mainly through myxomatosis), and mechanisation. The replacement of horses with tractors released land from fodder production for commercial crops, increased labour productivity, and enabled the working of new areas and facilitated greater speed and timelines of operations. Further developments in varieties, animal breeding and nutrition, and disease and pest control also contributed to the output expansion.

The late 1950s and 1960s were a period of labour shedding and increases in the output-to-labour ratio. While output nearly doubled over the two decades, employment rose from 466,000 in 1950/1 to a peak of 480,000 in 1953/4 and then declined to 440,000 in 1960/1 and 414,000 in 1970/1. Machines such as tractors, equipment for the bulk handling of grains, milking machines, and cane harvesting machinery and the growth in the size of farm equipment enabled the substitution of capital for labour. In part this process was fostered by increased real wages, by government assistance through taxation incentives and investment allowances, and by the labour-saving bias in new agricultural technology. Also important to an explanation of the rise in labour productivity was the switch of government policy from encouragement of closer settlement to reconstruction and farm amalgamation, and a recognition that continued support for labour-intensive agricultural industries (including dairying and fruit growing) was not in Australia's long-term interest. During the 1960s and 1970s average farm sizes increased, as did the output of the land- and capital-intensive cropping activities and of the extensive sheep and beef cattle industries.

The 1950s and in particular the 1960s witnessed another mining boom, with the exploitation of new minerals and oil, very large-scale capital-intensive operations, and modern techniques of search, quarrying, ore recovery, and management. Taxation incentives were implemented in 1946 and in subsequent years to encourage greater Australian investment in mining and oil exploration. The 1950s saw the development of Mount Isa as a major copper mine, a booming uranium industry to support the growing atomic power industry overseas, the mining of beach sands for the aerospace industry, and the use of tungsten from King Island for use in the production of high-speed cutting tools. Mechanisation of underground coal mines and a marked reduction of industrial disputation contributed to increased productivity and competitiveness of the coal industry. Between 1950/1 and 1966/7 coal output per man shift worked trebled. Even with these developments the share of the mining industy in national income and export receipts in 1959/60 remained at about the 1949/50 level of 2 percent.

Large new mining projects were developed from the late 1960s through the mid 1970s. Australia found a rapidly growing Japanese steel industry in need of iron ore and coking coal. Removal of the ban on iron ore exports in the early sixties, the development of very large-scale equipment, and the arrival of bulk carriers greater than 100,000 tonnes facilitated the large-scale open cut mining of iron ore in Western Australia and coking coal from Queensland. Bauxite mining and alumina refinery industries developed upon scientific exploration and enormous scale operations. Small quantities of commercial oil were found in 1960, followed by the discovery of the Bass Strait field in 1964. New technology played a major role in the offshore wells. The saving in oil import outlays following the oil discoveries had as important an influence on the balance of payments as did the growth of mineral exports. New sources of nickel, manganese, and phosphate rock were added to the list of resources of the Lucky Country. Between 1962/3 and 1972/3 real output of the mining industry increased threefold to represent 4 percent of national income. Mineral products by 1970/1 provided 25 percent of Australia's export receipts, and the oil discoveries resulted in a substantial fall in import outlays.

Mining industry development was characterized by large-scale operations, investments with a heavy dependence on overseas finance, long-term contracts, and high capital-to-labour ratios. Investments of hundreds of millions of dollars were involved. In most cases long-term contracts were important (see B. Smith 1982). About half of the funds were obtained from overseas, mainly the United States, the United Kingdom, and Japan. Employment in the mining sector rose about half as fast as output, reflecting dramatic increases in labour productivity and capital intensity.

1970s

The expansion of the mining industry continued through the 1970s. Dramatic increases in oil prices from $1.80 (U.S.) a barrel in 1970 to twelve dollars in 1974 and forty dollars in 1979 spilled over to increased demand for steaming coal. Between 1969/70 and 1979/80 Australian coal production doubled to 80 million tonnes per annum, with most of the growth being in steaming coal. After expansion in the first part of the decade, the production of oil, iron ore, nickel, and bauxite/alumina levelled off. The decline in world general economic growth after 1973/4 placed a brake on opportunities for development of new mining ventures other than those directly related to energy. Nonetheless, by 1980/1 the mining sector provided nearly 5 percent of national income and 26 percent of export receipts.

The 1970s were difficult years; the decade witnessed major adjustments in the rural sector. Commodity prices were at historically low levels during the beginning and middle years. Also, price volatility in export markets was exaggerated by the proliferation of nontariff trade barriers against agricultural products in the major importing and some export-competing countries. Cost flow-ons from the inflation experience in the general economy and the growing interdependence of the rural sector and the rest of the economy for inputs of goods and services together resulted in extreme price–cost pressures being placed on the rural sector. There was a substantial real appreciation of the exchange rate (see Chapter 5). Further, government policy exhibited greater emphasis on the importance of transmitting market prices to farmers rather than using price-insulating schemes. This was especially true of wheat, the meats, wool (even allowing for introduction of the reserve price schemes which, essentially, are buffer stock schemes), and the coarse grains, and there was a trend to allow more influence of market prices in the dairy and fruits schemes. The rural Green Paper of 1974 (Harris et al. 1974) and the Industries Assistance Commission were important forces in the policy shift. The trends of labour shedding and increased farm size continued throughout the 1970s. Despite the difficulties, the absolute level of agricultural output and exports increased over the 1970s; however, the sector's share of both national income and export receipts declined.

Around 1980

The mining and agricultural industries of the 1980s are, with a few exceptions, capital- and land-intensive activities dependent on the world market for over half their sales. Most farms are family farms with assets exceeding $300,000 (comprising 76 percent land and improvements, 15 percent machinery, and 9 percent livestock) operated by the owner and family with hired labour for peak period tasks. The extensive cropping and pastoral properties use relatively larger areas of land for a lower yield per unit area than their counterparts in Europe and North America. Subject to reservations about measurement, the family income of the average Australian farmer is approximately comparable with that of urban families. Even so, there is a proportion of the farm group with incomes below accepted poverty levels. In this sense the Australian farm sector has adapted to changing economic circumstances with more success than has been the European, Japanese, and probably also the North American experience.

Australian mining is dominated by large corporations using very high capital-to-labour ratios (often exceeding $1 million of capital stock per worker). Most of the output comes from mines that are very large scale and employ technologies that are state of the art or lead the world. There has been a trend to even larger operating units and lower labour-to-output ratios.

Over half of the agricultural and mining output is sold for export, and the natural resource-based industries provide nearly 80 percent of total export receipts. Around a third of the exports go to Japan, 14 percent to North America, and under 10 percent to Britain. Domestic prices are closely tied to world prices, although there are some two-price schemes that cushion the direct link. World prices for most of the mineral products as well as the agricultural products are highly variable relative to prices of manufactured goods and of services.

Modern agricultural and mining activities are heavily dependent on the rest of the economy for inputs of goods and services and they in turn provide inputs for use by upstream industries. Over 70 percent of gross farm receipts are spent by farmers on purchased inputs of machinery, fertilisers, services, and hired labour. In the mining industry just over half of gross receipts are spent on purchases of energy, plant and equipment, and materials. Most of the inputs come from domestic sources. In the case of domestic food sales, which absorb just under half of agricultural food production, it is estimated that 64 cents of the consumer's food dollar (for example, a wrapped loaf of sliced bread in an air conditioned supermarket) goes to off-farm activities of storage, transport, processing, and distribution and only 36 cents goes to the farmer (for wheat). Even for the export sales, off-farm outlays on storage and transport and in some cases further processing (for example, dairy products and animal slaughter) add 20 percent or more to the value at the farm gate. Smelting and refining add another 50 percent to the value of some mineral products. Estimates of the direct and indirect contributions to national income from changes in the natural resource industries (using input–output techniques) indicate multipliers of between 1.7 and 2.5. That is, while the direct contribution of the agricultural and mineral sectors to national income is only 6 percent and 5 percent respectively, their combined direct and indirect effect (including effects on upstream and downstream industries) is about double these percentages.

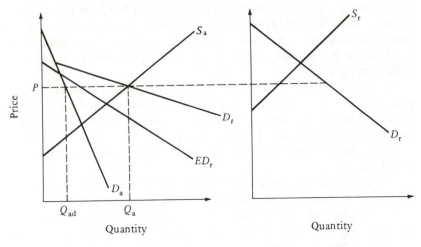

Figure 6.1. Static model.

6.2   Analysis of the growth process

A framework

A simple supply and demand model provides a convenient framework for assessing the effects and roles of different forces on the growth of production and trade and of prices for agricultural and mineral industries in Australia over the twentieth century. Consider first a competitive static situation. The world market is segmented into Australia (A) and rest of the world (R). Long-run demand and supply in R are denoted by D_r and S_r in the right-hand panel of Figure 6.1. From these curves, an excess demand curve ED_r representing the demand for Australian exports can be drawn as shown in the left-hand panel of Figure 6.1; for simplicity, transport costs and exchange rate issues are ignored at this stage. Long-run demand and supply in Australia are denoted by D_a and S_a. The aggregate demand for Australian production D_t is the sum of domestic demand and export demand. Market equilibrium yields price P, Australian production Q_a, Australian demand Q_{ad2}, and Australian exports $Q_{ae} = Q_a - Q_{ad}$.

A comparative statics model, building on the right-hand panel of Figure 6.1, can be used to evaluate the effects of developments over time. As in Figure 6.1, the initial period story for Australia in Figure 6.2 is represented by demand D_t, supply S_a, price P, and production Q_a. Over time, circumstances shift the demand curve out to D'_t and the supply curve out to S'_a. The task is to describe the factors shifting these curves. Domestic demand shifts stem from population growth, income

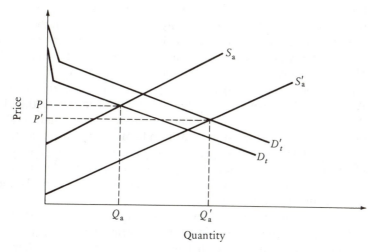

Figure 6.2. Comparative statics model.

supply curve out to S'_a. The task is to describe the factors shifting these curves. Domestic demand shifts stem from population growth, income growth and the income elasticity of demand, and changes in taste. Shifts in export demand are associated with overseas country demand shifts and supply shifts. The latter are influenced by technology, by input costs, and in the short run by seasonal conditions. Changes in transport costs and in government policies affecting the production, consumption, and trade of products in other countries also can be evaluated. Commodity policy in Australia and currency exchange conditions will influence the position of the export demand curve perceived by Australian producers. Technological change, changes in relative input costs, past investment activities, and seasonal conditions influence the rate of shift of the Australian supply curve. The net effect of the various shifts is modified by the responsiveness of supply and demand to market prices as summarised by own price elasticities.

This framework has been widely used in the analysis of the development of agricultural production and prices, with Schultz (1940) providing one of the early and very articulate presentations. A consensus for developed countries is that the supply shifts associated with technological change have exceeded the demand shifts associated with population and income growth, resulting in a pattern of rising agricultural production, a decline in the relative importance of agriculture, and a decline in agricultural prices relative to general prices. Trends in Australian agriculture over the twentieth century have been consistent with the Schultzian model and differ only in magnitude from the experience of other developed countries. Real output and exports have trended upwards. However, the growth rates have been slower than for the rest of the economy, so that the relative contribution of agriculture in national income and of agricultural exports in total exports has declined. At comparable levels of aggregate per capita incomes, the share of Australian agriculture in national income has been about double that of developed countries in the northern hemisphere, including the USA. The second part of the twentieth century is consistent with the hypothesis of declining relative prices for agricultural products, but it is not demonstrably the case that there has been a downward trend when looking at all of the twentieth century.

A more complex picture emerges with the mineral industries. At the global level, supply shifts for most minerals have been greater than demand shifts, which in turn have risen at a rate lower than general economic activity. Australian mineral production, which was more important at the turn of the century than in most other developed countries, declined in both absolute terms and as a share of national income during the first three decades to reach the international average. The minerals and energy boom of the late 1960s and 1970s reversed this trend, with Australian mineral and energy output rising in both absolute terms and as a share of national income and exports, a pattern shared only by Britain and Norway. It is not obvious from the available data whether the relative prices of Australian minerals have decreased, increased, or remained about constant when looking at the long period of the twentieth century.

To try to understand the principal factors determining the observed trends, the following discussion looks behind shifts in the domestic demand, export demand, and supply curves for Australian agricultural and mineral products over the twentieth century.

Domestic demand shifts

The domestic market was the dominant outlet for most food products throughout the twentieth century; except for wheat and sugar, over 50 percent of sales were domestic sales. In the case of wool, export demand has accounted for over 95 percent of sales. Population growth was the most important source of increased domestic demand, but only in the periods 1904/5 to 1913/14 and 1945/6 to 1973/4 did this effect exceed 2 percent per annum. The effect of income growth was much smaller. Available estimates of the income elasticity of demand for food range from 0.21 to 0.76 (see Richardson 1976 for a review article); they are higher for some products, including beef, and lower for others, including dairy products and cereals. Considered together with increases in real income per capita, these elasticity estimates imply that even in the high-income growth periods of the 1910s, 1950s, and 1960s income-induced shifts of the food demand curve were under 1 percent per annum. In short, the growth of domestic food demand was less than the rate of growth of the economy as a whole.

Domestic demand for minerals has been important in the case of coal (initially for trains, ships, and some industry, after the first world war for steelmaking, and in the latter part of the period also for electricity generation) and iron ore (for steelmaking after the first world war) and for small amounts of base metals used in the metal and allied industries; but domestic demand has not been important for some, such as gold and the sand minerals. In all cases the demand for minerals is a derived demand. Although no satisfactory estimates of key elasticities are readily available and known to me, it is apparent that the Australian domestic demand for its minerals grew at a slower rate than real gross national product. This is associated with income elasticities of demand for the products produced from these minerals being less than unity, particularly at the higher income levels of the post–World War II period. Too, since 1960 the declining relative importance of the Australian metal manu-facturing and associated industries, and improvements in the efficiency of production processes, particularly in the case of energy conversion, resulted in small shifts of domestic demand.

Overseas demand

A key issue for export demand for Australian agricultural and mineral products is the elasticity of export demand and in particular whether Australia can be described as a small country able to export as much as it wishes without significantly influencing the export price. With the exception of four products, Australia produces less than 10 percent of world production of various mining and agricultural industry products; the exceptions are wool (30 percent), bauxite and alumina (30 percent), mineral sands (33 percent), and, for a short period in the 1900s, gold. In a world of free trade, zero transport costs, and homogenous products, the export demand would be highly price-elastic (exceeding 10) for those products in which it has a small share of world production.[3] Even for

---

[3] Beginning with the identity $X = D - S$, where X is exports, D is rest of the world demand, and S is rest of world supply, the export demand elasticity x is given by $x = (D/X) (d - s) + s$, where d and s are the elasticities of demand and supply, respectively, in the rest of the world. To illustrate, if the supply and demand elasticities are 0.2 in

wool, bauxite, and mineral sands the elasticity would exceed unity. In practice, transport costs, product heterogeneity (whether intrinsic or due to diversified portfolio considerations), tariff and nontariff trade barriers, collusive behaviour, and perhaps long-term contracts are important. Each of these real-world factors effectively reduces the degree of price elasticity of rest of world excess demand curves for Australian exports.[4] There is a lively debate about the magnitude of the effects. Taking a longer-term and aggregate view of natural resource–based exports, the assumption that Australia faces a highly elastic, but still less than infinitely elastic, long-run aggregate export demand curve is a reasonable approximation for the twentieth century.

Distortions of the world free trade in agricultural food products grew in both importing and export-competing countries during and after the 1930s depression period. Largely for national agricultural and food policy reasons and in response to the potential political strength of agricultural interests, governments acted to protect their domestic agricultural sectors from the full force of world market prices – both the low average levels and volatility of prices. For the main part, developed countries in the northern hemisphere have supported domestic prices above world levels to maintain the parity of farmers' incomes with those of others in their growing economies. European and Japanese agriculture is heavily protected, North American dairy products, sugar, and meat are heavily protected by quotas, and at times subsidies have been paid on grain exports. By contrast, many developing countries have policies designed to keep food prices below world market levels. In all cases a battery of tariffs, quotas, export taxes and subsidies, and "understandings" work to modify and in selected cases such as the European Common Agricultural Policy actually eliminate any adjustment between domestic and world prices. These policies have significantly reduced the elasticity of demand for Australian food exports, and on balance they have reduced the average world price relative to a free market situation.[5]

In the case of wool and the mineral products, trade intervention has been limited and where applied it typically has taken the form of tariffs rather than nontariff barriers.

---

absolute terms, and if Australia's share of rest of world demand is 5, 10, and 30 percent, the export demand elasticity is -7.8, -3.8, and -1.0 respectively. If the elasticities are 0.5, the corresponding export demand elasticities become -19.5, -9.5, and -2.5.

[4] See, for example, Bredahl, Meyers, and Collins (1979), Cronin (1979), and Horner (1952).

[5] For an empirical analysis of the effects of these policies in the context of the 1970s see Tyers and Chisholm (1982).

The net effect of shifts in overseas demand for and supply of agricultural and mineral products on relative commodity prices over the twentieth century is far from clear. From around 1910 to the second world war there was a general downward trend for most commodity prices. Since the Korean war commodity boom there has been a downtrend in real agricultural product prices. However, relative prices at around 1980 were at levels similar to those experienced in the 1930s. There is no strong trend, either up or down, for most mineral prices over the post–World War II period. Real energy prices declined from the turn of the century until the OPEC-orchestrated increases of 1973, 1974, and 1979.

Short-term price fluctuations have been especially important. Seasonal shifts in supply have been the principal disturbing element for agricultural prices; demand shifts caused by changes in income growth rates and in expectations have been of lesser importance. In the case of the mineral products, shifts in demand with changing economic conditions have been the principal sources of price fluctuations. Government policies, by insulating domestic prices from world price changes, have exaggerated the variability of world prices in what is the residual market.

Four developments in the world demand for mineral products in the post–World War II period had an important positive influence on Australia's potential development. First was the rapid growth of the Japanese economy and in recent times of other economies in Southeast Asia. In general these countries have low levels of natural resources and they chose policies of importing most of their raw materials. Japan has been the most important market for Australia's iron ore, coking coal, and steaming coal and it has taken important quantities of other minerals. A second and complementary development was the advent of large bulk carriers, larger-scale port handling facilities, and land transport cost savings, which effectively lowered the real cost of transporting low-value bulky cargoes long distances. Third, post–World War II technological changes resulted in a marked increase in demand for such materials as uranium, mineral sands, bauxite/alumina, and special metal hardening additives. Fourth, the dramatic changes in real energy prices associated with the oil pricing policies of OPEC in the 1970s affected oil and substitute energy products including steaming coal and natural gas.

Australian agricultural supply shifts

Shifts in the productive capacity of Australian agriculture over the twentieth century reflect the adoption of new technology; investment in land improvements, livestock, machinery, and off-farm infrastructure; to a small extent, additional land in aggregate and the substantial addition of land under cultivation and improved pastures; and, up to 1940/1, additional labour. Changes in the availability of labour and its growing cost relative to capital and land, together with labour-saving technological change, also influenced the way in which agriculture was conducted. Since the incentive to conduct research into and adopt new technology and to proceed with investment programmes was influenced in part by levels of returns and available funds, these supply shifts were in part endogenous rather than pure exogenous forces on the sector. Government policies and actions influenced the paths of development.

The stock of available technology was augmented by findings overseas, by domestic research and development, and by "learning by doing". Overseas agricultural research with the exceptions of basic and mechanical research, required further on-site adaptive research to meet the peculiarities of the Australian environment. From the end of the nineteenth century to the present day, governments funded and conducted a major part of the rural research and extension effort. For example, the Australian Science and Technology Council (quoted in D. B. Williams 1982: 86) estimates that in 1976/7 $132 million, or 2 percent of the gross value of rural production, was spent on agricultural research and development; of this, 56 percent was spent by state departments, 31 percent by the Commonwealth Scientific and Industrial Research Organisation, 10 percent by universities, and 4 percent by private enterprise. Over 80 percent of these funds were direct government grants. The few studies that have assessed the economic benefits of rural research (see D. B. Williams 1982: chap. 4 for a survey) have reported relatively high rates of return, although caution is required in extrapolating the results of selected case studies to all rural research.

A number of motives have been adduced for the high level of government intervention. It seems that the market failure argument based on the public good nature of research and the atomistic structure of the agricultural sector has had little influence, and certainly it would not justify the high proportion of government subsidy unless the external spillovers beyond agriculture were absurdly high. Discussing the 1870–1914 period, when departments of agriculture and experimentation stations were established, McLean (1982: 296) argues, "The demand for government [research, extension and education] action arose when the process of rural development was threatened by problems of poor management, climatic variability, pests and out-migration encouraging politicians to cast around for solutions. The threatened revenue loss from land sold on credit sharpened this incentive." During the long periods of fixed exchange rates, agricultural expansion and exports were seen as a means of solving balance-of-payments problems in paying for imports for development of the manufacturing sector, and government subsidies for research were one way to expand production. At times government subsidies for rural research were justified because there was tariff assistance to the manufactured sectors; in the 1930s the argument was primarily one of equity; after the 1974 Green Paper (Harris et al. 1974), the argument was primarily one of second-best efficiency ("tariff compensation"). It is reasonable to conclude that a large segment of the new technology was provided to the agricultural sector rather than sought by the sector itself as part of an explicit investment decision.

Whereas the atomistic structure of the agricultural sector would seem to provide a fertile seedbed for the adoption of new technology, there are many examples of slow adoption. Crop responses to fertiliser were known in the nineteenth century, but the application of artificial fertiliser was not widely adopted until the twentieth century. The introduced legume–superphosphate pasture techniques widely diffused in the 1950s were developed two decades before, and even such mechanisation as tractors and milking machines was slow to be adopted. The reasons for slow adoption are not fully understood or quantified; probably they include the unavailability of funds to finance changes – and farmers have shown a preference for high levels of internal financing; expectations and social attitudes towards change; and questions about the effects of new technology on the local environment. Some explanation for the slow investment growth in the post–World War II period can be attributed to restrictions on the availability of equipment and fertilisers after the war, and to myxomatosis, which enabled effective control of rabbits that otherwise would have been the principal beneficiaries of improved pastures.

Overall, technological change has played a major role in agriculture's expansion of output throughout the twentieth century. However, it is interesting to note that several studies find a lesser role for technological improvement and a greater role for additional capital in the expansion of Australian agricultural output relative to the experience of North America (see, for example, D. B. Williams 1982). New and better varieties and bloodstock increased not only returns per unit area but also the areas suitable for more intensive production. Improved pastures and legume-cropping rotations increased output in the second part of the century as fertilisers had in the first part. Improved control of pests and diseases, including rabbits, raised production levels. Tractors released land previously required to feed horses, new machinery enabled additional land to be cleared and developed, and its contribution to time-liness of operations raised output. And there were gains in managerial efficiency.

Investment in the rural sector, both by farmers and the government, proceeded in an uneven fashion. Sustained private capital expansion took place during periods of land clearing for cropping in 1900 to 1930, land clearing and pasture improvement during 1950 to 1970, and machinery investment since the end of the second world war. Powell (in D. B. Williams 1982) estimates that from 1920/1 to 1975/6 the real farm capital stock increased four times, or about 2.5 percent per annum. A large part of the land improvements (the largest portion of the farm capital stock) was undertaken by on-farm labour and equipment, and the majority of the finance came from accumulated farm income. Even today, less than a fifth of farmer investment is financed by borrowed funds. The factors influencing levels of investment included the intended output level; the availability of funds, particularly as a determinant of the timing of investment; relative factor costs; and potential productivity gains with new capital-embodied technology. Governments have had direct and indirect effects on intended output. Examples include the "grow more wheat" campaign of 1929/30, market price support schemes from the 1920s onwards, lowering costs of investment (for example, provision of credit at concessional rates of interest, investment allowances in taxation assessment), and its own direct investment in infrastructure.

An important plank of government policy over the twentieth century has been expansion of the agricultural sector. In the first half of the century intensification of rural production was part of the policy of population expansion. Later, increased rural exports, particularly during the era of fixed exchange rates, were sought to finance the import needs of the manufacturing sector and to avoid balance-of-payments crises. Railway development continued through to the 1920s, and also road development to assist expansion of the wheat industry. A sequence of irrigation schemes from 1900 to the 1960s turned sparse grazing areas into intensive dairying, fruit, vegetable, rice, and sugar areas. Typically such infrastructure was provided at well below cost, and often below variable cost. Until the 1960s little concern was given to assessing the economic viability of the projects, and in many cases there were no remunerative markets for the extra output. Too, a large part of government infrastructure, including telephones, postal services, and electricity, has been provided to areas of low population density in the rural sector at less than cost (Kolsen 1983).

One expression of government policy to increase the Australian population was closer settlement schemes; they were also seen as a means of rewarding and resettling returned soldiers after the two world wars. These schemes involved government purchase of existing large agricultural holdings and their subdivision into smaller holdings. Typically the smaller holdings used the land more intensively. In many cases the new holdings proved to be too small during adverse periods (of droughts and price slumps), and many required additional assistance and/or amalgamation during the 1930s, the late 1950s, and the 1960s and 1970s.

From the 1960s onwards, land settlement policy shifted from closer settlement towards land amalgamation. In part the shift came from recognition that modern technology and factor prices favoured medium and larger farms, and that increased agricultural output, particularly of fruits and dairy products, was neither necessary for balance-of-payments reasons or consistent with the efficient use of scarce resources. And so was born the comprehensive State Grants (Rural Reconstruction) Act 1971 and the 1976 Rural Adjustment Scheme with explicit aims of farm buildup and expansion and assistance out of agriculture of nonviable farmers and their families. It is likely that the adjustment schemes have had a very small impact on aggregate output. Their principal effect has rather been to reduce the inputs used, and particularly labour, per unit of farm output.

Average farm size rose dramatically after the second world war. In part this was due to outside forces on the agricultural sector, including the rising price of labour relative to both capital and land, good employment opportunities elsewhere in the economy, new machinery embodying labour-saving technology, and a shift from labour-intensive activities (including fruits and dairying) to the extensive cropping and livestock activities. At the same time farmers have substituted off-farm inputs for farm inputs, including machines for labour; between 1948/9 and 1975/6 expenditure on off-farm inputs rose from 30 percent of the value of gross output to 50 percent. In aggregate the farm labour force fell 15 percent between 1954 and 1976 while real farm output doubled.

Estimates of supply elasticities are available only for the post–World War II period. Pandey, Piggott, and MacAuley (1982) estimate the aggregate agricultural supply elasticity in the long run to be between 0.6 and 1.0 and note that it has been increasing over time with increased dependence of agriculture on nonfarm inputs. Estimated supply elasticities for individual farm products are much greater because of the extra substitution opportunities.

Australian mineral supply shifts

Mineral resources, though part of a country's natural endowment, require skills and investment for their discovery, mining and refining, and transformation to product forms and transport to locations sought by willing buyers. Further, there is a diversity of mineral resources in terms of size of ore body, proportion of valuable minerals, chemical and physical structure of minerals and ore body, physical location, and other environmental aspects. Knowledge about known reserves, and about techniques of prospecting, mining, and refining in Australia have improved over the twentieth century. As well, changes in relative input costs associated with economic growth have influenced the supply of mineral products, and, as in agriculture, government policy and action have played a role in development of the industry.

Successful research in Australia and imported technology provided improvements in prospecting, mining, and extraction techniques, and these gains have played a major role in shifting outwards the supply curve for Australian minerals over the century. Most prospecting in the first half of the century relied on visual inspection of rock outcrops for the initial detection of valuable minerals. Only after the 1930s were geologists given a major role in mineral exploration. Techniques today include the use of satellites and detailed description and analysis of geological structures. Since its establishment in 1946 the Commonwealth Bureau of Mineral Resources has been active in coordinating the mapping and inventory assessment of the nation's mineral resources. An illustration of the importance of mineral discoveries is the absence from maps of Australia's mineral resources in 1960 of iron ore deposits in Western Australia, bauxite deposits, and nickel deposits. The 1965 Vernon Committee of Economic Inquiry observed that the mining industry was unlikely to be a major sector of activity and that mining exports would increase slowly. It took until the 1960s for the major offshore oil discoveries in Bass Strait to be made. Diamonds had not been located by 1970.

Techniques of mining have improved so that mines once considered uneconomic became viable prospects. Particular examples include offshore drilling for oil and gas, large-scale open cut mines, improved ventilation, and developments in underground mining techiques. To a large extent the new technology was capital-embodied and required large-scale operations dependent on the availability of export markets and often long-term contracts.

Developments in metallurgy have been responsible for a large part of the increased output of minerals. At the turn of the century zinc at Broken Hill was stockpiled in tailings dumps awaiting the flotation process developed in the 1910s. New smelting methods for lead, zinc, copper, and silver ores improved extraction rates, and once unprofitable goldfields benefited from cyanide and chlorination techniques. Each ore body had its own peculiarities, and typically teams of experts handsomely repaid their salaries in higher extraction rates and higher levels of purity in final products. Private companies met most of the research costs; obviously profit prospects influenced such investment decisions.

Mining techniques became increasingly capital-intensive, with most of the major developments of the 1960s and 1970s being dominated by investments of hundreds of millions of dollars and the processing each year of millions of tonnes of material. Large-scale techniques permitted the spreading of fixed overhead costs of infrastructure, enabled the successful mining of ore bodies with lower levels of mineral concentrations, and enabled greater mechanisation and scale economies in extraction and transportation. In part these techniques were encouraged by new technology and developments in both Australia and the rest of the world, by the rising cost of labour relative to the cost of machines (and in some cases by scarcity of labour), and by the availability of funds to finance such large investments.

The beneficial effects on labour productivity were dramatic. For example, between 1950 and 1970 production per man shift at the underground coal face trebled. Between 1960/1 and 1980/1 real mining output increased nearly sevenfold, or 10 percent per annum, while the mining work force rose 70 percent, or 3 percent per annum, giving a gain in labour productivity of around 7 percent per annum. A large part of the labour productivity gain can be attributed to the increased capital-to-labour ratio.

Assessment of the effects of government policy on the development of the mineral industry is extraordinarily complex; not surprisingly, a comprehensive study is not yet available.[6] In most cases governments financed railway and port infrastructure and charged mining companies less than full cost. An exception is the Pilbara region iron ore projects, where companies provided all the infrastructure. In some cases competition between state governments was important. For a few cases rail charges were used as a crude form of royalty. The pattern of royalty payments is described by Emerson and Lloyd (1983: 236) as "a veritable hotch-potch". Although royalties are relatively small (an average of 4.7 percent of the value of gross mining output in 1976/7), they have had a net depressing effect on output. On the other hand, a number of incentive schemes, particularly for gold and crude oil, in effect favoured mining activities relative to alternative investments in the economy. The

---

[6] For analyses of government policy towards the mining industry see Cook and Porter (1984), Emerson and Lloyd (1983), FitzGerald (1974), Industries Assistance Commission (1976), and B. Smith (1983).

Chifley government in 1946 introduced a number of income taxation incentives specifically for the mining and petroleum industries to encourage Australian, as opposed to foreign, expenditure on exploration and development. Following the FitzGerald report (1974), many of these advantages were removed in the 1974 federal budget, although favourable depreciation provisions were introduced in 1976. Government restrictions and conditions on the granting of prospecting licences tended to reduce incentives. The ban on iron ore exports between 1938 and the early sixties and government monopoly control of uranium mining in the early 1950s are prime examples of unfavourable government intervention. Controls on finance markets and the exchange rate and restrictions on foreign ownership and control adversely influenced returns and investment decisions. More recently, social concern for the effects of mining on the environment and the rights of aboriginals have added to the private costs of mining development.

To my knowledge no estimates have been made of the supply price elasticities for the Australian mining industry as an aggregate. K. G. Williams and Fraser (1985) estimate the long-run supply elasticity for Western Australian iron ore at 4.4 and for the short run at 0.6. A priori reasoning and press statements by the industry imply a low elasticity in the short run and a less than infinite long-run elasticity.

Rapid growth of the Australian mining industy in the late 1960s and 1970s can be attributed to discoveries of new ore bodies, the availability of entrepreneurial and capital resources, the use of large-scale modern mining, processing, and transport techniques, and a rapidly expanding new market in Asia in the 1960s and in energy in the 1970s. All these factors contributed to buoyant estimates of the expected profitability of investment.

6.3   Intersectoral linkages[7]

The natural resource industries have been closely interrelated with the rest of the economy, with lines of causation running in both directions. This section highlights some of the links as they have influenced general economic performance during the twentieth century.

Agricultural and mining industries directly and indirectly have provided incomes, and rising per capita incomes, to an important sector of the economy. At the turn of the century about a third of the population was directly employed, by the second world war about a quarter, and by 1980/1 just over 10 percent. These industries indirectly employed

---

[7] For a further discussion see Edwards and Watson (1978) and B. Smith (1983).

additional persons in downstream industries, for example machinery and material supply, and upstream industries, for example transport and processing. With increased specialisation these indirect multiplier effects have grown in importance over the century. Technological change and increased capital intensity, particularly in the 1900–20 and 1945–70 periods, have contributed to increased per capita output levels that have exceeded increases in the rest of the economy.

Incomes of the natural resource–based industries have been relatively more volatile than those of the manufacturing and tertiary sectors. This reflects the high level of dependence on seasonal conditions and export markets. In turn, the fluctuating incomes have given rise to variations in economywide consumption and, more important, investment expenditures, which added an element of instability to aggregate macroeconomic performance.

Reflecting Australia's comparative advantage, the natural resource–based industries have provided in excess of 80 percent of export receipts during the twentieth century. Particularly during the era of fixed exchange rates, the level of exports was a prime determinant of permissible imports. Many government policies to expand the natural resource–based industries were motivated by the need to expand exports (and reduce imports in the case of oil), and on occasion restraints on economic activity were made because of a perceived need to reduce the level of imports.

Price levels in the natural resource industries have had direct and indirect effects on general price levels. Food costs are a significant component of general indexes of living costs; in the 1920s food had a weight of 40 percent in the "C" series index, in the 1960s a weight of 30 percent in the consumer price index, and in the 1980s a weight of 20 percent. Mineral prices have indirect effects via their input cost component of steel and steel products (for example cars) and of other industries; oil prices have a direct effect. In turn, wage rates frequently have been adjusted with reference to changes in the price indexes under the guise of cost-of-living adjustments, indexation, and equity. The long-term tendency for relative food and mineral prices to fall has exerted a deflationary effect, while the short-term price swings have contributed to instability problems.

Economic growth in the general economy has had some effect on demand for natural resource–based industries. The direct income growth and population growth effects on nontraded foods, for example fresh milk, poultry, and vegetables, have been more important than for the traded goods, for example wool and bauxite/alumina, where overseas demand was the dominant factor. Domestic demand was the most important outlet for the coal and iron ore industries until the late 1960s, and cyclical fluctuations in general economic activity caused short-term demand disturbances. Over the longer term domestic demand for food and minerals grew at a slower rate than real national income.

Changes in relative factor prices and factor availability induced changes in production methods. Rising real labour costs, in conjunction with labour-saving technology biased towards the larger scale, helped induce the substitution of capital for labour and increases in the size of production units. The capital accumulation process was facilitated by greater flexibility and sophistication of the financial markets. At the same time, improvements in general education levels and communication assisted the movement of labour between sectors.

Government policies exerted an influence on development of the natural resource industries, both directly and indirectly. Policies of closer settlement in the first part of the century and the provision of infrastructure, usually at below cost, contributed to the development of more intensive forms of agriculture. In the 1970s these policies were reversed and aimed towards facilitating the buildup and amalgamation of farms into larger units. Government funds played a key role in the flow of new technology for the agricultural sector, whereas the mineral sector funded most of its research activities. Commodity price policies, though important for some products (mainly the labour-intensive dairy and fruit activities) and for some years, probably had only a small effect on long-term agricultural trends, particularly in the case of the export-oriented land-intensive cropping and livestock activities. In the case of mining the picture is very complex. Up to about 1973 it is likely that government provision of infrastructure at less than full cost and taxation incentives provided a net incentive to most mining activities. Restrictions on iron ore and uranium exports were important barriers to development. Since 1970 the importance of the taxation advantages has been eroded and has probably been more than offset by the hotch-potch of royalties and especially oil and gas excise duties. Indirectly, government assistance to the manufacturing industries has lowered the incentives for development of the export industries. The interdependence of sectors was highlighted in the 1929 Brigden report and resurfaced again in the Vernon report of 1965 and in various Green and White papers on the agricultural and manufacturing sectors released in the 1970s. These intersectoral links are developed further in the following chapter.

6.4   Conclusion

The high level of dependence of development of the Australian economy on the natural resource industries, especially for export income, provides part of a broader explanation of the poor performance of the overall economy relative to that of other developed countries. There has been a general tendency for the terms of trade to move against most agricultural and mineral products, primarily because of the low income elasticity of demand. This economic reality has been further aggravated by the growth of protectionist agricultural policies in the developed northern hemisphere countries. Australian policies of import protection for manufactures and maintenance of an overvalued exchange rate have added to the difficulties of developing further natural resource exports and output.

To some extent changes in product mix, development of new export markets, and adoption of new technology enabled the natural resource industries to adjust and actually to expand real output. The discovery and development of new mines in the 1960s and 1970s, encouraged by new market opportunities, provided a substantial boost to the Australian economy that was not available to other rural exporters such as New Zealand. Even with these adjustments, the relative importance of the natural resource industries in national income and employment has fallen dramatically over the last few decades.

Table 6.1. *Indicator statistics of the relative importance of agricultural and mining sectors in national output and average growth rates of real output over the twentieth century*

| Average of three years centered on | Real GDP (1966/7 prices) ($m) | Share of GDP at current prices | | Average annual growth rate over decade[a] | | |
| | | Agriculture (%) | Mining (%) | GDP (%) | Agriculture (%) | Mining (%) |
	(1)	(2)	(3)	(4)	(5)	(6)
1900/1	3,310	19.3	10.3	—	—	—
1910/11	4,533	23.5	5.1	3.5	8.2	0.1
1920/1	5,138	23.5	3.0	1.3	0.9	−5.7
1930/1	5,951	21.2	1.8	1.5	2.2	−3.4
1940/1	8,429	19.5	3.3	3.5	1.8[b]	5.5[b]
1950/1	11,402	24.0	2.3	3.1	N.A.	N.A.
1960/1	16,786	12.9	1.7	3.9	2.5	4.9
1970/1	28,101	7.4	3.1	5.3	1.6	15.2
1980/1	38,474	6.8	4.7	3.2	2.8	5.0

[a]Compound growth rate linking real output level at beginning of period and end of period.
[b]For period 1930/1 to 1938/9.
Sources: (1) and (4) from M. W. Butlin 1977 to 1973/4, and then from Norton, Garmston, and Brodie 1982; (2) and (3) from data in N. G. Butlin 1962 to 1938/9, and then from Australian Bureau of Statistics, *Australian National Accounts*; (4) and (5) from data in N. G. Butlin 1962 to 1938/9, from Haig 1966 for 1948/9 to 1961/2, and from Australian Bureau of Statistics, *Gross Product by Industry at Current and Constant Prices* for 1962/3 to 1980/1.

Table 6.2. *Indicator statistics for Australian exports over the twentieth century*

| Average of three years centered on | Real exports (1966/7 prices) ($m) | Share of exports in GDP (%) | Contributions to exports by | |
| | | | Agriculture, forestry, fishing and hunting (%) | Mining (%) |
	(1)	(2)	(3)	(4)
1900/1	674	23.2	56.2	37.7
1910/11	930	23.9	76.2	18.2
1920/1	927	20.8	79.3	14.4
1930/1	1,116	15.7	86.5	9.5
1940/1	1,585	17.7	73.7[a]	17.5[a]
1950/1	1,450	25.6	88.7	5.7
1960/1	2,431	15.6	78.3	7.3
1970/1	5,141	15.1	52.7	25.0
1980/1	7,505	18.0	45.3	27.3

[a]1938/9 only.
Sources: (1) and (2) from M. W. Butlin 1977 to 1973/4, and then from Norton, Garmston, and Brodie 1982; (3) and (4) from Australian Bureau of Statistics, *Overseas Trade*, various issues.

Table 6.3. *Indicator statistics of resources employed in agricultural and mining sectors over the twentieth century*

Year	Annual employment by industry		Estimated real private capital stock in 1966/7 values	
	Agriculture (000) (1)	Mining (000) (2)	Agriculture ($m) (3)	Mining ($m) (4)
1900/1	351.6	118.4	6,113	105
1910/11	422.2	98.3	10,094	188
1920/1	463.3	54.0	7,601	85
1930/1	513.8	47.2	11,933	98
1940/1	500.8	60.6	11,736	205[a]
1950/1	465.9	59.6	11,795	N.A.
1960/1	440.2	52.3	14,478	N.A.
1970/1	414.4	71.9	22,814	2,475
1980/1	381.9	89.3	23,308	4,009

[a]Figures for 1937/8.

Sources: (1) and (2) from Keating 1967 for 1900/1 to 1960/1, then for agriculture from Bureau of Agricultural Economics and for mining from Australian Bureau of Statistics (average mining employment times ratio of 1961 census figure to survey employment figure (= 1.48)). (3) from N. G. Butlin 1962 for 1900/1 and 1910/11, Powell 1974 for 1910/11 to 1970/1, and Bailey 1981 for last decade. The Butlin figures were spliced onto the Powell figures at 1920/1 and require caution in their interpretation because they ignore on-farm–produced investment. Figures were inflated to 1966/7 values using the GDP deflator. (4) from Butlin 1962 inflated to 1966/7 values using the GDP deflator, and for 1970/1 and 1980/1 from Bailey 1981 reinflated to 1966/7 values using the GDP deflator.

Table 6.4. *Estimates of productivity growth in the agricultural and mining sectors over the twentieth century*

Decade ending	Average annual growth of real output over decade		Average annual labour productivity growth over decade		Average annual total factor productivity growth over decade	
	Agriculture (1)	Mining (2)	Agriculture (3)	Mining (4)	Agriculture (5)	Mining (6)
1910/11	8.2	0.1	6.3	1.9	5.2	0.7
1920/1	0.9	−5.7	0.8	0.1	1.8	0.7
1930/1	2.2	−3.4	1.2	−2.1	0	−3.0
1940/1[a]	1.8	5.5	1.8	2.0	1.2	1.3
1950/1	N.A.	N.A.	N.A.	N.A.	N.A.	N.A.
1960/1	2.5	4.9	2.5	6.2	1.8	N.A.
1970/1	1.6	15.2	1.6	12.0	0.1	N.A.
1980/1	2.7	5.0	2.7	2.8	2.6	1.9

[a]For period 1930/1 to 1938/9.

Sources: (1) and (2) as in Table 6.1. (3) and (4) are measured as annual real growth rate for output less annual growth rate of persons employed using employment figures of Table 6.3. (5) and (6) are measured as annual real growth of output less weighted annual growth rate of persons employed and real private capital stock using employment and capital stock figures of Table 6.3 and weights of 0.67 for labour and 0.33 for capital.

Table 6.5. *Indicator statistics for selected price movements over the twentieth century*

	GDP deflator (1966/7 = 100) (1)	Price movements relative to GDP deflator (1966/7 = 100)					
		Average earnings (2)	Export deflator (3)	Wool price (4)	Wheat export price (5)	Gold (6)	Copper (7)
1900/1	13.3	38.3	109.2	93.8	N.A.	110.3	N.A.
1910/11	14.6	49.3	118.4	123.2	N.A.	101.3	N.A.
1920/1	26.3	48.3	124.3	101.7	179.3	88.3	113.6
1930/1	22.5	61.8	77.8	67.2	57.8	107.8	86.7
1940/1	26.1	62.5	95.4	91.3	79.1	223.3	81.8
1950/1	58.9	63.7	244.1	430.6	151.3	143.7	97.8
1960/1	86.3	86.0	106.0	106.1	111.5	98.9	114.8
1970/1	116.9	117.2	84.0	53.0	76.9	83.4	148.4
1980/1	334.9	135.4	91.2	73.8	79.1	346.2	97.4

Sources: (1), (2), and (3) from M. W. Butlin 1977 to 1973/4 and thereafter spliced series from Norton, Garmston, and Brodie 1982; (4) from Bureau of Agricultural Economics; (5) from Dunsdorf 1956 to 1948/9 and then spliced series from Bureau of Agricultural Economics; (6) and (7) from Kalix, Fraser, and Rawson 1966 and Australian Bureau of Statistics, *Mineral and Mineral Products*, various issues, and N. G. Butlin 1962 for the first two decades of gold prices.

References

Bailey, C. 1981. *Studies in National Accounting Current Costs and Constant Cost Depreciation and Net Capital Stock*. Occasional Paper. Canberra: Australian Bureau of Statistics.

Bambrick, Susan. 1979. *Australian Minerals and Energy Policy*. Canberra: Australian National University Press.

Barnett, D. W. 1979. *Minerals and Energy in Australia*. Sydney: Cassell.

Blainey, Geoffrey. 1978. *The Rush That Never Ended*. 3d ed. Melbourne: Melbourne University Press.

Boehm, E. A. 1979. *Twentieth Century Economic Development in Australia*. 2d ed. Melbourne: Longman Cheshire.

Bredahl, M. E., W. H. Meyers, and K. J. Collins. 1979. "The elasticity of foreign demand for US agricultural products: the importance of the price transmission elasticity". *American Journal of Agricultural Economics* 61: 58–63.

Brigden, J. B., et al. 1929. *The Australian Tariff*. Melbourne: Melbourne University Press.

Bureau of Agricultural Economics. 1973. *Statistical Handbook of the Sheep and*

Wool Industry. 4th ed. Canberra: Australian Government Publishing Service.

Butlin, M. W. 1977. *A preliminary annual database, 1900/01 to 1973/74.* Research Discussion Paper 7701. Sydney: Reserve Bank of Australia.

Butlin, N. G. 1962. *Australian Domestic Product, Investment and Foreign Borrowing 1861–1938/39.* Cambridge: Cambridge University Press.

Cook, L. H., and M. G. Porter. 1984. *The Minerals Sector and the Australian Economy.* Sydney: Allen & Unwin.

Cronin, M. R. 1979. "Export demand elasticities with less than perfect markets". *Australian Journal of Agricultural Economics* 23: 69–72.

Davidson, B. R. 1981. *European Farming in Australia.* Amsterdam: Elsevier.

Dunsdorfs, Edgars. 1956. *The Australian Wheat-Growing Industry, 1788–1948.* Melbourne: Melbourne University Press.

Edwards, G. W., and A. S. Watson. 1978. "Agricultural policy", in F. H. Gruen (ed.), *Surveys of Australian Economics,* vol. 1, pp. 189–239. Sydney: Allen & Unwin.

Emerson, C., and P. J. Lloyd. 1983. "Improving mineral taxation policy in Australia". *Economic Record* 59: 232–44.

FitzGerald, T. M. 1974. *The Contribution of the Mineral Industry to Australian Welfare.* Canberra: Australian Government Publishing Service.

Forster, C. (ed.). 1970. *Australian Economic Development in the Twentieth Century.* London: Allen & Unwin.

Haig, B. 1966. "Estimates of Australian real product by industry". *Australian Economic Papers* 5: 230–50.

Harris, S. F., et al. 1974. *The Principles of Rural Policy in Australia: A Discussion Paper.* Canberra: Australian Government Publishing Service.

Horner, F. B. 1952. "Elasticity of demand for the exports of a single country". *Review of Economics and Statistics* 34: 326–42.

Industries Assistance Commission. 1976. *Report on Petroleum and Mining Industries.* Canberra: Australian Government Publishing Service.

Kalix, Z., L. M. Fraser, and R. I. Rawson. 1966. *Australian Mineral Industry: Production and Trade, 1842–1964.* Bulletin No. 81. Department of National Development, Bureau of Mineral Resources, Geology, and Geophysics, Canberra.

Keating, M. 1967. "Australian workforce and employment, 1910–11 to 1960–61". *Australian Economic History Review* 7: 150–71.

Kolsen, K. M. 1983. "Effective rates of protection and hidden sectoral transfers by public authorities". *Australian Journal of Agricultural Economics* 27: 104–15.

McLean, I. W. 1982. "The demand for agricultural research in Australia 1870–1914". *Australian Economic Papers* 21: 294–308.

Norton, W. E., P. M. Garmston, and M. W. Brodie. 1982. *Australian Economic Statistics.* Occasional Paper No. 8A. Sydney: Reserve Bank of Australia.

Pandey, S., R. R. Piggott, and T. G. MacAuley. 1982. "The elasticity of aggregate Australian agriculture supply: estimates and policy implications". *Australian Journal of Agricultural Economics* 26: 202–19.

Powell, R. A. 1974. "Technological change in Australian agriculture 1920–21 to 1969–70". Ph.D. thesis, University of New England.

Raggart, A. 1968. *Mountains of Ore.* Melbourne: Lansdowne.

Richardson, R. A. 1976. "Structural estimates of domestic demand for agricultural products in Australia: a review". *Review of Marketing and Agricultural Economics* 44: 71–101.

Shaw, A. G. L. 1980. *The Economic Development of Australia.* 7th ed. Melbourne: Longman Cheshire.

Schultz, T. W. 1940. *Agriculture in an Unstable Economy.* New York: McGraw-Hill.

Smith, B. 1982. "Trade and investment issues in Australia's mineral developments", in C. R. Webb and R. H. Allan (eds.), *Industrial Economics: Australian Studies,* pp. 410–21. Sydney: Allen & Unwin.

    1983. "Resources and Australian economic development", in F. H. Gruen (ed.), *Surveys of Australian Economics,* vol. 3, pp. 77–123. Sydney: Allen & Unwin.

Tyers, R., and A. H. Chisholm. 1982. "Agricultural policies in industrialised and developing countries and international food security", in A. H. Chisholm and R. Tyers (eds.), *Food Security: Theory, Policy and Perspective from Asia and the Pacific Rim,* pp. 307–53. Lexington, Mass.: Heath (Lexington Books).

Williams, D. B. (ed.). 1982. *Agriculture in the Australian Economy.* 2d ed. Sydney: Sydney University Press.

Williams, K. G., and R. W. Frazer. 1985. "State taxation of the iron ore industry in Western Australia". *Australian Economic Review,* 1st Quarter: 30–6.

CHAPTER 7

Tariffs and the manufacturing sector

KYM ANDERSON

For at least fifty years Australia has been more protectionist towards its manufacturing sector than perhaps any other high-income country except New Zealand. This difference between Australia and other industrial countries became especially marked following the substantial post–World War II reductions in tariffs on manufactured goods imported by Western Europe, the United States, and Japan.[1]

This chapter first examines the development of the manufacturing sector in Australia and then discusses the role tariffs have played in that development and in achieving other social goals. It looks at why high levels of protection were adopted and what the effects of protection have been. The decade from 1973 saw some major changes in the level, composition, and instruments of protection in Australian manufacturing industries and in the sector's performance in the Australian economy. The chapter includes an assessment of this recent experience in the light of past developments. The final section comments on the efficacy of Australia's protectionist development strategy.

The importance of the manufacturing sector in high-income countries typically has risen over most of this century and then declined during the past decade or two. Australia has followed a similar path, but the sector's importance increased more rapidly and then decreased more rapidly than in most other industrial countries. Up to the 1970s, the sector's relatively rapid growth was stimulated by steadily rising protection from import competition. In other industrial countries, by contrast, manufacturing protection has tended to decline for at least the past half century. The relative decline in Australia's manufacturing sector (in terms of its share of GDP) during the 1970s has been attributed to several factors, the most important being the boom in the mining

---

[1] There are few studies that include Australia in comparisons of protection rates both across countries and over time. An early exception is that published by the League of Nations, *Tariff Level Indices* (Geneva, 1927). Other more fragmentary pieces of comparative evidence are reported in Anderson and Garnaut (in press). Much has been written about Australian tariff protection per se, however. Important sources are Brigden et al. (1929), Corden (1963), Lloyd (1978), Moffatt (1970), and Reitsma (1960), as well as the numerous annual and other reports of the Tariff Board and Industries Assistance Commission.

165

sector. Surprisingly, the pleas by affected industries in the mid 1970s for assistance from structural adjustment pressures were, with two important exceptions, not heeded by the Australian government of the day. On the contrary, many manufacturing tariffs were cut substantially for the first time in Australia's history. This policy redirection has been attributed to what is probably a permanent change in the climate of opinion in Australia away from sympathy for long-term protection.

7.1   The development of manufacturing

The broad picture in international perspective

Manufacturing activities, including the processing of primary products, accounted for only about 4 percent of Australia's GDP in 1861, the earliest year for which reliable data are available (Butlin 1962). Their contribution rose to 10 percent by 1876, then fluctuated between 10 and 12 percent until 1910 before rising to a peak of 29 percent in the late 1950s. Thereafter the sector's share fell steadily, so that by the early 1980s it was around 20 percent (Figure 7.1). The share of the Australian labour force employed in manufacturing has followed a similar hill-shaped trend. At the time of federation about 15 percent of the workforce was engaged in manufacturing. This share rose to a peak of about 30 percent around 1950, and has since fallen to under 20 percent.

Since 1900 manufacturing value added has grown at least 50 percent faster than value added in the primary and service sectors, and, at least up to the 1940s, employment growth in manufacturing was almost double that in other sectors (Boehm 1979: Table 6.3; Butlin 1962: Table 269; Keating 1973: Table 19.4). Exports of manufactured goods other than processed primary products, on the other hand, have always been of minor importance to Australia relative to exports of agricultural and mineral products. Prior to the 1950s manufactures accounted for less than 10 percent of Australia's exports. Their share gradually increased over the 1950s and 1960s but levelled out at a little over 20 percent in the late 1960s.

To judge how typical Australia's manufacturing development has been, it is useful to compare it with that of other countries. At the turn of the century, manufacturing was only half as important to Australia as to other high-income countries: Its contribution to Australian GDP and employment of less than 15 percent compared with between 20 and 25 percent in the United States and Canada and between 25 and 35 percent in the major countries of Western Europe (Kuznets 1971: Tables 22, 39). However, by the 1950s Australia had virtually eliminated this

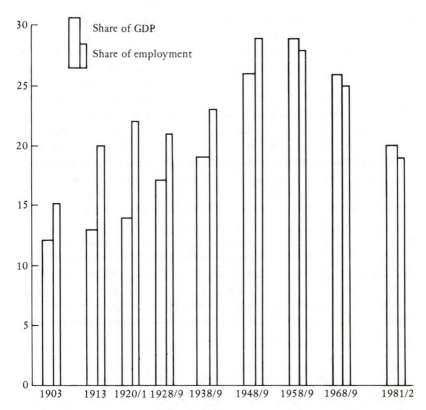

Figure 7.1. The manufacturing sector's shares of GDP and employment, Australia, 1903 to 1981/2. *Sources:* Butlin 1962; Butlin and Dowie 1969; Keating 1973; Australian Bureau of Statistics, *Australian National Accounts: Gross Product by Industry and Manufacturing Establishments*, various issues.

difference, with its manufacturing sector contributing almost 30 percent to GDP and employment, which was close to the average for other high-income countries. Since the 1960s these shares have declined in both Australia and other high-income countries, but more so in Australia (Table 7.1).

Also worth noting is that before the 1960s the Australian manufacturing sector's share of employment tended to be above its share of GDP, whereas the opposite is true for industrial countries as a group (Kuznets 1971: Tables 26, 44). This suggests that the labour intensity of Australia's manufacturing sector was above that of other industrial countries. Yet in an economy such as Australia's where labour is relatively scarce, one might expect to observe a degree of labour intensity below the average. Perhaps the major reason for the phenomenon is that in Australia manufacturers were protected by tariffs "made to measure"; that is, they tended to be set so as to compensate producers for the cost disability they suffered, relative to their competitors in the United Kingdom, as a result of Australia's higher wage rates. The effect of this procedure for setting tariffs in a relatively high-wage economy was to protect most highly the most labour-intensive manufacturing industries, which were the least suitable for Australia's environment.

The final column of Table 7.1 shows that with respect to exports, too, Australia is a most unusual industrial country. The share of exports from manufacturing in Australia is similar to that of developing countries, and only one-third the share for other high-income countries. This has been the case throughout the past century. In 1913, for example, all manufactures (including processed primary products) accounted for only 12 percent of Australia's exports, compared with more than 50 percent of the exports of other industrial countries (Forster 1970: Table 3.10; Maizels 1963: Tables A1, A3). The reason is quite simply that Australia, with its very high per capita endowments of agricultural land and minerals, has always had a stronger comparative advantage in primary rather than manufactured products.

The stages of manufacturing development

Prior to federation in 1901, the domestic market for manufactured goods was hampered by tariff barriers at the borders of Victoria, South Australia, and Tasmania and by large transport costs. The latter provided natural protection to light manufacturing industries such as textiles, clothing, and footwear (mainly from imported materials), food for local consumption, bricks, printing, preliminary processing of primary products for export (wool, meat, flour), and metal works and machinery (especially for repairs and maintenance).

After federation, the elimination of tariff barriers between the states encouraged specialisation to take advantage of economies of scale (although state-specific regulations restricted somewhat this opportunity for economising). The resulting higher rate of growth of manufacturing continued for a decade or more, with the opening of the Newcastle steelworks in 1915 symbolising the country's industrial take-off.[2] World War I provided some stimulus to Australian manufacturers, but the sector was insufficiently developed and too remote from the war scene

[2] For more details of the development of the iron and steel industry, see Hughes (1964a).

Table 7.1. *Share of manufacturing in* GDP, *employment, and exports, various countries and country groups, 1960, 1970, and 1981 (percentages)*

	Share of GDP			Share of employment			Share of exports 1970
	1960	1970	1981	1960	1970	1981	
Low-income countries[a]	11	12	16	7[b]	8[b]	15[b]	27
Middle-income countries[a]	20	22	22	15[b]	18[b]	21[b]	26
High-income countries[c]	30	28	25	26	28	24	78
Australia	29	27	20	28	26	20	27
Canada	23	20	19	25	24	21	60
EEC	33	31	26	30	31	27	82
Japan	34	36	31	21	27	25	94
New Zealand	N.A.	N.A.	N.A.	26	29	24	N.A.
United States	29	26	22	26	26	22	69

[a]These are the World Bank's two categorisations of developing countries.
[b]Includes mining, construction, electricity, water, and gas.
[c]OECD countries (that is, excluding high-income OPEC member countries).
Sources: World Bank, *World Development Report* (Washington, D.C. 1983; OECD, *Historical Statistics 1960–1981* (Paris, 1983).

Table 7.2. *Annual rates of growth of manufacturing and total* GDP *and employment, Australia, 1900 to 1981 (annual percentages in real terms)*[a]

	Manufacturing		Total	
Period	GDP	Employment	GDP	Employment
1900–13	4.9	4.3	4.2	2.0
1913–18	−4.1	0.0	−1.5	1.0
1918–29	4.9	2.0	2.4	1.1
1929–33	−4.7	−2.8	−0.0	−0.9
1933–9	5.9	6.3	2.6	3.0
1939–46	4.1[b]	4.1	N.A.	2.2
1946–60	6.5[c]	2.3	4.2[c]	1.9
1960–73	5.4[d]	1.5	5.5[d]	2.8
1973–81	1.6	−0.9	2.8	1.5

[a]Compound rates of growth between the two-fiscal-year average (three in the case of 1900) at the beginning and at the end of the calendar year periods shown. Output is valued at 1910/11 prices to 1939, at 1947–50 prices during World War II, at 1953/4 prices during the 1950s, at 1968/9 prices in the penultimate period, and at 1979/80 prices in the final period.
[b]For the period 1936–9 to 1947–50, from Maizels 1957.
[c]For the period 1949 to 1960, from Haig 1966.
[d]For the period 1963 to 1973, from Reserve Bank of Australia 1984.
Sources: Butlin 1962; Butlin and Dowie 1969; Haig 1966; Keating 1973; Maizels 1957; Reserve Bank of Australia, *Australian Economic Statistics: 1949–50 to 1982–83* (Sydney, 1984); Australian Bureau of Statistics, *Manufacturing Establishments*, various issues.

to assist greatly in meeting the war's needs. Employment in manufacturing actually declined slightly in 1914 and 1915 as large numbers joined the army. Recovery was slow. Quantitative estimates of manufacturing output and employment growth during this and subsequent periods are given in Table 7.2.

The second industrial growth spurt occurred immediately after this brief setback during the war (Figure 7.2).[3] As is detailed below, this was encouraged by a devaluation and large increases in tariff protection. The expansion of the 1920s was checked by the depression around 1930, but further protection increases and a devaluation at that time enabled manufacturing activity to lead the economy out of the depression in the mid and later 1930s (see Chapter 3). Thus when World War II broke out in 1939, Australian manufacturers were sufficiently developed to be

[3] See Forster (1964) for a detailed account of Australia's industrial development during this period.

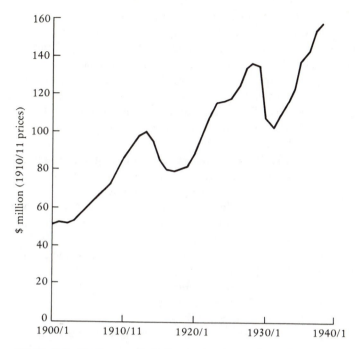

Figure 7.2. Real manufacturing GDP, Australia, 1900/1 to 1938/9.
Source: Butlin 1962: 461.

able to adapt to producing war material and equipment as well as civilian
needs, of which supply from overseas was interrupted by the war. One
index of this intrasectoral change was the drop by one-third, to 16
percent, in the share of manufacturing GDP contributed by food and
drink during the 1940s (Boehm 1979: Table 6.1).

Rapid industrial growth and diversification continued for the duration
of postwar reconstruction in the northern hemisphere, during which time
competition in Australia from imports was minimal. This growth would
have been checked by the reemergence of that competition from the
late 1940s had the federal government not intervened by raising protection levels further, this time via quantitative restrictions on imports.
These controls remained in force throughout the 1950s, during which
time real manufacturing GDP grew at more than 6 percent per annum
(Table 7.2). When import licensing was removed in 1960, it was replaced
with similarly protective tariffs on imports. This encouraged the continued expansion of the manufacturing sector through the 1950s and 1960s,
though not without some structural changes. In particular, labour-in-

tensive industries declined in relative importance as heavy industry expanded. The share of manufacturing value added contributed by textiles, clothing, and footwear, for example, fell from 16 to 10 percent in the two decades to 1968/9, whereas that due to industrial metals, machinery, and transport equipment rose from 38 to 48 percent (Boehm 1979: Table 6.1). Thus even though manufacturing GDP grew as rapidly as total GDP between 1960 and 1973, manufacturing employment grew only half as rapidly (Table 7.2). This was a period of rapid service sector employment growth (see Chapter 8).

From the early 1970s, however, a number of major structural and policy changes in the Australian and international economies have had profound effects on Australia's manufacturing sector. First, the outward shifts in the supply of and demand for Australian minerals and energy, and the associated inflow of development capital from overseas, caused the exchange rate to appreciate considerably relative to what its value would have been in the absence of the mining boom. This necessarily reduced the competitiveness of other tradable industries, including many manufacturing industries (Corden 1984; Gregory 1976; Snape 1977). As a result the share of the minerals sector in GDP and exports grew rapidly.

Second, rapid export-oriented industrialisation took place in Japan from the mid 1950s and in the Asian NICs (the newly industrialising countries of Singapore, Hong Kong, Taiwan, and South Korea) from the early 1960s. These countries are extremely poorly endowed with agricultural land and minerals relative to labour, are relatively open to international trade and capital flows, and are closer to Australia than to most other sources of industrial raw materials and food. As a result, since the early 1960s Australia has experienced extremely rapid growth in primary exports to – and manufactured imports from – these countries, just as it did with Europe in the nineteenth century (Table 7.3). For example, during the 1970s Australia's share of imports from East Asia's developing countries grew from 11 to 19 percent, whereas the share of other industrial countries' imports from that region increased only from 5 to 7 percent (Kym Anderson and Garnaut forthcoming: chap. 2). This trade growth put further pressures on Australia's manufacturing sector, particularly the labour-intensive segments, which are most vulnerable to competition from developing countries.

Third, Australians, like citizens of other advanced industrial countries, have in recent years increased their demand for nontradable services, including government-provided services, relative to goods. Thus even without the mining boom and rapid industrialisation in East Asia, it is likely that, for domestic demand reasons, manufacturing would

Table 7.3. *Direction of Australia's trade, 1951/2 to 1981/2 (percentages)*

	Exports			Imports		
Area	1951/2 to 1954/5	1968/9 to 1971/2	1978/9 to 1981/2	1951/2 to 1954/5	1968/9 to 1971/2	1978/9 to 1981/2
Industrial countries						
United Kingdom	36	11	4	45	21	9
Other Europe	27	16	17	15	19	17
United States	7	13	11	12	24	23
Japan	8	26	28	2	13	18
New Zealand	4	5	5	1	2	3
Total	82	71	65	75	79	70
Developing countries						
East Asia	6	12	18	7	7	13
Southwest Pacific	3	4	4	1	2	1
South Asia	4	3	2	6	2	1
Middle East	1	2	5	4	5	10
Africa	2	2	1	2	1	1
Latin America	1	2	1	1	1	1
Total	17	25	31	21	18	27

Note: The country groups shown account for between 96 and 99 percent of Australia's trade.
Source: Australian Bureau of Statistics, *Overseas Trade*, various issues.

have declined relative to the production of services from the 1970s, just as has happened in Western Europe and North America (Table 7.1). The fact that the decline has been relatively greater for Australia is attributable to the other factors examined in this chapter.

Fourth, from late 1972 to late 1975, Australia had a Labor government that did not discourage demands for real wage increases and that actively encouraged equal pay for women. As a result, during 1974 alone, award wage rates grew in real terms by 19 percent for males and 27 percent for females. By 1977 average earnings of females were only 12 percent lower than those of males, compared with 36 percent lower a decade earlier – the result of a conscious institutional move towards awarding equal pay for women (Gregory and Duncan 1981). There was also a significant compression of skill differentials over this period. The ratio of labourers' to skilled workers' awards (if the latter are represented by the rates for fitters and turners) also rose by about one-eighth between 1972 and 1977. These wage changes reduced further the international competitiveness of Australia's more labour-intensive tradable industries, which were primarily the same industries facing increasing import competition from manufacturers in East Asia.

Finally, during the mid 1970s marked changes were made to Australia's manufacturing protection policies. The dramatic reduction of all tariffs by one-quarter in July 1973, and some subsequent minor tariff reductions, affected greatly the more highly protected manufacturing industries, which included motor vehicles and most of the relatively labour-intensive industries. The major industries in the latter category were protected to some extent by import quotas from 1974, as discussed further below, but most manufacturing industries emerged in the 1980s with considerably less protection from import competition than a decade earlier.

The net effects of these five sets of influences on manufacturing output and employment were substantial. In fact, both declined absolutely. At 1979/80 prices, manufacturing output in 1975/6 was 5 percent below that of 1973/4, and it took a further three years to return to the 1973/4 level. Moreover, the number employed in manufacturing fell 9 percent in the two years to August 1975, and fell a further 6 percent in the subsequent twenty-four months, to 1.2 million.

The reduction in the average level of protection to manufacturers was not the primary reason for the rapid decline of the manufacturing sector's shares of GDP and employment during the decade from 1973. Of considerably more importance were the mining boom and, for unskilled labour-intensive industries, the growing competition from Asian imports.[4] During the preceding half century, however, the gradual increase in protection from import competition, particularly via tariffs, probably was the main reason the manufacturing sector expanded more rapidly in Australia than in other industrial countries to become just as important in terms of GDP and employment despite Australia's strong comparative disadvantages in manufacturing.[5] A brief summary of the

---

[4] For quantitative assessments of the relative importance of these various factors in the mid 1970s see Dixon, Parmenter, and Sutton (1978), Gregory and Martin (1976), and Marsden and Anderssen (1979).

[5] Government assistance to other tradable sectors had not been absent but had always been relatively minor compared with the tariff assistance afforded the manufacturing sector. Even during the 1920s and 1930s, when some agricultural industries were heavily protected, the (weighted) average rate of assistance to agriculture as a whole was still low compared with assistance to manufacturers.

evolution of protection is therefore an essential part of the history of the manufacturing sector.

7.2   The evolution of protection

Protection emerged as a political issue in Australia well before feder-ation. The discoveries of gold in the 1850s in Victoria and New South Wales caused the population of Australia to treble in less than a decade. Then, as the alluvial gold deposits were depleted during the 1860s there was concern about the likelihood of unemployment among the greatly enlarged workforce. Tariff protection for manufacturing was advocated as a way to increase the demand for labour, but its popularity was by no means universal. There were fierce parliamentary confrontations and narrow voting margins over protection policy in both colonies in the 1860s. As it happened, the protectionists won the day in Victoria while the free traders won in New South Wales. When the first federal par-liament met in 1901 these opposing views were clearly expressed. Within a few years, though, the free traders had merged with the protectionists to form an anti–Labor party coalition, and both the coalition and Labor became sympathetic to calls for protection.

A variety of considerations were important in explaining the emer-gence of a protectionist consensus in the first decade of the federation. Forty years of high protection in Victoria, and considerable protection in South Australia and Tasmania, had created many vested interests that lobbied hard for the retention of protection under federation. As well, import duties as a source of government revenue were seen as more feasible politically and administratively than were income taxes.[6] And third, the protectionist leadership from Victoria was able to woo the support of the Labor party. It did this by developing the concept of "New Protection", whereby the continued provision of protection was made conditional on employers' providing superior conditions of em-ployment, including high wages. When members of the Free Trade party were defeated decisively in the 1906 election, the party's survivors an-nounced that they interpreted the election outcome as an expression of the electorate's preference for protection.

Thus the first substantial protective tariff, the Lyne tariff, was imposed on manufactured imports in 1907/8. It doubled many of the existing

---

[6] That this need for raising revenue was not pursued to the point of also taxing domestic import-competing production to offset the tariff's protective effect was the result of the other two considerations.

revenue duties, and the average increase was almost a third (Crawford 1934). But its real significance was not in the height of the duties (for they were little more than twice the natural protection provided by ocean transport costs between Australia and Britain, according to Pope and Manger 1984) but in the victory of protectionist forces.

Manufacturing was boosted somewhat towards the end of World War I under the stimulus provided by the disruption of normal import supplies. The disappearance of that stimulus after the war and the decline in ocean transport costs led the government to raise the level of tariff protection in 1920/1 to about one-third above the height of the Lyne tariff. Its purpose was to support infant industries, such as the iron and steel and the motor body building industries, in the wake of the sharp decline in natural protection. This Greene tariff met with little criticism, for by this time opposition to protection had virtually disappeared. Defence became an additional justification for protection, along with employment considerations and national pride in watching the industrial sector develop.

Tariffs were raised further in the mid 1920s as production costs overseas fell and as the postwar boom ended. They were increased again for a wide range of commodities by the Scullin tariff adjustments of 1929/30. These increases, which were part of the emergency measures of the depression, applied to British as much as to other goods. The Scullin tariff was accompanied and followed by some quantitative restrictions on imports as the depression deepened, and by further tariff increases in 1930/1. Manufacturers were protected even further by the 25 percent devaluation of the Australian pound against sterling in 1931.

One set of estimates of the average level of import tariffs in Australia, by Carmody (1952), is reproduced in Figure 7.3. Some of the changes, such as the decline in 1908 and in the period from 1914 to 1918, are due not to policy changes but to declines in the ad valorem equivalent of specific duties. But the main policy changes are clearly evident: the Greene tariff increases around 1920, the further increases of the mid 1920s, and the large Scullin adjustments around 1930. Australia lowered its British preferential tariff rates following the Ottawa agreement of 1932, but the general tariff remained high throughout the 1930s. This paralleled similar trade policy moves by the United States, which, along with its main trading partners, began to reduce tariffs bilaterally after the U.S. reciprocal Trade Agreement Act was passed in 1934.

As mentioned above, manufacturing activity received another natural protection boost by the disruption of supplies during and immediately following World War II. Again the government raised artificial barriers

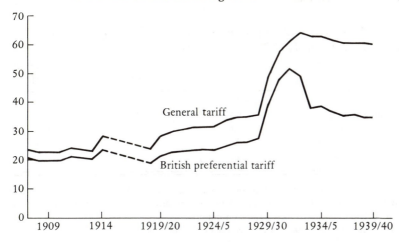

Figure 7.3. Average rates of import tariffs on manufactured goods, Australia, 1907 to 1939/40. Weights used in determining averages are based on the pattern of domestic consumption. *Source:* Carmody 1952.

to imports as this stimulus disappeared following postwar reconstruction. This time, import licensing rather than the tariff was used extensively, at least until 1960. This was seen as a policy instrument also capable of helping to achieve balance-of-payments equilibrium during this period of fixed exchange rates (Moffatt 1970). Licensing provided even more protection than the tariff, so that when it was abandoned in 1960 numerous tariffs were raised to maintain protection levels.

Australia did not participate in the multilateral tariff reductions negotiated in the Dillon and Kennedy rounds of GATT talks in the 1950s and 1960s (Arndt 1965), just as it had not participated with the United States in reducing tariffs bilaterally in the 1930s. However, in 1973 all tariffs were reduced unilaterally by 25 percent. This was Australia's first major liberalisation of imports, a historic turning point in protection policy. Having taken that decision, the government cut tariffs further on some items in the mid 1970s as part of an overall review of tariffs, and on other items in early 1977 following a currency devaluation. The latter cuts brought the average tariff reduction since 1973 to 40 percent, sufficient for Australia to qualify as a participant in the Tokyo round of GATT negotiations.

Thus the mid 1970s saw a major turnaround in tariff assistance to Australian manufacturers. This occurred despite the very considerable structural adjustment pressures on the sector, mentioned in the preced-

Table 7.4. *Effective rates of protection to manufacturing industries,*
Australia, 1968/9 to 1981/2ᵃ (percentages)

Industry	1968/9	1973/4	1981/2
Textiles	43	35	54
Clothing & footwear	97	64	204
Motor vehicles & parts	50	38	124
Other manufacturing	32	23	14
Total manufacturing	36	27	26

ᵃThe Industries Assistance Commission estimates are described as effective rates of assistance. However, in the case of manufacturing, virtually all of the assistance is provided
via tariffs and quantitative restrictions on imports.
Sources: Industries Assistance Commission 1976, 1980, 1983.

ing section. The only industries exempted were textiles, clothing and
footwear, and motor vehicles and parts. For other manufacturing industries, the effective rate of protection was reduced from 32 to 23
percent in 1973, and fell steadily thereafter to 14 percent by 1981/2
(Table 7.4). On the other hand, quotas were applied to imports of
textiles, clothing, footwear, and motor vehicles from 1974, which became increasingly protective over time as Australia's competitiveness in
these industries declined. The average rate of effective protection to
these quota-protected industries trebled from 45 percent in 1973/4 to
130 percent by 1981/2. Thus the average effective rate of protection for
manufacturing as a whole, which remained around 27 percent during
the decade from 1973, masks both the tendency for considerably reduced
protection in most industries and a phenomenal increase in quota protection for two industry groups.

In short, the period from federation to 1973 was one of gradual increases in protection from manufacturing import competition, while the
decade since then has been one of protection cuts for most manufacturing industries. This Australian experience contrasts markedly with
that of other industrial countries. The evidence in Table 7.5 suggests
that manufacturing tariff reductions have been the norm in most other
industrial countries throughout much of the period since 1900. Australia,
with New Zealand, has been one of the most protected of the industrial
countries since the 1920s. (It is true that in 1925 tariffs were higher in
the United States than in Australia, but this was an aberration in U.S.
tariff history. U.S. tariffs have been on a long-term decline since 1900,
except for a sharp blip from 1920 to the mid 1930s [Kindleberger and
Lindert 1978: 221].) This evidence is consistent with that in Table 7.6,

Table 7.5. *Average manufacturing tariff rates, selected industrial countries, 1902, 1913, 1925, 1970, and 1975 (percentages)*

Country	1902	1913	1925	1970[a]	1975[b]
Australia	6	16	27	23	13
Belgium	13	9	15	—	—
Canada	17	26	23	14	8
Denmark	18	14	10	—	—
EEC[c]	—	—	—	8	8
France	34	20	21	—	—
Germany	25	13	20	—	—
Italy	27	18	22	—	—
Japan	10	20	13	12	11
Netherlands	3	4	6	—	—
New Zealand	9	N.A.	N.A.	23	N.A.
Norway	12	N.A.	N.A.	11	N.A.
Sweden	23	20	16	7	5
Switzerland	7	9	14	3	N.A.
United States	73	44	37	9	6

[a] The 1970 estimates are not comparable with earlier estimates because the earlier estimates used f.o.b. export prices of other countries as indicators of border prices, instead of c.i.f. import prices for the country concerned. Thus the earlier rates are somewhat overestimated. This has little effect on the intercountry comparison for each year, however.
[b] The 1975 estimates, which were compiled by the Industries Assistance Commission from information supplied by the GATT, may not be perfectly comparable with the 1970 and earlier estimates.
[c] Belgium, France, West Germany, Italy, Luxembourg, and the Netherlands in 1970; also Denmark, Ireland, and the United Kingdom in 1975.
Sources: League of Nations, *Tariff Level Indices* (Geneva, 1927), as quoted in Little, Scitovsky, and Scott 1970: 162–3; General Agreement on Tariffs and Trade, *Basic Documentation for the Tariff Study* (Geneva, 1972); and Industries Assistance Commission 1978: Table 1.3.3.

showing the decline in the openness of the Australian economy relative to other industrial economies, as measured by exports plus imports as a percentage of GDP. It is therefore appropriate to ask why Australia took such a strongly protectionist stance until the 1970s, and why it altered that stance in the mid 1970s.

7.3   Reasons for high protection levels to the 1970s

One of the strongest conclusions in neoclassical trade theory is that protection against imports reduces the average level of income in countries like Australia whose economies are too small to influence inter-

Table 7.6. *Share of national product traded, selected industrial countries, early 1900s to 1970s (percentages)*[a]

Country	Early 1900s	1920s	1950s	1960s	1970s
Australia	42	37	35	32	31
Austria	N.A.	N.A.	45	54	68
Belgium	N.A.	N.A.	62	75	93
Canada	32	42	39	41	47
Denmark	62	57	66	61	61
Finland	N.A.	N.A.	46	48	58
France	35	N.A.	27	28	39
Germany	38	31	31	37	45
Italy	28	26	27	34	49
Japan	30	36	20	20	24
Netherlands	N.A.	N.A.	96	92	100
Norway	69	64	87	84	89
Sweden	40	32	46	45	56
Switzerland	N.A.	N.A.	56	61	65
United Kingdom	44	38	44	42	55
United States	11	11	9	10	15

[a]For the period since 1950, the World Bank's data refer to the ratio of exports plus imports of commodities and nonfactor services to GDP. The earlier data from Kuznets refer to the ratio of exports plus imports of commodities to GDP (or GNP in the case of Australia, Canada, Italy, the United Kingdom, and the United States).

It has not been possible to get data for years that correspond exactly across countries. The percentages in the first two columns, from Kuznets, refer to the following years for each country: Australia 1911–13, 1924–9; Canada 1911–13, 1926–9; Denmark 1910–14, 1921–9; France 1908–10; Germany 1910–13, 1925–9; Italy 1911–13, 1925–9; Japan 1908–13, 1918–27; Norway 1905–14, 1920–9; Sweden 1911–13, 1921–30; United Kingdom 1909–13, 1924–8; and United States 1904–13, 1919–28. The final three columns, from the World Bank, refer to 1950–60, 1960–70, and 1970–7.

Sources: Kuznets 1966: Table 6.4; World Bank, *World Tables (1980 Edition)* (Washington, D.C., 1980).

national prices.[7] Nonetheless, a number of public interest arguments have been used to support the case for protection. These include the infant industry argument as well as the arguments that protection could boost real wages and thereby redistribute income and attract more im-

---

[7] It has been argued in the past that Australia may have been able to influence the price of wool. In the 1920s wheat was also considered by some authors to have a low export demand elasticity (Brigden 1925; Brigden et al. 1929; Giblin 1936). Others, however, strongly disagreed that Australia would have monopoly power even in wool and wheat (Benham 1926; Viner 1929). See Reitsma (1960: chap. 6) for a detailed discussion of the debate on the terms-of-trade argument. With strong competition from synthetic and other natural fibres, and with the growth in the wool industry in a number of other

migrants, could alleviate unemployment problems, could overcome balance-of-payments problems, and could ensure a more "balanced" economy that was less specialised in primary production.

Infant industry protection, wages, and immigration

Supporters of protection have claimed that there is a dynamic economic case for protection aimed at stimulating new manufacturing activity because the general atmosphere engendered by manufacturing is more conducive to economic growth than that surrounding primary activities. Protection was necessary, it was argued, to ensure that entrepreneurs would risk their capital during the early years before an industry could stand on its own feet. This argument was used in Australia during periods of high growth optimism, such as from the 1860s to the 1880s, and in the two decades following World War II (Reitsma 1960: chap. 7), but in recent times it has been taken much less seriously.[8]

In Australia, a belief that protection raised real wages or allowed a larger workforce to be employed at a given real wage played an extremely important part in moulding public opinion in favour of protection. This proposition, first espoused formally by Brigden (1925), was incorporated into a major official report on the Australian tariff (Brigden et al. 1929) and was further clarified by Reddaway (1937). It was argued that protection of the import-competing manufacturing sector would raise the demand for labour. This would have two effects that were judged to be socially desirable: It would support greater employment at given real wages and so attract immigrants, and it would implicitly tax some of the rents of the relatively rich landowners. That is, protection was seen as an instrument capable of both redistributing national income more equitably and increasing Australia's population of European settlers.[9]

countries, it is likely that any monopoly power in wool that Australia may have enjoyed in the past has now virtually disappeared. (See Freebairn 1978 for a recent survey of estimates of Australia's export demand elasticities.) In any case, the more efficient policy if any such monopoly power existed would be a tax on exports of that product rather than taxes on every item imported. This is because the latter approach not only would involve higher tax collection costs but would, through the tariff's effect on the exchange rate, provide disincentives to exporters of export products other than wool.

[8] This school of thought was popularised by List (1985). Marshall (1890) used the presumed presence of these supply conditions in industry and in agriculture to argue that protection was less costly in the United States, then mainly an exporter of primary products, than in Britain, an exporter of manufactures. For a discussion of why the infant industry argument should not be taken as a serious justification for import protection see Baldwin (1969) and Corden (1974: chap. 9).

[9] In the process, moderate tariff levels could raise tariff revenue for the government, so

Brigden's proposition survived despite considerable controversy and refinement.[10] Its supporters knew they were arguing a second-best case, and they were suspicious that average incomes would be lower because of protection. However, the first-best redistribution policy, namely taxing land rents for the purpose of raising living standards of wage earners, was seen by them as politically impractical because it was more overt than the tariff, as well as being difficult to administer. Critics, on the other hand, argued that if direct income redistribution was necessary it could be achieved most efficiently through rent or income taxation (Viner 1929). But their arguments were insufficient to win the public or even the economists' debate at the time.

Had the Australian discussions continued in the Brigden–Reddaway tradition, the protectionists' case would soon have weakened with the increased feasibility of using superior instruments of taxation for redistributing income to wage earners. Income taxation, for example, has been applied widely since the 1940s.

As it happened, though, the relationship between protection and income redistribution increasingly came to be understood in terms of a model that invited conclusions excessively favourable to protection. This was the model presented in the celebrated article by Stolper and Samuelson (1941). The model had two tradable sectors, agriculture and manufacturing, and two homogeneous and domestically mobile factors, which were called land and labour. The authors concluded, in reference to the Australian situation,[11] that protection of the relatively labour-intensive tradable sector, manufacturing, would unambiguously raise real wages and reduce the real return to land. By ignoring the fact that land is nonhomogeneous and is specific to the primary sector, this model inappropriately distracted attention from the more efficient means of redistributing income mentioned above.

In recent years the belief that protection is desirable because of its effect on relative factor rewards has waned considerably. The anxiety to stimulate immigration of European workers has diminished, and the

reducing the need for other (and perhaps more administratively expensive) forms of taxation, although this point was not included in the argument at the time. On the perceived importance of peopling Australia with European settlers see Borrie (1963).

[10] Supporters of the position taken by Brigden (1925, 1927a and b) included Copland (1931, 1935) and Giblin (1927, 1936). Both were members of the Brigden committee that produced the 1929 tariff report. Critics included Benham (1926, 1927) and Viner (1929). An account of the debate is given in Cain (1973).

[11] The Australian situation had been discussed at that time in a number of theoretical papers published in the *Quarterly Journal of Economics* Karl Anderson 1938, 1939; Copland 1931; M. C. Samuelson 1939). Interest in the history of thought concerning the so-called Australian case for protection was rekindled recently in an exchange between P. A. Samuelson (1981a and b) and Manger (1981a and b).

real incomes of wage and salary earners, at least since the mid 1960s, have been above the average of farm household incomes. Also, it has become increasingly apparent that the real income of a household of workers may not be enhanced by protection if their particular skills are not used intensively in the protected industries, or if a relatively large share of their expenditure is on goods that are highly protected (Lloyd 1982). The fact remains, though, that this belief was an important contributor to the raising of Australia's manufacturing tariff in the first few decades after federation.

Employment protection

A variant of the Brigden proposition – that protection for manufacturing allows higher levels of employment to be maintained at a given real wage – has been influential during lengthy periods of high unemployment. The argument is persuasive to the layman, especially in the Australian environment, where, for institutional reasons, real wages tend to be more than usually rigid in the face of market pressures for their reduction.

The reality is that general unemployment can be addressed effectively only by measures that either raise aggregate demand (which is feasible only when the economy is operating within its balance-of-payments constraints) or raise productivity relative to real wages (through raising average productivity, reducing real wages, or a combination of the two).

In practice, protection is likely to have very little effect on employment, except in the short run. This is because protecting one set of industries is equivalent to taxing all other industries via the effect of protection on the exchange rate, so that any employment gains in the first set of industries will be more or less offset by employment losses in the second set. The reduced job opportunities in agriculture, however, might take some time to be reflected in the employment statistics; they might in the interim take the form of underemployment on farms, which is not measured in the statistics. What is observed, therefore, namely fewer threats of retrenchments in the protected industry itself, is only part of the story. But it is the part that impresses the voter in times of higher unemployment, such as around 1930.

More often, protection is sought for the maintenance not of overall employment but of employment in certain industries or regions. Society is often concerned to cushion workers and owners of enterprises facing large declines in their fortunes, especially when those declines coincide with high general levels of unemployment. Protection is never the first-best policy instrument for this purpose, even if the cause of the problem is increased import competition. Direct subsidies would be a less wasteful means of assisting the industry until the industry's problem disappears. If the cause of the problem is a permanent (rather than temporary) decline in competitiveness, once-only assistance for structural adjustment would be even more sensible than handouts every year to prop up the industry. However, protection tends to be used because, unlike subsidies, it does not involve budgetary outlays. As already mentioned, this argument for protection to maintain an industry's existing level of output was used in Australia following the first and second world wars.

Balance of payments

Prior to the movement towards more flexible exchange rates in the 1970s, it was often argued that protection was necessary at times for the maintenance of equilibrium in the balance of payments. This was especially so in the 1950s in Australia when the sterling area currencies were pegged to the pound, which in turn was pegged to but not freely convertible into the U.S. dollar.

This argument was never strong, since a country's competitive weakness could be corrected by demand policies that led to lower rates of inflation than those ruling in other countries. It lost all credibility among economists when exchange rates became adjustable in the early 1970s. If a deficit in external payments results from excessively high domestic costs and not solely from excessive domestic demand, a real devaluation is more appropriate than increased protection. This is because the former boosts export industries as well as discouraging imports, whereas the latter discourages both exports and imports. Conversely, the first-best response to a surplus in the balance of payments of an economy free of distortions is real currency appreciation, through inflationary demand policies or through nominal currency appreciation. However, if the economy were distorted by import protection (in the absence of offsetting export subsidies), then the most efficient strategy would be to reduce that protection first, and to appreciate only if the payments surplus persisted after all import barriers had been removed.

In practice, when the balance of payments is tending towards surplus, the correction of this tendency is often associated with pressure for some tradable industries to contract. Perhaps the best-known example is where there has been strong growth in mineral exports – whether as the result of the discovery of minerals or of an increase in their relative prices on world markets (Corden 1984). The consequent rise in the real effective exchange rate reduces the competitiveness of other tradable sectors and so may generate public sympathy for their assistance. A protection increase in these circumstances would be an inefficient means of providing assistance, however. Apart from the loss to consumers of importables, protection only assists industries that compete with imports and not other export producers such as farmers. The burden of adjustment for the established industries producing tradables could be eased as well by slowing the rate of real appreciation of the currency. This provides what Corden (1981) has called "exchange rate protection" to tradable relative to nontradable industries. Though it still has welfare costs, such action may provide short-term assistance more efficiently than many other forms of assistance because it is temporary and does not distort resource allocation within sectors.

A more "balanced" and "self-sufficient" economy

Many societies have protected import-competing industries in order to have a more "balanced" economy, despite the cost in terms of income forgone. This desire has resulted from anxieties about the availability of imported supplies of essentials in times of war, or from an idea that it is somehow wrong or unnatural for the intersectoral composition of economic activity to diverge markedly from that of other countries, or at least from that of the advanced industrial countries (Johnson 1965). It has also been argued that protection allows an economy to be less specialised and hence less vulnerable to changes in the fortunes of particular commodities on world markets. This is the argument used in Europe and Japan to justify protection of their agricultural industries.

The balanced economy argument for protection of manufacturing has always been influential in Australia. Without protection, it is probable though by no means certain that the Australian manufacturing sector would have been smaller and would have accounted for a smaller proportion of employment and domestic product than the manufacturing sectors of the major industrial countries.

Public sympathy for protection on these grounds arises because many persons' perception of the Australian economy without manufacturing protection is of many farms and mines and few cities. By far the largest sector, services, is usually ignored or viewed as unproductive ("taking in each other's washing") and therefore unimportant. Also overlooked is the fact that protection reduces the share of GDP that is traded, so that exports are from a narrower range of industries – are more specialized – than would be the case without protection.

Conclusion: the role of private vested interests

This discussion reveals flaws in each of the arguments that traditionally have been used to justify protection in Australia from society's point of view. However, it also shows how these ideas nonetheless at times have supported and encouraged a climate of public opinion favourably disposed towards protecting the import-competing manufacturing sector in a country as richly endowed in natural resources as Australia.[12] The more the public wishes to assist manufacturers, the lower the political cost of providing protection and hence the more protection those industries are likely to receive, ceteris paribus. Thus the arguments that the tariff would redistribute income away from wealthy landowners to workers and would encourage emigration from Britain to Australia were used to influence public opinion in favour of protection. So too were the arguments that manufacturing boosted national defence and diversified the industrial base. Public sympathy also ran high for industries that sprang up to help the war effort and then later faced increased import competition after postwar reconstruction and during the 1929–33 depression. All these factors kept down the political cost of introducing protection policies to a growing number of manufacturing industries during the first few decades of federation. Tariff protection rather than more efficient forms of assistance such as direct subsidies was used, presumably because it raised rather than depleted government revenue and was less overt in that it was not subject to annual budget scrutiny.

Once established, a protection policy has considerable value to the small number of groups benefiting from it. These groups therefore have an incentive to spend part of their benefit in lobbying for the retention of that policy. Groups adversely affected by it, on the other hand, are large in number and so have more difficulty organising to lobby against the policy. In addition, the loss to each of the latter groups is small relative to the gain to each protected group. And since there is considerable inertia in the political system anyway, in the sense that governments have time to deal only with what they perceive as the issues of highest priority, protection policies once in place tend to remain in place until the pressures for change exceed some threshold level.

Australia's protectionist stance might have been eroded during the 1950s and 1960s as other industrial countries wound down their tariffs

---

[12] No attempt is made in this chapter to explain the interindustry distribution of manufacturing protection in Australia. To do so requires drawing also on the private interest theories of government policy making. See Kym Anderson (1980).

following the Dillon and Kennedy rounds of multilateral trade negotiations. But this was not to be. Australia justified its high-protection stance to the international community by arguing that since agricultural protection was excluded from the negotiations, Australia would receive no quid pro quo for a reduction in its manufacturing protection (Arndt 1965). Domestically there was little opposition to the stance, not least because manufacturing and primary production were expanding rapidly. In any case, the government argued that the stance was necessary during the 1950s for balance-of-payments reasons. Then, in the 1960s, the Country party found it convenient to continue propagating the apparent virtues of manufacturing protection (along with assistance to the least competitive agricultural industries), in order to boost party funds and thereby retain its influence in parliament despite the declining importance of rural votes.

By the mid 1960s, however, more people were recognising that Australia's postwar economic growth performance had been much weaker than that of most other industrial countries, and that protection policies were partly to blame. In fact, as is made clear in Chapter 1, Australia's per capita income growth had been relatively low for much of the century. It would be unreasonable to conclude that protection was the only cause for this relatively poor performance. Other domestic market regulations may also be more distortional in Australia than elsewhere (Pincus and Withers 1983). However, the consensus among economists that protection must have been one of the main contributors has received increasingly wider acceptance among leaders over the past two decades.[13]

7.4   Reasons for protection cuts in the 1970s

The effect of the growing awareness of the costs of protection on the political market for protection has been to increase the political cost of maintaining or increasing existing levels of protection. Thus in 1971 the

---

[13] Growth in Australia would be slower in part because protection reduced competition and thereby removed the impetus for technological innovation and domestic entrepreneurship. On the dynamic gains from trade see, for example, Haberler (1959: 1–14), Keesing (1967), and Krueger (1978). Empirical evidence on the relationship between trade and growth is provided also in Kravis (1970) and Michaely (1977). In addition, Balassa (1982) and Krueger (1978) report results of empirical research showing the positive effects on growth of the recent liberalisation of trade in a number of developing countries that, like Australia, had import-substituting industrialisation policies. Corden (1974: 327–9) suggested that some of these arguments can be put in comparative static terms whereby trade provides the domestic economy with more knowledge, which in turn expands wants (which induces people to work harder); suggests better ways of producing goods; etc.

government approved a systematic review of the whole tariff structure. This review generated a steady stream of recommendations for seven years from 1974 for reductions in protection to particular manufacturing industries. Most recommendations were accepted at least partially by both Labor and conservative governments. The industries affected accounted for about 10 percent of manufacturing value added, and their average effective rate of protection was halved.

More important, the changing climate of opinion concerning the national interest in protection made it easier for the Labor government in 1973 to reduce all tariffs by 25 percent as a way of reducing the inflationary pressures it inherited on taking office in late 1972. It was not difficult politically for the returned conservative government to add some further tariff reductions in January 1977, two months after a devaluation, in order to participate in the Tokyo round of multilateral trade negotiations.

As discussed earlier, these three sets of changes ensured that the rate of protection to most manufacturing industries fell substantially during the 1970s. It is true that protection for textiles, clothing, footwear, and motor vehicles and parts increased enormously during the decade. But what is remarkable about that series of policy changes is not that protection for textiles and cars increased in response to declining international competitiveness; this occurred also in North America and Western Europe.[14] It is that other manufacturing protection was reduced by so much. The latter is remarkable not only because it signifies a major turnaround in Australia's policy stance but also because it occurred at a time when manufacturing output and employment were declining absolutely and when the rate of overall unemployment was high and rising. That is, it occurred at a time when one might expect to see protection being increased. That the latter did not occur has been attributed largely to the changed climate of opinion concerning the national interest in

---

[14] The main reasons the textile, clothing, and footwear industries and the motor vehicle industry were singled out for protection increases in the latter 1970s and 1980s included the following: These are industries that had well-established lobbying capacity before 1973, because for decades they had been highly dependent on protection; both groups of industries employed large numbers of workers (representing a total of 20 percent of the manufacturing workforce in 1973); the motor vehicle industry is particularly important to the economies of South Australia and Victoria, and so also receives strong support from the governments of these states when seeking federal government protection; they enjoyed the highest tariff protection in 1973 and so were affected most by the 25 percent tariff cut; and the textile, clothing, and footwear industries, being very labour-intensive, were the industries affected most by the real wage increases and increasing import competition from industrialising Asia. Thus the expected net benefit from lobbying for protection was probably much higher for these than for other manufacturing industries.

protection (Kym Anderson and Garnaut in press: chap. 6). The Australian economics profession became increasingly outspoken against protectionism during the 1960s and by the early 1970s was advocating trade liberalisation with near unanimity and with increasing technical sophistication. A similar change occurred within the bureaucracy and in the financial press. These views were reflected in numerous official reports commissioned by the government, and were adopted by an increasing number of politicians. A leading role was played by the Industries Assistance Commission (formerly the Tariff Board). Private interest groups also responded to the changing trade policy atmosphere. In particular, the National Farmers' Federation made liberalisation of manufactured imports a major part of its political lobbying and public education programmes.

7.5   Was the tariff a good thing for Australia?

If not recently, was the tariff a good thing for Australia in the past? The conventional wisdom has been to answer this question in the affirmative. This chapter, however, has sought to cast doubt on the validity of this standard answer. True, the tariff probably increased the intersectoral dispersion of GDP and of employment, though not necessarily of exports. The corollary to this is that the primary and service sectors have been given less opportunity to contribute to the growth of the Australian economy than would have been the case without protection. In addition, the tariff retarded per capita income growth.[15] In a more open Australian economy, primary production would have contributed a little more to employment, somewhat more to GDP, and substantially more (especially in volume terms) to exports. The greater income from primary production would have been spent partly on tradable manufactured goods and services (both domestically produced and imported) but mainly on nontradable goods and services, so expanding employment and output prospects in the tertiary sector.

It has often been claimed that, regardless of its effect on incomes,

[15] An additional reason for the tariff being costly is that in the Australian federation of states, state governments have tended to compete with each other to attract direct foreign investment, by providing free land and other inducements. An indirect effect of this has been the encouragement of suboptimal scales of operation within each state or in a number of states (see Hughes 1964b). For a discussion of the importance of economies of scale in the Australian setting see Forster (1970). An important consequence of the smallness of the protected Australian market relative to the minimum efficient plant size for many manufacturing industries is that such industries have tended to be highly concentrated and therefore not always subject to the discipline of competition (Brown and Hughes 1970).

protection has contributed to population growth in Australia. Over the past century, Australia's population growth averaged 2 percent per year, twice the average for other high-income countries. Most of this difference is explainable in terms of the high rate of immigration from Europe (especially the United Kingdom) to Australia. And this high immigration rate is in turn often attributed to the effect protection had on raising the demand for labour in Australia's manufacturing industries.

It is, however, debatable whether immigration would have been slower without high levels of protection, especially if Australia had been less selective in its sources of immigrants. The population growth rates of Canada and the United States were not much lower than Australia's, for example, despite their much higher base population. Had Australia chosen a less protectionist trade policy, it is conceivable that per capita incomes would have risen more rapidly and that this would have enticed at least as many immigrants. As just pointed out, there might have been just as many jobs created under a free trade policy as were created under the protectionist strategy. The main difference between the two strategies may be not so much in the number of new jobs as in which industries they appeared. In the former case more of them may have arisen in industries producing nontradable goods and services.

In summary, the manufacturing sector contributed a larger share of the GDP cake than it would have in the absence of protection. But the cake itself might have been considerably larger under freer trade, certainly per head of population and possibly even in aggregate terms, insofar as higher and more rapidly rising incomes attract immigrants and foreign capital inflows. Thus the tariff may not have been necessary to boost Australian immigration, particularly if more immigrants had been sought from Europe or Asia and fewer from industrial centres in the United Kingdom. The tariff may also have been unnecessary for achieving income redistribution goals, given that more direct policy instruments were available, notably export and (later) income taxes. Balance-of-payments and employment goals too could have been achieved more efficiently with other instruments. In short, the only objective for which the tariff was clearly the best policy instrument was the diversification of the economy towards more industrial activity. Whether the extent to which it achieved that objective warranted the cost is a moot point.

References

Anderson, Karl. 1938. "Protection and the historical situation: Australia". *Quarterly Journal of Economics* 53(4): 86–104.

1939. "The Australian case for protection re-examined: comment". *Quarterly Journal of Economics* 54(4): 149–51.

Anderson, Kym. 1980. "The political market for government assistance to Australian manufacturing industries". *Economic Record* 56(153): 132–44.

Anderson, Kym, and R. Garnaut. 1987. *Australian Protectionism: Extent, Causes and Effects.* Sydney: Allen & Unwin.

Arndt, H. W. 1965. "Australia – developed, developing or midway?" *Economic Record* 41(95): 318–40.

Balassa, B. 1982. *Development Strategies in Semi-Industrial Economies.* Baltimore: Johns Hopkins University Press.

Baldwin, R. E. 1969. "The case against infant industry protection". *Journal of Political Economy* 77(3): 295–305.

Benham, F. C. 1926. "The Australian tariff and the standard of living: a reply". *Economic Record* 2: 20–42.

1927. "The Australian tariff and the standard of living: a restatement". *Economic Record* 3: 239–48.

Boehm, E. A. 1979. *Twentieth Century Economic Development in Australia.* 2d ed. Melbourne: Longman Cheshire.

Borrie, W. D. 1963. "The peopling of Australia", in H. W. Arndt and W. M. Corden (eds.), *The Australian Economy: A Volume of Readings,* pp. 101–23. Melbourne: Cheshire.

Brigden, J. B. 1925. "The Australian tariff and the standard of living". *Economic Record* 1(1): 29–46.

1927a. "The Australian tariff and the standard of living: a rejoinder". *Economic Record* 3: 102–16.

1927b. "Comment on Mr. Benham's restatement". *Economic Record* 3: 249–51.

Brigden, J. B., et al. 1929. *The Australian Tariff: An Economic Enquiry.* Melbourne: Melbourne University Press.

Brown, P., and H. Hughes. 1970. "The market structure of Australian manufacturing industry, 1914 to 1963–64", in C. Forster (ed.), *Australian Economic Development in the Twentieth Century,* pp. 169–207. Sydney: Allen & Unwin.

Butlin, N. G. 1962. *Australian Domestic Product, Investment and Foreign Borrowing, 1861–1938/39.* Cambridge: Cambridge University Press.

Butlin, N. G., and J. A. Dowie. 1969. "Estimates of Australian work force and employment, 1861–1961". *Australian Economic History Review* 9(2): 138–55.

Cain, N. 1973. "Political economy and the tariff: Australia in the 1920s". *Australian Economic Papers* 12: 1–20.

Carmody, A. T. 1952. "The level of the Australian tariff: a study in method". *Yorkshire Bulletin of Economic and Social Research* 4(1): 51–65.

Copland, D. B. 1931. "A neglected phase of tariff controversy". *Quarterly Journal of Economics* 45(1): 289–308.

1935. "Notes on tariff theory with special reference to the Australian tariff". *Economic Record* 11 (suppl.): 33–9.

Corden, W. M. 1963. "The tariff", in A. Hunter (ed.), *The Economics of Australian Industry,* chap. 6. Melbourne: Melbourne University Press.

1974. *Trade Policy and Economic Welfare.* Oxford: Oxford University Press (Clarendon Press).

1981. "Exchange rate protection", in R. N. Cooper (ed.), *The International Monetary System under Flexible Exchange Rates,* pp. 17–34. Cambridge, Mass.: Ballinger.

1984. "Booming sector and Dutch disease economics: a survey". *Oxford Economic Papers* 36: 359–80.

Crawford, J. G. 1934. "Tariff level indices". *Economic Record* 10: 213–21.

Dixon, P. B., B. R. Parmenter, and J. Sutton. 1978. "Some causes of structural maladjustment in the Australian economy". *Economic Papers* 57: 10–26.

Forster, C. 1964. *Industrial Development in Australia* 1920–1930. Canberra: Australian National University Press.

1970. "Economies of scale and Australian manufacturing", in Forster (ed.), *Australian Economic Development in the Twentieth Century,* chap. 3. Sydney: Allen & Unwin.

Freebairn, J. W. 1978. "Projections of Australia's world trade opportunities: mid and late nineteen eighties". IMPACT Working Paper No. I–07. Industries Assistance Commission, Melbourne.

Giblin, L. F. 1927. "The Australian tariff and the standard of living: a note on Mr. Benham's statistics". *Economic Record* 3: 148–56.

1936. "Some economic effects of the Australian tariff". The Joseph Fisher Lecture in Commerce, University of Adelaide, June 23.

Gregory, R. G. 1976. "Some implications of the growth of the mining sector". *Australian Journal of Agricultural Economics* 20(2): 71–91.

Gregory, R. G., and R. C. Duncan. 1981. "The relevance of segmented labour market theories: the Australian experience of equal pay for women". *Journal of Post Keynesian Economics* 3(3): 403–28.

Gregory, R. G., and L. D. Martin. 1976. "An analysis of recent relationships between import flows and import prices". *Economic Record* 52(137): 1–25.

Haberler, G. 1959. *International Trade and Economic Development.* Cairo: National Bank of Egypt.

Haig, B. 1966. "Estimates of Australian real product by industry". *Australian Economic Papers* 5(7): 230–50.

Hughes, H. 1964a. *The Australian Iron and Steel Industry 1848–1962.* Melbourne: Melbourne University Press.

1964b. "Federalism and industrial development in Australia". *Australian Journal of Politics and History* 10: 323–8.

Industries Assistance Commission. 1976. *Assistance to Manufacturing Industries in Australia, 1968–69 to 1973–74.* Canberra: Australian Government Publishing Service.

1978. *Annual Report 1977–78.* Canberra: Australian Government Publishing Service.

1980. *Trends in the Structure of Assistance to Manufacturing*. Canberra: Australian Government Publishing Service.

1983. *Annual Report 1982–83*. Canberra: Australian Government Publishing Service.

Johnson, H. G. 1965. "An economic theory of protectionism, tariff bargaining and the formation of customs unions". *Journal of Political Economy* 73(3): 256–83.

Keating, M. 1973. *The Australian Workforce, 1910–11 to 1960–61*. Canberra: Australian National University Press.

Keesing, D. B. 1967. "Outward-looking policies and economic development". *Economic Journal* 77: 303–20.

Kindleberger, C. P., and P. H. Lindert. 1978. *International Economics*. 6th ed. Homewood, Ill.: Irwin.

Kravis, I. B. 1970. "Trade as a handmaiden of growth: similarities between the nineteenth and twentieth centuries". *Economic Journal* 80(320): 850–72.

Krueger, A. O. 1978. *Foreign Trade Regimes and Economic Development: Liberalization Attempts and Consequences*. Cambridge, Mass.: Ballinger for the NBER.

Kuznets, S. S. 1971. *Economic Growth of Nations: Total Output and Production Structure*. Cambridge, Mass.: Harvard University Press.

List, F. 1885. *The National System of Political Economy*. London: Longman, Green. Translated from the German text first published in 1841.

Little, I., T. Scitovsky, and M. Scott. 1970. *Industry and Trade in Some Developing Countries: A Comparative Study*. London: Oxford University Press for the OECD.

Lloyd, P. J. 1978. "Protection policies", in F. H. Gruen (ed.), *Surveys of Australian Economics*, pp. 241–96. Sydney: Allen & Unwin.

1982. "Protection for whom?" *Economic Papers* 1(2): 1–16.

Maizels, A. 1957. "Trends in production and labour productivity in Australian manufacturing industries". *Economic Record* 33(65): 162–81.

1963. *Industrial Growth and World Trade*. Cambridge: National Institute of Economic and Social Research.

Manger, G. J. 1981a. "The Australian case for protection reconsidered". *Australian Economic Papers* 20(37): 193–204.

1981b. "Summary upon the Australian case for protection: comment". *Quarterly Journal of Economics* 96(1): 161–7.

Marsden, J. S., and W. E. Anderssen. 1979. "Employment change in manufacturing: the role of imports, productivity and output growth". *Australian Bulletin of Labour* 9(3): 48–72.

Marshall, A. 1890. *Principles of Economics*. London: Macmillan.

Michaely, M. 1977. "Exports and growth: an empirical investigation". *Journal of Development Economics* 4(1): 49–53.

Moffatt, G. G. 1970. *Import Control and Industrialization: A Study of the Australian Experience*. Melbourne: Melbourne University Press.

Pincus, J. J., and G. A. Withers. 1983. "Economics of regulation", in F. H. Gruen (ed.), *Surveys of Australian Economics*, vol. 3, pp. 9–76. Sydney: Allen & Unwin.

Pope, D., and G. Manger. 1984. "The tariff and Australian manufacturers' international competitiveness: 1901–1930". University of New South Wales, Sydney. Mimeograph.

Reddaway, W. B. 1937. "Some effects of the Australian tariff". *Economic Record* 13: 22–30, 249–50.

Reitsma, A. J. 1960. *Trade Protection in Australia*. Brisbane: University of Queensland Press.

Samuelson, M. C. 1939. "The Australian case for protection re-examined". *Quarterly Journal of Economics* 54(4): 143–9.

Samuelson, P. A. 1981a. "Summing up on the Australian case for protection". *Quarterly Journal of Economics* 96(1): 147–60.

   1981b. "Justice to the Australians". *Quarterly Journal of Economics* 96(1): 169–70.

Snape, R. H. 1977. "Effects of mineral development on the economy". *Australian Journal of Agricultural Economics* 21(3): 147–56.

Stolper, W. F., and P. A. Samuelson. 1941. "Protection and real wages". *Review of Economic Studies* 9(1): 58–73.

Viner, J. 1929. "The Australian tariff". *Economic Record* 5(9): 306–15.

CHAPTER 8

The service sector

MICHAEL CARTER

Our typical view of work involves manual work in the factory or on the farm. Yet in 1981 nearly two out of three Australian workers were not engaged in the factory or on the farm but in the production of services. At the same time services accounted for nearly 60 percent of the total output of the economy (GDP). In terms of their relative shares of employment and output, the agricultural and the manufacturing sectors are the bit players in the modern Australian economy. Services have the leading role.[1]

The precise composition of the service sector will concern us later. For the present it will suffice to indicate broadly the scope of economic activity that is regarded as services. Typical services include transport, communication (telephones, postal services, etc.), the distribution of goods (wholesale and retail trade), banking, insurance, government, health, education, recreation, entertainment, and personal services such as hairdressing.

The prominence of the service sector in the modern Australian economy raises a number of questions that are considered in this chapter. Has the relative importance of the service sector increased over time, and if so, what accounts for this development? How has the evolution of the service sector influenced the overall development of the Australian economy? How does the history of the service sector in Australia compare with that in similar economies? And finally, has the composition of the service sector changed in the course of the twentieth century?[2]

The author gratefully acknowledges the substantial help provided by Colleen Carter, Christopher Findlay, Bryan Haig, Allan Hall, Eva Klug, Ted Rymes, and the editors, Rodney Maddock and Ian McLean, while absolving them of any blame for remaining errors.

[1] The classic work on the service sector is Fuchs (1968), which deals with the U.S. economy. The basic reference for Australia is Dowie (1970), which is similar in spirit to Fuchs. The volume edited by Tucker (1977) contains studies of a number of service industries. Other relevant material on the Australian service sector may be found in Dowie (1966) and Haig (1975). My interest in this topic was stimulated by reading Gershuny (1978).

[2] Two important aspects of the development of the service sector in Australia have been slighted for lack of space. The first of these omissions, the role of government regulation, has been well covered elsewhere–see for example Butlin, Barnard, and Pincus (1982),

Because of the number and diversity of industries included in the service sector, it is impossible within the scope of this chapter to deal with each in detail. Furthermore a separate discussion of each industry would not help us answer the questions just posed. We need an organising framework. The most conventional framework for analysing the service sector is known as the Fisher–Clark hypothesis. In the next section this framework is outlined. In the following sections I shall employ this theory to examine the development of the service sector. Superficially Australian economic development appears to conform well to the hypothesis. However, as decreasing levels of aggregation in the statistical evidence are examined there emerges a considerably more complicated picture. This view is reinforced by considering in more depth some particular service industries. In the final section of the paper this leads to a reassessment of the appropriateness of the Fisher–Clark hypothesis to the Australian historical experience and the posing of a more complicated explanation of the role of services in economic development and structural change.

8.1　Economic development and structural change: the service economy

It has long been conventional wisdom that economic progress in the long run is associated with the gradual transformation of the economy from agriculture to manufacturing and then to services. Underdeveloped economies are primarily agricultural. Initially economic development proceeds by transferring resources from the agricultural to the manufacturing sector. After a period of industrialisation, there follows a further transfer of resources from manufacturing to services, so that, in a mature economy, most of the workforce will be engaged in the production of services.

The idea that development was necessarily accompanied by changes in the industrial structure is usually attributed to Fisher (1935) and Clark (1940).[3] Both were concerned with elaborating the conditions of eco-

---

especially part 4, and the references cited there. Regulation of the financial sector is dealt with in Chapter 9. The second omission is trade in services, the importance of which has only recently been appreciated in Australia (see for example Tucker, Seow, and Sundberg 1983). Trade in services promises to become much more important as a result of technological improvements in communication. This is now an active area of research by many economists, although little of this work is yet available in published form.

[3] An extended discussion of the writings of Fisher and Clark on the growth of the service sector can be found in Dowie (1970). Perhaps the idea of the relationship between economic progress and structural change should be attributed to the colonial statisticians

nomic progress. They concluded that structural change (which included a relative growth in the service sector) was a necessary concomitant of economic progress. Fisher emphasised the demand for services, arguing that services were luxuries – that is, services had a relatively high income elasticity. Therefore, as incomes rose, the proportion of services in final expenditure would also rise, necessitating a relative increase in service employment. Clark, on the other hand, emphasised the supply side. He argued that the rate of productivity growth was usually lower in services compared with agriculture and manufacturing. Even if there was no change in output shares, the differential productivity growth rates in goods and services would require that an increasing proportion of the workforce be employed in the production of services. The high income elasticity of demand for services would magnify this effect.

The empirical implication of the Fisher–Clark hypothesis is the expectation that a strong correlation will be observed between per capita income and the share of output and employment in service industries. This should be evident both within the same country over time and looking across different countries at the same point of time. This correlation was indeed documented by Clark and subsequently by Kuznets (1966) and other writers.

Australia has frequently been noted as an exception to the rule (see for example Kuznets [1966: 97, 111]). The view that Australia is atypical was strongly reinforced by Dowie (1970). Comparing Australia with the United States he concluded: "As far as services are concerned, the Australian story is thus far from the dramatic one ... [found] in the United States. Indeed, the series go a long way towards reinforcing the suggestion, most implicit in Kuznets' work, of an atypicality in the Australian experience" (p. 222). We now examine the development of the service sector in Australia to see whether this conclusion is justified.

8.2   The service sector in the Australian economy

The definition of the service sector

One of the difficulties of charting the development of services through time is that different authors adopt different definitions of the service

Coghlan (New South Wales) and Johnston (Tasmania), who in 1891 persuaded their fellow statisticians to reorganise the classification of the workforce to reflect the industrial structure of the economy and proposed an industrial classification that is essentially used throughout the Western world today. As far as I am aware, this was the first use of a modern industrial classification of the workforce that in turn made apparent the structural changes that accompany economic growth.

sector and some authors even change their definitions from time to time. This reflects a lack of precision and agreement as to the essential characteristics of a service and the distinction between services and goods.[4]

For empirical purposes the following sectoral aggregation has been adopted:

Primary	*Industry*	*Services*
Agriculture, etc.	Manufacturing	Trade
Mining	Electricity, gas,	Transport & communication
	& water	Finance & business services
	Construction	Public administration &
		defence
		Community services
		Entertainment & personal
		services
		Ownership of dwellings

In comparing the data presented here with other sources, it should be borne in mind that other writers have adopted different sectoral divisions. For example Fuchs (1968) includes transport and communications in the industry sector. In his treatment of the Australian service sector, Dowie (1970) treats electricity, gas and water, and construction as forming part of the services sector.[5]

The share of services in employment and output

A superficial examination of the historical evidence suggests that the Australian economy has developed as suggested by the Fisher–Clark hypothesis. Table 8.1 shows that over the course of this century the percentage of employees engaged in producing services has increased from around 40 percent in 1900/1 to more than 60 percent in 1980/1. Over the same time period the share of primary employment (agriculture and mining) has fallen from 32 percent to 8 percent. On the other hand,

---

[4] It would not be appropriate to dwell on this issue here. The interested reader is referred to discussions in Dowie (1970), Fuchs (1968), Greenfield (1966), Tucker (1977), and especially Hill (1977), whose definition underlies the classification adopted in this chapter.

[5] We should also recognise that the sectoral and industrial divisions of output and employment recorded in national income statistics do not reflect the true division of economic activity in the economy, because (among other reasons) a substantial amount of economic activity goes unrecorded. However, there is no reason to suggest that the measured sectoral shares are biased in any particular direction. For an extended discussion of the hidden economy I refer the interested reader to Carter (1984) and the references cited there.

Table 8.1. *Sectoral shares in selected countries (percentages)*

Employment				Output			
Years	Primary	Industry	Services	Years	Primary	Industry	Services
Argentina							
1900/4	39	25	36	1900/4	38	13	49
1925/9	36	27	37	1925/9	32	17	51
1947	27	30	43	1950	17	32	52
				1980	11	36	53
Australia							
1901	32	26	40	1900	30	19	51
1933	27	30	43	1930	23	23	55
1947	18	38	45	1950	33	31	36
1981	8	28	64	1980	12	30	57
Canada							
1911	39	27	34	1926	23	26	51
1921	37	27	37	1935	18	26	56
1950	22	35	44	1950	17	36	47
1980	7	27	66	1980	11	31	59
United Kingdom							
1901	15	42	44	1907	13	33	55
1931	13	43	44	1935	7	37	56
1950	9	46	46	1950	9	42	49
1980	4	37	59	1980	7	33	60
United States							
1899	39	25	36	1899/1903	21	23	56
1929/37	23	25	52	1927/37	11	26	62
1950	14	35	51	1950	10	36	54
1980	5	30	66	1980	6	30	64

Source: Calculated from Tables 8.2, 8.3.

the percentage of employees engaged in industry is today approximately the same as it was at the beginning of the century. That is not to say that the share of industrial employment has remained constant. During the first half of the century the share of industrial employment rose from 26 percent in 1901 to around 39 percent in the 1950s. This growth in the relative share of manufacturing has been reversed in the last twenty years (see Chapter 7).

Considering the changing composition of output, services accounted for 51 percent of GDP (in current prices) in 1900/1 whereas in 1980/1 the figure was 57 percent. The relative growth of services in output has been much less pronounced than the changes in the share of service employment. Furthermore the changes in the relative shares in aggregate output of the other two sectors (primary and industry) have been more dramatic than the changes in the share of services.

From the perspective of the early 1980s, any conclusion that "Australia is different" appears quite unjustified. Table 8.1 compares sectoral shares in employment for Australia and four other countries: Argentina, Canada, the United Kingdom, and the United States. On this evidence Australia certainly does not stand out as being atypical, especially as regards the share of the service sector. At the beginning of the period, the share of services in employment in Australia is slightly greater than that of Canada and the United States and slightly less than that of the United Kingdom. By the end of the period, these rankings are reversed. However, the differences between nations at a point in time are far less than the changes over time. Nor does Australia stand out in terms of the other two sectors. All four nations experienced a substantial decline in the share of agricultural employment that was accompanied by a rise and then subsequently a fall in the share of manufacturing. This is less pronounced in the case of the United Kingdom, but the experience of Canada and the United States is remarkably similar to that of Australia. With respect to sectoral shares of output, Australia again is quite typical. It has a slightly smaller service sector than Canada, the United Kingdom, and the United States, but a service sector that has experienced approximately the same increase over the last eighty years as in the other three countries.

The composition of the service sector

The relative growth of service sector employment has not been shared equally by the various service industries (Table 8.2 – Australia). The "growth" industries in the service sector have been finance and property and public administration and defence, accompanied to a lesser extent by wholesale and retail trade.[6] The share of employment engaged in finance and property in 1980/1 is six times what it was in 1910/11, most of the growth having occurred during the last twenty years. Wholesale and retail trade has grown steadily over the last seventy years from 12

---

[6] Finance and property include banks and other financial institutions, insurance companies, real estate agents and developers, as well as architectural, legal, accounting, and other business services. Prior to the census of 1971, business services were included in community services. Public administration includes all federal, state, and local government establishments mainly engaged in public administration and regulatory activities, as well as the judicial system and the defence forces. It excludes public enterprise (e.g. Telecom) and health, education, and welfare services.

percent in 1910/11 to 18 percent in 1980/1. Indeed the distribution of goods now accounts for as much employment as does their manufacture. Growth in public administration and defence has not been steady. The greatest expansion occurred during and after the second world war. However, whereas the defence component was largely reversed after the war, public administration remained at its wartime level for many years. It declined somewhat in the late 1950s and early 1960s but has grown again in recent years.

The share of employment involved in transport and communication has remained essentially constant over the last eighty years at around 8 percent of total employment. The remaining category, "Other services", employs approximately the same share of the workforce today (22 percent) as it did in 1901 (19 percent), although its share had fallen as low as 14 percent in the period after World War II. Moreover the composition of "Other services" employment is quite different today from what it was eighty years ago. At the beginning of the century domestic service was prominent in employment, whereas today the number employed as domestic servants is negligible. On the other hand, health and education are much more prominent employers than they were at the turn of the century. We shall examine the composition of the category "Other services" in more detail in the next section.

Turning now to output shares (Table 8.3), the picture is somewhat different. With one exception (finance and property), the share of the service industries in GDP in 1980 is little different from the corresponding shares in 1900. However, the only industry that can genuinely claim a relatively constant proportion of output is transport and communication, although with the exception of the thirties and of course the war years, the proportion of output devoted to public administration and defence has varied only between 3 and 4 percent. In wholesale and retail trade and "Other services" there has been considerable intertemporal variation. The percentage of output involved in distribution reached 21.3 percent in 1920/1 and had fallen to 12.8 percent by 1980/1. The variation in the output of other services reflects changes in composition of this industry, mentioned above. Changes in the output share of finance and property are dominated in the early years by changes in the share of imputed income to owner-occupied dwellings. These presumably reflect changes in the quantity and the quality of the housing stock. Only in recent years has the output of the industry finance and property excluding the rent to owner-occupied dwellings become a significant proportion of the economy. By 1980/1 it represented 10 percent of total GDP compared with 2.4 percent in 1960. However, these figures must be treated with caution. The output of the financial sector is in part

Table 8.2. *Changes in shares of employment in selected countries (percentages)*

Year	Agriculture	Mining & quarrying	Manufacturing	Electricity, gas, & water	Building & constr.	Transport & comm.	Wholesale & retail trade	Finance & property	Public admin. & defence	Other services
Argentina										
1900/4	39.2	0.2	19.8	0.8	4.5	4.6	N.A.	N.A.	3.6	27.3
1947	26.7	0.5	23.5	0.5	5.6	6.4	N.A.	N.A.	N.A.	36.8
1970	16.2	0.5	21.6	1.2	8.7	7.2	16.1	3.1	N.A.	25.4
Australia										
1901	32.3	—	25.8	—	—	7.4	13.5	N.A.	N.A.	18.9
1947	15.9	1.8	28.5	1.2	7.9	8.5	14.7	2.5	5.2	13.8
1981	6.5	1.5	19.2	2.2	6.8	7.8	18.9	9.1	6.1	21.8
Canada										
1911	37.1	2.3	27.1	—	—	8.0	10.4	N.A.	N.A.	15.1
1950	19.6	2.0	26.4	1.2	6.8	7.8	16.6	N.A.	N.A.	19.5
1980	5.5	1.8	19.8	1.2	5.8	7.3	17.2	5.7	N.A.	35.8
United Kingdom										
1901	9.2	5.5	33.5	—	7.9	7.9	14.0	7.9	N.A.	14.0
1950	5.1	3.8	37.5	1.6	6.4	7.7	14.0	N.A.	N.A.	23.9
1980	2.7	1.4	28.4	1.4	6.9	6.5	17.3	6.4	N.A.	29.0
United States										
1899	36.9	2.5	20.0	—	4.9	7.7	10.8	1.2	4.1	11.9
1950	12.5	1.7	27.6	1.4	6.4	7.2	19.0	N.A.	N.A.	24.3
1980	3.6	1.0	22.1	1.4	6.3	5.2	20.3	8.4	N.A.	31.8

Notes

(1) Unless specified separately, "Electricity, gas, & water" and "Building & constr." are included under "Manufacturing." (For Australia in 1901, "Manufacturing" also includes "Mining & quarrying".)

(2) "Other services" includes all services not otherwise specified.

Sources

Argentina: 1900/4: Diaz Alejandro 1970: Table 1.5.
1947: Bairoch 1968: Table A4.
1950/80: ILO, *Year Book of Labour Statistics*, annual issues, Table 2.

Australia: 1901: Bairoch 1968: Table A2.
1947: Keating 1973: Table 19.4.
1981: Australian Bureau of Statistics, Australian census.

Canada: 1911: Bairoch 1968: Table A2.
1950/80: ILO, *Year Book of Labour Statistics*, annual issues, Tables 2 and 3B.

United Kingdom: 1901: Deane and Cole 1967: Table 31.
1950/80: ILO, *Year Book of Labour Statistics*, annual issues, Tables 2 and 3B.

United States: 1899: *Historical Statistics of the United States* (Bureau of the Census, Washington, D.C., 1975), F251–60.
1950/80: ILO, *Year Book of Labour Statistics*, annual issues, Tables 2 and 3B.

203

Table 8.3. *Changes in shares of output in selected countries (percentages)*

Year	Agriculture	Mining & quarrying	Manufacturing	Electricity, gas, & water	Building & constr.	Transport & comm.	Wholesale & retail trade	Finance & property	Public admin. & defence	Other services
Argentina										
1900/4	38.1	0.3	9.9	0.4	2.7	4.4	13.9	14.5	6.7	9.0
1950	15.6	1.0	23.4	1.1	7.4	17.1	10.0	7.2	9.1	8.2
1980	8.8	1.9	25.3	2.2	8.5	16.1	7.2	14.4	N.A.	15.5
Australia										
1900/1	19.4	10.3	12.2	—	7.0	6.8	15.2	12.0	3.4	13.9
1950/1	30.8	2.3	22.6	1.6	6.7	6.8	12.5	4.6	3.2	8.8
1980/1	5.7	6.4	20.4	3.0	6.5	6.8	12.8	18.5	4.4	14.4
Canada										
1926	20.3	3.2	21.7	—	4.2	12.9	11.6	10.0	3.4	12.9
1950	13.2	4.0	28.6	2.4	5.3	8.6	14.0	8.2	4.9	10.7
1980	4.3	6.5	21.5	3.4	5.8	8.0	11.0	10.6	N.A.	29.8
United Kingdom										
1907	6.3	6.3	27.1	1.6	3.9	10.0	18.9	18.5	3.2	4.0
1950	5.8	3.5	34.6	2.1	5.3	8.2	13.9	5.8	6.5	14.4
1980	2.1	5.3	23.4	2.8	6.3	7.5	9.4	14.7	6.9	21.5
United States										
1899/1903	18.2	2.9	18.6	—	4.3	10.3	16.6	12.7	6.0	10.3
1950	7.0	3.2	29.3	1.9	4.4	7.2	18.0	11.0	9.5	8.5
1980	2.8	3.6	22.9	2.6	4.6	6.4	16.7	20.0	12.2	8.1

Notes

(1) Unless specified separately, "Electricity, gas, & water" is included under "Manufacturing."

(2) "Finance & property" includes the imputed rent to owner-occupied dwellings.

(3) "Other services" includes all services not otherwise specified.

Sources

Argentina: 1900/4: Diaz Alejandro 1970: Table 1.6.

1980: UN, *National Accounts Statistics*, vol. 1, part 1, various years.

Australia: 1900/1: Butlin 1962: Table 3.

1950/1: Australian Bureau of Statistics, *Australian National Accounts, National Income and Expenditure 1971/72* (7.1), app. C, Table C.

1980/1: Australian Bureau of Statistics, *Gross Product by Industry, 1981–82* (5221.0) (unpublished data for 1970 provided by ABS.

Canada: 1926: Urquhart and Buckley 1965: Series E46 to E61.

1950: *National Accounts of OECD Countries, 1950–78* (Paris: OECD).

1980: *National Accounts of OECD Countries, 1963–83*, vol. II (Paris: OECD).

United Kingdom: 1907: Deane and Cole 1967: Tables 40, 41.

1950: *National Accounts of OECD Countries, 1958–78* (Paris: OECD).

1980: *National Accounts of OECD Countries, 1963–83*, vol. II.

United States: 1899/1903: *Historical Statistics of the United States* (1975), F251–60.

1950: *National Accounts of OECD Countries, 1950–78.*

1980: *National Accounts of OECD Countries, 1963–83*, vol. II.

imputed and a portion of this rise may be due to a change in the treatment of the financial sector in the national accounts.

In comparing the industrial structure of the Australian economy (and especially the service sector) with that of comparable countries (Tables 8.2 and 8.3), the similarities are again more striking than the differences. For the industries for which separate figures are available, there are few differences among countries in either the level or the pattern of inter-temporal variation. In no way can a convincing case be made that the economic structure of Australia is historically atypical.

There is one exception to this conclusion, namely, the share of output devoted to transport and communication in the prewar period. At the beginning of the period the share of output originating in transport and communication in Australia is only half that of Canada and two-thirds that of the United Kingdom and the United States. This appears coun-terintuitive given Australia's large size and low population density. It also conflicts with the view that Australia overinvested in transport facilities (especially railways) in the early years (Butlin, Barnard, and Pincus 1982: chap. 10). That the output share of transport services in Australia was substantially less than in Canada, the United Kingdom, and the United States while the employment shares were comparable implies that transport and communication were markedly less productive in Australia in the early part of this century relative to comparable countries. The reasons for this are unclear. A possible explanation is that Australia had substantially different transport requirements than for example Canada because of its high degree of urbanisation. Another possibility is that the output share of transport is systematically under-stated in the data used. The question warrants further investigation.

Productivity

Accurate measures of productivity require accurate measures of both input and output. In the case of many service industries (for example health, education, and public administration) the usual difficulties of measuring inputs (particularly capital) are compounded by the lack of an independent measure of output. In such cases it is customary to value the output of the industry as the sum of the value of the inputs. This measurement convention rules out any possibility of productivity growth. Therefore the productivity of the service sector is biased down-wards in comparison with manufacturing and agriculture. Furthermore I shall here follow a common practice and be satisfied with a partial measure of productivity, total output per employee or labour produc-tivity. Since the service sector is on average less capital-intensive than manufacturing, this measure is further biased in favour of manufacturing. The bias is increased to the extent that working hours are shorter in the service sector and part-time employment is more prevalent.

With these provisos in mind, we can see in Table 8.4 output, employment, and output per employee in 1980 and their growth rates over the decade 1970/1 to 1980/1 for ten industries. The table also shows earlier figures (for the period 1949/51 to 1959/61) reported by Dowie (1966). Table 8.4 supports the view that the service industries have a lower rate of productivity growth than agriculture and manufacturing. However, the growth rate of productivity should be carefully distinguished from its level. In 1980/1 finance and property produced 30 percent more output per worker than manufacturing; on the other hand, the value of output per worker in wholesale and retail trade, community services, and entertainment was little more than 60 percent of that of manufacturing.

Once again transport and communication emerge as having an atypical experience. This is explained when we recall that the 1970s was the decade of massive energy price rises, which were reflected in the price of transport services. Thus the value in current prices of the output of transport service rose relative to the value of other goods and services. This highlights one of the limitations of relying on current-price time series. They make it impossible to distinguish between price and quantity changes. As long as prices in all industries rise at the same rate, changes in relative shares will reflect changes in relative quantities. But if relative prices change, some of the changes in relative prices will be due to price changes rather than to quantity changes. For reasons on which I shall elaborate later, the price of services has risen relative to that of goods. This implies that the change in relative shares of output at current prices will overstate shifts from goods to services.

I have not taken any account of differences in capital inputs, working hours, and full- and part-time work, all of which might be expected to bias the productivity measure of the services sector downwards. With these reservations in mind, this evidence does tend to support the conventional wisdom that service industries on the whole produce a lower output per worker and have increased their productivity at a lower rate than manufacturing or agriculture.[7]

---

[7] The differential productivity between goods and service industries has been documented in many countries (Fuchs 1968). In his comparative study of Australia, the United Kingdom, and the United States, Dowie (1966) found that, although productivity growth rates were significantly higher in goods-producing as compared to service industries in all three countries, the differential in Australia was considerably higher than in the other two countries.

Table 8.4. *Real output, employment, and productivity growth rates 1949/51 to 1959/61 and 1970/1 to 1980/1*

	Agriculture	Mining	Manufacturing	Construction	Wholesale & retail trade	Transport & comm.	Finance	Community services	Entertainment
Levels (1980)									
GDP ($m)	7,038	7,329	24,178	7,932	16,420	8,358	12,906	12,288	4,665
Employment (000)	407.2	84.3	1,233.6	483.3	1,265.4	341.8	510.5	1,007.8	386.4
Productivity ($)	17,284	86,940	19,600	16,412	12,976	24,453	25,281	12,193	12,073
Growth rates (1970/1 to 1980/1) (%)									
GDP	1.5	4.0	2.1	1.1	2.4	5.5	2.7	5.9	2.0
Employment	−0.6	0.3	−0.7	0.6	1.5	1.3	2.9	5.6	1.8
Productivity	2.1	3.7	2.8	0.5	0.8	4.2	−0.2	0.4	0.2
Growth rates (1949/51 to 1959/61) (%)									
GDP	2.1	4.4	6.6	3.4	3.5		5.7	2.7	
Employment	−0.4	−0.7	1.6	2.1	2.1		4.5	2.5	
Productivity	2.5	5.2	5.0	1.3	1.4		1.3	0.1	

Sources
1970/1 to 1980/1: Australian Bureau of Statistics, *Gross Product by Industry, 1981/82* (5221.0) (with unpublished data for 1970/1 provided by ABS; id., *The Labour Force, 1978, 1980* (6204.0).
1949/51 to 1959/61: Dowie 1966.

Industrial structure and Australia's growth performance

It is well known that large productivity gains can be achieved from the transfer of underemployed labour from the agricultural sector to industry and to services. This is one of the fundamental wisdoms of development economics. In part these are accounting rather than real gains obtained by increasing the proportion of economic activity covered by the market and hence included in national income statistics. Nevertheless the flight from the farm to the factory (and the financial institution) will be accompanied by an increase in recorded output and reflected in growth statistics.

Australia, in common with Canada, the United Kingdom, and the United States, exploited these gains early and so by the beginning of our period of study had a relatively mature industrial structure. Therefore the subsequent growth performance appears disappointing when compared with that of the newly industrialising countries. For example, in 1950 Japan still had 50 percent of its workforce employed in agriculture compared with 15 percent in Australia. Today agricultural employment in Japan has declined to 10.7 percent compared with Australia's 7.9 percent.[8] It is little wonder therefore that Australia's growth rate compares unfavourably with Japan's over this period. Australia matured early.

8.3   Selected service industries

We now go down one further level of aggregation and look at certain service industries that provide some historical colour to this chapter and illustrate its themes. Particular attention is given to transport, as it provides a good illustration of many of the points I wish to establish. Some other service industries are discussed elsewhere in the book.[9]

Transport services

During the period of this study there have been startling developments in the modes of transport that flow from important technological developments around the turn of the century, such as the internal combustion engine and powered flight. Also transport services have been

---

[8] Employment data for Japan were obtained from *Year Book of Labour Statistics* published by the International Labour Organisation.

[9] Butlin (Chapter 9) deals with financial services, Withers (Chapter 10) discusses education in relation to labour market, and Pincus (Chapter 11) deals with government and public administration.

central to the development of the Australian economy over the last eighty years.[10]

Since most Australians live in cities, it is appropriate to consider first urban passenger travel, which predominantly involves the journey to work. In a recent book, Ian Manning (1984: 1) documents that "In . . . [the last] hundred years, in Australia as in other wealthy countries, the normal means of getting about in cities changed twice, first from walking to trams, trains and buses, and then from public transport to the motor car."

Urban public transport in Australia began in the 1850s with the first suburban railways, followed by the introduction of horse buses and tramways in the 1860s. Mechanically powered trams were introduced in the 1880s. Prior to this the only means of transport available to the nonaffluent was walking. The introduction of buses, trams, and trains did not immediately alter the mode of transport of the working class, since, although a significant increase in the potential speed of urban travel was obtained, fares were comparatively high. Only when the electrification of the tramways led to a considerable reduction in fares was there a dramatic increase in patronage. The trams then replaced walking as the most popular mode of transport for medium-length urban journeys. This suggests that it was not rising incomes but falling prices that provided the major impetus to the growth of public transport.

Although the private motor car first appeared before the first world war, expense limited ownership to the wealthy. Car ownership grew gradually during the 1920s, but this trend was interrupted by the depression and then by the second world war. "Though the motor car was brought to a reasonable level of technical reliability seventy or eighty years ago, and though it was first mass-manufactured six decades ago, mass motorization dates only from the end of the second world war" (Manning 1984: 30). The arrival of mass private motoring signalled the decline of public transport.

---

[10] Transport in Australia is one of the most intensely studied of the service industries. A short survey of the Australian transport system can be found in Forsyth (1982) and in several relevant papers in Webb and McMaster (1975). Much of the material on urban transport is derived from Manning (1984). Davison (1978) describes the impact of public transport on the suburban development of Melbourne in the 1880s. The evolution of the transport system in Australia is intimately associated with the story of government enterprise and regulation. This aspect is aptly covered in Chapter 10 of Butlin, Barnard, and Pincus (1982). The development of freight forwarding and its impact on the transport system is the subject of Rimmer (1977). Stubbs (1983) surveys the Australian maritime industry. Conlon (1982a and b) discusses the impact of transport costs on Australia's international trade and industrial structure. Domestic airline services and regulation are discussed by Hocking (1982) and Forsyth (1982). Findlay (1983) discusses Australian international aviation policy.

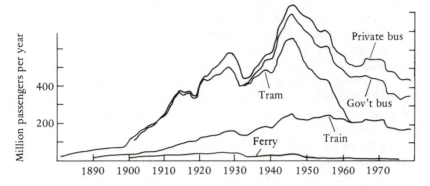

Figure 8.1. Public transport passengers carried, Sydney, 1881–1978.

The rise and fall of urban public transport are illustrated in Figure 8.1, which shows total passengers carried in Sydney for the period 1881 to 1978. The supremacy of the trams from 1910 to 1947 is clearly evident, as is their rapid decline in the postwar period. Though some tram passengers transferred to buses after the war, most found other means of transport, that is, the private car. Train travel had experienced a slower growth than trams and has not suffered the same loss of passengers. The hump of Figure 8.1 becomes more remarkable when it is recalled that the decline of public transport passengers during the postwar period occurred in the face of a rapidly expanding population and workforce in Sydney.

Turning to the transport of freight, a reasonable claim can be made that it was not federation but changes in the technology of freight transport that brought about the integration of the Australian economy. Prior to 1939 interstate trade was severely inhibited by the system of land transport to the extent that Rimmer (1977: 171) claims: "Individual states functioned to some extent as self-sufficient regional islands." Rail transport was constrained by the nonuniformity of gauges and road transport frustrated by inadequate vehicles and railway protection taxes. The dominant mode of interstate freight transport was coastal shipping, which was inefficient and costly.

The postwar boom in the production and use of motor vehicles affected freight in the same way as it affected urban passenger travel. Despite the protective taxes and regulations favouring rail, road transport flourished in the postwar boom. Its success was aided by the deterioration in the rail system during the war and by the proliferation of owner drivers induced into the industry by the availability of war surplus trucks and war service gratuities to spend on them. Road transport quickly replaced rail as the dominant mode of intrastate freight transport and challenged rail and coastal shipping for interstate trade. The railways and coastal shipping retained a substantial share in the movement of such bulk cargoes as iron ore and coal. A recent development has been the growth of private railways associated with mineral exploitation – private rail now nearly matches public rail in terms of tonne kilometres of freight carried. Of course shipping retains its dominant role in trade between Tasmania and the mainland.

The development of Australian transport services during the postwar period was considerably affected by the growth of a new type of transport service – freight forwarding. The freight forwarder "assumes responsibility for the movement of goods from door-to-door as part of a total package of transport services" (Rimmer 1977: 168). The freight forwarder chooses the most economical mode of transport and arranges for any intermediate transport and handling, thus exploiting the benefits of economies of scale and specialisation. The development of freight forwarding helped stem the flow of traffic from the railways and from coastal shipping by offsetting some of the advantages of road transport.

Like private motoring, air travel was available prior to the second world war. But it was not until the postwar improvements in speed and comfort and reductions in costs that patronage was assured. From 1950 to 1975 air travel was the fastest growing mode of transport. Measured in passenger kilometres, domestic air travel grew steadily in excess of 8 percent per year (Butlin, Barnard, and Pincus 1982: 289). In Australia air transport is embroiled in even more extensive government regulation than land transport. The federal government has controlled competition in domestic air transport through the two-airline agreement and in international air transport through its ownership of Quantas. The effect of the two-airline agreement in raising the price of air travel and reducing the quantity consumed is notorious (Kirby 1981). Less attention has been paid to the effect of airline regulation in suppressing the development of the air freight market in Australia. Air transport would seem well suited to Australia's vast distances and sparse population. However, until recently the market was effectively confined to the two domestic airlines by regulation. Consequently the rate of growth of Australia's domestic air freight activity over the period 1961 to 1976 was only a little over half that of the world average and less than half that of Canada. In the same period the world average freight rate fell, whereas Australia's domestic average freight rate rose (Gawan-Taylor 1984: 32–5).

Declines in the relative costs of transport applied internationally as well as nationally, stimulating the international division of labour and the growth of world trade. This placed other pressures on domestic producers, pressures that were in part resisted by the tariff. A complicated story remains to be told detailing the effect of changes in costs and technology of transport on the location and structure of Australian industry and consequently on the patterns of population growth. Overall real freight costs have declined substantially and led to increases in the volume of freight. This has had ramifications for the location of industry and the structure of development. Better transport services have allowed better rationalisation of production, thus realising economies of scale.

Domestic and personal services

Whereas in 1981 the number of domestic servants was negligible, in 1911 seven percent of the workforce was engaged in domestic service (Table 8.5). Females outnumbered males nearly ten to one. Writing of Australian urban life in the 1880s, Twopeny (1883: 49) reports:

Where mistresses are many and servants are few, it goes almost without saying that large establishments are out of the question. Given equal incomes, and the English mistress has twice as many servants as the Australian, and what is more, twice as competent ones. Even our friend Muttonwool only has six – coachman, boy, cook, housemaid, nurse, and parlourmaid.

Writing of Melbourne in the same period, Davison (1978: 202) records that

The income levels for domestic service in Melbourne were pitched rather higher than in London. A family on £200 was fortunate to employ a girl, that on £300–400 could barely afford a maid of all work. A large family on £500 might have a nurse as well, while a £600 establishment included a boy, a nurse and a general servant. At a princely £800–1000, a lady commanded two women and a man servant.

The upper-income categories (£600 and over) would cover the professions (doctors, lawyers), bankers, managers, and merchants; £300–400 would have included shopkeepers and many self-employed tradesmen and senior office workers. Many more skilled workers could have expected £200 per year. On this basis we can conclude that the proportion of households employing at least one domestic servant would be quite large.

Still, there was unsatisfied demand. Davison (1978: 202) reports that "the servant shortage was a vexing and apparently interminable problem to middle-class matrons". This is partly because wages for domestic service were considerably higher than in England. Even at the going rate, demand for domestic servants exceeded supply. It seems that fac-

Table 8.5. *Employment shares – selected service industries (percentages)*

Year	Finance & investment	Insurance	Property & business	Health	Education, museums, libraries	Welfare & religious insts.	Other community services	Enter-tainment, recreation	Rest. clubs, hotels	Personal services	Domestic service
1901		2.0		1.3	2.1	0.5	2.6	0.4	3.8	1.3	6.9
1911		2.3		1.7	2.0	0.5	2.1	0.7	3.3	1.2	6.0
1921		1.8		2.2	2.2	0.5	2.7	0.8	3.3	1.1	4.7
1933		2.1		2.0	2.1	0.6	2.8	0.9	2.7	1.5	4.8
1947		0.8		2.7	2.2	0.7	1.4	1.1	3.4	1.3	1.7
1954	1.2	0.8	0.7	3.0	2.5	0.6	1.8	1.0	3.0	1.1	1.0
1961	1.4	1.1	0.9	3.6	3.2	0.7	2.4	1.0	2.9	1.3	0.8
1966	1.6	1.2	1.0	4.0	4.0	0.8	2.7	1.2	2.9	1.4	0.7
1971	2.4	1.3	3.5	4.8	4.2	0.7	1.6	1.0	2.8	1.2	0.2
1976	2.6	1.2	4.0	6.0	6.0	0.8	1.7	1.1	3.0	1.1	0.0
1981	3.0	1.2	5.0	6.6	6.7	1.1	1.8	1.4	3.2	1.1	0.0

Source: Australian Bureau of Statistics, Census reports.

tories offered more attractive employment. Twopeny (1883: 57) complains: "Unfortunately, but a very small proportion of the daughters of the poorer colonial working-class will go into service. For some inexplicable reason, they turn up their noses at the high wages and comparatively light work offered, and prefer to undertake the veriest drudgery in factories for a miserable pittance." The "inexplicable reason" appears to be the independence and shorter hours offered by factory work coupled with the egalitarian spirit of the colony. The price required to compensate for the strictures of life as a domestic servant appears to have been too high for the colonial employer.

Though the percentage of the workforce engaged in domestic service has declined steadily at least since the beginning of the century, the most dramatic decline occurred during and immediately after the second world war. This was also the time of the widespread production and use of such home appliances as washing machines and vacuum cleaners, which served as substitutes for domestic servants. Whether the new appliances priced domestic servants out of the market or appliances were mass produced to meet an excess demand for servants is an open question.

Another perspective on the decline of domestic service is given by Snooks (1983), who has estimated the value of total household production for the period 1891 to 1981. His estimates suggest that the percentage of total household services produced by domestic workers in private employment declined from 9.0 percent in 1901 to 0.3 percent in 1981. These data probably overestimate the decline in purchase of household services, since they do not include services purchased externally, such as contract cleaning and gardening (now included in personal services), child care, and food prepared outside the home. It is likely that such purchased services have increased in importance in recent years. Unfortunately data to measure this change are not readily available.

The category "Personal services" includes hairdressers, laundries, domestic cleaners, gardeners, photographers, funeral directors, and miscellaneous other activities. Employment in personal services has changed very little over the last eighty years, and these activities have consistently occupied a very small fraction (approximately 1 percent) of the working population (Table 8.5).

Entertainment and recreation

Entertainment has also seen remarkable changes since 1900. In the latter part of the last century the only available forms of purchased entertainment were live entertainment – theatre, concerts, music halls, and vaudeville. Motion pictures were first shown in Australia in 1896 and rapidly gained popularity. By 1920 there were 750 picture theatres in Australia and attendances exceeded 67 million annually (that is twelve per capita per year). Moreover during the next decade attendances almost doubled.[11] The cinema enabled a substantial increase in the productivity of entertainment services: Once produced, a movie could be shown to a wide audience at little additional cost. A similar productivity increase was achieved by the phonograph, although contemporary examples suggest that quality was poor.

The next major change in the provision of entertainment services was the introduction of broadcast radio. The first commercial radio station in Australia opened in Sydney in 1923. This enabled a very considerable rise in productivity, since additional listeners could be serviced at no marginal cost. The introduction of radio broadcasts may have had some impact on the popularity of the cinema, since the latter failed to maintain its previous rate of growth. In 1955, the year prior to the introduction of television, cinema attendances were only slightly greater than they had been in 1929 despite a 43 percent increase in the population and greater affluence.

A more severe challenge to public entertainment arrived with the introduction of television to Australia in 1956. The then current expectations of the complete demise of the movie theatre proved unfounded, but audiences shrank and many movie theatres were closed. The style of motion picture and the form of presentation were changed, the decor of the theatres updated. The nature of the service was changed somewhat. An interesting side effect was the disappearance of movie news from the programme. Visual news could be provided better by television.

Though television did not eclipse the movie theatre, recent developments seem likely to be a more serious threat. Home video recorders and laser disk players provide the consumer with the ability to provide similar entertainment at home. Further potential for individual provision of such services will arise from satellite broadcasting supplemented perhaps by cable and subscription television.

A feature of Australian leisure activity is the prominence of outdoor pursuits such as fishing, swimming, surfing, and sailing, which are promoted by the climate and the proximity of the major cities to the sea. Land-intensive sports such as tennis and golf, which are primarily the reserve of the rich in many countries, attract mass participation in Aus-

---

[11] Figures for cinema attendances are taken from the article on the Australian film industry in the *Australian Encyclopedia* (1983: vol. 4, p. 132), which provides references for further reading. Dates for the introduction of radio and television come from Media Information Australia (1981).

tralia. Such recreational activities do not require much service employment to support them.

Reflecting on the development of recreation and entertainment in Australia, it should not be surprising that employment in this industry has grown only moderately over the last eighty years, although there is evidence for a significant increase in the most recent census. Another perspective on the changing nature of entertainment activity is provided by Table 8.6, which shows the composition of expenditure on recreation and entertainment for selected years over the period 1920/1 to 1966/7. The declining importance of movies and live entertainment is shown in the percentage of expenditure devoted to admissions, which declines from about 40 percent in 1920/1 to under 10 percent in 1966/7. The difference is accounted for by the purchase of leisure and entertainment goods such as televisions and boats.

Employment in restaurants, clubs, and hotels has not shown any growth despite the recent boom in eating away from home and the proliferation of licensed clubs. Against this development must be set a decline in the number and patronage of hotels and taverns. It would seem that public drinking as a form of entertainment has in fact declined dramatically over the years. The nature of the services provided by restaurants, clubs, and hotels has changed substantially even though their relative importance in the economy has not.

8.4   Economic growth and structural change: a reassessment

At first sight, then, the Fisher–Clark hypothesis appears to be very well supported by the data. In Australia, as in comparable countries, a steadily increasing proportion of the workforce has been engaged in the production of services rather than goods. At the same time it is evident that productivity growth in the service sector has been slower than in the other two sectors. The net result has been only a small increase in the share of output originating in the service sector. These facts have been interpreted by Fuchs (in the United States) and Dowie (in Australia) as lending support to the Clark variant of the Fisher–Clark hypothesis – namely, that the motivating force for the transformation comes from the productivity differentials, not from differences in income elasticity.

As we have investigated successive levels of disaggregation in the preceding sections, a less clear picture has emerged. Rather than advancing steadily on all fronts, the relative growth of the service sector has been far from uniform. The emergence of services as the dominant sector in the economy reflects diverse histories in the various service

Table 8.6. *Composition of expenditure on recreation and entertainment, selected years 1920/1 to 1966/7 (percentages)*

Years	Admissions	Musical instruments	Radios, radiograms	TV sets	Radio, TV licenses	Cameras, films	Boats, trailers, caravans	Reading matter	Toys, games, sporting goods	Miscellaneous (clubs, parks, fireworks)
1920/1	38.7	10.8	1.4	—	—	1.9	—	34.0	4.2	9.0
1930/1	29.0	5.2	2.9	—	1.9	2.9	—	42.4	6.2	9.5
1938/9	27.6	2.3	7.6	—	4.0	2.7	—	36.5	9.0	10.3
1950/1	21.9	3.9	12.0	18.1	1.7	2.6	0.9	35.4	11.5	10.1
1960/1	12.4	4.1	7.3		4.0	2.9	2.5	30.0	9.8	8.9
1966/7	8.6	5.5	8.1	8.2	5.1	3.6	7.1	31.8	11.1	10.9

Source: Unpublished data provided by Bryan Haig.

industries. Some services, of which domestic service is the most prominent example, have in fact declined. Many service industries, such as personal services, entertainment and recreation, and miscellaneous community services have maintained a more or less constant share of employment throughout the period. Growth has been confined to health, welfare, and financial and business services. It is the latter industries that have brought about the dominance of the service sector in the modern Australian economy.

What is remarkable about this picture is that it is precisely those services for which the Fisher–Clark hypothesis would have predicted the most dramatic growth that have remained static or in fact declined. Entertainment, personal services, and domestic services are luxuries par excellence. They are also characterised by low productivity growth. According to Fisher and Clark, we could confidently have expected a dramatic increase in their share of output and employment. The example of these industries suggests that the development of the service sector cannot be explained on the grounds of high income elasticity and low productivity growth alone.

At least two important factors are missing from the conventional explanation of the development of the service sector. These are the impact of relative price changes on the demand for final services and the impact of specialisation on the demand for intermediate services.[12]

Relative price effects – the household production unit

Fisher, Clark, and other authors underestimated the potential effects of changes in relative prices. If productivity in the production of services grows less rapidly than the productivity in the production of goods, there will be a change in relative prices. The price of services will rise relative to the price of goods, and the consumer, wealthier though he may be, will be encouraged to substitute goods for services in his consumption. For many services this price effect has dominated the income effect.

Services can either be purchased directly as final commodities in the market or be produced by the consumer with goods purchased in the market.[13] Transport is a good example. Over the last one hundred years

[12] The impact of changes in relative prices and specialisation has been noted by other writers. Bauer and Yamey (1951) made similar observations in a perceptive critique of the Fisher–Clark hypothesis on both theoretical and empirical grounds. Changes in relative prices are emphasised in Baumol (1967); Greenfield (1966) emphasises specialisation and the demand for producer services. See also Gershuny (1977, 1978). A pioneering attempt to estimate the interaction of demand and supply effects in the demand for services was made by Haig (1975).

[13] For the underlying economic theory see Becker (1965) and Lancaster (1966).

the modal choice of the provision of urban transport services has changed twice. One hundred years ago urban transport was essentially a self-service. The ordinary urban Australian walked about the city. Fifty years later, urban transportation was largely a purchased service. For a fee the passenger was bodily conveyed nearer to his or her destination by means of the application of factors owned and controlled by others. Personal exertion and time were saved at some cost. Another fifty years on, urban transport is once again largely self-produced. The motorist combines personal labour with capital equipment (namely, a car) to produce the transportation service.

The reasons for these changes are not hard to discern. Rising incomes and falling relative prices account for the growth in mass public transport in the first half of this century. The introduction of motorised transport in the latter half of the last century offered an impressive advantage in speed over the next best alternative, walking. High fares limited its adoption for the journey to work. Falling relative prices and rising incomes led to steadily increasing patronage. The growth of mass public transport is a good example of the Fisher–Clark thesis. In those early days public transport was a luxury.

Similarly, rising incomes and falling prices account for the exodus from public transport in favour of the motor car. From its introduction early this century, the motor car has fallen steadily in relative price. According to Manning (1984), by the mid 1970s the purchase price of cars relative to wages had fallen to only 25 percent of the immediate postwar price. Similarly the price of petrol fell to such an extent that by 1978 petrol prices as a percentage of wages were only 20 percent of what they were in 1950. On the other hand, public transport fares have kept pace with wages over the postwar period, even with the assistance of subsidies. Operating costs have in fact risen relative to wages (Manning 1984: 17).

Furthermore not only out-of-pocket costs are relevant. Public transport often involves considerable walking and waiting. The passenger walks (or drives) to the station (or bus stop), waits for the bus or train, and then walks from the bus stop (or station) to the ultimate destination. The motorist has no waiting time and can often drive much closer to his or her destination than the bus or train takes its passenger. Although public transport (especially trains) may attain greater speeds in urban travel, it usually requires longer elapsed times. A study in Sydney in 1971 found that a car was three times faster than the fastest public mode (bus) for short journeys (one to two kilometres). The car retained its advantage over public transport (train) even for journeys of twenty kilometres (Manning 1984: 23).

Transport, both private and public, requires a substantial input of time on the part of the passenger. As wages rise, the opportunity cost of the elapsed time of the journey rises. We should therefore expect people to choose faster forms of transport as their incomes grow. Private motoring is cheaper in its use of time than public transport.[14] Taking account of both the out-of-pocket costs and the opportunity costs, it is not surprising that Australians took to the motor car in the millions.

Here we have the Fisher effect in reverse. Rising incomes have caused consumers to substitute the private motor car for public transport services. Consumption of transport services (as recorded in the national accounts) has been correspondingly reduced with a rise in the consumption of manufactured goods. There is a rise in the consumption of such ancillary services as service stations, motor mechanics, and motoring organisations, but these do not entirely offset the transfer of employment from running trams and buses to the manufacture of motor cars. Private motoring becomes the luxury good, transport services the inferior good.

In Lancaster's (1966) theory of demand, goods are purchased to produce characteristics that are the objects of final consumption. He distinguishes two substitution effects, the efficiency substitution effect and the private substitution effect. The first results from a change in relative prices, making a different bundle of purchased inputs the most efficient (least costly) method of producing given characteristics. This also affects the relative price of the various characteristics; any consequent change in the optimum bundle of characteristics is the private substitution effect. Changes in relative prices, especially the relative reduction in the capital and running costs of private motoring, mean that private motoring is now a relatively cheaper means of producing a given transport service. Further, since private motoring offers greater comfort and speed, there is in addition a private substitution effect – the purchase of relatively more comfort and speed in the form of private motoring.

Entertainment provides another example of the changing locus of production. Technological change and mass production have combined to lower the costs of the self-production of entertainment services. By purchasing a home video recorder and hiring (or purchasing) a movie, the household can provide itself with essentially the same service that can be purchased by attending a cinema. The service is not identical. The home-produced movie lacks the ambience of the theatre, the feeling

[14] Two provisos to this statement immediately arise. First, the advantage of private over public transport can be offset by the effects of congestion on public roads. Second, part of the elapsed time on public transport can be used for some other task, such as reading the newspaper.

of going out and being part of a crowd. In compensation it offers greater comfort and convenience and requires no transport cost. The essential characteristic of the movie, that is, images on a screen, is the same in both cases. The cost of producing that characteristic has swung heavily in favour of home production. This makes the attainment of the other characteristics of the cinema – ambience, etc. – relatively more expensive. This substitution effect will reduce consumption of the public service. Table 8.6 gives some insight into the extent of these changes. The composition of expenditure on entertainment has moved away from direct purchases of service and towards the purchase of goods for the self-production of entertainment – televisions, radios, boats, and sporting goods.

With two prominent exceptions (health and education), relative price effects have led to a reduction in the percentage of services in the consumer's budget. What, then, has maintained the overall share of services in GDP? This is the subject of the next section.

Specialisation and the demand for intermediate services

By no means all services are consumed by final consumers. A large proportion of the output of the service sector is used as inputs into production by other enterprises. Some services, such as wholesale trade and accounting services, are almost entirely performed on behalf of other enterprises rather than for final consumers. Many other service industries, such as insurance, banking, legal services, and transport, produce both for other industries and for final consumers.

The reason that the share of services in output has remained steady or even increased is that the switch of final consumption demand from services to goods has been matched by a steadily increasing demand for business services. This has nothing to do with income elasticity or even relative productivity growth rates; it is simply a result of increasing specialisation and division of labour.

Once again, transport is a good example. At the turn of the century many farmers would use their own horses and carts to obtain supplies and transport output to the market or railway. Today the farmer is more likely to employ the services of a transport firm. We can speculate that this development has been brought about by an increase in the average distance over which the goods are carted and a rise in the capital cost of the necessary equipment. The availability in the postwar years of much larger trucks means that the transport firm can exploit economies of scale in servicing many farms in the one journey.

In a similar manner manufacturing and construction firms have tended to substitute hired transport services for their own transport equipment. This is evidenced by the growth of freight forwarding mentioned previously. The freight forwarder specialises in the provision of routing, packaging, and documenting services that would otherwise have been provided internally even if the firm purchased the actual cartage externally.

Similar examples abound. Security firms have displaced watchmen. Computing bureaux have replaced internal office staff. There has been in recent years a proliferation of accounting, distribution, consulting, and advertising firms, which thrive by offering specialised services to other businesses. In their absence these services would have to be provided internally. This is a comparatively recent development and is in large part responsible for any increase in the employment in the service sector in recent years. The impact of these changes can be seen in the dramatic increase in the share of employment in the finance and property category in Table 8.5 and especially in the subcategory property and business services.[15]

In addition, a large proportion of education and health expenditure should properly be regarded as intermediate rather than final services. As Glenn Withers has documented in Chapter 10, the growth in participation in education has been most marked in the tertiary sector. This development can be interpreted as the substitution by firms of formal education for on-the-job training and is another example of firms purchasing specialised services externally. Many would go further and argue that the primary function of schooling is to socialise the industrial workforce and therefore that virtually all education should be regarded as an intermediate service. Similarly health expenditure cannot be regarded in its entirety as a final service. Occupational accidents compose a significant proportion of health expenditure. As is now becoming apparent, many diseases are occupationally related and the services devoted to treating them could reasonably be regarded as intermediate rather than as final consumption. As with the expenditure, the employment involved in the production of health services must be regarded as being shared between intermediate and final services.

In summary, the growth in employment and output has been in intermediate rather than in final services (with the exception of educa-

---

[15] Table 8.5 overstates this development, since there was a change in classification between the censuses of 1966 and 1971. Business services such as accounting and legal services were transferred from "Other community services" to the category "Property and business". At the same time certain financial activities such as building societies and finance companies were transferred from "Property and business" to "Finance and investment" (previously confined to the banking industry).

tion and health). This can be attributed to a process of specialisation and division of labour accompanying the maturation of the economy and spurred on by certain technological developments. Even education and health cannot be simply regarded as examples of the increasing demand for final services – a large part of their activity must be regarded as intermediate production.

8.5   Conclusion

Much of the conventional wisdom regarding economic development and structural change is founded on a myth. The Fisher–Clark hypothesis explains the relative expansion of the service sector in terms of the income elasticity of demand and growth rate of efficiency of supply of services. The natural phenomenon they were concerned to explain, namely, the relative expansion of the service sector, has persisted. However, with the benefit of further experience and a different perspective, we find that the explanation they advanced is inadequate. Those services for which income elasticity might be expected to be highest and productivity growth lowest, such as personal services and entertainment, have remained static or declined. The growth in the service sector is rather attributed to demand for business services brought about by increasing specialisation.

Similarly, hindsight allows us to dispose of a second myth regarding the Australian service sector. Contrary to a longstanding supposition, Australia's development does not differ significantly from that of comparable advanced countries such as Canada, the United Kingdom, and the United States. Considering both the total relative size of the service sector and the composition of various industries within that sector, Australian experience during the twentieth century does not differ in any significant way from that of comparable countries. What is notable when comparing services historically across these countries are the similarities rather than the differences.

References

Australian Encyclopedia. 1983. Vol. 4. Sydney: Grolier.

Bairoch, P. 1968. *The Working Population and Its Structure.* International Statistics, vol. 1. Institut de Sociologie, Université Libre de Bruxelles.

Bauer, P. T., and B. S. Yamey. 1951. "Economic progress and occupation distribution". *Economic Journal* 61: 741–55.

Baumol, W. J. (1967). "Macroeconomics of unbalanced growth: the anatomy of urban crisis". *American Economic Review* 57: 415–26.

Becker, G. S. 1965. "A theory of the allocation of time". *Economic Journal* 75: 493–517.

Butlin, N. G. 1962. *Australian Domestic Product, Investment and Foreign Borrowing, 1861–1938/39.* Cambridge: Cambridge University Press.

Butlin, N. G., A. Barnard, and J. J. Pincus. 1982. *Government and Capitalism: Public and Private Choice in Twentieth Century Australia.* Sydney: Allen & Unwin.

Carter, M. G. R. 1984. "Issues in the hidden economy: a survey". *Economic Record* 60 (September): 209–21.

Clark, C. 1940. *The Conditions of Economic Progress.* London: Macmillan.

Conlon, R. M. 1982a. "Overseas transport costs and industrial structure", in Webb and Allan 1982, pp. 254–69.

1982b. "Transport cost and tariff protection of Australian manufacturing". *Economic Record* 58: 73–81.

Davison, G. 1978. *The Rise and Fall of Marvellous Melbourne.* Melbourne: Melbourne University Press.

Deane, P., and W. A. Cole. 1967. *British Economic Growth, 1688–1959.* 2d ed. Cambridge: Cambridge University Press.

Diaz Alejandro, C. F. 1970. *Essays on the Economic History of the Argentine Republic.* New Haven, Conn.: Yale University Press.

Dowie, J. A. 1966. "Productivity growth in goods and services: Australia, USA, UK.". *Economic Record* 42: 536–54.

1970. "The service ensemble", in C. Forster (ed.), *Australian Economic Development in the Twentieth Century,* pp. 208–65. London: Allen & Unwin.

Findlay, C. C. 1983. *Australian International Civil Aviation Policy and the ASEAN–Australia Dispute.* ASEAN–Australia Economic Papers No. 1. Kuala Lumpur and Canberra: ASEAN–Australia Joint Research Project.

Fisher, A. G. B. 1935. *The Clash of Progress and Security.* London: Macmillan.

Forsyth, P. J. 1982. "The transport industry: a perspective", in Webb and Allan 1982, pp. 243–53.

Fuchs, V. R. 1968. *The Service Economy.* New York: Columbia University Press for the National Bureau of Economic Research.

Gawan-Taylor, M. 1984. *The Australian Domestic Air Freight Market: Consequences of Partial Deregulation.* Discussion Paper No. 87. Centre for Economic Policy Research, Australian National University.

Gershuny, J. I. 1977. "The fallacy of the service economy". *Futures* 9: 103–14.

1978. *After Industrial Society? The Emerging Self-Service Economy.* London: Macmillan.

Greenfield, H. I. 1966. *Manpower and the Growth of Producer Services.* New York: Columbia University Press.

Haig, B. D. 1975. "An analysis of changes in the distribution of employment between manufacturing and service industries, 1960–70". *Review of Economics and Statistics* 57: 35–42.

Hill, T. P. 1977. "On goods and services". *Review of Income and Wealth,* ser. 23, no. 4: 315–38.

Hocking, R. D. 1982. "The Australian two airline policy: a case study", in Webb and Allan 1982, pp. 201–8.

Keating, M. 1973. *The Australian Workforce 1910/11 to 1960/61.* Canberra: Department of Economic History, Research School of Social Sciences, Australian National University.

Kirby, M. 1981. *Domestic Airline Regulation: The Australian Debate.* Sydney: Centre for Independent Studies.

Kuznets, S. 1966. *Modern Economic Growth: Rate, Structure and Spread.* New Haven, Conn.: Yale University Press.

Lancaster, K. J. 1966. "A new approach to consumer theory". *Journal of Political Economy* 74(2): 132–57.

Manning, I. 1984. *Beyond Walking Distance.* Canberra: Urban Research Unit, Australian National University.

Media Information Australia. 1981. "History of Telecommunications in Australia". *Media Information Australia,* February: 71–2.

Rimmer, P. J. 1977. "Freight forwarding: changes in structure, conduct and performance", in Tucker 1977, pp. 167–207.

Snooks, G. 1983. "Household services and GDP, 1891–1981". Paper presented to the Spring Workshop in Economic History, Australian National University, Canberra.

Stubbs, P. 1983. *Australia and the Maritime Industries.* Melbourne: A.I.D.A. Research Centre.

Tucker, K. A. (ed.). 1977. *Economics of the Australian Service Sector.* London: Croom Helm.

Tucker, K. A., G. Seow, and M. Sundberg. 1983. *Services in ASEAN–Australian Trade.* ASEAN–Australia Economic Papers No. 2. Kuala Lumpur and Canberra: ASEAN–Australia Joint Research Project.

Twopeny, R. 1883. *Town Life in Australia.* Repr. Harmondsworth: Penguin Books, 1973.

Urquhart, M. C., and K. A. H. Buckley (eds.). 1965. *Historical Statistics of Canada.* Toronto: Macmillan of Canada.

Webb, G. R., and J. C. McMaster (eds.). 1975. *Australian Transport Economics: A Reader.* Sydney: Australia & New Zealand Book Co.

Webb, L. R., and R. H. Allan (eds.). 1982. *Industrial Economics: Australian Studies.* Sydney: Allen & Unwin.

PART III

Input markets

CHAPTER 9

Capital markets

MATTHEW W. BUTLIN

This chapter sets out some features of the development of the Australian capital market between 1900 and 1980 and, in particular, of the institutional framework of those markets. The changes between those dates are profound and of necessity the account in this essay is narrowly focused.

There are three themes in the following account. First, the institutional environment of the capital market responded, albeit slowly at times, to the changing demands for capital reflecting the pattern of economic development and other factors. Second, the capital market became increasingly effective in mobilising domestic savings, particularly from the household sector. Third, public policy towards the regulation of capital markets and financial intermediaries, significantly influenced by attitudes shaped by the financial collapse of the 1890s, played a major role in shaping the institutional framework of the capital market.

9.1   The Australian capital market in 1900

At the beginning of the twentieth century the Australian capital market was rudimentary by contemporary European standards. The lingering financial and monetary implications of the depression in the first half of the 1890s continued to exert a strong inhibiting influence on the recovery of domestic financial markets.

During the second half of the nineteenth century, an array of financial institutions had developed to service the special characteristics of the contemporary economic structure. Trading banks organised on a widespread branch network were by far the most important domestic institutions dealing primarily with local and foreign deposits. These funds serviced the demands on the one hand of a rapidly expanding and capital-intensive rural sector, primarily pastoral, and of the financing of overseas

Noel Butlin, Rod Maddock, Ian McLean, and other participants in this volume provided useful comments on earlier drafts. I am particularly grateful to Alan Hall for thorough and constructive criticism that substantially improved the coverage and argument of the analysis. The views expressed herein are my own and do not necessarily reflect those of my employers.

trade, and on the other hand of government banking business and the accessing of overseas funds on government account. Two specialist financial intermediaries had grown to considerable prominence: pastoral finance companies fed by the accounts of pastoralists, wool broking and private raisings in Britain, and funding the acquisition and transfer of rural properties and their capital expansion; and "land banks", which also were domestic and foreign deposit institutions and dealt primarily in the funding of urban real estate transactions.

Somewhat lower down the scale, but still very prominent by comparison with their overseas counterparts, Australian building societies had acquired considerable substance, encouraged by the strong demands for home ownership in a wealthy and relatively egalitarian society and by demands for housing as a speculative investment. These societies depended on domestic deposits but immediately before the 1890s depression had followed the other financial intermediaries into the acceptance of foreign deposits. Savings banks also existed, but not in a well-developed form, although their predecessors were established in the form of post office savings banks. Insurance companies had not yet become major institutions.

At perhaps the lowest level of significance, stock exchanges of a restricted kind existed, principally in Sydney and Melbourne, and were concerned with raising equity capital and engaging in the business of share transfers. The main activities of these institutions were concerned with mining, a limited range of investment activity, and, to a lesser extent, transfers of government securities.

The capital demands of agriculture (excluding pastoral activity), services, and manufacturing were primarily met from retained profits and personal financial associates, supported by limited overdraft facilities extended by banks and commercial enterprises with whom business was transacted. The essential focus of the capital market was in pastoral activity and goldmining in the private sector and the funding of infrastructure in the public sector. Lending was based on agreements backed by collateral security and generally took the form of mortgage or overdrafts, the latter reflecting the needs of rural industry.

This structure and orientation were severely disrupted after 1890. The financial collapse in 1890 and 1891 associated with the puncturing of the land boom in the late 1880s saw the failure or reorganisation of around half of the trading banks in existence in 1890 and the failure, on a broad scale, of land banks. Building societies, although generally on a sounder footing than the land banks, also suffered from the lack of public confidence in intermediaries whose assets largely comprised land. A drastic process of reconstruction followed the downturn as domestic and particularly foreign institutions concerned were forced into reconstruction of rural properties and sought to foreclose on mortgages.

Both processes had important implications for the structure and operations of the capital market in 1900 and, in many areas, until as late as 1910. The land banks disappeared, building societies dwindled, and pastoral companies were faced with the problem of disposing of foreclosed properties – this situation being compounded by the drastic rundown in Australian livestock numbers during 1896–1904. The focus of the pastoral companies shifted more towards broking business and to the direct operation of pastoral properties.

In contrast, the stock exchanges sustained and expanded their role by the growth of mining in the period 1890–1910, following the discoveries in Western Australia, by the continuation of government financial requirements and stock transfer, and by a strengthening of the weak market in government securities that had emerged in 1890.

The prominence of the Australian banks increased as a result of the dire problems of these other intermediaries and the enforced risk aversion in bank management to which the financial collapse gave rise. The private banks were reduced in number by outright failures and mergers, which reduced competition and, in 1900, had placed them in a position in which smaller numbers could reap any advantage from subsequent recovery. At the same time, the banks were faced with a large-scale repatriation of foreign funds from the private sector, a process that continued until 1907. Moreover, their traditional funding role was severely constrained because the capital demands of the pastoral industry did not recover and, indeed, remained relatively slight during the first thirty-five years of the century. So far as the private banks were concerned, their opportunities for recovery were limited by the formation, in particular, of government rural banks during the 1890s to service the capital requirement of farmers. None of this was a propitious opening to the twentieth century for the capital market.

9.2   The Australian capital market in 1980

By 1980 the domestic capital market encompassed a broad and highly developed set of institutions that effectively mobilised domestic savings, servicing a wide range of demands including housing, economic development (including both industrial expansion and resources development), working capital of business, household requirements, and the purchase of existing assets. A broader range of financial assets were traded, ranging from the very short term (overnight money) to very lengthy debt instruments.

These outcomes reflected the changing attitudes towards regulation and the evolving financial demands for finance arising from the changing industrial and demographic structure of the Australian economy.

Partly reflecting this, a broader range of financial intermediaries existed: The additions included credit cooperatives, finance companies, merchant banks, and dealers in short-term securities. The financial system in 1980 was, on the whole, more heavily regulated, although the burden of regulation fell differently than in 1900. A central bank, the Reserve Bank of Australia, had evolved. In addition, there had been a reordering of the financial intermediaries existing in 1900 in response to the structural changes in the economy since that time and their implications for the capital demands of businesses, households, and the public sector.

The preeminent position of the banking system, and trading banks especially, had been severely eroded by the rapid growth of other financial institutions, particularly in the postwar period. Nonetheless, banks remained the largest single group of intermediaries, with assets amounting to somewhat less than two-fifths of the assets of Australian intermediaries.

Banks serviced a broad range of business and consumer needs. The overdraft secured by land or by a floating charge over assets, the predominent lending instrument in 1900, had given ground relatively to a wider and more flexible range of instruments including term loans, leasing, commercial bill finance, and consumer credit in the form of personal instalment loans and credit cards. This proliferation partly related to regulations framed in terms of bank overdrafts. At the same time, savings banks provided a substantial share of housing finance largely through crédit foncier loans and, reflecting banking regulations, were major captive lenders to government.

In 1980 regulations also prevented banks from accepting very short-term deposit liabilities: Over time, this provided a niche in which a large number of nonbank money market corporations functioned.

The official money market initially stemmed from initiatives by the Reserve Bank to encourage trading in short-term assets as a means of facilitating monetary policy. By 1980 the market comprised the official and nonofficial segments, both of which dealt in differing degrees in short-term negotiable securities of the public and private sectors. The authorised dealers, which had access to central bank credit, were required to deal in a restricted group of assets comprising commonwealth government securities and selected private paper and drew their funds from professional operators including businesses. Though small in size, the authorised dealers were an important element in short-term monetary management by the monetary authorities.

Money market corporations bulked substantially larger than the authorised dealers, ranking fourth in terms of the nonbank financial intermediaries, and held a broader range of short-term public and especially private paper. Funds were raised both domestically, on a short-term basis reflecting the coverage of maturity controls on bank deposits, and from overseas. Overseas fund raising was facilitated by the participation of foreign equity, frequently banks, in the ownership of many money market corporations. Money market corporations were frequently merchant bankers and, as such, assisted in many cases by connections with foreign parents, raised substantial amounts of overseas debt finance for their clients, including funds for economic development.

Life offices and pension funds were second to banks in size of asset portfolios (a bit more than two-thirds of bank assets), having peaked in relative importance in the 1960s, and drew on premium contributions from domestic residents. The proceeds were primarily invested in equities and debentures of corporations and, partly reflecting financial regulations, in government securities. As such, life offices played a largely complementary role to banks in providing longer-term direct and indirect finance compared with the trading banks' orientation towards shorter-term finance.

Finance companies, some of which were affiliated with banks, were next in importance, providing debt finance to businesses and households using a broad range of instruments, including leasing and term loans; like banks, they drew on domestic deposits and debenture raising to finance their activities.

Consumers and households also obtained finance from permanent building societies and credit cooperatives, both of which occupied prominent positions in the financial hierarchy and both of which drew exclusively on domestic deposits to fund their activities. Permanent building societies, after finance companies and the life offices the largest group of nonbank financial intermediaries, lent almost exclusively for housing and competed closely with savings banks in this field. Credit cooperatives generally made term loans to individuals, with or without security, for the purchase of consumer durables and made limited loans for the purchase of or improvements to homes.

Pastoral companies had dwindled to unimportance reflecting the reduced relative significance of pastoral activities in the national economy.

Direct finance from domestic sources was largely directed through stock exchanges that had developed into sophisticated institutions deal-

ing with share flotations, debenture raisings, and stock transfers. Trading
in government paper was much less important than in 1900, with secondary market trading in government securities increasingly being conducted off exchange. Whereas the focus of capital raising in 1900 had
been largely on mining, in 1980 a broader range of enterprises sought
funds through the stock exchanges.

9.3   The development of the capital market 1900–39

1900 to 1914

In this period, the private sector increased its claims on the rest of the
world by around $60 million, mostly associated with high gold exports.
In net terms, therefore, domestic savings more than satisfied capital
demands in Australia.

Much of this period was spent in recovering from the lingering effects
of the 1890s financial collapse. For the first ten years of the century, the
principal focus of the capital market was, in the private sector, goldmining and the pastoral industry and, in the public sector, sale of government   securities   to   finance   economic   expansion   and   related
infrastructure. From 1910 until the first world war capital needs broad-
ened with an expansion of the industrial and commercial sectors and
some slowing in domestic debt issues by governments.

The stock exchanges flourished in the years leading up to World War
I, with major issues of new shares being sought in most areas apart from
mining and banking. Stock transfers and dealings in government securities, the latter reflecting the increased role of the domestic market in
financing government requirements throughout the period 1900–14, also
supported stock market activity.

The surpluses of public enterprises and debt raisings both in the London capital market and in domestic markets provided the finance for
government requirements. Estimates of N. G. Butlin (1962) suggest that
the gross operating surpluses of public enterprises amounted to around
half of the gross product of that section prior to World War I, thereby
making a substantial contribution to financing the capital needs of the
public sector. The balance of the remaining requirements were largely
met one-third from overseas borrowing and two-thirds from domestic
borrowing.

Table 9.1 provides details of the assets of selected intermediaries
between 1902 and 1914. The marked expansion of banking institutions
catering for household savers is apparent, a development that closed a
gap at the turn of the century. Governments encouraged this expansion;

Table 9.1. *Australian assets of selected intermediaries (£ million)*

Year	Trading banks[a]	Savings banks[a]	Building societies[b]	Life offices[c]	Friendly societies[c]
1901	116.8	32.9	N.A.	N.A.	N.A.
1905	114.0	38.3	N.A.	N.A.	N.A.
1909	131.8	52.7	4.6	35.6	4.9
1914	175.1	87.8	N.A.	43.8	6.7
1920	269.5	142.7	6.7	71.8	8.7
1924	333.8	188.0	N.A.	95.5	11.0
1929	365.4	247.1	13.2	129.0	3.9

Sources: [a]S. J. Butlin, Hall, and White 1971.
[b]Hill 1959; figure for 1920 is actually 1919.
[c]Commonwealth Bureau of Census and Statistics, *Finance Bulletin*, various issues.

it suited their own requirements, both by providing an asset and by founding new banks (following a practice long established before 1900). By 1914 around two-thirds of the assets of savings banks were government securities or deposits with state treasuries. In 1912 the Commonwealth Bank was established; significantly, the savings bank function commenced first.

Trading banks, by contrast, grew slowly. The reconstructions forced by the earlier bank failures, coupled with the loss of confidence by British investors (those who had not lost their capital) in Australian financial institutions, had led to a high degree of risk aversion by bank managers. Funds were drawn largely from Australian sources.

Statistics on the *pattern* of bank lending in this part of the century are very limited. By 1912, 36 percent of all of the Bank of New South Wales's advances were for pastoral purposes, 25 percent were for agricultural purposes, and 23 percent were to merchants and storekeepers (Holder 1970: 547). These figures, while illustrative, reflect the extremely cautious lending policy, which emphasised internal liquidity: Speculative or risky propositions were avoided; short-term self-liquidating advances were preferred; and large collaterals were required (Guille 1975: 192).

Over 90 percent of advances by the Bank of New South Wales were by means of overdraft. That form of lending was well suited to borrowers with substantial collateral but little liquidity. However, it was inappropriate for enterprises with little capital and uncertain prospects. Unlike banks in some other countries, Australian banks did not hold equities and did not, as a rule, provide long-term finance. That, for the most part, was obtained through entrepreneurs' capital, retained earnings, and, to a much lesser extent, share markets.

Pastoral companies were also active in financing rural activity on terms broadly similar to bank terms, lending to improve or purchase properties and to finance working capital, with loans typically being secured by property or future revenue. In addition to rural advances, the pastoral companies also profitably operated a substantial number of foreclosed properties during the first decade and de facto acquired direct equity participation.

Housing finance was generally limited during this period. Investment in housing was perceived as being speculative, following the experience of the 1890s and the substantial – perhaps excessive – expansion of housing in the lead-up to that period. As a result, specialist institutions, such as building societies, had only a limited capacity to attract funds. Funds were also available through life offices, which lent on mortgage, with only a modest contribution from the savings banks.

Overall, the capital market prior to World War I met the demands placed upon it without much strain. The problem it faced was principally one of scale, since there were no fundamentally new factors at work. Therefore, the adjustments to the institutions in the market were limited: The market remained rudimentary and, in respect of lending instruments, unresponsive to the requirements of sectors other than agriculture, commerce, and government.

1919 to 1929

In the first decade following World War I, demands on the domestic capital market were intense, reflecting, in the private sector, a rapid expansion and reorganisation of industry that called for substantial quantities of funds as businesses were founded, expanded, and incorporated, and, in the public sector, a headlong rush into the creation of infrastructure for economic development. Domestic savings were inadequate to meet these demands, calling for a significant topping up from foreign savings.

Against this background, the intermediaries catering for household savers, (building societies, savings banks, and life offices) grew rapidly both in response to the rapid expansion of the population and the increasing needs of government for borrowed funds.

The postwar expansion of the public sector required substantial quantities of finance that was met largely by overseas borrowing supplemented by domestic borrowing. That trend partly reflected the limited size of the domestic market given the scale of the requirement and partly the favourable conditions under which dominion and state governments could borrow in London. In addition, the public enterprises were generating smaller surpluses: In 1926 the gross operating surplus was 26 percent of gross product, compared with 38 percent in 1910.

Retained earnings, particularly in the manufacturing sector, principally funded businesses' requirements (Forster 1964); reliance on bank credit and trade creditors fell relatively. At the same time, however, the domestic stock exchanges flourished as existing enterprises incorporated or were publicly listed, and as a result of new raisings stemming from the expansion of service industries and manufacturing industry (Were and Son 1954: 802) and continued domestic loan placements by governments.

The evidence available on foreign investment in manufacturing during the twenties indicates that overseas savings made little contribution to the growth in manufacturing. Forster's (1964) estimates suggest that between 1919 and 1929 foreign investment in manufacturing from the United States and Britain may have amounted to around $72 million, compared with the estimated total investment in manufacturing between 1919/20 and 1929/30 of around $292 million (N. G. Butlin 1962).

In the unsettled financial conditions of the late twenties foreign and domestic capital markets perceived that, with a deterioration in Australia's terms of trade and a belief that the overseas raisings were not generating an adequate stream of exports, Australia had a severe debt servicing problem. By 1929/30 interest on public debt domiciled externally amounted to around 25 percent of exports.

Finance for housing: The high rate of immigration into Australia and the consequent high rate of family formation during the 1920s spurred by government initiatives to expand home ownership provided the basis for an expansion of those intermediaries lending directly for housing. Building societies grew rapidly during this period and more than doubled the value of outstanding balances between 1919 and 1929 (Hill 1959: 13); the growth of savings banks was only marginally less. By contrast, the liabilities of the trading banks grew by 34 percent over the same period. The most important group of lenders for housing was the savings banks, which in 1929 held some $50 million in housing loans, up from $9 million in 1919. Trading banks and life offices supplemented these funds. In 1929, mortgages held by life offices amounted to $71 million (or 26 percent of their Australian assets), of which perhaps half was in urban districts. How much of this was for housing is uncertain.

From early in the twentieth century, the states actively encouraged home ownership. New South Wales established a housing board in 1912 to purchase land and build dwellings on it for sale or lease. The scheme was extended in 1919 to enable the board to make advances to individuals. Similar encouragement was provided by other states. A substantial contribution was also made by the War Service Homes Commission, which was established by the federal government after World War I to help provide homes for ex-servicemen and their dependants. In 1929 government housing authorities had outstanding advances of $23.4 million, compared with $36 million by the War Service Homes Commission in 1930 and around $24 million by building societies in 1929.

One outcome of these developments was that the rate of home ownership rose from 50 percent in 1911 to 55 percent in 1933, and the proportion of persons purchasing by instalment rose from 5 percent in 1911 to 13 percent in 1933.

1929 to 1939

The depression and the effective closure of external capital markets to public borrowings from 1930/1 forced major adjustments on the domestic capital market. For the thirties as a whole, Australia drew only modestly on world savings. Part of the adjustment involved severe restraint on the demand for capital by the private sector, whilst the public sector turned almost exclusively to the domestic capital market to fulfil its requirements.

Stock exchanges were adversely affected by the depression. New issues were limited, with few signs of a pickup in activity until late in the decade when the pace of industrialisation quickened.

Notwithstanding the severity of the economic adjustments, the trading banks weathered the storm without loss, in striking contrast both to the experience in the 1890s and to overseas. Most other groups fared worse, though, for the most part, better than forty years earlier (see Schedvin 1971).

Relatively comprehensive statistics covering most of the financial system exist for the year 1936. In 1936 the Australian financial system consisted of trading and savings banks, pastoral companies, life offices, trustee companies, building societies, finance companies, and stock exchanges. Table 9.2 provides details on the gross assets and liabilities for many of these institutions. Whilst a consolidation of the balance sheets of the various institutions to provide a flow-of-funds matrix is not possible, the figures highlight the importance of the banking system to the financial system as a whole.

The activities of the trading banks continued to be directed towards the provision of working capital and other short-term finance to the private sector and to holding liquid assets such as government paper. In 1936 almost half of bank lending went to the agricultural and pastoral

Table 9.2. *Financial intermediaries in 1936: selected assets and liabilities in Australia ($ million)*

Institutions	Deposits & borrowings	Other liabilities	Cash	Deposits with banks	Australian government securities	Advances	Other assets
Trading banks[a]	687.5	40.1[b]	75.6	N.A.	171.4	583.8	N.A.
Savings banks	451.6	30.9	2.4	65.6[c]	268.4	20.8	125.3
Trustee companies	438[d]	5.4	N.A.	N.A.	125.7	75.0	242.7
Life offices	N.A.	N.A.	4.6	N.A.	199.6	132.4	43.2
Building societies[e]	5.0	20.0	N.A.	N.A.	N.A.	21.6	3.4
Pastoral companies	30.6[f]	49.6	N.A.	N.A.	N.A.	50.5	29.7
Credit cooperatives	N.A.	N.A.	N.A.	N.A.	N.A.	N.A.	N.A.

[a]Includes Commonwealth Bank: assets and liabilities in Australia.
[b]Australian liabilities only.
[c]Includes deposits with Commonwealth Bank.
[d]Includes approximate investment of trust funds administered by trustee companies.
[e]Figures for 1935
[f]Includes debenture capital and deposit and customers' credit balances.
Source: Royal Commission on Banking 1936.

Table 9.3. *Classification of advances within Australia by nine trading banks (percentages)*

Advance to persons or institutions engaged in	1927	1931	1935	1936
Manufacturing and mining	11.9	9.6	8.8	9.2
Commerce, transportation, & distribution	22.6	20.4	18.3	19.0
Finance, insurance, etc.	4.6	4.6	5.6	5.9
Agricultural, pastoral	41.5	47.4	49.8	47.7
Professions, entertainments	5.5	5.4	5.1	5.0
Others (building, government)	13.9	12.6	12.4	13.2
Total	100.0	100.0	100.0	100.0

Source: S. J. Butlin, Hall, and White 1971.

industries, with the next largest borrower being the commerce, transport, and distribution group. Bank advances to "other pursuits including building and to public bodies" – and, presumably, to private individuals – accounted for just over 13 percent of the total. Table 9.3 provides further details.

A comparison of Table 9.3 with the previously cited statistics on the breakup of lending by the Bank of New South Wales in 1912 reveals a shift in lending patterns by the trading banks away from agriculture in response to the changing industrial structure of the economy. However, the onset of the depression tended to reverse that trend.

Notwithstanding the success of the banking system during the depression, the federal government in 1936 set up the Royal Commission into Monetary and Banking Systems (hereafter Banking Commission). The commission was significantly influenced in part by contemporary theories of central banking, by a distrust of the banking system born of the 1890s' financial collapse, and by the extremely tight monetary conditions in 1929/30 and 1930/1.

The Banking Commission criticised the banking and financial system for inadequate provision for fixed and longer-term lending and considered that overdrafts that carried the condition of repayment on demand and the uncertainty of term and interest rate were inappropriate to "fixed capital purposes or term finance".

The commission also criticised the lumpiness of capital issues and the aversion of the intermediaries to particular classes of risk. In particular, the facilities available to borrowers of limited means who had been successful on a small scale in a secondary industry that was capable of expansion "and deserving of encouragement in the public interest" were felt to be limited. There was some substance to these claims. At the time banks were free to charge rates of interest that reflected risk and expense associated with new enterprises. Development projects were unattractive to banks at any price.

The recommendations of the Banking Commission were largely directed towards strengthening and defining the central banking functions of the Commonwealth Bank (then comprising principally the note issue) and providing controls over the banking system. The recommendations became a blueprint for legislation during the forties and fifties.

9.4   Further development and regulation 1939–80

During the years 1937 to 1949 the views embodied in the Banking Commission gained currency and were reflected in legislation, many of the initiatives being a product of (mostly) wartime governments between 1941 and 1949.

At the war's end, portfolios of all intermediaries and especially banks were extremely liquid. Concerns over that development gave rise to the Banking Act and the Commonwealth Bank Act, both of 1945. This legislation modified some of the Banking Commission recommendations, continued practically the whole wartime procedure for control of banking and exchange, and abolished the note issue reserve. Notwithstanding the change in government in 1949, the principles of this legislation remained the basis of subsequent banking legislation until 1980.

Finance for postwar economic development

Throughout the postwar period Australia was a substantial importer of capital, drawing heavily on foreign savings to supplement an internationally high savings rate.

In the postwar period private enterprises sought funds, both equity and long-term debt, to meet the capital requirements of economic development on a broad scale. Share raisings were limited by the size of the domestic market; consequently domestic raisings were supplemented by injections of foreign capital, particularly in the fifties and sixties, or direct investment associated with the establishment or expansion of Australian subsidiaries. In later years, foreign capital came in as borrowing rather than as direct finance and its importance declined somewhat relative to domestic raisings.

Domestic stock exchanges expanded their operations for much of this period, although with the advent of higher inflation and slower economic growth in the decade following 1972 equity raisings diminished in relative importance. The manufacturing and service sectors, the latter comprising finance and property, were the chief borrowers for much of the period. During the decade prior to 1980, there were two share booms building on the mineral discoveries in the early 1970s and shifts in the relative price of energy during the period.

Life offices and superannuation funds were increasingly important, long-term investors transforming their portfolios from predominantly mortgages (to business and to households), with relatively few equities or debentures, to predominantly equities.

In the postwar period, longer-term finance has not, as a rule, been provided by the Australian banking system which has concentrated on providing finance for business operations. An exception is term lending (and farm development loans) by the banks, which was introduced in an explicit form during the 1960s. However, whilst it now is a significant element of bank lending, it was not something then undertaken by choice by the trading banks but was actively encouraged by the Reserve Bank.

Housing finance

In the postwar period the trend to increased home ownership continued, with savings banks and the building societies remaining predominant, supplemented by life offices and finance companies. Throughout the period governments have provided substantial incentives for home ownership through tax and subsidy arrangements.

The tax concessions available to persons investing in housing for commercial purposes have been substantial. The capital gains tax that has limited application to longer-term investment in real estate meant that housing income could be taken in the form of capital gains: an important consideration in time of high inflation when nominal rates of return on other assets were fully taxed. Moreover, the steady increase in housing prices, together with the scope for a high degree of gearing, meant that the profits could be magnified.

On balance, there was a substantial inducement to investment in housing. Particularly in the postwar period, a number of key price distortions have encouraged home ownership by selected groups. Tax exemptions on interest payments for mortgages (including the partial and complete exemptions at various times), the effect of interest rate ceilings on home mortgage interest rates, and the taxation (or lack of it) of capital gains on property held for more than a year have all worked to raise the demand for housing.

It is a moot point as to whether there has been an overinvestment in housing relative to other assets: The distortions favouring housing must be weighed against benefits accruing to other forms of investment, including accelerated depreciation, investment allowance, deductibility of business interest payments, and so on. Rates of residential capital formation in Australia are broadly in line with contemporary international experience.

That said, Yates (1982) has shown that interest rate ceilings have been largely regressive in effect, assisting the middle class at the expense of the lower income groups.

Development of financial intermediaries

The Banking Act of 1945 entrenched the pattern of wartime regulations on the domestic banking system. At that time the banks accounted for almost three-quarters of the assets of Australian financial intermediaries. Notwithstanding the attempt in 1947 by the government of Prime Minister Chifley (who had been a member of the 1936 Banking Commission) to nationalise the banks and the legislative changes by the later Menzies government, the broad thrust of that legislation towards regulating financial markets remained.

There were three basic elements to bank regulation. In the first case, banks were subject to directives from the Commonwealth Bank and subsequently from the Reserve Bank concerning the areas of lending business that they could pursue and the terms on which deposits could be accepted and loans made. Second, the trading banks were required to lodge deposits with the central bank (initially Special Accounts and subsequently Statutory Reserve Deposits–SRD), and the banks also agreed to hold a specified portion of their portfolios in the form of liquid assets and commonwealth government securities (LGS). In addition, the banks faced restrictions in relation to their deposit maturities: They were unable to accept either very short-dated interest-bearing deposits or deposits of very long maturity.

Against that background, the subsequent general development of the financial system contains a good deal of economic logic. The regulations prohibited the banks from lending directly to particular sectors; consequently nonbank intermediaries (some of which were owned or partly owned by the trading banks) moved in to pick up the business that banks might otherwise have acquired. An example of this is the rapid expansion of the finance companies between 1953 and 1961, reflecting the restrictions on the banks for lending to the household sector to finance hire purchase agreements. Lending by bank-owned finance companies accounts for a substantial fraction of lending by all finance companies.

The SRD and LGS requirements added to the effective cost of funds to the banks, with the impact of these arrangements depending on the level of market interest rates. The high inflation rates and high nominal interest rates of the seventies sharply increased the returns from financial innovation during this period, stimulating the growth of nonbank intermediaries. Banks made greater use of forms of lending (for example, bill finance) that did not require deposit funds and did not attract the SRD impost. This stimulated the commercial market: That development, coupled with the bank deposit maturity controls, provided a niche for the merchant banks.

Extensive regulations on savings banks, including those on the nature of deposits that could be offered, on assets that could be held, and on interest rates that could be charged on housing loans, placed this group at a competitive disadvantage compared with other intermediaries.

The relative importance of the banking sector therefore diminished in relation to the financial system as a whole. The share of the banks in the total liabilities of the financial system fell from 66 percent in 1956 to 46 percent in 1976. By 1980 banks held less than two-fifths of the assets of financial intermediaries (Norton and Garmston 1984: 73).

By the sixties the impact of regulation in reducing the market share of the banking system was well recognised, particularly by the monetary authorities. A wide variety of institutions outside the direct umbrella of regulation had emerged, with the result that the banks, though still the largest group, had been diminished in importance. Further, the profusion of different intermediaries implied an efficient exploitation of scale economies in funds management.

These trends led to a greater reliance on market-oriented instruments of policy and a progressive easing of the regulations on the banks and other intermediaries. Interest rates on negotiable certificates of deposit were deregulated in 1973, and the regulations governing savings banks were progressively reduced.

The advent of money market corporations was prompted by a gap arising from the needs of business and others to invest and borrow significant sums at short notice. The establishment of the official money market dealers in the early 1960s went some way towards meeting that gap, but the regulations governing the types and quantities of assets that could be held placed this group at a competitive disadvantage in selected areas compared with the unofficial money market corporations. Moreover, deposit maturity controls limited the ability of banks to compete with nonbank financial institutions at the short end of the maturity spectrum.

The extended inflation of the seventies and eighties brought further pressure on the banking system. Corporations and the financial markets became more attuned to international capital markets as a source of short-term as well as long-term finance (in this the merchant banks appear to have played an important role). These considerations placed the banking system at an increasing competitive disadvantage, particularly at a time of rising interest rates; one result in December 1980 was the decision to deregulate interest rates paid on deposits of maturities longer than a month. Further changes were made to savings bank regulations to increase their competitiveness.

Perhaps the clearest recognition of the need to make the Australian financial system more competitive came with the establishment in 1979 of the Committee of Inquiry into the Australian Financial System (the Campbell committee), which was to inquire into the system and to make recommendations on the improvement of the structure, operations, and regulation and control of the financial system. The Campbell committee reported in 1981 and recommended sweeping changes to the financial system aimed at increasing its efficiency and competitiveness, but at the same time proposing different approaches to the regulatory structure. The Campbell committee report was followed in 1984 with the report of the Martin committee, which broadly confirmed the thrust of the Campbell recommendations, although it set them in a somewhat different context. Since the Campbell committee began its deliberations in the late seventies, there have been a number of moves to foster a less overtly regulated financial system, including the removal of controls on bank deposit interest rates in 1980, deregulation of share brokerage rates, the removal of notice of withdrawal requirements for savings bank deposits, and the lessening of controls over savings bank balance sheets. More recently, the exchange rate was floated and exchange controls were largely removed (in December 1983), and from August 1, 1984, the deposit maturity controls on banks were substantially liberalised. It seems certain that these moves towards greater flexibility in financial markets will have as profound an effect on the financial system as the 1936 Banking Commission.

9.5   Conclusion

There are three main conclusions regarding capital markets in Australia arising from the preceding account of their operation during the twentieth century.

The capital market institutions were responsive to market forces. That is, institutions adapted to the requirements of a changing set of demands for capital as they emerged during the twentieth century. Demands for housing encouraged the growth of specialist intermediaries such as building societies and savings banks that drew their funds from deposits of the household sector. Different capital requirements from new or expanding business sectors called for a wider variety of lending instruments in addition to bank overdrafts, particularly in the postwar era. That said, the capital market has been considerably more effective in responding to these pressures during the last twenty years than it was in the first sixty: That is at least partly a reflection of the conservatism of financial management during the forty years after the 1890s collapse.

Second, the market was not merely rudimentary in 1900 but also inefficient as a mobiliser of savings. One of the marked features of the development of capital market institutions during the twentieth century was this expansion of intermediaries that functioned to mobilise household savings and that also provided an incentive for further savings on the part of that sector. This development was reflected in the rapid expansion of savings banks up to the start of World War I. Subsequently, the relative importance of these intermediaries continued to grow with the proliferation in the postwar period of credit cooperatives, permanent building societies (particularly after the introduction of mortgage insurance during the 1960s), and finance companies.

Third, financial regulation has played a major role in shaping the financial system over time and reflected a longstanding mistrust of banks. In the mid thirties and the subsequent decade, policy makers (and by extension the Australian electorate) brought forth a regulatory structure for domestic financial intermediaries that focused on banking. Curiously, that approach appears to have been coloured by the bank failures of 1891 and 1892 and their subsequent impact on the perceptions of banking, rather than by the events of the depression of the thirties (which was the milieu of the 1936 Banking Commission). Australian banks weathered the depressed economic conditions of the 1930s very successfully by comparison with international experience.

The use of nonmarket regulatory devices brought, in time, the inevitable consequence of the proliferation on a large sale of nonbank financial intermediaries that conducted, to some extent, activities related to those of the banks. The main economic loss in this development has been the loss of economies of scale by banks through the decentralised market organisation. The growth of nonbank intermediaries accelerated at a time of high inflation, when interest rates rose and the economic rents from the gaps in the regulatory structure increased. On the other hand, the efficiency of financial intermediation between savers and lenders has been increased.

References

Butlin, N. G. 1962. *Australian Domestic Product, Investment and Foreign Borrowing 1861–1938/39*. Cambridge: Cambridge University Press.

Butlin, S. J., A. R. Hall, and R. C. White. 1971. *Australian Banking and Monetary Statistics 1891–1945*. Occasional Paper No. 4A. Sydney: Reserve Bank of Australia.

Forster, Colin. 1964. *Industrial Development in Australia 1920–1930*. Canberra: Australian National University Press.

Guille, C. W. 1975. "The financing of Australian manufacturing during the inter-war years: a case study of 26 listed general engineering firms: 1923–24 to 1936–37". Master's thesis, University of Sydney.

Hill, M. R. 1959. *Housing Finance in Australia 1945–1956*. Melbourne: Melbourne University Press.

Holder, R. J. 1970. *Bank of New South Wales: A History,* vol 2: *1894–1970.* Sydney: Angus & Robertson.

Norton, W. E., and P. M. Garmston. 1984. *Australian Economic Statistics 1949–1950 to 1982–83,* vol. 1: *Tables.* Occasional Paper No. 8A. Sydney: Reserve Bank of Australia.

Royal Commission on Banking. 1936. *Royal Commission into Monetary and Banking Systems.* Canberra: Government Printer.

Schedvin, C. B. 1970. *Australia and the Great Depression: A Study of Economic Development and Policy in the 1920s and 1930s.* Sydney: Sydney University Press.

Were, J. B., and Son. 1954. *The House of Were 1839–1954.* Melbourne: McCarron, Bird.

Yates, J. 1982. "The distributional impact of interest rate regulation on the household sector", in *Australian Financial System Inquiry Commissioned Studies and Selected Papers, Part 4,* pp. 157–245. Canberra: Australian Government Publishing Service.

CHAPTER 10

Labour

GLENN WITHERS

Consider a workforce that is literate, urban, and employed predominantly in the service sector. It is affluent, but with some major unemployment. About 40 percent of the population is in the workforce. It is a workforce deriving importantly from international migration (including government-assisted immigration) and possessing compulsory conciliation and arbitration and a high degree of public employment. Factories and Shops Acts seek to prevent unsafe and unhygienic working conditions, and Workers' Compensation Acts seek to compensate for injuries. There is considerable population mobility but settlement stability. Technical training is provided substantially by apprenticeship within industry, at industry expense. The workforce is strongly segmented by sex. Australia in 1984? Yes. But also Australia in 1900.

Clearly there are strong elements of continuity in the Australian labour market this century, perhaps more so than in any other industrial economy. But at the same time there are major changes to be discerned. To the average worker the most important might be the change in scale of the firm, and hence social relations at the workplace, improved comfort in the workplace, improved social security in the labour market, and increased real wages and shorter working hours for the employed. At a more aggregate level, this century also saw the full force of the economic cycle and its consequences for the labour market, and it also saw the longer-term moves to more advanced education for the workforce and to massively expanded female employment and to substantially increased female relative earnings.

This mix of stability and change will be reviewed closely and the central question will be posed as to whether that mix and the overall operation of the Australian labour market has been to the benefit or detriment of Australian economic performance.

The author is grateful to Yvonne Sheard for research assistance and to Owen Covick, Norman Fisher, Michael Keating, Don Rawson, Bernie Yates, and the co-authors and referees of this book for comments. The usual caveats apply.

10.1   The legacy of the 1890s

The labour market story must begin prior to 1900, for the depression of the 1890s marks a major watershed for Australian labour. During the long boom to 1891, Australia had developed a relatively flexible labour system. By international standards, unions were prominent on a craft basis, but they covered under 5 percent of the workforce. Employment was small scale and the workplace ethos was dominated by the personal relationship between owner managers and employers. The average number of workers per factory in 1890 was only fifteen. Individual bargaining, supplemented by some collective bargaining in a few areas, largely determined wages and conditions for workers. Continuing relative scarcity of labour meant that these wages were high by world standards, though there were significant elements of insecurity and instability in work. Nevertheless "there may have been alienation, [but] it was difficult to locate" (Parsons 1980: 56).

In the 1890s the attempt by key unions to affirm various bargaining principles, including closed shop principles, in the face of depression was totally defeated by united employer organisations, and their strikes were broken. The unions concerned were pastoral, mining, and maritime, but employers and workers in general were concerned at the legacy of bitterness and at the consequent uncertainty facing future labour relations and working standards. The outcome was important. In the labour market it led directly to the device of compulsory arbitration and conciliation as an attempt to guarantee fair and equal bargaining power between workers and employers. In politics it led to the formation of Labor parties, instead of reliance upon likeminded "good-as-Labor men" among the liberals in the parliaments (Hagan 1983).

In the labour market more centralised, formalised processes, based significantly on legal adversary relationships, began to replace previous more informal, more decentralised, and more personal arrangements at the workplace, a change that was later accentuated by the emerging technological and managerial change to larger-scale enterprise.

The worker motivation for these institutional changes is clear, given the personal and collective insecurities and defeats of the 1890s. What of employer acceptance? It was grudging and not universal, but it was gradually achieved. Indeed from the 1930s to the 1970s it was the employers who came to champion the arbitration system. But the earlier employer acceptance came only at a price. This price was the falling of real wages from 1900 to 1914 and, most important and enduring, the "New Protection": the provision of tariff guarantees to urban employers to offset the labour costs incurred under compulsory conciliation and arbitration, and the provision of publicly assisted immigration to help employers. Both of these were received without union opposition because of wage protection. This compact is analysed further in Chapter 7 of this book. Employers "failed to take advantage of the weakness of the labour movement at the turn of the century. With few exceptions they opted for the quiet life" (McIntyre 1983: 111).

Hence the jewel in the crown of Australian labour, the unique Australasian experiment in compulsory arbitration, one that excited overseas comment early in the century (then as part of "socialism without doctrine", to use French labour minister Métin's phrase) and that still excites comment today (as in Nobel laureate James Meade's [1982] depiction of Australian-style arbitration as an exemplar institution for effective incomes policy).

The system has not been without its opponents. The commonwealth industrial power underpinning the commonwealth conciliation and arbitration court was carried only narrowly at the federal convention of 1898, and governments have attempted to alter this constitutional power with a view to undermining arbitration, but those efforts resulted in the failure that traditionally accompanies Australian constitutional referendums. In the case of Prime Minister Bruce in 1929, his attempts to amend the industrial power led ultimately to an election in which the government was defeated spectacularly and the patrician Bruce himself lost his seat to a union leader recently fined for an unlawful strike.

10.2   The conciliation and arbitration system

The first fifty years

At the 1898 federal convention particular stress was laid on the conciliation function, as it was at the time of the introduction of the enabling federal legislation to parliament in 1903. Attorney General Deakin, outlining the modest role envisaged for the proposed court, said, "It removes friction where friction occurs, but it does not authorise or justify an interference where there is no friction, nor does it authorise or justify any greater interference than is necessary to remove the friction" (CPD, 1903, 15: 2865). In the states the picture was mixed, with some states opting for regulatory arrangements and others for conciliation bodies. But by the 1930s two major evolutionary developments had become clear: The commonwealth court had become preeminent, and conciliation had given way to arbitration in matters of wages.

As regards Commonwealth dominance, the percentage of total wage changes affected by the commonwealth court rose from 6.7 percent in 1913 through 13.6 percent in 1920 to 58.9 percent by 1929 (Hancock 1979). Nevertheless separate wage-determining authorities continued to coexist, so that a focus on the Commonwealth does some injustice to the story of wage settlement during this early period. Only in 1937 did New South Wales arbitral authorities adopt federal basic wage rulings automatically. The federal basic wage was from that time unequivocally the focus of the arbitral system, though it had been so effectively for some time.

The basic wage represented the minimum wage that could legally be paid to an adult male performing unskilled labour, and the history of its determination by the Commonwealth court illustrates the emerging commitment to arbitration.

The federal basic wage underlay the wage system from 1907 to 1967. It derived initially from the 1907 Harvester judgment and was said then to be a wage determined by social need: a fair and reasonable wage sufficient to provide a condition of frugal comfort for an unskilled male worker with a wife and three children. Justice Higgins, the dominant presence in the early history of the commonwealth court, found this to be seven shillings per day in 1907. On top of this basic wage, various margins for skill were also established, and "appropriate" award wages for females and youths were determined as a proportion of the basic wage. In 1914 the female wage was set at 48.2 percent of the male wage.

Whereas the basic wage was said to reflect social need, the level actually chosen may have very much reflected the prevailing market conditions of the time (as did secondary wages or margins) and hence, by one view, had as much an economic as a social basis (McCarthy 1969). This became clear when the royal commission on the basic wage in 1921 found that the true cost of living was much above the Harvester standards. The arbitration court declined to act on this finding, so abandoning its original principle and conceding some of the constraints imposed by what it saw as economic realism. Equally clear cut is that when the basic wage was indexed to price movements from 1912, though initially on a discretionary basis, in order to guarantee real purchasing power, and especially when it was automatically indexed on a quarterly basis from 1922, then the arbitration function gained obvious preeminence over conciliation concerns. The wage-setting processes of the court were no longer a response to any particular disputation or industrial relations problem, but rather a routine and, for the most part, mechanical laying down of a wage that applied across a large part of the economy, whether disputation existed or not, and that was determined in clear recognition of economic factors. Moreover, this national wage-fixing process became the focus of the court's interest and of public appreciation of the court's activities, and the innovation of the full bench reflected this change of emphasis. The court was now neither an industrial fire brigade nor a social welfare agency, whatever the intentions or pretensions of its founding fathers.

Automatic indexation of the basic wage remained until 1953, and the Harvester standard itself remained sacrosanct until 1931. In 1931, again in explicit response to economic conditions and not to social factors, the court instituted a 10 percent cut in the basic wage, on the basis of the economy's capacity to pay. (The 1930s experience was also important for macroeconomic understanding and is discussed in Chapter 3. The point to note here is that control of the basic wage was not control of all nominal wages. Moreover nominal wages are not real wages. In 1931 the money wage cut was followed by a real wage increase.) This was a major act of independent economic policy making, since the court diverged from the federal government, which in 1931 was still pledged to maintain the worker's standard of living. Later, "prosperity loadings" were awarded in the improved economic circumstances of 1937, 1946, and 1950.

Margins in this whole period to 1950 emerged by the ill-defined process of "work value inquiry", and much of the less prominent but detailed and time-consuming work of the court in the foundation years and the interwar period was individual determination of margins without resort to any general principles to govern the relative wage structure that emerged, though resort was had to wage comparisons across trades on an ad hoc basis from time to time. Nevertheless resultant margins were not random and, indeed, displayed considerable rigidity, indicating the force of historical relativities originally developed through free bargaining.

The postwar period

After World War II new economic conditions prevailed. The court had to adjust to full employment and, especially during the Korean boom, to substantial inflation. The court lost congruence with the wage system under these circumstances as earnings moved ahead of awards. To regain parity, and in the name of containing inflation, in 1953 automatic indexation of the basic wage was abandoned, and a system of national wage cases was substituted that took account, in some unspecified mix, of a range of economic and industrial relations factors. Also joint hearings of both basic wage and metal trades margins were subsequently adopted, since it was recognised that the metal trades case had emerged as a yardstick for the margins structure. On grounds of comparative wage justice, the metal trades decision flowed through to other award margins. Hence it was clear that the metal trades award should also be based on national economic criteria. Work value cases still permitted some individual relativity divergences initially, but these also became a source of flow-ons by the 1960s. In the period immediately after abandonment of automatic indexation, state awards reemerged for a time as wage leaders.

The logic of the integration of basic wage and margins became further acknowledged in 1967 with the adoption of the "total wage" concept, whereby the distinction between basic wage and margins was eliminated. A total wage was assessed on national criteria. A separately determined minimum wage was still declared on a social need basis, but this was no longer the basic wage that provided a floor to the whole wage structure. This decision of 1967 placed wage determination centrally in the process of macroeconomic regulation and on a continuing basis until loss of commission control again became a problem.

In the tight labour market of the early 1970s overaward payments and consent decrees by the commission (whereby the commission rubber-stamped private agreements brought to it for registration) produced substantial wage increases. This time the commission sought control by reversion to indexation, in a neat reversal of the position in the early 1950s. Indexation was applied from 1975 to 1981, but it was neither full nor automatic. Partial indexation and "plateau" indexation often applied, so that price movements were discounted and not necessarily awarded in full to higher-paid workers.

But with continuing high inflation and unemployment, in 1977 the commonwealth and state governments sought a voluntary wage freeze, which came to nothing. Private collective bargaining now developed apace again, as it had in the early 1970s. The commission abandoned centralised wage fixing in July 1981 and wages escalated even further as government talked up expectations of a mineral boom, which failed to materialise. A wage pause initiated by the Fraser government in 1982 was more successful in reducing wage increases, though limited by the arbitration commission to six months and then extended to ten months when the pause was taken over by the incoming Labor government and used as the basis for a prices and incomes strategy, developed at a national summit of union and employer delegates and negotiated subsequently with the union movement. The accord reached with the Australian Council of Trade Unions (ACTU) included a commitment by government to provide appropriate tax and welfare measures in return for a commitment to wage restraint by unions. The accord was integrated with centralised wage fixing through arbitration commission compliance, and was supported by the device of threat of denial of indexed national wage increases to unions breaching accord principles.

It is notable in the recent period that the actions of the commission have been determined by the willingness of the parties to adhere to its strictures. Long emerging and unmistakable since the O'Shea case of 1969, the inability of the commission to enforce its decisions has meant that it presides, not rules. The system can thus be characterised now as one of voluntary compliance, not literal arbitration (Isaac 1984: 13–14). The forms of legal adversary relations remain, but the sanctions do not, at least as far as the unions are concerned. It is not surprising that in this environment the ACTU, formed in 1927, has become more influential. Suasion from within the union movement is needed to hold incomes policies together in the absence of external sanctions and of underlying cooperative relationships between unions and employers.

Thus, the transformation was complete, 1904 to 1984. Three phases can be discerned. From a body with modest industrial peace intentions, the Commonwealth Arbitration Commission had been developed first as a major vehicle for social justice (what Higgins called a "new province of law and order") and then, as the economic constraints on this social purpose became explicitly recognised, as an independent centrepiece for economic policy making. Latterly the commission has become an element of corporatist economic practice, depending crucially upon the voluntary compliance of the parties before it. The underlying dilemma of social versus economic purpose had been resolved early on, though some occasional trade-offs of industrial relations versus macroeconomic objectives still persisted. Nevertheless the important reality was the early demise of the limited conciliation function, the subsequent centrality of judicial arbitration through wages, and finally the emergence of an ancillary role in consensual incomes policy.

10.3   Unions

The consequences of arbitration for unionism in Australia are important. The unions are as much creatures of arbitration as they were its creators, albeit through sympathetic liberal parliamentarians. Unions had organised under 5 percent of the workforce by 1890, but the depression and their defeat in the great maritime strike decimated union membership and strength. Victorian Trades Hall Council–affiliated membership fell from a peak of 30,000 in 1890 to a low of 2,230 in 1895 (Parsons 1980). A particular advantage of the adoption of arbitration arrangements was that the system required union registration to operate effectively. Unions rendered dispute notification a manageable process, and weak unions could, in principle, as readily seek favourable awards for their members as could strong unions. (At the same time once awards were determined they applied to relevant union and nonunion workers, so that the benefit of union membership to individual workers was, to that extent, muted. This was true of most state jurisdictions from the early days of arbitration and for federal awards after the *Burwood Cinema* case of 1925.) By World War I a quarter of the workforce was unionised. By 1954 a peak of 49 percent was reached; thereafter the figure remained there or a little below. In terms of employees this level represented 58 percent, compared with 47 percent for the United Kingdom (and rising) and 30 percent for the United States (and falling). For Australia the most dramatic periods of union membership growth were early in the century and after the two world wars.

A further advantage offered to unions by the arbitral system was the restriction on new competitive unions. The registration system determines the legitimacy of unions for arbitral purpose and so inhibits breakaway movements and props up otherwise industrially irrelevant unions. Admittedly, it also inhibits breakaways of elite craft groups that could then use their strategic leverage selfishly, but this point reaffirms equally the conservative nature of the registration system. In consequence the total number of unions has changed little since World War I, despite a fourfold growth in membership. The outcome has been a growing average union size, but a particular concentration in the dynamically growing unions, including public sector and white collar unions and unions in areas of growing female employment, while other small trade unions continue to exist under the aegis of the arbitral system. Today, half the unions have fewer than a thousand members and account for under 2 percent of all trade unionists in Australia. The economic implications of this lack of union adaptation are undoubtedly important. The predominance of the craft basis for unions and the ubiquity of small-scale unions have major consequences for contemporary industrial relations, for example demarcation disputes, as does the pervasive lack of dynamism inherent in the protection offered to all registered unions by the arbitral system. As Howard (1983: 243) puts it:

If the system required unions to exist, the operation of the system did not require a wide and conventional range of industrial relations activity from them. So far as the conciliation and arbitration system was concerned, unions were required to bring disputes in manageable and orderly proportions before the tribunal, but unions were not needed to resolve disputes or administer agreements.

But the growth of unionism in Australia should not be attributed solely or even mainly to arbitration. Between 1890 and the first world war there was a remarkable growth of trade unionism in most of the major industrial nations. The union percentage of occupied persons was as follows (Phelps-Brown 1966: 1):

	France	Germany	Sweden	UK	USA	Australia
About 1890	2.2	4.0	2.1	8.1	5.1	4.1
About 1913	14.4	25.2	26.4	26.9	18.3	24.1

It is true that Australian unionism did remain high thereafter, whereas United Kingdom and especially United States levels fell away. And this might be ascribed to arbitration. But the Australian levels are not exceptional by some European standards. Perhaps what is more clearly different in the twentieth century is the form that unionism takes under the aegis of the arbitration system.

This difference, discussed above, is also reflected in that most tangible of measures, strikes. Considerable contemporary concern is evinced over Australia's allegedly unreliable industrial relations record and, in particular, over reliability as an international supplier. What is evident, however, is that strikes have become shorter since the turn of the century and particularly since 1951. Since the war they have averaged only one or two days, despite the mid 1970s being the highest strike period this century in terms of strikes per worker. Accordingly production disruption is relatively limited.

Of course, industrial concentration of strikes is important, and coal, metals, building, and stevedoring do account for the bulk of work days lost. (It is notable that the coalmining and maritime industries were at the heart of the great strikes of the 1890s.) Direct production effects may therefore be greater in these industries. But strikes may be more for the purpose of bringing disputes to notice and resolution quickly and, sometimes, for influencing the outcome of any arbitration, though the Arbitration Commission does generally decline to hear matters currently the subject of strike action. To the extent that short strikes are directed more often at grievances without resort to arbitration, it can still be argued that employer intransigence and the lack of effective industry grievance procedures may to some extent be attributable to the existence of arbitration for a wide range of industrial issues. A further difference in Australian unionism that might be attributable to the arbitration system is the increasing resort in recent decades to bans, restrictions, limitations, and other production disruptions, which still constitute a dispute for arbitral purposes but do not involve loss of pay.

Of course many of these considerations apply equally to employers and employer organisations, and this should be stressed. The reduced incentive to resolve workplace problems directly is equally applicable to employers, as is evident in the relatively limited attention paid by management to human resource matters. The industrial relations manager typically occupies a low-pay and low-prestige position in the Australian management hierarchy. Similarly the arbitral arrangements provide an inducement for management to accept short strikes as an integral part of dispute settlement. Nevertheless some debate over how much can be attributed to arbitration is possible. For instance, United Kingdom industrial relations are not dissimilar to Australian despite the absence of a history of compulsory arbitration.

10.4 Employment structure

Within the distinctive system of arbitration and the associated high level of unionisation, what have been the major trends in the level and structure of the Australian workforce this century?

Labour is required by industry as a factor input for production. The total amount of labour required is determined by gross national output and by (average) labour productivity. Real gross product from 1900 to 1984 increased twelvefold in Australia. But the labour force has increased a little less than fivefold, implying a little over a doubling in labour productivity levels over the course of the century to date.

Labour force expansion has occurred in train with the expansion of the Australian population. The total dependency ratio was around 58 percent in 1900 and has not varied greatly from that level through to today, despite significant changes in population composition and labour force participation composition (Table 10.3 below). What has varied more, within the relatively constant 40 percent workforce ratio, has been the relative level of employment and unemployment, considered below.

For those in the employed labour force, industry of employment derives directly from the composition of demand for the products of industry and from the industry pattern of labour productivity. The outcome of these factors has been a steady diminution in the employment share in agriculture and mining and a gradual increase in manufacturing share, accelerating during World War II and reaching a peak in the late 1950s of 29 percent of employment, but thereafter diminishing in favour of service growth, particularly in areas such as community services, finance, property and business services, recreation and entertainment, and personal services (Table 8.2). Chapter 8 provides a detailed analysis of the development of this service sector. What is important to emphasise here is that Australia was already a very highly urbanised and service-oriented society at the turn of the century relative to other countries. Indeed it is estimated that even in 1890 Australia had only 25 percent of the workforce in agriculture as opposed to 40 percent for the United States, 48 percent for Canada, 37 percent for New Zealand, and 40 percent for Argentina (Jackson 1977). And this comparison refers to countries of new settlement that lacked historically large rural populations, unlike Europe.

Another type of broad change over time has been in workforce status. There has been a long-term shift away from employer and self-employed status, though this has been partly arrested and reversed in the late 1970s and early 1980s. For example, the self-employed represented about 9 percent of the workforce early in this century, declining especially after World War II to 6 percent in the 1960s and rising again from 1974 to 9 percent in the early 1980s. The long-term trend was clearly associated with the declining agriculture contribution and with the rise of large-scale manufacturing enterprise. The reversal since the mid 1970s partly reflects manufacturing recession but may also be related to a greater awareness of tax minimisation strategies available to nonwage and nonsalary earners, and to resort to self-employment as a flexible margin during recession, a phenomenon also observed in the 1930s (Covick 1983).

Nonwage and nonsalary earner employment and part-time employment have been the major sources of contemporary employment growth since the onset of recession in the mid 1970s. In the case of part-time employment, this represented 8.6 percent of the labour force in 1964 and had risen to over 17 percent by 1984: a doubling in twenty years. The shift has not been adequately explained, but descriptively it is associated with the increased role of married women in the Australian workforce in recent times; this will be discussed further below.

Public sector employment

One further dimension of workforce structure that requires attention is public sector employment. This is of interest because it is largely funded by compulsory taxation rather than by charges for services, and because terms and conditions of that employment may differ from that of private employment. As regards the latter, many public sector employments eschew strike action. Similarly much public sector employment offers formal job security and retirement provision beyond levels common in the private sector. But the rise of large bureaucratic private employers had reduced, though not necessarily eliminated, the disparity between public and private employment conditions, and there has been recent legislation to permit retrenchment of public employees. Today, therefore, some of the difference is more between large and small employers than between public and private, though differences of the latter kind do remain. In particular it can be argued that public sector unions can be more effective against their employers because those demands can be met from resort to consolidated revenue and the underlying power to tax.

Public employment is of greater importance as an indicator of the extent of government involvement in the economy – of concern because of differing views over the consequences of such involvement for the nation's achievement of its economic objectives. But it is noteworthy that, insofar as public employment is a useful indicator of the extent of government activity, big government is historical feature of the Australian labour market: There has been no major sustained increase in the public employment share in the period since World War II. The major periods of rising shares of public sector employment were 1906 to 1915 and 1940 to 1942. There is a further but smaller increase in public sector share after 1974, a period of high unemployment. In 1900 government employed 8.7 percent of the civilian workforce. By 1946 this had risen to 18.9 percent, but by 1974 the figure was still 19.9 percent (Barnard, Butlin, and Pincus 1977). In 1984 the percentage had risen to 25.0 percent.

The significance of these figures is that overseas notions of big government, which are reflected in public employment figures (Rose 1980), do not import readily into Australia. Indeed it seems clear that government employment in Australia is not now as big as in most OECD countries, and has not grown much for forty years, except for the current recession. The international picture can be seen in the following data from Aitkin (1983), showing public employment share in total labour force:

	Australia	Ireland	Italy	Sweden	UK	USA
About 1951 (%)	20.5	14.5	8.9	21.1	27.0	16.4
About 1976 (%)	21.4	26.3	21.2	32.2	30.4	18.5

Of course, more subtle interpretations of growth of big government in Australia are possible. For example there can be increased resort by government to regulatory powers not requiring substantial labour input, and this is well documented for the postwar period in Australia (Pincus and Withers 1983). Further, the historical trend in Australia this century has been to alter the composition of public employment away from production activities such as rail, posts, and telegraph towards other functions of government. Perhaps the most important dimension of this change is the shift from provision of physical capital infrastructure in transport and communication under the "colonial socialism" of the nineteenth century, through the expansion of urban infrastructure such as roads, electricity, water, and sewerage in a phase of "independent socialism" extending to the 1930s, followed by a dramatic shift to human capital provision after the second world war (N. G. Butlin, Barnard, and Pincus 1982). The implications of the switch to human capital outlays (and associated employment) will be considered further below.

Occupational composition

Finally, consider the occupational structure that results from the industry pattern of labour requirements. It might be thought that occupation patterns might develop somewhat independently of industry, but work by Carey (1979) shows, for the period 1947 to 1966, that occupation employment shares within industries vary little over time in most industries. What varies are the industry shares in total employment. Given the differences in occupational composition across industries, it is these industry employment movements (in response to changing output and productivity patterns) that generate changing occupational composition of the total workforce.

This is seen in Table 10.1, where the changing occupational distribution of workforce 1911 to 1981 is summarised. The industry pattern already discussed flows through to produce a corresponding decline in the role of rural and mining occupations and a rise of occupations related to the service industry. But even more than the industry figures, it shows the consequences for the skill and education levels of the workforce of the industry changes. There has been a major shift away from manual and trade work to professional and clerical employment, a change supported by the particular form of human capital outlays referred to above.

10.5   Workforce characteristics

Economic demography

The aggregate and structural labour requirements of industry must be matched with the level and composition of the workforce. At the broadest level population movements determine the size of workforce, so that

Table 10.1 *Occupational distribution of the workforce, 1911–81 (percentages)*

Occupation group	Census year						
	1911	1921	1933	1947	1961	1971	1981
1 Upper professional	1.8	1.7	1.8	1.4[a]	2.8	2.60	4.36
2 Graziers	1.7[b]	1.6[b]	2.8	2.3[b]	2.3	1.52	1.60
3 Lower professional	3.2	3.5	3.9	4.5	5.9	8.26	10.26
4 Managerial	5.0	3.7	4.5	5.9	7.1	7.22	5.83
5 Shop proprietors	1.3	1.7	2.8	[c]	1.2	0.71	0.76
6 Farmers	11.8[b]	11.3[b]	7.6	11.4[b]	4.6	3.40	2.85
7 Clerical workers	4.1	6.6	9.9	13.9[a]	15.6	19.48	20.76
8 Armed services, police	0.6	0.6	0.5	1.6	1.5	1.67	1.61
9 Craftsmen	17.3	17.0	12.2	15.9	16.4	15.05	14.15
10 Shop assistants	6.3	5.9	4.7	7.0[c]	5.0	5.27	5.94
11 Operatives	7.5[d]	8.8[d]	8.4	10.0	11.2	10.69	8.50
12 Drivers	5.2	5.4	5.1	5.5	5.0	4.39	3.98
13 Service workers	11.4	11.1	11.3	7.6	7.6	8.33	9.58
14 Miners	4.8	2.5	2.2	1.2	0.8	0.68	0.61
15 Farm workers	10.4	8.8	10.0	2.0	3.9	2.61	1.73
16 Labourers	7.7[d]	9.7[d]	12.3	9.9	9.2	7.87	7.21
Total (000 = 100%)	1,831	2,166	2,696	3,072	4,171	5,235	6,223

[a] Accountants included with bookkeepers in group 7. Professional engineers included with mechanics in group 9.
[b] Wheat and sheep farmers included with other farmers in group 6.
[c] Shop proprietors included in group 10.
[d] Some labourers included in group 11.
Source: Broom and Jones 1976, updated from unpublished figures provided by F. L. Jones.

net natural increase and net migration, and their associated age composition, have determined the boundaries of the Australian labour force.

Since the 1890s natural increase has been the major continuing source of increase in Australia's population. The most important influences upon natural increase trends in the twentieth century have been the secular decline of birth rates and the somewhat slower secular decline of death rates. Imposed on this has been the cyclical influence of a further reduction in birth rates during the depression in the 1930s and their sustained revival in the postwar period until the mid 1970s, whereafter depression levels of fertility have again applied (National Population Inquiry 1975). The basic demography underlying the labour market is obviously subject to major economic influence. And this also applies to immigration, which has strongly supplemented the natural increase in population, except for the war and depression years. In the

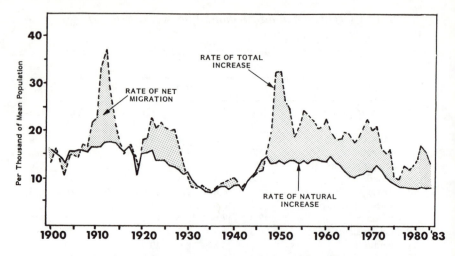

Figure 10.1. Rates of natural increase, total increase, and net migration 1900–83. *Notes:* Troop movements are excluded. Data are for calendar years. *Sources:* Commonwealth Bureau of Census and Statistics, *Demography Bulletin*; Australian Bureau of Statistics, *Year Book* and *Population and Vital Statistics*.

latter case both the willingness to migrate and the government willingness to assist migrants are typically reduced. The cyclical behaviour of both fertility and migration have had important echo effects for the age distribution of the Australian population (Hall 1963). Overall population growth averaged 1.9 percent per annum for the period to World War I and 1.5 percent for the interwar period, rising to 2.1 percent for the period from 1947 to 1976. This pattern is illustrated in Figure 10.1, and the composition of migration by source is indicated in Figure 10.2. From the latter the shift over time from Britain through northern Europe to southern Europe to West Asia to East Asia is clear, and therefore marks an important change in the nature of the Australian population and workforce. Predominantly of British and Irish origin at the turn of the century, it has become much more diverse today.

Looking directly at the contribution of migrants to the population of working age, the annual average contribution of overseas arrivals less departures aged fifteen to sixty-four, relative to the change in the population aged fifteen to sixty-four, was 38 percent in the 1920s, falling to − 4.5 percent in the 1930s and 1940s and then for the post–second world war period contributing an average of 45 percent to the growth of the working age population (H. P. Brown 1979). If the children of migrants are also accounted for, the postwar contribution is larger – of the order

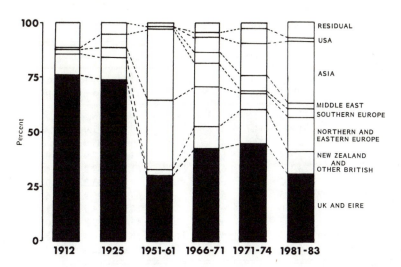

Figure 10.2. Net migration gain by origin 1912–83 (percentage share).
Notes: Origin refers to country, 1912 and 1925; nationality, 1951–61;
birthplace, 1966–74, 1981–3. The Australian born are excluded from
the last two classifications. "Residual" refers to "other" and "not
stated". *Sources:* Commonwealth Bureau of Census and Statistics. *Demography Bulletin*; Charles Price and Jean Martin, *Australian Immigration: A Bibliography and Digest* (Department of Demography,
Australian National University, 1975), no. 3, part 1, Table 2; Australian Bureau of Statistics, *Overseas Arrivals and Departures, Country
of Birth*.

of 60 percent. The government role in this process has been to induce
and select migrants, to subsidise passage to Australia, and to facilitate
settlement with a range of post-arrival services. Of the 3.35 million
postwar migrant arrivals, 2.02 million have received government passage
subsidy.

Labour force participation

From the working age population so determined by economic demography, the aggregate workforce depends upon labour force participation
behaviour. Table 10.2 shows the labour force share of total population
and of population aged fifteen to sixty-four, for census years 1901 to
1981. The overall stability previously mentioned is evident. But it is also
apparent that substantial changes have occurred within the labour force.
The most notable of these are the declining participation of younger

Table 10.2 *Population and labour force, 1901–81*

Census year	Total pop. (000)	Pop. 15–64 (000)	Labour force (000)	Labour force participation (%)					
				All ages	15–64	Females 10+	Males 15–19	Males 65+	Married women
1901[a]	3,774	2,296	1,615	42.8	70.3	N.A.	N.A.	N.A.	N.A.
1911	4,455	2,853	1,990	44.7	69.8	22.5	90.0	87.0	N.A.
1921	5,436	3,470	2,329	42.8	67.1	21.0	86.4	85.9	N.A.
1933	6,630	4,379	2,744	41.4	62.7	18.1	73.0	37.9	2.0
1947	7,579	5,970	3,196	42.2	63.0	19.0	81.1	38.2	3.4
1954	8,987	5,677	3,702	41.2	65.2	19.0	79.7	33.2	7.0
1961	10,508	6,437	4,225	40.2	65.6	20.4	69.6	26.9	9.6
1966	11,550	7,172	4,856	42.0	67.7	25.0	66.2	24.9	14.1
1971	12,928	8,021	5,563	43.0	69.4	26.7	55.7	22.2	18.0
1976	13,916	8,876	6,131	44.1	69.1	32.4	56.0	16.8	22.3
1981	14,927	9,747	6,719	45.0	68.9	34.5	61.0	12.3	22.2

[a]The 1901 census in Queensland did not include labour force questions. Queensland is therefore imputed at New South Wales rates.
Source: Census of Australia.

and older males and the increased participation of women, particularly married women. The change in the latter case is dramatic, from a low 2 to 3 percent of the female workforce in 1947 to around 22 percent of a much expanded female workforce in 1981: a tenfold increase in share. Thus within the seeming stability of the aggregate growth of the population and of the workforce there have been major compositional changes: What was a male workforce of British origin in 1900 has become a much more diversified workforce, with major non-British and female presence, and mostly this has happened since the second world war.

The joint significance of these postwar changes is well illustrated in recent work by Zagorski (in press), who finds that social mobility between economic sectors and branches in the postwar period has come from migrants initially expanding and then sustaining manufacturing employment, and married women facilitating the expansion of the service sector, particularly in the "post-industrial" areas. It was these new entrants to the workforce and not relocation by established workers across industries that provided essential mobility for structural change. School leavers tended to replicate the existing structure. It is important therefore to examine the implications of low migration and ultimate limitations on continued increases in married female labour force participation for future structural change in Australia. In many other countries structural change is facilitated by drawing upon a low productivity rural labour force. Australia had no such reserves. Migration and married women have been the source of augmentation and adjustment instead. On the other hand, the low share of manufacturing employment in Australia does reduce the retraining burden required for expansion of service employment, not the case in Europe.

Education

A final major change in the nature of the workforce has been in the education levels of workers. At 1900 schooling was compulsory to age thirteen years, and government primary schools were free or nearly free and open to all. Private schools were not subsidised, and secondary and tertiary education was subsidised but had substantial fees and very small enrolments. The workforce was literate but not well educated. This position changed gradually over the next forty-five years. Government-financed high schools were established, as were technical schools and colleges. But admission to high schools was highly restricted and based on competitive entry, and technical education was mostly part time, geared to the needs of apprenticeship, and provided as a supplement to on-the-job training. In consequence public education outlays as a share of GDP had drifted up from under 0.9 percent early in the century to only 1.4 percent in 1938/9.

The period after the second world war saw tremendous change. Partly in response to a belief in the strategic importance of education for economic growth, state outlays on education burgeoned. The 1964 Martin report was quite explicit in its commitment to a human capital approach: "Education should be regarded as an investment which yields direct and significant economic benefits through increasing the skill of the population and through accelerating technical progress" (Committee on the Future of Tertiary Education in Australia 1964: vol. 1, p. 4). In 1950/1 public education outlays were 1.75 percent of GDP. By 1982/3 they were 5.4 percent.

Resources available to primary education had expanded, secondary education for all was opened up, and tertiary education funded by government was expanded dramatically, including the new sector, the college of advanced education. Moreover, government direct provision and operation of education facilities, free or nearly free of fees, were supplemented by subsidy of private schools and provision of cash benefits to students. Australian education has expanded 4.5 times in enrolments since 1901, and, on top of that, there has been a tenfold increase in real resources per enrolment.

The postwar era has truly been a golden age for education. But there was a Cinderella. This was technical education, where the philosophy of predominant industry provision of training still prevailed. Technical enrolments did grow, but funding was not nearly commensurate. This pattern was reversed a little from the mid 1970s with improved attention, organisation, and funding, but technical education has only just begun to awake from a long slumber of seventy-five years. It is only in quite recent times that alternative ideas such as pre-apprentice training, block release, sandwich courses, group training, general technical education, and the like have gained currency (Committee of Inquiry into Labour Market Progress 1985). In its review of Australian technical education, the OECD (1977) pointed out that, in terms of resources devoted to it, technical education was the smallest sector of public education but had twice the enrolment equivalents of the universities and colleges combined.

The historical neglect by government of technical education has been based on private provision of training within Australia and has been facilitated by the ability to resort to immigration of skilled workers during periods of skill shortages. It is therefore appropriate that when the Whitlam Labor government deliberately sought to reduce migration inflow it also sought to expand technical training in Australia.

The expansion of educational opportunity in the postwar period is dramatic by prewar standards. But it is important to put this achievement into international perspective. If enrolment rates or expenditure rates are compared internationally, Australia still ranks towards the lower end of the education spectrum for the industrial countries. Figures from the OECD (1977) for enrolment rates in full-time education in 1975 are given in Table 10.3.

Undoubtedly an important part of the difference in enrolment rates is due particularly to the restrictions on technical education (Australia Tripartite Mission 1969). It is not clear that substantial expansion in most other areas of education would provide commensurate benefits for Australia. In the one study of rates of return to postsecondary education in Australia that includes trade education, Selby-Smith (1975) found social and private benefit–cost ratios for certificate, trade technician, and trade courses that uniformly and substantially exceeded those for College of Advanced Education (CAE) and university courses at all levels.

10.6   Labour market operation and performance

Real wages

A primary measure of labour market success for workers is the growth of real wages provided. This can come either from productivity growth

Table 10.3 OECD *education enrolment rates, 1975 (percentages)*

Country	Ages 15–19		Ages 20–24	
	Males	Females	Males	Females
Australia	45.0	43.9	6.7	4.1
Canada	67.3	65.4	18.3	10.7
France	50.5	56.0	14.8	8.6
Germany (West)	52.9	43.0	15.0	9.8
Italy	48.1	38.2	20.5	12.9
Japan	76.1	75.0	19.8	9.0
Netherlands	64.4	50.3	17.7	6.7
New Zealand	43.3	39.3	7.9	4.7
Sweden	58.3	55.6	14.1	14.6
United Kingdom	44.4	44.8	9.3	6.1
United States	72.1	71.9	24.4	18.8
Mean	56.6	53.0	15.3	9.6

Source: OECD 1977.

or from changing share of wages in output. In the long run, real wages have accorded closely with productivity growth in Australia, as is seen in Table 10.4. This has meant a threefold increase in real wages since the turn of the century.

The close trend correspondence between labour productivity and real wages implies a long-run uniformity in share of the benefits of growth as between labour income and profits. However, where there is a divergence of productivity and real wages in particular periods, so there is a variation in labour's share of national product. The divergence is known in contemporary jargon as "real wage overhang", and there have been five major periods of such divergence historically. An escalation of real wages above productivity took place in the early 1920s and became locked in through the 1920s by the adoption of quarterly indexation in 1923 (Pope 1982b). A second shift took place in the late 1920s but quickly dissipated with the onset of depression. A third major shift in wages occurred during and immediately after World War II, but thereafter general decline is evident until a very marked increase in labour's share of GDP took place in the early 1970s, when, in contrast to the 1920s, real wage gains did not become locked in despite a form of indexation of wages. A further real wage push was experienced in 1981 (Covick 1982).

It is notable that each of these periods of overhang (or marked increase in labour's share of GDP) is characterised by an increase in union share of workforce and of industrial strike activity (Table 10.6). However, the

Table 10.4. *Wages and productivity, 1900–81*

Financial year	Labour productivity[a]	Real wages (hourly award, males)	Nominal wages (hourly award, males)	Weekly hours of work[b]	Labour share of manufacturing value added (%)
	Index 1913–14 = 100				
1901	85	105	79	N.A.	N.A.
1914	100	100	100	48.9	55.2
1921	105	102	164	47.1	57.9
1929	103	128	193	45.3	55.9
1932	110	133	168	45.5	53.3
1939	108	136	184	44.9	54.2
1949	136	163	336	40.0	60.2
1959	177	177	693	40.0	53.9
1969	222	211	1,048	39.2	52.3
1976	254	278	2,520	37.1	56.0
1981	267	273	4,013	36.6	52.3
1984	285	280	5,299	36.4	51.2

[a]Real GDP per person employed.
[b]Excluding overtime.
Sources: Boehm 1979; Pope 1982; and updated from Australian Bureau of Statistics, *Year Book Australia*, "Award Rates of Pay Indexes" (6312.0), June 1985, and *Manufacturing Establishments, Summary of Operations* (8202.0), 1983–4.

gains made during such expansionary and active phases are lost in subsequent phases of the cycle, so that the long-run trend is to keep real wages in accord with productivity growth and not to induce permanent shifts in factor shares of income.

In 1921 the jump in real wages came also with major increases in awards, but in the immediate postwar, early 1970s, and 1981 experiences earnings moved ahead of awards. The more common denominator is union aggressiveness in the face of accelerating inflation. Of course, cause and effect here are difficult to disentangle, but there is evidence of the significant contribution of union pressure (Perry 1981). At most – and even this does not necessarily follow – it seems that the arbitral system may have kept real wages from fully adjusting downwards subsequently, because of full or partial indexation, but did not bring about the initial wages explosion.

Similarly, despite some common preconceptions to the contrary, international evidence for the bulk of the postwar period found Australian real and nominal wage responsiveness to be actually significantly less sluggish than the collective bargaining–based United Kingdom system and marginally less so than the free market United States system of wage determination. To that extent Australian arbitral arrangements did not rigidify our economic adjustment processes. On the other hand, postwar Australian wage flexibility has been a little less than for Sweden and much less than for countries such as Austria and Japan, where a strong link between wage determination and market imbalance does persist (Coe and Gagliardi 1985; Grubb, Jackman, and Layard 1983).

Relative wages

Concern over whether wages adjust in response to market imbalance also applies to relative wages. The economist's idealised image of a well-functioning market is the auction market, whereby relative prices adjust quickly to accommodate changes in underlying supply and demand forces. Along these lines the Treasury (1979: 53) has concluded that "the arbitral tribunals, awards, national wage cases and other paraphernalia of the Australian system (including, notably, unions and employers insulated from competitive forces) must, in important respects, have led to less favourable results than those which might have been attained under a more market-orientated system".

What have been the historical movements in wage relativities in Australia? A plethora of relativities could be considered, but the most important are industry and occupation differentials on the requirements side of the market and differentials by sociodemographic groups on the social side of the labour market. As for industrial differentials, Keating (1983) shows for the postwar period to 1979 that there is a considerable stability in relative industry earnings, the major changes being a trend increase in the chemicals and construction groups' relativities and a decline in commerce and finance and business services' relativities.

As for occupational differentials, comprehensive data are largely unavailable on a long-term basis. Some insight can be gained from award rates for skilled and unskilled categories. Hancock and Moore (1972) show a countercyclical compression of skill relativities for the period 1914 to 1966, and this relationship persists if their study is updated to the more recent period. The award pattern underestimates relativities to the extent of overaward payments, as documented for the metal trades for the period to 1929 by Forster and Harris (1983) and for the postwar period by Isaac (1965). Making allowance for overaward pay, the Australian skill relativity experience looks similar to the historical pattern in countries such as the United Kingdom, the United States, and Germany (Bray and Boschan 1962).

On the sociodemographic side, a major feature of the postwar labour market is that increased female employment has been accompanied by increased female wage relativities. It is not often appreciated that in almost all of the twenty years after 1960 average female wages and employment rose by a greater percentage than for males (Gregory and Duncan 1981). The longer-term picture is female award wages set at 48.2 percent of male rates in 1914 and remaining at that level until 1939, when the ratio increased to 53.6 percent. Further increases came in 1945 (to 60.6 percent) and in 1950 (to 70.4 percent), and there were small increases in the 1960s and 1970s; the equal pay decision of 1972 lifted the relativity from 74.2 percent to 77.8 percent in that year and to 86.4 percent by 1974. By 1981 the average adult male award was only 5 percent greater than the female award. In 1969 the arbitration commission conceded the principle of equal pay for equal work. In 1972 the principle became equal pay for work of equal value.

It is sometimes claimed that the male–female wage differential represents discrimination in the labour market. Similar claims also apply for migrant and nonmigrant wages, though no awards are made on the basis of birthplace. However, if the contributing influence of differing education, experience, and language proficiency is allowed for, then it is found that the wages discrepancy diminishes greatly within industries or occupations. In the case of migrants it largely disappears, but for women some residual difference remains (Chapman and Miller 1982). It is clear that any discrimination really relates more to factors influencing occupational preparation and choice within the family and the education system than to discrimination within the labour market. This is an important distinction in terms of appropriate policy response. In the case of women's employment, the choice now is whether to move further to equal pay for comparable worth (that is, to even stronger parities across occupations without significant reference to demand for the work relative to supply of labour), which is being pressed for in the United States, or to move directly to reducing the occupational segmentation by which women typically concentrate in a narrow range of occupations. The former is an arbitrator's nightmare and the latter is an uphill battle, since it involves the whole area of attitude formation. Power (1975) shows that the degree of employment segmentation for women has changed little since the 1890s, despite the other dramatic changes in women's employment and wages since World War II. The expansion of women's employment has come from traditionally female occupations. In 1911, 75 percent of the total female workforce was in occupations where over 50 percent of the workforce is female. In 1977 this figure remained exactly the same (Power 1975). Lewis (1983) shows that segregation has not declined since 1977.

One final area of wage relativity much discussed in recent years is youth wages relative to adult wages. The rising level and share of youth unemployment since the mid 1970s have drawn attention to the possible contribution thereto of youth wage relativities. Youth award wages have risen steadily from 62.2 percent of adult awards in 1970 to 66.2 percent in 1982. A recent Bureau of Labour Market Research study (1983) finds that this change can explain some part of changes in youth unemployment, but only a part.

Given these movements in relative wages, how much have they been determined by market imbalance? The Treasury view quoted earlier was that the Australian wage-fixing system causes marked divergence from appropriate flexibility and hence from efficient reallocation of labour. And work by Pope (1982b) for the period 1900 to 1930 and by Freebairn and Withers (1977) for the period after World War II finds wage changes by industry and occupation quite unresponsive to market imbalance as measured by relative unemployment and job vacancies. Market adjustment seems to take place more through quantities ("job opportunities") or quality (including "credentialisation") than through wage movements (Blandy and Richardson 1982). The countercyclical movement in the skilled to unskilled ratio observed by Hancock and Moore (1972) is said to reflect an equity motivation on the part of tribunals to allow skilled workers to take the brunt of economic adjustments, and Pope (1982b: 126) concludes that "wage regulation was not without cost to the working class".

But this conclusion is premature. As with absolute real and nominal wage movements, it must be asked what would have happened in the absence of arbitration. An attempt to answer this is provided by Withers, Pitman, and Wittingham (1983), who examined the relationship between labour market pressure and relative wage changes for common industries and regions for four countries over a common time period. The countries were the United States, the United Kingdom, Sweden, and Australia, reflecting a wage-fixing spectrum from free market through decentralised collective bargaining and centralised "consensus" bargaining to arbitration. The conclusion was that the Australian experience was common to all four countries, irrespective of wage-fixing system. It seems that underlying relative wage determinations are more fundamental economic and social forces than mere wage-fixing institutions. Phrases such as "implicit contracts", "internal labour markets", and "interdependent utilities" begin to capture some of the phenomenon (Thurow 1982) and to explain the general historical rigidity of even the U.S. wage system.

For these reasons it is also not very surprising to find that the Australian industrial and occupational relativity structure does not diverge very significantly from overseas countries such as the United States and the United Kingdom, despite the institutional and other differences (Brown et al. 1978; Hughes 1973; Norris 1980). What is called "comparative wage justice" by Australians is to be found in the United States labelled as "pattern bargaining" and in the United Kingdom as "fair comparisons". Indeed the doctrine of comparative wage justice itself was well entrenched in Australia before tribunals came on the scene (Isaac 1985: 20).

Much of the evidence here is in terms of occupations and industries, but the same point may even apply to some sociodemographic differentials such as female relativities. Mitchell (1983) thought that Australia's equal pay decisions were the most important demonstration of the autonomous role of arbitral tribunals. But he failed to discern the similar movements in European countries (OECD 1980). Only in the United States amongst major industrial countries was there no such movement in the early 1970s, so that the United States, not Australian, experience most needs special explanation. An apparently faster and greater change of female relativities in Australia may owe something to the arbitration commission.

Mitchell (1983: 12) also thought the rise in relative wages for youth after 1974 was due to arbitration. Indeed, then retiring Treasury Secretary John Stone asserted in 1984 that there was no single fact more disgraceful to the conduct of our national affairs than youth unemployment, which fact he ascribed directly to "a system of wage determination under which trade union leaders and people preening themselves as 'Justices' of various arbitration benches combine to put young people in particular, but many others also, out of work" (*Australian Financial Review*, August 28, 1984, p. 8). But Deputy President Isaac of the commission has pointed out that these decisions were ratifications of private agreements (Isaac 1985: 28). Isaac could have added that Britain has youth relativities similar to Australia's, despite the absence of compulsory arbitration.

In all, the Australian experience with arbitration-based wage fixing does not appear to have produced relative wage outcomes very different from overseas experience. There are some exceptions to this, but the general position seems clear. Accordingly Keating (1983) has similarly concluded that Australian industrial relativities have met the needs of the postwar labour market reasonably well, though he gives wage flexibility (and high response elasticities) a higher role than the Withers et al. (1983) study indicated is the case. In both cases considerable emphasis is laid upon a highly mobile and adaptable workforce. It is therefore interesting to put this into longer-term perspective (see the next section).

Table 10.5 *Job mobility: median duration in current job*

Country	Year	Median duration (years)
Australia	1981	3.3
Canada	1983	4.3
France	1978	7.2
Germany (West	1972	5.3
Italy	1972	5.0
Japan	1982	13.0
Netherlands	1972	5.1
United Kingdom	1979	5.5
United States	1983	4.2

Source: OECD, *Employment Outlook*, September 1984.

Mobility

Mauldon (1928) collected labour market gross flow data and found that the number of workers leaving an employer in any twelve-month period was above a minimum of 19 percent of average employment. The Australian Bureau of Statistics finds that for the late 1970s around 15 percent of workers change jobs within any twelve-month period.

Another measure of mobility is internal migration. The Australian historical pattern since 1900 has been that of high population mobility but overall settlement inertia. The establishment of Canberra is the only really substantial settlement change in Australia since 1900. But perhaps the high population mobility that has accompanied this settlement rigidity may begin to diminish now as a result of married female labour force participation and the mobility difficulties thereby faced for two-income families. Be that as it may, it is telling that one indicator of internal mobility, Australian-born persons resident in a state other than that of birth, was 10.6 percent in 1901 and 11.7 percent in 1981. The intermediate census figures fluctuate between these levels, indicating considerable stability in movement levels over eighty years (Brosnan 1984; Rowland 1979).

A related measure is the average duration of current jobs. Table 10.5 provides some international perspective to Australian experience; it is observed that, despite the major differences in wage-setting institutions, Australian and North American median job durations are not markedly divergent. Indeed Australia had the highest job mobility of any OECD

country in the 1970s and early 1980s. The marked contrast, as is often
the case, is with the Japanese system.

Industrial peace

It is valuable to extend the exercise of international comparisons further
and consider industrial peace. The Australian history has been considered above (see also Table 10.6). What can now be added is that, even
in its historically most strike-prone decade, the 1970s, Australia is only
in the middle range of OECD countries in terms of the most statistically
reliable strike indicator, namely working days lost per thousand
employees.

For the period 1970 to 1979, and for all industries and services, extreme rates of 1,516 and 1,403 days lost per thousand employees were
recorded in Italy and Iceland, with lows between 2 and 54 days lost for
Switzerland, Sweden, Austria, West Germany, and Norway. The Australian figure was 675, compared with 572 for the United Kingdom and
515 for the United States (Creigh and Makeham 1982).

What is also interesting is that Creigh and Makeham find that if they
statistically control for inflation and unemployment as explanations of
strike behaviour, they account for a significant proportion of stoppage
variation, and that only Canada, Italy, and Spain experience significantly
greater stoppage rates than might be expected given inflation and unemployment rates.

This finding still leaves open the possibility that industrial relations
institutions may influence strike activity through their effects on inflation
and unemployment. Insofar as this influence could operate through
wages, it has been concluded above that there has been little to choose
in the past between the Australian, United Kingdom, United States,
and Swedish styles of system in relation to microeconomic efficiency
and that there is at least a small Australian advantage in relation to
aggregate wage responsiveness vis-à-vis the United Kingdom and perhaps even the United States. The improved wage flexibility of the United
States in the mid 1980s may not be due to any change in labour market
structure; it may owe more to the import shock effect on manufacturing
of the overvalued U.S. dollar. Further, in relation to aggregate wage
flexibility, such countries as Norway, Austria, Germany, Switzerland,
and Japan evinced a clear superiority to both the United States and
Australia. Bearing this in mind, let us move to one further criterion of
economic performance, namely, productivity growth.

Table 10.6 *Australian unionisation since 1913*

Years	No. of unions	Average size of unions (000)	Union share of workforce (%)	No. of strikes per worker	Days lost per worker involved due to strikes
1913–20	404	1.41	26.78	0.19	16.41
1921–30	377	2.15	33.23	0.16	14.13
1931–40	363	2.27	29.41	0.09	6.86
1941–50	372	3.54	39.98	0.27	4.43
1951–60	368	4.84	46.24	0.34	2.01
1961–70	345	6.11	44.08	0.31	1.63
1971–80	332	8.31	45.28	0.39	2.45
1981–4	324	9.29	43.36	0.32	3.04

Source: Australian Bureau of Statistics, *Labour Reports*; *Trade Union Statistics*.

Productivity growth

This section on labour market operation and performance began with the observation that productivity growth determines long-run real wage movements. But whereas Australia's aggregate growth performance has been impressive (partly because of immigration), its productivity performance (closely related to GDP per capita) is less so. The historical trend is discussed in Chapter 1, but it is worth recalling here that in the postwar period productivity has progressively declined, decade by decade. Productivity growth of 2.9 percent in the 1950s reduced to 2.4 percent in the 1960s and an average of 1.9 percent in the 1970s.

Long-run productivity decline for Australia might be expected with the changing structure of industry. The decline in the share of output from agriculture for a country that starts with high-productivity agriculture means that continued productivity growth cannot be obtained when low-productivity rural workers move into manufacturing. Instead of drawing on domestic surplus labour in the form of an abundant domestic rural population, Australia has drawn on international labour via immigration. The picture is partially brightened if we acknowledge the income increases experienced by migrants relative to home country incomes, and if Australia's advanced movement to shorter working hours is incorporated. These and other factors related to interpretations of movement in the standard of living are considered in Chapter 12.

Another part of the explanation is the measurement convention of valuing services at input cost. As an economy shifts more toward services, the measured productivity growth will decline, ceteris paribus. Similarly, in recession a productivity retardation can also be due to underutilised labour employed. However, these factors are broadly common to the advanced industrial nations and so do not explain major cross country differences as opposed to intertemporal trends. Accordingly what is not basically altered by such measurement factors is the fact that, in international terms, what was possibly the world's wealthiest nation (in per capita terms) in 1890 had fallen decisively to the second rank of nations by 1984. But so had Britain and New Zealand, and so will soon the United States and Canada.

Partial answers to enhanced productivity growth for Australia might be sought in product market and services deregulation, especially tariff and quota reductions. The historical link between protection and arbitration was noted above; it is therefore clear that arbitration has played an indirect role in reducing productivity growth in this way. The tariff issue is pursued further in Chapter 7. However, it should be pointed out, lest too much be expected, that most of the successful economies are riddled with regulatory restrictions too (Withers 1983).

More compelling is the evidence regarding extensive, modern, and well-supported systems of industrial training in these countries. There is little correlation between general tertiary education and productivity growth across countries. There does seem more correlation with industrial training support and effectiveness. In the United States, the United Kingdom, and Australia, primitive systems of training apply, though recent United Kingdom reforms are promising. The long neglect of technical and further education as part of education in Australia was discussed above. Even more, the long neglect of state support of on-the-job training must now be stressed. In 1983/4 the federal government appropriation for education was $4,211 million. By contrast, the appropriation for trade and skills training was $141 million, or 0.03 percent of the education outlay. It is reasonable to assume that ready access to overseas labour supplies is a major explanation of Australia's poor training performance.

Successive federal and state government policies appear to have assumed that industry training is a matter for industry finance, not public finance. Yet the government funds the greater part of training costs for a whole host of other occupations, and education costs for private consumption. The equity of this funding arrangement is not clear, nor is its efficiency. Predominant reliance upon private employer initiative alone is quite inadequate in the presence of the market imperfections inherent in the training process. It is also relevant to recognise that in West Germany and Switzerland apprentices average 20 percent of adult pay rates. In Britain the figure is 60 percent and in Australia 66 percent. The activity surrounding the 1984 Committee of Inquiry into Labour Market Progress (Kirby inquiry) indicates an increasingly widespread recognition of the importance of these training issues. The Commonwealth and state governments have begun to increase support for industrial training by the young, and, at the same time, active debate was emerging in the mid 1980s over the issue of increased "freeing up" or "privatisation" of the traditional postsecondary education sector.

There is undoubtedly much, much more to the economic success of the countries identified than wage flexibility and training. Some of these factors are covered elsewhere in this book. But one additional and fundamental labour market factor might now be stressed. This is prompted by recognition that what characterises the high-productivity advanced industrial nations is that their whole industrial ethos is different; it can be summed up as "cohesion" or "consensus" or "cooperative prosperity". The difference is not so much the institutional structure of labour markets in these countries, but the attitudes of the parties.

It is here that the historical perspective on Australian labour 1900 to 1984 may be pertinent. Australia's industrial system is based on legally imposed adversary relationships in which the relevant parties take no responsibility for encouraging sound workplace relationships. There might have been a chance under the conciliation function for this to be otherwise, but the determination of Australian industrial judges to become and remain arbitral centralised wage fixers, and the compliance of employers and unions in this, could have nullified any such achievement. This could be a real cost of the arbitral system – not any direct effects on wage levels, relativities, or strikes, but the subtle effects on workplace cooperation and functions.

This conclusion must be tentative, since it remains true that the United Kingdom's record of bad workplace industrial relations is similar to Australia's, and arises without benefit of arbitration tribunals. The argument would have to be that Australia lacked the entrenched class hostility of the United Kingdom and had a chance to revive and build on the relatively harmonious working relationships of the second half of the nineteenth century in order to continue to provide a more cooperative working society than Britain did. This chance may have been lost by the resort to a compulsory arbitration system that operated via formal adversary relationships. Of course, an alternative view can be advanced that holds that institutions and attitudes common to all the Anglo-American countries have produced productivity retardation in all of those countries alike.

Actually the arbitration system, with a finely honed sense of self-preservation, is currently evincing a renewed interest in working life issues, as seen in the federal tribunal's 1984 job protection decision and the Victorian Industrial Commission's technological change consultation decision of the same year. Such working life issues are also being assiduously pursued directly by governments, as in equal opportunity, industrial democracy, and occupational health and safety. Of course workplace matters have long been the day-to-day essence of Australian industrial relations. But they have been relegated to inferior status, treated on an ad hoc basis, and handled badly. This is changing in the 1980s, and this is appropriate. Whether Australia's poor performance on constructive workplace cooperation is due to arbitration or not, it is clear that, like the United Kingdom, Australia needs a new industrial relations. It also seems clear that this is an area less suited to centralised arbitration procedures, so that it is possible that tribunals' attempts to involve themselves extensively in such issues might need to be resisted, given evidence of a desire for constructive reform emanating increasingly from the workplace itself and from government when some uniformity is required.

Unemployment

Real wages for Australian workers in employment have historically been high. But the Australian achievement has become soured by two things. One is the decline in relative international wage levels over the century, as discussed above. The other is the problem of unemployment.

Before World War II there was hardly a period when unemployment fell below 4 percent of the workforce, and during the great depression it reached 25.3 percent (Forster 1985). During the long postwar boom the position was better, and Australia did record one of the lowest average levels of unemployment amongst industrial countries over thirty years, with unemployment varying from 1.5 percent to 3 percent. However, since 1974 the relative deterioration in the unemployment position has been even greater for Australia than for most OECD economies (Norton and McDonald 1981), and the levels of unemployment in the mid 1980s of nearly 10 percent are above those for any time this century in Australia except for the great depression. In 1945 the Curtin government issued an epochal paper on full employment (White Paper on Full Employment in Australia 1945) that committed it to the maintenance of full employment. That commitment has not been fulfilled since 1974, and prospects for its restoration are not promising, given a decade now of high unemployment.

However, there is a major difference in post–second world war unemployment, including that since 1974. In the pre-1939 period the predominant attitude was that to provide adequate unemployment compensation would induce "bludging" at public expense. Sustenance and relief work were provided by the states during the depression. But before then government assistance to the unemployed comprised either indirect assistance in the form of subsidies granted to private charities or special financial assistance to destitute persons. The exception was Queensland, which passed an Unemployed Workers Insurance Act in 1923.

It was only in 1945 that commonwealth unemployment benefits were commenced. They were established providing differential rates for juniors and adults and for single and married unemployed persons, but the benefits were funded from general revenue, they were not income-related, and they could be received as long as unemployment continued. Many overseas systems of unemployment are based on insurance and are income-related and of fixed duration. It is argued by some that unemployment benefit improvements in the 1970s have contributed to unemployment since 1974 (Harper 1979). It is also possible that the availability of such benefits alters attitudes in negotiations over wages.

It is only in the 1970s that manpower programmes have begun to be adopted as an ongoing part of an active labour market policy in Australia. Since then a range of programmes involving training, retraining, and job creation have been instituted – the two largest schemes being the Regional Employment Development Scheme (REDS) of the Whitlam Labor government and the Community Employment Program (CEP) of the Hawke Labor government. It is said that such schemes help disguise true levels of unemployment, so that official unemployment figures underestimate underlying unemployment. The REDS and CEP schemes are explicitly public sector job creation schemes, which may reduce the job creation potential below that which would result from the same public outlay on private sector wage subsidies. Private sector support is already an accepted principle in other parts of the manpower programme structure, but these other schemes currently receive much less funding. And overall funding for Australian manpower programmes is small. In 1979/ 80 Australia spent $126 per head on manpower programmes compared with $174 for West Germany, $232 for the United States, $274 for Canada, and $551 for Sweden (McMahon and Robinson 1984). Swedish official unemployment remained under 2 percent. Those who assert that manpower programmes cannot sustain full employment have Boulding's Law to contend with: "If it exists, it is possible." What might have more substance are claims that the costs of such an approach are too high. But this needs to be articulated, not asserted.

Another source of hidden unemployment is discouraged workers. Since official statistics record only persons actively seeking work, those discouraged from seeking work because they believe suitable work will not be found are excluded from the regular statistics. Some estimates put total unemployment, including discouraged workers, at almost twice the official recorded level (Sheehan and Stricker 1982). A further complication is that when persons can pursue other social services in the face of job market problems, this too can make interpretation difficult; for example early retirement for the older unemployed (Merrilees 1982; Sheehan and Stricker 1983). Other problems of interpretation arise when considering the issue of the "black", or hidden, economy, which is alleged to have increased in recent decades and which can absorb significant unrecorded employment (Carter 1983). The hidden economy may have involved employment of around 150,000 persons in the early 1980s (Fisher 1983).

Work hours and conditions

In addition to increased real wages, shorter working hours can be a major benefit to workers that results from the evolution of the labour market. In Australia skilled tradespeople had achieved relatively low hours by 1890, but the bulk of workers worked considerably longer. The range then was from forty-four to forty-eight hours for the skilled trades up to seventy hours or more for unskilled transport workers (New South Wales *Statistical Register* 1889: 433).

With the establishment of the arbitral system at the turn of the century, the spread of shorter hours became a major aim of the union movement. A forty-eight-hour working week was taken as the initial arbitration norm by the commonwealth court, but a reduced working week was progressively awarded to trades with difficult working conditions. Weekly hours of work from 1913/14 are indicated in Table 10.4. In 1920 Justice Higgins sought to extend the forty-four-hour week further, using as a pace setter the timber workers' case, and he explicitly used the passing on of productivity increase in shorter hours as a criterion (Maddock and Carter 1984). This decision was opposed by the government, and Prime Minister Hughes amended the court's legislation to require a three-judge court for cases considering standard hours. Higgins resigned in protest over this and other issues of political interference, and the union movement turned to state legislation and awards to provide for reductions in hours. These were achieved in 1925 in New South Wales and Queensland and were gradually extended across other states and at the federal level throughout the 1920s, through a mixture of legislation and awards. By the end of the 1920s most workers were on a forty-four-hour standard week.

The next great reduction in the standard working week came in 1948, with the federal court having agreed to a reduction to forty hours. The Labor government in New South Wales had anticipated this decision and legislated there for the shorter week from July 1947. Again, pace-setter unions had preceded the general hours decisions, but in 1947/8 "flow on" was rapid, as it had not been in the 1920s.

Thereafter the standard work week remained at forty hours until the late 1970s. There was little concerted effort by the union movement for a reduction until the launching of the thirty-five-hour-week campaigns based upon specific industry factors in the late 1970s, followed by more general campaigns in the 1980s.

Overall the result is a drop in weekly hours from around fifty hours in 1900 to under thirty-seven hours by 1981, excluding overtime. However, overtime has increased so that the effective reduction in hours is less than the standard hours changes would indicate.

Of significance equal to or greater than standard hours changes is the move to part-time work. Associated with increased married female labour force participation, and particularly evident since 1974, the part-time workforce share of employment numbers rose from 11.9 percent in 1974 to 16.5 percent by 1981. Though this is consistent with broad overseas trends, the Australian increase was greater than elsewhere, putting Australia at 1981 second only to Sweden with its part-time workforce share of 25 percent (*Economist,* June 16, 1984).

The changes in weekly hours have been supplemented by changes in other paid leave provisions. Paid annual leave of one week was first introduced in commonwealth awards in 1936 and was extended to two weeks in 1945, three weeks in 1963, and four weeks in 1974. Other improvements include extended sick leave provisions and long-service leave entitlements.

The whole process of determination of working conditions has been sporadic and fragmented. The result has been a greater diversity of conditions than is common for wage movements. In part this is due to the often discontinuous nature of such changes – and hence the more ready involvement of state governments as well as tribunals. It is also due to a greater intrinsic need for diversity to reflect particular occupational and industrial work situations. General principles have not

been readily forthcoming in this area; the difficulties facing recent re-
newal of interest by tribunals in such working life issues were discussed above.

It appears that Australian work hours were much shorter than in many
other countries earlier in the century, but they are now closer to common
international practice. The recent thirty-five-hour-week push started earlier in Australia than in most countries, but there is clearly a general
movement in this direction developing overseas, for example in West
Germany in 1984.

It might be mentioned that many nonwage conditions of employment,
including paid sick leave, leave loadings, and annual leave, raise the
cost of labour to firms beyond the direct wages paid. This is also true
of imposts such as compulsory worker's compensation levies and payroll
tax. It is likely that such indirect labour costs have risen significantly as
a share of total labour costs in the last fifteen years, as they have in all
OECD countries except Italy. The Australian 1983 guesstimate of 34.5
percent nonwage labour costs is at the high end of the spectrum for the
Anglo-American countries and Japan, but is below the continental European norm, which is 40 to 45 percent (*Economist,* June 16, 1984: 39).
This higher rate of growth of "on-costs" than wages means they are of
increasing relative significance in influencing employment growth in
Australia.

Finally, brief attention might be given to workplace health and safety.
Brief, because the basic system of regulation was laid down at the turn
of the century and remained relatively unchanged until a recent revival
of interest in the 1980s. Towards the end of the nineteenth century some
liberal concern over "sweating" and racist concern over domestic
Chinese labour competition arose and led to a combination of Factories
and Shops Acts and Early Closing Acts that sought to provide for minimum standards of safety and hygiene at the workplace. Enactments
began in the 1890s and were in place in all states by the end of the first
decade of the century. Factory inspections were the main vehicle for
regulatory enforcement (Coghlan 1918). The same period also saw the
enactment of Australia's worker's compensation legislation covering
workplace injury and removing the liability from the employee for self-
insurance or demonstration of employer negligence. This complex of
worker protection legislation has remained in place relatively unchanged
for eighty years, another element in the remarkable institutional labour
market stability in Australia. However, rising consciousness of occupational health and injury problems on the part of workers and concern
over rising insurance costs for employers have begun to force a revision
of these arrangements.

10.7   Conclusion

By early in the twentieth century the predominantly laissez-faire Australian labour market of the second half of the nineteenth century had been transformed. The elements of a significant regulatory structure had been erected and institutions put in place that would remain into the 1980s. These included compulsory arbitration and comprehensive legal minimum wages, high levels of (craft-based) unionisation, apprentice-based trade training, government-supplied formal education, occupational safety and health legislation based on factory inspection, and use of compulsory employer-paid accident compensation schemes.

Substantial stabilities are also evident in other aspects of the labour market over this long period since federation. The paid workforce remained at around 40 percent of the population at the end of the period just as it was at the beginning. The government employment share had not altered dramatically, and the workforce was highly urban, postindustrial, and literate, with high real wages. A large proportion of workers were overseas born, and employment was significantly segmented on the basis of sex.

Naturally such stability has not been without cyclical variation. Unemployment rates, participation rates, wage–skill relativities and wage shares, immigration levels, unionisation rates, and the like all varied with the ups and downs of economic activity.

But there were also major trend changes, especially after the second world war. The scale of the workforce itself grew fivefold over the eighty-four years and average real wages increased fourfold. Paid work hours per worker declined by 25 percent. Agriculture and mining declined as a share of the workforce. Average union size increased and strike days lost per worker declined. But perhaps the most notable of the changes that took place were the burgeoning formal education of the workforce, the incorporation of married women and non-British migrants into the workforce (and the earlier retirement of older workers), and the establishment of a comprehensive unemployment benefit system. These latter were all post–World War II changes and were associated with a degree of structural change in the industrial and occupational composition of employment that was quite marked compared with the prewar period. In particular the postwar period saw the rise and decline of the Australian manufacturing sector. This process of structural adjustment seems to have operated mainly through quantity and quality adjustments in labour markets, reflecting the pattern of unemployment and job opportunities and the increasing importance of education and the educated workforce.

It is likely that even more adaptability than has been shown in the past is now necessary. By the end of the period the economy was continuing in a prolonged stagflation state that had first clearly emerged in 1975, and it faced important adjustment pressures from international trade and technological changes, as well as various sociodemographic and attitudinal pressures from within the labour market, particularly those relating to issues such as equal opportunities, immigration change, and unemployment of long duration. It is thus highly probable that some further improved responsiveness in the labour market, especially in the areas of industrial relations and industrial training, is needed for successful accommodation to continuing present problems and to the needs of the remainder of the century and beyond.

Whether the appropriate direction is one of deregulation and a return to nineteenth-century basic structures is less clear. The emergence in the mid 1980s of a labour market deregulation movement is notable, though proponents of such deregulation had still to define precisely the nature of the deregulation proposed and the likely benefits, based not on a priori analysis of ideal markets but on historical and international evidence of how less regulated labour markets do function. This is important because with too competitive a marketplace for labour some static efficiency (resource allocation) improvements may come only at the expense of losses in dynamic efficiency (that is, even lower productivity). Some rigidities may be the price of workplace cooperation and skill acquisition and transmission. It is for this reason that the major alternative direction of reform being mooted in the 1980s is towards institutions of greater cooperation and consensus in the labour market. This direction of change can suffer its own problems, including those of enhancing the privileges of the cooperating parties at the expense of excluded groups, for example the unemployed.

The challenge is to get the mix of stability and flexibility right. The ideal is to maximise real wage growth while minimising unemployment and inflation. Achieving these objectives simultaneously is no easy task, and Australia has only occasionally approximated it in the past. Thus it seems clear that the present historical stability in Australian labour markets is in need of change. And there is increasing evidence of recognition of this and a widespread willingness to contemplate necessary changes. Mancur Olson (1982) has expressed the view that long-term entrenchment of interest group power most explains the economic decline of nations. If this is true it no doubt applies with some force to Australia's labour market, given the long-run rigidity in basic institutions revealed here.

References

Aitkin, D. A. 1983. "Where does Australia stand?" in G. A. Withers (ed.), *Bigger or Smaller Government?* pp. 13–31. Canberra: Academy of the Social Sciences in Australia.

Australian Tripartite Mission. 1969. *The Training of Skilled Workers in Europe.* Canberra: Australian Government Publishing Service.

Barnard, A., N. G. Butlin, and J. J. Pincus. 1977. "Private and public sector employment in Australia". *Australian Economic Review,* 1st Quarter: 43–52.

Blandy, R., and S. Richardson. 1982. *How Labour Markets Work: Case Studies in Adjustment.* Melbourne: Longman Cheshire.

Boehm, E. A. 1979. *Twentieth Century Economic Development in Australia.* 2d ed. Melbourne: Longman Cheshire.

Bray, G., and C. Boschan. 1962. "Secular trends and recent changes in real wages and wage differentials in three Western industrial countries: the United States, Great Britain and Germany". Paper presented at Second International Conference of Economic History, Paris.

Broom, L., and F. L. Jones. 1976. *Opportunity and Attainment in Australia.* Canberra: Australian National University Press.

Brosnan, P. 1984. "Australian net interstate migration: 1911 to 1961". *Australia Economic History Review* 24(2) (September): 150–72.

Brown, H. P. 1979. *Australian Demographic Databank.* Vols. 1–2. Canberra: Department of Economics, Research School of Social Sciences, Australian National University.

Brown, W., et al. 1978. "How far does arbitration constrain Australia's labour market?" *Australian Bulletin of Labour* 4(4) (September): 31–9.

Bureau of Labour Market Research. 1983. *Youth Wages, Employment and the Labour Force.* Canberra: Australian Government Publishing Service.

Butlin, M. W. 1977. *A Preliminary Annual Database, 1900/01–1972/73.* Research Discussion Paper 7701. Sydney: Reserve Bank of Australia.

Butlin, N. G., A. Barnard, and J. J. Pincus. 1982. *Government and Capitalism.* Sydney: Allen & Unwin.

Carey, T. 1979. *Australian Labour Force Data, 1947 to 1971.* Discussion Paper 38. Adelaide: National Institute of Labour Studies.

Carter, M. 1983. *The Hidden Economy–What Are the Issues?* Discussion Paper 84. Centre for Economic Policy Research, Australian National University.

Chapman, B., and P. Miller. 1982. "Determination of earnings in Australia", in K. Hancock et al. (eds.), *Japanese and Australian Labour Markets: A Comparative Study,* pp. 228–59. Canberra: Australia–Japan Research Centre.

Coe, D., and F. Gagliardi. 1985. *Nominal Wage Determination in Ten OECD Economies.* Working Paper No. 19. General Economics Division, OECD. March.

Coghlan, T. 1918. *Labour and Industry in Australia.* 4 vols. Oxford: Oxford University Press.

Committee on the Future of Tertiary Education in Australia (L. H. Martin, Chairman). 1964. *Tertiary Education in Australia*. 3 vols. Melbourne: Government Printer.

Committee of Inquiry into Labour Market Progress. 1985. *Report.* Canberra: Australian Government Publishing Service.

Covick, O. 1982. "Relative wage shares in Australia", in K. Hancock et al. (eds.), *Japanese and Australian Labour Markets: A Comparative Study,* pp. 372–417. Canberra: Australia–Japan Research Centre.

Covick, O. (ed.). 1983. *Understanding Labour Markets in Australia.* Adelaide: National Institute of Labour Studies.

Creigh, S. W., and P. Makeham. 1982. "Strike incidence in industrial countries: an analysis". *Australian Bulletin of Labour* 8(3) (June): 139–55.

Department of Labour and Immigration. 1975. *Labour's Share of the National Product: The Post-War Australian Experience.* Canberra: Australian Government Publishing Service.

Fisher, N. W. F. 1983. *An Expenditure Approach to Estimation of the Hidden Economy and Informal Labour Markets.* Working Paper No. 12. Canberra: Bureau of Labour Market Research.

Forster, C. 1985. *Unemployment and the Australian Economic Recovery of the 1930s.* Discussion Paper in Economic History No. 45. Australian National University. August.

Forster, C., and P. Harris. 1983. "A note on engineering wages in Melbourne 1892–1929". *Australian Economic History Review* 23(1) (March): 50–7.

Freebairn, J., and G. Withers. 1977. "The performance of manpower forecasting techniques in Australian labour markets". *Australian Bulletin of Labour* 4(1) (December): 13–31.

Gregory, R. G., and R. C. Duncan. 1981. "The relevance of segmented labour market theories: the Australian experience of the achievement of equal pay for women". *Journal of Post-Keynesian Economics,* Spring: 403–28.

Grubb, D., R. Jackman, and R. Layard. 1983. "Wage rigidity and unemployment in OECD countries". *European Economic Review* 21: 11–39.

Hagan, J. 1983. "Unions: context and perspective 1850–1980", in B. Ford and D. Plowman (eds.), *Australian Unions,* pp. 30–59. Melbourne: Macmillan.

Hall, A. R. 1963. "Some long-period effects of the kinked age distribution of Australia, 1861–1961". *Economic Record* 39(85) (March): 43–52.

Hancock, K. J. 1979. "The first half century of Australian wage policy – part I". *Journal of Industrial Relations* 21(1): 1–19.

Hancock, K. J., and K. Moore. 1972. "The occupational wage structure in Australia since 1914". *British Journal of Industrial Relations* 10: 107–22.

Harper, I. R. 1979. "The relationship between unemployment and unfilled vacancies in Australia: 1952–1978". *Economic Record* 56(154) (September): 231–43.

Howard, W. 1983. "Trade unions and the arbitration system", in B. Head (ed.), *State and Economy in Australia,* pp. 238–51. Melbourne: Oxford University Press.

Hughes, B. 1973. "The wages of the strong and the weak". *Journal of Industrial Relations* 15(1): 1–24.

Isaac, J. E. 1965. "Wage drift in the Australian metal industries". *Economic Record* 41: 145–72.

1985. "Professor Mitchell and the labour market", in *Papers Arising from the Brooking Survey of the Australian Economy: The Australian Labour Market,* pp. 1–24. Discussion Paper No. B2. Centre for Economic Policy Research, Australian National University. January.

Jackson, R. V. 1977. *Australian Economic Development in the Nineteenth Century.* Canberra: Australian National University Press.

Keating, M. 1983. "Relative wages and the changing industrial distribution of employment in Australia". *Economic Record* 59(167) (December): 384–97.

Lewis, D. E. 1983. "The measurement and interpretation of segregation of women in the workforce". *Journal of Industrial Relations* 25 (September): 347–52.

McCarthy, J. 1969. "Justice Higgins and the Harvester judgment". *Australian Economic History Review* 9: 17–38.

McIntyre, S. 1983. "Labour, capital and arbitration, 1890–1920", in B. Head (ed.), *State and Economy in Australia,* pp. 90–113. Melbourne: Oxford University Press.

McMahon, P., and C. Robinson. 1984. "Labour force programme expenditures: an international comparison". *Bureau of Labour Market Research Bulletin"* (July): 22–6.

Maddock, R., and M. Carter. 1984. *Working Hours in Australia.* Melbourne: Committee for the Economic Development of Australia.

Mauldon, F. R. E. 1928. "Labour mobility in Australian industry". *Economic Record* 4(6) (May): 15–26.

Meade, J. 1982. *Wage-Fixing.* London: Allen & Unwin.

Merrilees, W. J. 1982. "The mass exodus of older males from the labour force – an exploratory analysis". *Australian Bulletin of Labour* 8(2) (March): 81–94.

Mitchell, D. J. B. 1983. *The Australian Labour Market.* Working Paper No. 59. Institute of Industrial Relations, University of California at Los Angeles.

National Population Inquiry (Borrie inquiry). 1975. *Population and Australia: A Demographic Analysis and Projections.* 2 vols. Canberra: Australian Government Publishing Service.

Norris, K. 1980. "Compulsory arbitration and the wage structure in Australia". *Journal of Industrial Relations* 22 (December): 219–63.

Norton, W. E., and R. McDonald. 1981. "Implications for Australia of cross-country comparisons of economic performance". *Economic Record* 57(159): 301–18.

OECD 1977. *Australia: Transition from School to Work or Further Study.* Paris: OECD.

1980. *Women and Employment.* Paris: OECD.

Olson, M. 1982. *The Rise and Decline of Nations: Economic Growth, Stagflation, and Social Rigidities.* New Haven, Conn.: Yale University Press.

Parsons, T. G. 1980. "Learning the rules of the game: some notes on the labour movement in the Melbourne manufacturing industries, 1870–1890". *Journal of Australian Studies* 6 (June): 56–62.

Perry, L. J. 1981. "Inflation in the UK, USA and Australia: some comparisons". *Economic Record* 57(159) (December): 319–31.

Phelps-Brown, P. M. 1966. "The economic consequence of collective bargaining", *Minutes of Evidence before the Royal Commission on Trade Unions and Employers' Associations* 38: 1–26. London: HMSO.

Pincus, J. J., and G. A. Withers. 1983. "Economics of regulation", in F. H. Gruen (ed.), *Surveys of Australian Economics,* vol. 3, pp. 7–75. Sydney: Allen & Unwin.

Pope, D. 1982. "Wage regulation and unemployment in Australia, 1900–30". *Australian Economic History Review* 22(2) (September): 103–26.

Power, M. 1975. "Women's work is never done – by men". *Journal of Industrial Relations* 17(2): 225–39.

Rose, R. 1980. *Changes in Public Employment.* Glasgow: Centre for Public Policy.

Rowland, D. T. 1979. *Internal Migration in Australia.* Canberra: Australian Bureau of Statistics.

Selby-Smith, C. 1975. "Rates of return in post-secondary education in Australia". *Economic Record* 51(136) (December): 455–85.

Sheehan, P. J., and P. P. Stricker. 1982. *Dimensions of Unemployment.* Melbourne: Institute of Applied Economic and Social Research.

1983. "Welfare benefits and the labour market", in O. Covick (ed.), *Understanding Labour Markets in Australia,* pp. 200–21. Adelaide: National Institute of Labour Studies.

Thurow, L. 1982. *Dangerous Currents: The State of Economics.* Oxford: Oxford University Press.

Treasury. 1979. *Job Markets: Economic and Statistical Aspects of the Australian Market for Labour.* Canberra: Australian Government Publishing Service

White Paper on Full Employment in Australia. 1945. *Commonwealth Parliamentary Papers,* 11, sess. 1945–6, vol. 4.

Withers, G. A. 1979. "Social justice and the unions: a normative approach to cooperation and conflict under interdependence", *British Journal of Industrial Relations* 15 (November): 322–37.

Withers, G. A. 1983. "Government and economic management: discussion", in G. Withers (ed.), *Bigger or Smaller Government?* pp. 95–106. Canberra: Academy of the Social Sciences in Australia.

Withers, G. A., D. Pitman, and B. Wittingham. 1983. *Relative Wages and Labour Market Adjustment: A Cross-Country Causality Approach.* Working Paper. Canberra: Bureau of Labour Market Research.

Zagorski, K. In press. *Social Mobility into Post-Industrial Society – Socioeconomic Structure and Fluidity of the Australian Workforce.* Canberra: Department of Sociology, Australian National University.

Government and economic welfare

Government

JONATHAN J. PINCUS

White settlement in Australia began as a penal colony, initiated by government. Although it is possible, even likely, as some North American and southern African examples might indicate, that private settlers would eventually have established themselves in a society less shaped by public coercion, nonetheless it was as an extreme type of command economy that the country began. Whether as a real consequence or merely as an intellectual echo of those beginnings, the story of Australian economic development has often been written in terms of public policy, with considerable and proper stress placed on the developmental roles of government.

This chapter is not concerned with judging whether the size of government has been too great or too small, especially when size is measured, as is done commonly, by government shares in aggregate final consumption or investment or employment: See Table 1.3 above and Boehm (1979: 220, 316). An explanation of some of the reasons for the present deemphasis is given below, especially in section 11.2.

This chapter is rather concerned with a tentative and preliminary assessment of the means and extent of public sector encouragement for economic growth and development. The government programmes most closely influencing the pace and shape of Australian economic development were those that altered the size and characteristics of the population; provided or arranged provision of intermediate inputs for use in private production activities, and of final goods and services for private consumption; and otherwise influenced the pattern of private production, consumption, savings, and investment. (Some of these interconnected programmes are discussed more fully in other chapters.) In carrying out these activities, government made use of its exclusive resource – law, and regulation pursuant to law – directly in ordering changes to private behaviour, and indirectly in raising revenue via taxes, charges, and loans. As is usually the case, government actions aimed at altering the level or composition of output had consequences for the distribution of economic wellbeing between individuals and groups, and vice versa, so that our discussion cannot be narrowly focused upon what were proclaimed specifically to be developmental policies.

Preliminary matters need to be discussed concerning difficulties encountered when measuring the contribution made by government towards the enjoyment of economic wellbeing. At the beginning of the century, governments in Australia were notable for the size of their public enterprise activities. Where governments sell their output, the methods for including their productive activities in GDP do not differ in kind from those for the inclusion of private market activities:[1] The contribution to GDP is equal to the cost of production plus or minus any operating profit or loss. (The proposition that measured GDP is not an accurate index of economic wellbeing is illustrated in Chapter 12, especially in relation to goods and services like leisure, which are not exchanged in the market.) As this century progressed, Australian governments shifted the emphasis of their resource-using activities from marketed to unmarketed outputs, so the considerations discussed in Chapter 12 became more pressing (see Table 11.1 below).

Consider defence, the improvement of which was one of the aims of federation, and which is taken here to be a final consumption item. For national accounting purposes, aggregate consumption is calculated by summing individual valuations. When a consumption item has a price and is not rationed, the price is the (common) weight used when performing the summation. When unpriced, the valuations vary across individuals and are generally not observable, so national accountants include defence at its cost of production, rather than attempt to estimate the value of its consumption. Ignoring for simplicity any difference between average and marginal costs, the value of aggregate consumption exceeds the cost of production of a public good if it is supplied in less than optimal amounts, and falls short of cost if it is supplied in more than optimal amounts. Although I attempt in this chapter no quantitative assessment, there are some reasons on balance to expect that the former situation – too small a supply – was often the case for public goods, and that the reverse was the case for private goods supplied by the government at less than cost.

Where government produces an unpriced intermediate input, there will be an increase in GDP, one that appears in private factor prices or rents. In particular, the maintenance of a legal framework within which

[1] Although it should be noted that some problems may be greater in quantity. For example, because of the greater power of government to engage in cross subsidization, profits or losses as measured by usual accounting methods do not always carry the same implication for economic welfare; in particular, an enterprise might "break even" by offsetting losses in one "market" against profits elsewhere. In general, the losses can represent misallocated resources; but so do the profits when they arise from the exercise of monopoly power.

specialisation of economic activity can take place can greatly increase GDP or GDP per capita, although national accountants do not usually attribute the increase to the public sector. On the contrary, some early national accountants regarded all government expenditure on law and order as intermediate outlays, not to be included in GDP. The more conventional treatment, which is to count them as final expenditures, nonetheless can understate their true contribution.

11.1   Law and order

An outstanding characteristic of white Australian society has been the low level of violence to persons. Civil order has been scarcely disturbed by communal strife, and never by civil war. (The rule of law – freedom from arbitrary arrest, imprisonment, or death; the state's near monopoly of violence – it must be stated, did not extend equally to all groups, especially to the Aboriginal population nor to the early Chinese and Melanesian immigrants. And some groups among the white population did better out of the arrangement than did others.) What were originally potentially explosive mixtures – convicts and their jailers; Irish Catholics, and English and Scottish Protestants – coexisted in a surprisingly peaceful community (Smith 1982). Possibly because the threat of violence was so great, laws and practices sprang up that defused internal conflict, not the least by excluding from our shores groups seeming to threaten the homogeneity that was felt necessary for the maintenance of internal calm. Chinese and Melanesians who had moved to Australia were expelled; darker-skinned Europeans who did not speak English were admitted in significant numbers only after World War II. To anticipate a later theme, it can be said that the great trade-off was not between equity and efficiency, but between progress and security, or between material income and risk reduction.

The claim that Australia's stable political environment was beneficial to growth has to be set against some aspects of Olson's theory of growth (1982: 121–32), which postulates that periods of constitutional fixity are, eventually, detrimental to economic progress, being associated with the accretion of selfish and growth-retarding interest groups. It might be expected, therefore, that a political federation like the one begun in 1901 would have been conducive to fairly rapid economic growth to the extent that the new constitution disrupted arrangements previously restricting economic competition: trade associations, professional cartels, private or government bodies controlling entry into occupations or raising barriers to geographical mobility of workers and entrepreneurs, and so on. However, the disruption in 1901 was very small. It is indeed

possible that federation created opportunities for new or stronger restrictive groups, in particular through the enhanced legal status of labour
unions[2] and, in the interwar period, the powerful combination of federal
control of foreign trade and the establishment of marketing boards and
two-price schemes for rural products. The Australian customs union of
1901, although it possibly produced some gains from increased trade
between the states, relatively quickly became protectionist.[3] A federal
constitution, not born of armed struggle or revolution and not imposed
by victorious enemies, did little to discourage the activities of self-pro-
tective and growth-retarding groups.

We are stuck, then, with what appears to be a negative influence on
growth, namely, a social and political environment that encouraged the
formation of selfish interest groups. However, no one would seriously
maintain the proposition that a stable legal framework was wholly negative in its effects: The potential disadvantages of insecurity in property
rights, of costly and uncertain enforcement of contracts, of civil strife
or war, of predations by uncontrolled private bandits are all too obvious
to be ignored. The benefits bestowed by a stable legal order, nonetheless, are rarely guessed at.

The issue is important in that liberal political theorists and, especially,
libertarian ones tend to assign chiefly to government the task of maintaining internal and external security. What might then be called the
fundamental tasks of government, without the fulfilling of which private
economic activity would be greatly discouraged, may not give rise to
measured government "output" in proportion to the actual contribution
made by government. My unquantified suggestion is that our stable
political environment, with its tradition of relatively uncorrupt, disin-
terested, and competent bureaucracy and judiciary, has added greatly
to the growth of Australian wellbeing, if not to the growth of measured
GDP. In his recent survey of the literature on growth in the third world,
Reynolds (1983: 964) remarked that

---

[2] Howard (1983) argues that the Conciliation and Arbitration Act 1904 solved two contemporary problems of organised labour: how weak unions could force recognition (all
that mattered was that the court recognise a dispute); and how to render nonunion
labour less attractive (awards covered union and nonunion employees alike). This article
contains an excellent discussion of the creation of Australian unions by the state and
by the requirements of the arbitral system itself.

[3] In his discussion of the Australian case, Olson (1982: 132–6) stresses the costs of tariff
protection as the chief consequence of political stability. Note also that, in Olson's
theory, although members of narrow groups have disproportionate power, the dispro-
portion diminishes but does not disappear over time in stable societies (p. 41). While
there is time, there is hope.

Nothing is easier than to prevent or stifle economic growth. A government which is unable to maintain internal order, or which lacks minimal administrative capacity, or which is so little interested in growth that it fails to provide the necessary physical or human infrastructure, or which follows trade and tax policies strongly biased against exports, can readily prevent a country from reaching a turning point [into a phase of growth per head].

(See also Myrdal 1968.) Australian governments have, to a remarkable degree, maintained internal order and offered more than a minimal administrative capacity.

11.2   Fiscal measurements of government

The long-term trends in the proportion of the workforce engaged in the public sectors of Australia, the United Kingdom, and the United States are traced in Figure 11.1. With their ownership of large enterprises in transport and communications, Australian governments at federation employed a comparatively large share of the workforce. By 1913, after a period of rapid expansion, public enterprises employed six out of every ten public workers, a proportion held until the onset of the great depression. At the end of the 1970s, fewer than three out of ten public employees were engaged in producing marketed services, and so, to a substantial extent, the growth of government employment after 1913 was concentrated outside those fields that gave rise in the nineteenth century to the description "colonial socialism".[4] That is to say, governmental activity broadly classed as developmental or productive, like the building and operation of railways, ports, power stations, and dams, became relatively less important owing in part to the burdens those activities imposed on the public finances during the depression, in part to technological developments in road and air transport, and in part to political decisions about the appropriateness of charging consumers for public education, insurance, and health services.

A somewhat different picture from that given by Figure 11.1 is provided by the data in Table 11.1 on the ratio of public sector outlays to GDP. The early increase in public sector employment, so obvious in the figure, does not show up in public expenditure data because these include only two elements of public enterprise finances, namely, gross capital outlays and the net operating result (deficit or surplus). The expenditure series does, however, echo the jumps in government activity due to

---

[4] For detailed data on Australian public employment, see Tables 2.2, 2.4, and 2.6 of a book that this chapter draws freely upon, Butlin et al. (1982). A brief comparative discussion of the experiences of OECD countries is contained in Eichenberg (1983).

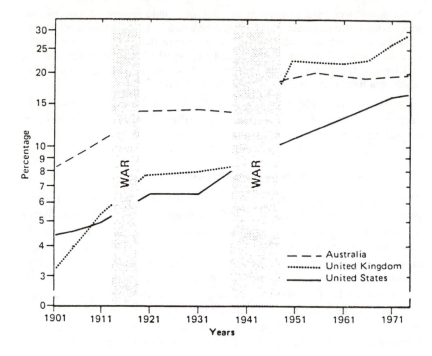

Figure 11.1. Public employment: total workforce percentage (excluding defence). *Source:* Butlin, Barnard, and Pincus 1982: 6.

world wars, and the plateaux that followed them. The limited details of expenditures also set out in the table indicate the shift in emphasis from investment to current outlays and, especially after the second world war, towards education, health care, and welfare, which rely more heavily on the use of cash transfers.

Table 11.1 also displays changes in the sources of government finance. Initially, borrowing was mainly on account of the public enterprises, and it diminished in importance along with those enterprises (although changes in the willingness and ability of governments after World War II to finance enterprise investment from taxation and from retained earnings were also important factors). In terms of taxation sources there has been, particularly since the uniform taxation legislation of 1942, a switch towards income taxes and away from property taxes and indirect taxes, especially customs and excise taxes.

I shall digress a little in order to address the question of the growth of government. For all levels of governments combined, the ratio of

Table 11.1. Government receipts and outlays by type 1900–79 (percentage of GDP)[a]

	1900	1910	1919	1929	1939	1949	1959	1969	1979
Receipts									
Customs and excise	3.9	3.6	3.1	4.8	5.2	5.8	4.9	4.1	5.2
Income taxation	0.3	0.4	3.2	3.1	4.6	12.5	9.7	11.3	15.7
Other taxes	0.9	0.8	1.7	2.5	5.8	6.4	7.2	6.9	8.1
Total taxes	5.2	4.8	8.1	10.2	15.6	24.8	21.9	22.4	29.0
Enterprise surplus[b]	2.1	3.5	4.2	5.6	3.5	1.7	3.5	2.4	1.6
Other current	3.0	2.4	1.5	1.2	—	—	—	—	1.8
Total current	10.3	9.3	13.9	14.7	19.1	26.0	24.8	24.8	32.4
Net borrowing and other capital	2.8	2.3	12.9	3.5	2.6	0.3	2.2	3.5	6.6
Total receipts[c]	13.1	13.0 (11.6)	26.8 (25.3)	20.6 (18.1)	21.7	26.7 (26.3)	27.6 (27.0)	28.4 (28.4)	39.0
Outlays									
Law and order	[d]	0.6	0.5	0.7	[e]	0.6	0.7	0.6	1.1
Defence	0.3	0.4	12.1	0.8	1.4	1.9	3.0	3.4	2.4
Net interest[f]	3.9	3.2	5.1	5.3	5.1	3.6	2.1	1.9	1.9
Education	0.9	0.9	0.9	1.4	[e]	1.4	2.5	2.6	4.9
Health and welfare	[d]	1.1	2.3	3.0	[e]	6.4	7.2	5.3	13.8
Other current[g]	4.8	0.6	0.6	0.6	[e]	4.6	1.7	5.6	6.3
Total current	10.0	7.0	21.5	11.7	15.1	18.4	17.3	19.4	30.6

Table 11.1. (*cont.*)

	1900	1910	1919	1929	1939	1949	1959	1969	1979
Investment in public enterprises[c]	2.0	3.8	2.7	4.9	3.4	4.4	5.8	4.5	4.3
Other nondefence investment[g]	1.0	2.2	2.6	4.0	3.2	3.9	4.5	4.5	4.1
Total investment	3.1	6.0	5.3	8.9	6.6	8.3	10.4	9.0	8.4
Total outlays	13.1	13.0	26.8	20.6	21.7	26.7	27.6	28.4	39.0

[a]Subtotals and totals do not always equal sums of components, because of rounding.

[b]Does not always exclude expenses of all state business undertakings; see also note c.

[c]For 1910–29 and 1949–69, revised investment data from Butlin, Barnard, and Pincus 1982 have been used, and corresponding revisions made to the data for "Enterprise surplus", "Total receipts", and "Total outlays". The figures in parentheses are those without the adjustment having been made to "Total receipts". For 1939, the revised data were used, but the other necessary adjustments were not made.

[d]Included in "Other current".

[e]Details not available.

[f]"Net interest" for some years includes other public debt charges.

[g]There being no convenient way to distribute the adjustment made in Butlin, Barnard, and Pincus 1982 to the official estimates of "Other nondefence investment", this particular adjustment was absorbed into "Other current" outlays for 1910–29 and 1949–69.
Sources: Butlin, Barnard, and Pincus 1982; Mathews and Jay 1972; Australian Bureau of Statistics, *Australian National Accounts, National Income and Expenditure*, various years.

outlays to GDP rose from 13 percent in 1900 to 39 percent in 1979, the first being a relatively high and the second a relatively low figure by their own contemporary standards; and the ratio of taxes collected to GDP rose more sharply, from 5 to 29 percent. Although both these measures have been used to assess growth in the "size" of government, they have their disadvantages because neither accurately traces the effects of government actions on relative prices, and neither gives us a good estimate of the increasing influence of government on the distribution of economic wellbeing among individuals, groups, and classes. It is open to a government to achieve a desired effect by various means, each placing a different burden on the budget: by the passage and enforcement of laws and rules pursuant to laws, or by the use of taxes and subsidies, or by direct public provision of items of consumption or investment. And within each means, the budget implications vary according to the exact method chosen.

For an example that is important in view of the significance of customs duties for federal finance until the 1940s, consider the fact that the effects of an import tariff on production, consumption, and foreign trade can be duplicated, with some practical difficulties, by combining a tax on Australian consumption with a subsidy to Australian production of import-competing goods. The surplus of consumption tax receipts over production subsidy payments would be equal to the customs revenue forgone, but the ratios of both outlays and taxes to GDP would be higher under the tax-cum-subsidy arrangement than under the tariff. The Industries Assistance Commission put at over $7,000 million the production subsidy equivalent of manufacturing import protection in 1977/8, so that if the alternative fiscal method had been used, the ratio of government outlays to GDP would have risen by about 8 percent to 47 percent. The reallocative pressure of taxation is better estimated by calculating its impact on relative prices than by estimating the amount of tax revenue raised. In a mixed economy, the allocation of resources responds to changes in relative prices, and these responses are indicated but roughly by the volume of tax revenue raised.

A similar warning, one that is more rarely heeded, has to be sounded about public outlays, in that the growth in public provision of a particular good or service does not always indicate an equivalent increase in the absorption of that commodity or its substitutes by the economy as a whole (Brennan and Pincus 1983). Production of public housing since 1961 has resulted in a smaller private housing stock (Williams 1982); and one would expect that public provision of free education and hospital and medical treatment has substantially displaced private outlays on education and health service.[5] Undoubtedly, public provision of goods and services has been a powerful way of making more equal the distribution of economic wellbeing in Australia; it is its effect on the allocation of resources that is more uncertain, especially in the years immediately after a particular form of public provision was first introduced.

11.3 Populate or perish

In what was regarded as a hostile physical and economic environment, one that was a huge distance from the British sources of population, law, and culture, a sense of community was a valuable social and economic resource. An increase in the population of Australia was sought, as a "public good", for reasons of defence and security, and, possibly, to foster a sense of community.[6]

The presence of strongly held and shared values among Australians – in this instance the desire for a larger homogeneous population – made it more likely that the "public goods" satisfying those values would be supplied through the electoral process in amounts approximating the optimal quantity. The exact nature of the population programme, however, was also influenced by the aspirations of politicians, the visions of public men, and the judgments of bureaucrats. In practice, the shared values meant that the machinery of the state that existed for the sake of what Hancock (1930: 72) called the "divine average" was constrained to produce an equalising result in each major area of operation. State action had to be justified in a polity that rejected too flagrant an apparent favouritism towards particular groups, regions, or classes.

Around federation an increase in the white English-speaking population, a goal frequently enunciated by politicians, was difficult to achieve, there having been population (and capital) outflow in the aftermath of the depression of the 1890s and the drought at the turn of the century. In the Great War, massive armies were hurled one against the other, with huge loss of life – over 50,000 Australians killed – reinforcing the belief that in population lay the security of this far-flung outpost of Britain. With the decline in immigration after the early 1890s, the proportion of foreign born in the population had fallen from one-third in

---

[5] Williams (1984), however, does not find this displacement in education; rather, a dollar extra from the public sector, whether spent on state or private schools, produced a dollar increase in education outlays in Australia in recent decades.

[6] In addition, there were expected to be benefits that show up more readily in national income statistics, such as economies of scale and increases in the size of the home market, reducing the average costs of infrastructure, spreading the tax burden, and encouraging the attainment of a more diversified economic structure.

1891 to one-sixth by 1911. Despite this, the vast majority of Australians had either been born in the British Isles or had one or both parents born there, and it was from there that migrants were recruited.

The migration programme was coordinated with British policies, especially through the empire settlement scheme under which the British government shared in the costs of subsidies to migration and in the costs of promotion of closer settlement: See Chapter 2. Australian public policies designed to support and assist the population goal had room for a significant British input. In particular, British manufacturers were invited to put their case before the Tariff Board (formed in 1921), and tariff rates were set so that British producers were given "full opportunity of reasonable competition on the basis of relative costs of economical and efficient production".[7] The interests of residents of "the home country" were given considerable weight. They could immediately register to vote, whereas others had first to serve a "naturalisation" period.

The migrants who flocked to Australia after 1908 were not escaping tyrannical governments or desperate economic conditions, but were attracted by somewhat better economic prospects than were offered at home, passing up the more varied opportunities provided by destinations in the Americas and southern Africa. Half the immigrants were aided by a passage subsidy from government.[8] It may not be too fanciful to suggest that, although possibly less risk averse than their brothers and sisters who remained at "home", these Englishmen and women who migrated to Australia were not the most adventurous of migrants, and in this respect were not atypical of Australian residents. They stuck predominately in the cities, despite efforts (which fell far short of the American "free settlement" laws) at encouraging closer rural settlement. Part of the attraction of Australia was the increasingly regulated labour market in which, aside from the catastrophe of unemployment, the effect of variations in demand and supply filtered through wage boards and commissions seriously applying the "basic wage" standard, and through a Tariff Board.

During the first quarter century of rapid growth in public enterprise

---

[7] As Article 10 of the 1932 Ottawa agreement put it. This article formalised and to some extent strengthened the role of British producers in the tariff process and marked the first British acceptance of repeated Australian offers of tariff preferences to British goods.

[8] The effect of subsidising passages is not to be judged simply by noting that half the immigrants were assisted. The other half came without public assistance, and so, presumably, would some of those who actually received assistance. See Chapter 2 for a discussion of migration that translates passage assistance into change in the relative prices of locational decisions.

activity the rail system doubled in length while catering to increases in urban transit and branch line traffic. The other great public enterprise, the post office, was held back initially through the complications of integrating the separate state departments and by the peculiarities of federal finance. Only after a substantial loan-financed programme was initiated in the early 1920s did the post office respond to the huge boom in demand for telephones. In addition to public transport and communications, the urban gas, power, and water supply services expanded rapidly, helped along (as in urban transit) by public takeovers of private businesses.

Because these enterprises by and large covered costs from receipts until the later 1920s, there was no overall subsidy to or tax upon the user of their services, and in this sense neither encouragement nor discouragement of complementary and substitute activities.[9] However, increasingly the enterprises practised cross subsidisation, favouring country customers at the expense of city ones and, more generally, elastic demanders at the expense of inelastic demanders. What, then, was their contribution to Australian development? A convincing answer would require application of recent developments in the theory of natural monopolies:[10] Were the cross subsidies *necessary* to enable natural monopolies to cover costs (in which case the cross subsidies, and the restrictive regulations supporting them, improved the efficiency in use of economic resources) or not?[11]

Public ownership of the large capital-intensive public utilities put half the reproducible capital stock into public hands.[12] By contrast, over 90 percent (by area, not value) of land remained publicly owned. Private capitalists, therefore, were less exposed to one form of sovereign risk, namely, simple expropriation. The struggle familiar from United States history between regulatory agencies and owners of capital was largely avoided in Australia. In its place was a conflict between the private customers and public suppliers (and between different classes of customers) over price and other conditions of delivery, mediated directly

---

[9] The accounting methods used by the enterprises do not correspond to those required to allow this claim to rest on a secure statistical basis.

[10] An enterprise serving a variety of types of customers is a natural monopoly if it can produce any given mixture of outputs more cheaply than could a group of two or more enterprises. See Sharkey (1982) for a theoretical exposition; Butlin et al. (1982) for some more Australian facts.

[11] Many of the activities making losses (in particular, the rail branch lines and other works aimed at assisting closer settlement) were relatively recent additions; hence, whatever the balance of advantages in the nineteenth century, it was rapidly being eroded in the 1920s (see Sinclair 1970).

[12] Financed largely by foreign borrowing, which was difficult to service when export demand fell in the late 1920s and the price level collapsed.

through parliamentary processes (ministerial direction; questions in parliament; official commissions of inquiry) rather than through special regulatory bodies. A population grew up for whom the consumption of some important goods or services came to be a matter of citizens' rights, not dependent upon the good will of private producers. They regarded private ownership of important resources as being a "privilege", the continued enjoyment of which was contingent upon the service of "social" rather than "selfish" ends.

11.4 Sharing the burden

According to Hancock (1930: 73), to Australians the state meant collective power at the service of individualistic "rights". The structure of state-guaranteed rights and the stability of Australian society were tested in the depression of the 1930s more severely than before or since. The government's response, like those in other countries, was pragmatic, erratic, and contradictory, but it retained a distinctively Australian flavour, with an emphasis on the application of notions of fairness and on the modification, not radical restructuring, of existing institutions. A fuller discussion of public policy in the great depression is contained in Chapter 3. Here, the main measures are recapitulated to demonstrate how some individual rights were preserved and others were infringed. It was recognised that the falls in world demand and in the supply of foreign loans entailed a burden, one that had to be borne as reductions in living standards and prospects. Public policy modified the incidence of those reductions so that the price signals sent from world markets, already muffled in the 1920s by closer settlement schemes, by rural marketing agencies, and by manufacturing tariffs, were not simply transformed into variations in the economic wellbeing of farmers, factory operatives, train drivers, rentiers, and bureaucrats. The burden was not borne as it fell, but neither was it shared equally.

The scope for fiscal action was reduced by the weight of the public debt and by the huge losses sustained by public enterprises – for rail alone, £11 million in 1930/1, an amount equal to about one-third of state taxation revenues. The federal government was able quickly and repeatedly to raise import tariffs without the delay of subjecting the rates to the vague procedures of the Tariff Board in its pursuit of made-to-measure tariffs, so that by 1931 rates were almost double their levels of 1929. In contrast to the American efforts to restrict output, but in keeping with the longstanding encouragement to closer settlement, the federal government exhorted wheat farmers to grow more wheat, and they responded with a record harvest in 1930. This proved no remedy for the farmers' financial problems, despite an increase in export receipts. Only when financial and legislative difficulties were overcome in 1931 (Sawer 1963: 18) was a bounty paid to growers for wheat marketed, which cost £4.3 million in 1934/5. Assistance also came in the form of debt moratoriums in 1930, and later by relief payments. By 1937, wheat growers were able to adopt the kind of two-price system that had been developed earlier for dairy, fruit, and meat producers, with a high domestic price defended by the federal import restrictions and with exports dumped on world markets (Sieper 1982).

Temporarily unable to raise loans, and with their revenues slashed, state and federal governments, on the advice of the Bank of England, attempted to balance their budgets by expenditure reductions and by increased charges and taxes. A more modest plan, which called for a 20 percent reduction in expenditures and for increased revenues, was adopted in June 1931. Pensions were cut, except those for certain dependants, but by less than prices had fallen, so that those previously relying solely on public social security payments were not disadvantaged. Wages had been cut already during 1930 by the wage-fixing authorities, somewhat in line with falling prices, and a further cut was made by the commonwealth court early in 1931 in an effort to reduce real wages. Prices continued to fall, so that the value of pretax real wages did not diminish significantly despite the unprecedented level of unemployment. As a part of the June 1931 plan, nominal interest rates were also reduced in "an indubitable breach of contract" (William Morris Hughes, quoted by Sawer 1963: 22).[13]

At first, wheat growers were the only sizeable group to receive relief through the federal budget. Others had to look to the states, which responded on a grudging scale: sustenance at first, then the miserly dole, and finally, as taxation rates rose – state income taxes on even modest incomes, federal sales taxes that exempted goods of common consumption – and as the loan market freed up, assistance by employment on public works (Butlin et al. 1982: 181–5). The unemployed, a new group of claimants against the state, without previously established rights except in Queensland, were not treated with anything like the generosity afforded to holders of rights to the "old" pensions and benefits, or to those who by their continued employment held on to the right to a "living wage".

The consequences for the sectoral shares of economic activity – rural, manufacturing, services – of the mixture of policy interventions of the

---

[13] By the Commonwealth Bank Act 1929, holders of gold in the form of coin and bullion were forced to exchange it for notes.

1920s are uncertain. By itself the tariff would have tended to raise real wages and to expand the manufacturing sector at the expense of grazing and farming interests and activity (Stolper and Samuelson 1941). But the tariff cannot be considered in isolation from the encouragement of immigration by way of passage and other subsidies. Whereas in theory protection should have enabled Australian producers to pay higher real wages than otherwise, immigration lowered the market clearing wage rate (and labour market regulation interfered with the clearing of the market, so that unemployment in the 1920s rarely fell below 5 percent). In addition, the policy of subsidising labour-intensive rural activities, especially small mixed and irrigated farming, to the extent that it decreased the drift to the cities and decreased the supply of manufacturing labour, offset the stimulation that the tariff gave to secondary industry. And the losses made by urban transit systems in carrying workers to their employments in the central business districts of the cities offset that offset. The response to pressures from particular private interests, and from the advocates of particular visions of the appropriate character of Australian development, was a bundle of policies the net effect of which was to shift labour and population from Britain, but which to some extent cancelled each other with respect to the sectoral balance of the Australian economy.

This was "protection all round". N. G. Butlin (Butlin et al. 1982: 75) has suggested that "the common view that actions by government that cancel one another out are merely pointless may miss a basic object – maybe the basic object – of the use of public means". The basic object that he had in mind was, perhaps, the socialisation of risk. Although the benefits that workers and capitalists in a protected industry obtain from tariff protection are mostly temporary as the higher rewards attract new entrants, a *system* that raises tariffs when imports threaten is a valuable form of "social insurance". Home price support schemes for rural industries have some of the same character, that of social insurance for producers against industry-specific risk. What was lacking in the 1930s was a public system of social insurance against general or economywide risk and for those who became unemployed as a consequence.[14]

11.5 Postwar reconstruction

War changed government in Australia. Power became more centralised, and there were increases in the extent and depth of public action, ex-

---

[14] For a discussion of how employment contracts, implicit or explicit, sheltered the core of employed persons from reductions in real wages in recent recessions see Gregory 1982.

emplified by the imposition of record high tax rates and of extensive controls (including conscription) over private economic activity, squeezing real private consumption in 1943/4 by 10 percent and private investment by more than half of their values of 1939/40. The experience of this "command economy", albeit one with considerable room for private decisions, had lasting effects on rulers and ruled alike, and reinforced the "lessons" learned from the 1930s depression. Planning for postwar reconstruction combined a determination to avoid the massive unemployment of the early 1930s, with some new concepts and relatively new instruments of economic control. The chief ideas of Keynes (1936) found a very receptive audience in Australia: The depression was due to the instability of private investment; low interest rates, although desirable, were not enough to ensure sufficient investment; the balance of payments could impose a severe constraint on stimulatory policy measures.

The fear of recurrence of the massive unemployment of the early 1930s was heightened by concern about managing the transition to a postwar economy. Although a postwar rise in the price level of 50 percent was contemplated with some equanimity by the economic experts gathered by the Commonwealth Bank in late 1943 – it could and did help relieve the burden of the public debt (Giblin 1951: 308–9) – it was believed in some influential circles that a postwar slump was almost inevitable, unless policy measures were taken. The sources of concern were external and internal. As to the former, the lesson of the 1930s was that governments (and this meant state governments) should never again borrow so heavily on external account. In June 1931, external interest payments, public and private, were equal to over 7 percent of national income. Although this proportion had fallen by half by June 1939 and again by half through the war, the fear that the balance of payments would seriously constrain full employment policies was reinforced by uncertainty as to the postwar shape of the international trade and payment system. Australian politicians and their economist advisors, with the heady experience of running the wartime economy almost behind them, argued in international meetings for a concerted, internationally coordinated effort to achieve full employment. If all nations expanded together, balance-of-payments difficulties would be less than if Australia, for instance, alone ran an expansionary course. A self-contained stability being impractical, the currency was tied to sterling (at some considerable cost), with seasonal and world trade fluctuations to be accommodated through local monetary variations or dampened by fiscal and regulatory policy.

Plans for postwar reconstruction revolved around the maintenance of full employment in a society that was to be transformed by social welfare measures. Economic management at the macro level required federal hands on the fiscal and monetary levers, and was to be assisted by the maintenance of price, capital issue, and other controls, of the kind enforced during the war under national security regulations, as well as by nationalisation of private banking and other enterprises and the establishment of new public enterprises. The federal government was also in the position to be able to encourage private foreign capital inflow into selected industries, like motor vehicle production. A shelf of blueprints for public capital works was developed to be available if and when the slump occurred. As in other fields, monetary control by the federal authorities had been enhanced by the war, and the Commonwealth Bank Act of 1945 finally made it clear that that bank was to give effect to the policy of the government. However, Labor failed in a series of referendums to gain acceptance of proposals to amend the constitution: postwar reconstruction, 1944; primary product marketing, 1946; regulation of employment conditions, 1946; price and rent control, 1948. And some nationalisation and monopolisation attempts were defeated by the courts: airlines, 1945; pharmaceutical prescriptions, 1945; banking, 1945 and 1947. The specific means chosen by government to expand its role were not available to it, so other methods of achieving its general policy goals were substituted.

The federal constitution held the possibility or, on some readings, the certainty of eventual domination of the states by the central government. The drive towards centralisation was fuelled by the combination of federal powers to tax and to make conditional grants to the states, and was aided by constitutional interpretations and, to a lesser extent, constitutional changes. Its speed, which depended on political and ideological considerations, was generally faster when the Labor party was in power (Butlin et al. 1982: 54–5, 80–1; Groenewegen 1983). Under the 1901 constitution the federal government had exclusive power to collect customs and excise taxes (which yielded 75 percent of all taxes until the start of the Great War), but was to return its "surplus" revenues to the states. The power to tax, however, proved to be the power to spend, and by 1938/9 federal outlays had risen to equal one-half of state outlays, from a share of one-sixth that they had represented in 1909/10. During the 1910s and 1920s, the federal government began to share with the states and threaten to displace the states from spending activities that were not included in the list of commonwealth powers set out in section 51 of the constitution, using conditional grants to the states (for example, the 1926 Federal Aid Roads Act); and to enter into fields of taxation in competition with the states (for example land taxes, estate taxes, and the income tax). It was the eventual exclusion of the states from income taxes that proved decisive to the federal fiscal balance.

The divergent practices of the states were an obstacle to the full use of the income tax during the second world war. In contrast to, for instance, the control of economic activity via the national security regulations, the constitutional validity of the form of taxation implemented did not expire upon the conclusion of the war and a period of postwar reconstruction. The states were thus deprived of independent access to income taxes. Federal control of state borrowing, already strong in the Loan Council, was reinforced by the availability to the commonwealth of surplus taxation revenues and by the fear, especially strong in the Labor party, of the burden of external interest payments.

The restrictions on the states' fiscal resources prevented them from dealing quickly with some of the shortages arising in the immediate postwar years in electricity and gas and in transport (although state financial accounts had been improved by their record rail business in the war, maintenance and renewals had been postponed). Commonwealth instrumentalities, in contrast, were not held back by any lack of funds, although they were affected by the same shortages of materials, especially imports. In dealing with market shortages, the Labor government used price control, capital issue control, and rationing, ultimately unpopular measures. (Labor's defeat in 1949 was set up by the bank nationalisation fiasco: Sawer 1963: 220.)

At the end of the war the states retained primary responsibility for law and order, public health services, public education, public housing, and, through state instrumentalities or local government, supply of water, electricity, gas, and public transport. Into most of these functions the commonwealth had already entered and was increasingly to displace the states or reduce the states to agents of the federal power. The effects were not confined to a mere transfer of functions from the state to the central government: Without the increase in centralisation, the growth in the extent of government activity could not have proceeded as early nor as rapidly. The process went furthest in social welfare. At the end of the war the states had provided assistance to widows, deserted wives and their children, and others in need, basically covering the gaps in commonwealth assistance. Commonwealth benefits included old age and invalid pensions, child endowment for the second child and subsequent children, a means-tested widow's pension, allowances to dependants of invalid pensioners, and, from 1945, income-tested unemployment and sickness benefits. Most of these had been introduced by Labor governments, as had daily bed subsidies for certain hospital patients. The more ambitious parts of Labor's nationalised health system foundered on the opposition of the medical profession, which was overcome only in the early 1950s by the Menzies administration. The issue between the political parties at the federal level was not so much whether Australia would have a social welfare system something along the lines of the British or New Zealanders, but what form such a system would take. By and large, Liberal/County party coalition governments (1949 to 1972) preferred to rely upon subsidies to private activity in the welfare, health, and education fields, with less emphasis on public provision of those services; and they also attempted to make the subsidies non-means-tested and, in that sense, universal.[15]

11.6 Federation in maturity

The final two sections are concerned with broad changes in the nature of public sector encouragement of Australian economic development since the late 1940s. As elsewhere in the chapter, the themes relate to factor inflows from abroad, public investment, and the effects public policies had on economic growth and economic security. A brief summary of the main issues follows.

Ties with Britain, although still strong, were loosened in matters of defence, immigration, capital inflows, and foreign trade, so that Australia became less of a British outpost, less concerned with its isolation from "home", and more integrated, economically at least, with the Asian and Pacific regions. During this period, the sense of alienation from the regional environment continued to diminish, and the pressure for racial and cultural homogeneity lessened. The period began with high targets set for immigration. In terms of a development strategy, there was no longer much hope that the rural sector would be an important provider of jobs. These were found during the 1950s and 1960s in manufacturing, a dynamic sector that was protected first by import quotas and then by tariffs. With the onset of economic troubles in the 1970s and the increasing difficulty that Australian manufacturing had in coping with high imports and high wages, and for other reasons, the enthusiasm for massive migrant inflows waned. Because most new jobs

---

[15] A crude measure of fiscal centralisation is given by the following: in 1909/10, when an amount equal to about 13 percent of GDP was laid out by governments, the federal government spent £3 for every £10 spent by the states; in 1968/9, when governmental outlays approached 28 percent of GDP, the federal government spent $32 for every $20 laid out by the states. For 1978/9, the final year reported in Table 11.1, the federal government received 80 percent of all taxes and 77 percent of all governmental receipts, and made 53 percent of all governmental current outlays and 46 percent of all outlays. (The difference between the federal receipts and outlays is mostly accounted for by federal grants to other levels of government.)

were in urban areas, public investment was directed at urban services, many of them unmarketed, implying less public concern with the promotion of economic growth (as it is usually measured) and more with achieving a greater degree of uniformity in the consumption of particular goods and services. Rather than merely serving the general interest by providing the framework within which private market activity could take place – the administrative, legal, human, and physical infrastructure that Reynolds referred to in the quotation cited in section 11.1 – government became increasingly concerned with catering to particular interests. The debatable question, which is taken up in the final section, is the extent to which this concern reflects a widespread desire on the part of the population of Australia generally for a government system providing specific forms of socialisation of risk, or instead reflects a system in which privileged sections were increasingly being created and served.

After the fall of Singapore to the Japanese in 1942, and increasingly during the gradual disbanding of the British empire in the later 1940s and the 1950s as Britain, with its poor economic recovery after the war, showed itself increasingly unable or unwilling to attempt to control regions "east of Suez", Australian political leaders looked to the Americans for a more secure defence alliance. Economic as well as strategic ties to Britain were being weakened. It was a part of American strategy in the cold war to forge stronger links among the Western European nations, including Britain, and this involved encouragement to the formation of the European Common Market in 1959 and strong American pressure for the ending of British imperial trade preferences. Although Britain did not agree to join the European Community until 1973, it had been forced in the interim to form a defensive trade bloc with the European "outer seven". In 1957 Australia signed two new trade agreements. The first gave trade preferences to Britain; the second, by agreeing to most favoured nation treatment for Japan, foreshadowed the ultimate ending of those preferences. Japan was too promising a customer for Australian wheat, wool, and, later, minerals to be discriminated against, and became the largest export market by 1966/7, the same year in which the United States overtook the United Kingdom as the chief source of Australian imports and in which Australia first extended qualified trade preferences to less developed countries.

A postwar immigration target of 1 percent of the population, or about 80,000, could not readily be filled from Britain, but was met twice over in the late forties when Australia accepted refugees from Europe. Europeans, now assisted by government passage subsidies, made up about one-half in the 1950s and a third in the 1960s of population inflow. A decisive change occurred in the late 1960s with the end of the "white

Australia" policy and the cautious admission of a small number of Asians (who accounted for a little over 1 percent of the population in 1971). Although two out of every five immigrant Australians in 1971 had been born in the British Isles, the ethnic mix was changing significantly, and the Australian culture was becoming more diverse.[16]

The experience of huge deficits in the public enterprises during the 1930s, and a gradual change in the economic and ideological framework, had their effects on the level and pattern of public investment. In the second half of the nineteenth century and in the first third of this one, public investment had combined with other programmes to form the "colonial socialism" in which private economic activity was supported by the public provision of physical infrastructure, especially in transport and communications, and by the public encouragement of population growth. For the first seven or eight years after the second world war the emphasis in public investment was on restoring the rail network and breaking energy bottlenecks. Rail soon ceased to be the largest single claimant on public investment funds, overtaken in the mid 1950s by roads and in the early 1970s by the post office (including Telecom), which then absorbed 12 percent of public investment funds. Between 1901 and 1930, rail alone had absorbed about one-third of such funds. After 1962, the share of enterprises in public investment persistently fell below 50 percent; in 1912 it had been 65 percent. Government involvement in immigration was more detailed and close after than before the 1939 war, particularly in arranging settlement of the early rush of refugees and the later arrivals from continental Europe. Apart from the Snowy Mountains scheme and some ill-conceived attempts at northern development, most public investment was in urban Australia. More public capital than was the case before the war was directed towards activities producing unmarketed or rationed services of roads, housing, hospitals, schools, universities, etc. This raises the problem of the definition of capital formation in that public (and private) current expenditures, on education especially, created a stock of human capital. Thus, even the revised estimates of Barnard and Butlin (1981) – which show public investment in about the same proportion to GDP during the 1950s and 1960s as in the period 1901–39, but lower in relation to private investment – may substantially underestimate public capital formation, broadly conceived. (For non-Australian evidence see Kendrick 1976.)

Remarkable changes occurred in the financing of the public enter-

---

[16] Rather than stress the assimilation of immigrants and the reestablishment of the cultural homogeneity that the former policies had sought, the Fraser Liberal/County party government funded "multiculturalism", including the teaching of English as a second language.

prises in this period. For the first two decades or so after the war, federal cash surpluses – taxation receipts in excess of current spending – were channelled into state and commonwealth public capital formation.[17] In the early postwar years, with their queues, blackouts, and rationing, the average rate of surplus to product (and possibly to capital) in the public enterprises was very low, but rising. Gradually, the surplus increased sufficiently to permit a progressive change from external funding to self-financing of capital works through retained earnings. In effect one form of taxation – the federal income tax – was replaced by another – a type of indirect taxation used to finance capital works. This switch was possible despite a considerably freer use of the enterprises for the cross subsidisation of particular groups of customers by other customers.

For that more rapidly growing part of public capital, which was used to produce unmarketed services, there is some evidence that public authorities were little interested in conventional economic efficiency (although we often lack the kind of accounting data that are needed for an accurate assessment). For example, political considerations long delayed the tentative application to roads of an economic calculus like benefit–cost analysis (Mathews and Jay 1972: 269–77).

The ratio of private investment to private disposable income rose in the 1950s and 1960s, implying either that capital productivity increased from the low levels of the 1930s or that governments contrived to stimulate investment or both.[18] In addition to public spending and tax measures (for example variations in company tax rules and rates, in payroll taxes, in investment allowances), a great variety of policies influenced the rate and composition of private investment (see Butlin et al. 1982: 111–47). Of particular interest were the rules relating to foreign investment, which was forbidden in rural activities, civil aviation, broadcasting, and banking, and at first encouraged (mostly from America) in manufacturing – there were in effect competitions among the states for the siting of plants – and, increasingly after 1972, regulated within a flexible and negotiable set of guidelines. The story in mining was similar – except that the miners competed with each other, through inefficient works programmes, for exploration rights.

There is a general pattern to be noticed here. It is that the income

[17] The effects of this form of forced savings depended partly on the extent to which taxation reduced private consumption rather than private savings, and the extent to which the private sector regarded government programmes as substitutes for private savings. In the event, private savings rates fell sharply through the 1950s, although the private investment ratio rose, driven partly by foreign capital inflows.

[18] See Chapters 4 and 5 for discussions of the extent to which government policy was responsible for the long boom of the 1950s and 1960s and for the less than satisfactory economic performance since the early 1970s.

or profit to be earned from productive activity, especially entrepreneurial activity, came to depend more and more on the conditions imposed by government or negotiated with government. The usual description, regulation of industry, fails to capture an important feature, namely, that the regulations were not fixed, unalterable, and known in advance, but were variable. The system of protecting against imports well illustrates the point. Australia has not had a fixed schedule of tariffs, or even a fixed schedule of tariff changes, but a complex set of bureaucratic and political arrangements whereby, with luck and lobbying, a more favourable import tariff or quota may be granted. Millions of import licenses were issued from the reimposition of quantitative controls in 1952 to their virtual abolition in 1960. Once the (prewar) tariff was reinstated as the chief protective technique, bylaw exemptions, under which an intermediate input could be obtained abroad with payment of no duty, could make or break a small manufacturer, and were decided by a few clerks applying spurious tests of "comparability" between foreign and domestic products. The Tariff Board, later Industries Assistance Commission, advised governments on changes to the level and nature of import portection, so that entrepreneurs naturally had to be vitally concerned with influencing the outcome. Mention has already been made of the negotiations between state governments and mining companies and manufacturers. To obtain a banking license in Australia has been a mysterious process of implicit and explicit negotiations. Insurance companies are threatened with a change of rules under which they operate when they cater too successfully to sections of the population (for example offering cheap health insurance for young adults). The examples could be multiplied. They point to the possibility that the business of business has become government, or at least the business of attempting to elicit favourable terms from government.

11.7   Public choice and private choice

In their pursuit of "the greatest advantage to the people of Australia" – the general objective set the central bank in 1945 – federal governments had wide choice between and within monetary, fiscal, and regulatory instruments. The macroeconomic performance of the economy does seem to influence the voters in representative democracies, as when Menzies almost lost power in 1961. Voters, nonetheless, are not affected equally or even in the same direction by, for instance, variations in the general price level: Whereas everyone may benefit in some long-run sense from the existence of a stable currency, debtors gain from particular episodes of inflation and creditors lose. A basic "goal" of macroeconomic policy during the 1950s and 1960s was "external balance", that is, the avoidance of devaluation of the exchange rate under pressure of a loss in international reserves. Now, it is possible to make an argument that a fixed exchange rate is a "public good" in that it protects citizens from unwise domestic monetary policy; or that in an unstable exchange market devaluation sets up self-fulfilling expectations of further devaluations. Decisions to alter the exchange rate in the postwar period were, however, as much or possibly more influenced by sectoral interests of exporters as by the desire of politicians to advance the common weal.

Alternatives to exchange rate variations ranged through a great variety of monetary measures, exchange regulations, budget changes, import controls (1952–62), all with differential effects on various politically sensitive interests who might be willing to see the general welfare to some extent sacrificed to their particular advantage. A similar contrast between general and particular interests can be made about growth in income per head. The pursuit of macroeconomic goals like growth and stability and full employment, however noble an action, has been tempered by political or ideological considerations, especially those concerning the extent to which voters and interest groups were willing to forgo those sectional gains that came at the expense of the general interest.

An enlarged national income, the "public good" that Giblin claimed was accepted as a national goal in the late 1930s, although it continued to be publicly avowed, had by the early 1970s been downgraded in favour of other objectives. In that the economy was able to deliver, during the 1950s and 1960s, reasonably steady and high rates of growth, public policy tended to shift to issues other than growth. The change in the character of migration policy has been discussed above. Enthusiasm for massive inflows of population somewhat waned with the importation of environmental concerns from societies richer and more crowded than Australia's, and with the emergence of persistently high levels of unemployment. There was certainly more concern with the "equity" of the distribution of economic wellbeing, which, when satisfied, tends to have the effect of reducing *measured* GDP because of the altered pattern of incentives that are introduced. In 1974/5, a man with a taxable income equal to average weekly earnings paid 22 percent by way of income tax and faced a marginal tax rate of 44 percent. In June 1975, unemployment benefits for a man with a dependent wife and child were virtually tax free, and equalled 43 percent of male average weekly earnings. It is reasonable to expect a small influence on the aggregate supply of effort, flowing from the wealth effects of the two sides of the government fiscal budget: Taxes reduce disposable income or wealth, which could induce a person to work harder or longer to make up some of the loss, whereas cash subsidies and free provision of goods and services have the opposite effect. We are then left with a massive change in opportunity costs, that is, in the relative "prices" of work in the income taxable sectors and of work outside it. Only the results of the former kind of work appear in GDP data.[19]

I have touched upon the progressive development of devices designed to protect sections of the gainfully employed population from the vagaries of the competitive market, of what Corden (1974) has aptly called the operation of a "conservative social welfare function". Two factors are fundamental to the efficacy of protective devices. The first is their degree of flexibility, of adaptation to changes in the economic environment; the case of variable import protection was briefly discussed as an illustration. The second factor is the strength of the barriers to entry into the industry or occupation to be favoured by a protective device, for, without such barriers, the rents generated would be dissipated quickly, thereby reducing the incentive of rent seekers to try to influence public policy (although, of course, the static cost of the distortion continues to be imposed on the economy). For the public enterprises, the picture is mixed, in that the defence of the market power of the public enterprises was unsuccessful in rail transport, in face of the growth of private ownership of motor vehicles and a series of constitutional cases based on section 92 of the constitution, but was much more successful in communications, where technical advances that could have reduced the demand for public output were either handicapped or assigned to the public sector. Private initiative was in many ways constrained by the actions of the public enterprises. But this was only an example of a general phenomenon. Within the private sector itself, until 1974 most private restrictive trade practices were permissible (although the opportunities for domestic competition were being enhanced by the integration of Australia into a national market). A great extension of publicly supported restrictive practices – marketing schemes, occupational licensing, unionisation – were further developed, so that the Australian economy came to justify the claim that it exhibited "all the restrictive practices known to man" (Butlin et al. 1982: esp. chap. 5). Earlier, I suggested that the existence of sectional, industry, profes-

---

[19] Of course, Australians had concern for the welfare of other Australians, including those they did not know or meet, and so did not vote solely in the hope of improving their own lot. Their level of concern, it should be pointed out, was, possibly, not extremely high: Only about one-quarter of respondents to opinion polls in the years 1977–82 nominated unemployment as their problem of most concern in a period when unemployment was rising from a rate of about thirty-five per thousand of population aged over fifteen, to more than eighty per thousand (Pagan 1983: 80–1).

sional, or occupational restrictions worsened the effect of the economywide recession of the 1930s insofar as it insulated selected sectors of
the economy from price signals. Similarly, and here Olson's (1982) argument seems to have an especial force, the effect of public and private
restrictive practices has been to slow down the rate of growth of measured GDP.

There has been a long-term trend towards less reliance on private
arrangements[20] and more on public. An interpretation of that trend, its
reasons and consequences, is important to any assessment of the role
of public policy in Australian economic performance. The interpretation
given in this chapter is that there has been a progressive shift of public
policy away from serving the general interest and towards serving particular interests; that is, a gradual increase in the relevance of the "private interest" theory of public policy that is associated particularly with
the work of Stigler (1975; for an Australian survey see Pincus and Withers 1983). As Kemp (1983: 218) suggests, the early Australian tradition
of the popular control of authority has created a paradox. The "very
trust in, and access to, authority...has almost certainly been a key
factor in the spread of authoritative regulation through Australian social
and economic life". However, the same trust and access have created
a system of powerful institutions, the existence of which has seriously
weakened popular control.

References

Barnard, A., and N. G. Butlin. 1981. "Australian public and private capital
    formation, 1901–75". *Economic Record* 57: 355–67.
Boehm, E. A. 1979. *Twentieth Century Economic Development in Australia.* 2d
    ed. Melbourne: Longman Cheshire.
Brennan, G., and J. J. Pincus. 1983. "Government expenditure growth and
    resource allocation: the nebulous connection". *Oxford Economic Papers*
    35: 351–65.
Butlin, N. G., A. Barnard, and J. J. Pincus. 1982. *Government and Capitalism:
    Public and Private Choice in Twentieth Century Australia.* Sydney: Allen
    & Unwin.
Corden, W. M. 1974. *Trade Policy and Economic Welfare.* Oxford: Oxford
    University Press (Clarendon Press).
Eichenberg, R. C. 1983. "Problems in using public employment data", in C.
    L. Taylor (ed.), *Why Governments Grow: Measuring Public Sector Size,*
    pp. 136–53. Beverly Hills, Calif.: Sage.

---

[20] These arrangements have been neither always competitive (Karmel and Brunt 1962)
nor always voluntary exchanges in "the market".

Giblin, L. F. 1951. *The Growth of a Central Bank: The Development of the Commonwealth Bank of Australia 1921–1945*. Melbourne: Melbourne University Press.

Gregory, R. G. 1982. "Work and welfare in the years ahead". *Australian Economic Papers* 21: 219–43.

Groenewegen, P. D. 1983. "The political economy of federalism, 1901–81", in Head 1983, pp. 169–95.

Hancock, W. K. 1930. *Australia*. London: Benn.

Head, B. W. (ed.). 1983. *State and Economy in Australia*. Melbourne: Oxford University Press.

Howard, W. A. 1983. "Trade unions and the arbitration system", in Head 1983, pp. 238–51.

Karmel, P. H., and M. Brunt. 1962. *The Structure of the Australian Economy*. Melbourne: Cheshire.

Kemp, D. A. 1983. "The national economic summit: authority, persuasion and exchange". *Economic Record* 59: 209–19.

Kendrick, J. W. 1976. *The Formation and Stocks of Total Capital*. New York: National Bureau of Economic Research.

Keynes, J. M. 1936. *The General Theory of Employment, Interest and Money*. London: Macmillan.

Mathews, R. L., and W. R. C. Jay. 1972. *Federal Finance: Intergovernmental Relations in Australia since Federation*. Melbourne: Nelson.

Myrdal, G. 1968. *Asian Drama: An Inquiry into the Poverty of Nations*. New York: Pantheon.

Olson, M. 1982. *The Rise and Decline of Nations: Economic Growth, Stagflation, and Social Rigidities*. New Haven, Conn.: Yale University Press.

Pagan, A. 1983. "Who's afraid of inflation?" *Economic Papers* 2: 79–93.

Pincus, J. J., and G. A. Withers. 1983. "Economics of regulation", in F. H. Gruen (ed.), *Surveys of Australian Economics*, vol. 3, pp. 9–76. Sydney: Allen & Unwin.

Reynolds, L. G. 1983. "The spread of economic growth in the third world". *Journal of Economic Literature* 21(3): 911–80.

Sawer, G. 1963. *Australian Federal Politics and Law 1929–1949*. Melbourne: Melbourne University Press.

Sharkey, W. W. 1982. *The Theory of Natural Monopoly*. Cambridge: Cambridge University Press.

Sieper, E. 1982. *Rationalising Rustic Regulation*. St. Leonards, NSW: Centre for Independent Studies.

Sinclair, W. A. 1970. "Capital formation", in C. Forster (ed.), *Australian Economic Development in the Twentieth Century*. London: Allen & Unwin.

Smith, F. B. 1982. "Australia and Britain". *Critical Review* 24: 80–93.

Stigler, G. J. 1975. *The Citizen and the State: Essays on Regulation*. Chicago: University of Chicago Press.

Stolper, W. F., and P. A. Samuelson. 1941. "Protection and real wages". *Review of Economic Studies* 9: 58–73.

Williams, R. A. 1982. *An Australian Housing Model.* Discussion Paper No. 58. Centre for Economic Policy Research, Australian National University.

1984. "Interactions between government and private outlays: education in Australia, 1949–50 to 1931–82". *Economic Record* 60: 317–25.

CHAPTER 12

Economic wellbeing

IAN W. McLEAN

Australians possess a powerful folklore about the high levels of material prosperity that they have long enjoyed, and about their relatively easy access to a share in that prosperity. A stylised rendering of the historical elements in this view might proceed as follows. Immigrants to Australia came largely because it offered economic prospects superior to those faced in Europe. Through hard work the settlers tapped the abundant mineral riches and brought vast areas of land into productive use. Gold and wool thus underpinned for a rapidly expanding population an average standard of living that by the late nineteenth century was above that in Britain. Further, the most important source of colonial wealth, rural land, had been redistributed without violence by government legislation from the few to the many, thereby weakening a nexus among economic, social, and political power that persisted in the United Kingdom.

In the 1890s, when an interruption to economic expansion occurred, colonial governments assumed new responsibilities for the maintenance of working conditions and the mitigation of hardship for the poorest members of society. By 1920 a legal basic minimum wage had been legislated, and a tariff policy was being implemented partly in order to protect the living standards of urban/industrial workers. After a second economic collapse during the 1930s governments more explicitly assumed responsibility for the improvement of living standards through policies to promote economic growth, and also for the provision of more comprehensive health, education, and social welfare programmes financed by an expanded system of taxation. Thus Australians have created a society whose material prosperity and the evenness with which it is shared have been for the last hundred years or more either the best in the world or close thereto.

This romantic view of some central themes in Australian history was

Frank Jones, John Piggott, and Sue Richardson, together with several contributors to this volume, offered helpful comments, and Margaret Morrissey provided valuable research assistance. Support from a University of Adelaide research grant in 1983 and from a Visiting Fellowship in Economic History at the Australian National University in the summer of 1984 is also acknowledged.

built up from an amalgam of contemporary observation and social ide-
alism, and nurtured by the collective belief that the experiment of white
settlement in Australia had succeeded in realising the economic goals
of those who came from Europe to a land frequently referred to by its
white inhabitants as the Lucky Country. What is the conformity between
folklore and fact?

12.1   Concepts and hypotheses

It is the purpose of this chapter to assess how far the economic activity
and associated economic policies that have been discussed in earlier
chapters have resulted in improvements in the economic wellbeing of
Australians. This ambitious goal is made more so by the dearth of
evidence on and analytical studies of the subject.[1] However, we are
assisted if we adopt the position that special significance should be given
to two dimensions of what is a complex and nebulous concept. These
are the average standard of living and the degree of economic inequality.
An additional advantage is that quantitative measures of both are at
least in principle obtainable. Frequently used measures of the former
are real per capita GDP, a ratio that may be varied by substituting
alternative denominators (the total workforce, civilian employment, labour input) or numerators (total consumption, private consumption).
Economic inequality can variously be defined with respect to income,
consumption, wealth, or some variation of these, and expressed in a
variety of summary forms – the most common being the Gini coefficient,
the Lorenz curve to which it is related, and reference points along the
cumulative distribution such as deciles. The basic economic unit used
in such studies is most frequently the individual, but the family or household may be preferred.

In this chapter trends in the economic wellbeing of Australians since
1900 will be discussed partly in terms of these conventional economic
concepts and measures. Nonconventional measures of living standards
and economic inequality complement the usual indicators, but do not
always tell the same story. The aim is to improve understanding of
the ways in which the wellbeing of Australians has been affected by the

---

[1] The unsatisfactory state of knowledge on the topics considered here is the reason why
more space than in other chapters is devoted directly to a survey of the limited evidence,
to establishing what the basic historical trends were, and to reporting the results of
very recent (sometimes unpublished) research germane to the issues discussed. An
earlier survey of evidence is offered by Boehm (1979: chap. 8).

growth, fluctuations, and structural changes that have occurred in the economy over the past eighty years.[2]

Before turning to the historical evidence, it is appropriate to consider the long-run relationship *between* standards of living and the degree of economic inequality.[3] For example, would a reasonable prior belief be a positive association between rising material conditions and a more equal sharing in the benefits of growth? It is not difficult to conceive of mechanisms that might produce simultaneous increases in living standards and reductions in inequality in an economy that had reached the stage of economic development attained by Australia at federation. As personal incomes rise, for example, differences in the income elasticity of demand for various domestically produced goods or services will lead to differences in their rates of output growth, ceteris paribus. If the industries that are expanding most rapidly are relatively intensive users of low-skilled labour, and the stagnant industries are relatively intensive users of skilled labour, the changing pattern of derived demand in the labour market may reduce margins for skill and hence narrow the distribution of wage and salary earnings. An alternative story might be based on the bias of technological change. If new technology saves skilled relative to unskilled labour, the margins for skill may again be reduced.[4] In the following sections I shall be alert to the possibility that interactions such as these may have occurred in the Australian experience.

12.2 Living standards

The historical record suggests strongly that the average Australian enjoyed a higher standard of living, broadly defined, at the outbreak of World War II than at federation. On present evidence, however, it seems that much of this gain occurred in ways that are not (fully) captured in output or income-based indicators – such as through increased life expectancy and shorter working hours. This period was marked by considerable variation in economic prosperity, with the depression of the

[2] There is a sense in which the perspective adopted in this chapter is ahistorical. The discussion is embedded in concepts drawn mainly from economics, although the topic cannot be easily confined to the economist's domain. And the concepts are those currently employed, the questions those currently asked. It is likely that the very meanings of economic growth, inequality, poverty, living standards, and other terms frequently used in the chapter have undergone some evolution, subtle but significant, since 1900.

[3] The classic discussion of this question is that of Kuznets (1955).

[4] For an elaboration of these points and a recent survey of the historical evidence on the nexus between growth and inequality see Lindert and Williamson (1985).

1930s the most serious interruption to gains in wellbeing. The historical record also suggests that an acceleration in the improvement in living standards occurred in the postwar boom to 1973, that this embraced higher rises in real income per person as well as in nonconventional measures, and that the period was remarkable for the almost uninterrupted nature of the improvement that occurred. Since 1973 the underlying growth rate in the economy has slowed, and wider fluctuations in economic activity have reappeared.[5] A decade is too short an interval to announce confidently the onset of another long period of slower and more variable growth in living standards than that which characterised the golden era of 1945–73. But we have been reminded of the possibility.

Economists' measures

One of the striking features of Australian economic history is the slow growth in living standards between 1890 and 1940 when measured by real per capita income (McLean and Pincus 1983). Perhaps the simplest illustration is to cite directly the underlying estimates. From a late-nineteenth-century peak in 1889 of $941 (in 1966–7 prices), GDP per capita grew by only 11 percent over the next half century to $1,045 in 1938–9. There are wide fluctuations during this period, with marked falls occurring in the 1890s and early 1930s. But there were few years in which a level of real income higher than that for 1938–9 was recorded. With available estimates, the impression persists of a half century of virtual stagnation in living standards however those estimates are massaged. By contrast with the 1890–1940 period, real income per capita doubled over the next thirty years (Table 12.1), a contrast that raises several questions. Was the economic prosperity of the late nineteenth century – Australians may have had the world's highest average incomes at that time – so based as to be inherently difficult to sustain? Did the rapid population growth (from 3.1 to 6.9 million over the fifty years following 1890) reduce the rate of per capita growth relative to what would have been recorded had there been a lower level of immigration? Does measured GDP understate increases in living standards more broadly defined during this period relative to earlier and later periods? And just how firmly based are the existing estimates of GDP?

---

[5] An increase in output or income variability need not per se decrease economic welfare. First, it is consumption that is important to wellbeing, and its variation tends to be less than that of personal disposable income. Second, if the variability is fully anticipated, no loss of welfare need result. A reduction in *uncertainty* concerning future variations in income would increase welfare. Whether or not such reductions occurred along with the postwar decline in fluctuations in economic activity may be debated, as might the contribution thereto of government macrostabilisation and social welfare policies.

Table 12.1. *Growth of real per capita* GDP *and consumption, 1889 to 1973/74*

Five years centred on:	1889		1911/12		1937/8		1971/2
A. Real GDP per capita							
(i) $ 1966/7	913		1,038		1,059		2,267
(ii) Change (%)		13.7		2.0		114.7	
(iii) Average annual							
growth rate (%)		0.6		0.1		2.3	
B. Real consumption per capita							
(i) $ 1966/7	743		799		805		1,592
(ii) Change (%)		7.5		0.8		97.8	
(iii) Average annual							
growth rate (%)		0.3		0.0		2.0	

Source: Data from McLean and Pincus 1982: App. table. The per capita GDP and consumption figures are averages for the five years centred on the years shown. The consumption expenditure excludes defence spending.

Some indication of possible weaknesses in the existing GDP estimates seems appropriate.[6] In the first place, there is a paucity of good price indexes, especially for the late nineteenth century, though the work of Bambrick (1970) is important for the years since 1910. Second, the direct deflation of aggregate consumption between 1890 and 1940 reported by McLean and Pincus (1983) raised by one-third the rate of growth of per capita real GDP during that period, illustrating the sensitivity of the Butlin-based estimates to plausible revision. A related point is that the estimates of aggregate consumption reported in Table 12.1 are residually obtained. Thus they include errors and omissions not only in the current price GDP estimates obtained largely by summing sectoral value added, but also in the estimates of nonconsumption expenditure items then deducted from GDP (defence, investment, changes in stocks, balance of payments). For the study of living standards, consumption-based series are especially relevant, but they are the weakest component of the historical national accounts estimates currently available.

Turning to evidence for the period from 1900 to the present, Table 12.2 contains four national accounts-based measures of living standards. Although the four measures generally fluctuate together, some diver-

[6] The primary source for the period before 1940 is N. G. Butlin (1962), and despite adjustment and extension, discussion of the long-run trends in economic activity in Australia prior to 1940 remains heavily dependent on this one set of estimates. The Butlin estimates of Australian GDP are critically evaluated by Boehm (1965) and Clark (1963).

Table 12.2. GDP *and consumption per person and per worker 1901 to 1981*

Period	Real private consumption per capita	Real total consumption per capita	Real GDP per capita	Real GDP per worker
$ (1966/7 prices)				
1901	651	672	819	2,071
1914	800	811	1,046	2,440
1921	719	727	971	2,422
1929	823	830	980	2,424
1933	736	741	934	2,259
1939	773	798	1,045	2,455
1947	854	907	1,179	2,762
1961	1,155	1,203	1,627	3,901
1974	1,747	1,801	2,398	5,508
1981	1,922	1,993	2,632	5,762
Annual average growth rate (%)				
1901–14	1.6	1.5	1.9	1.3
1914–21	−1.4	−1.4	−1.0	−0.1
1921–9	1.7	1.7	0.1	0.0
1929–33	−2.6	−2.6	−1.2	−1.7
1933–9	0.8	1.3	1.9	1.5
1939–47	1.2	1.7	1.5	1.5
1947–61	2.2	2.1	2.3	2.5
1961–74	3.2	3.2	3.0	2.7
1974–81	1.4	1.5	1.4	0.7

Sources: Australian Bureau of Statistics, *Australian National Accounts* and *Labour Report*; M. W. Butlin 1977; McLean and Pincus 1982; National Economic Summit Conference, *Information Paper on the Economy* (1983). All data refer to years ended June 30.

gences are evident. For instance, differences between the series of per worker and per capita GDP reflect variations in the age structure and workforce participation rate: In the early part of the postwar boom the population grew more rapidly than the labour force, and since 1961 the reverse has occurred.

There are many possibilities for varying the subperiods and the subsets of GDP and the population in order to create more cells in Table 12.2. However, the general outlines of the Australian experience of real per capita growth in GDP this century seem clear enough: marked fluctuations around a very slowly rising trend to the late 1930s; a sustained boom over the next three decades; and a marked slowdown in the 1970s but to rates of growth that were still above those typical of the period between 1900 and 1940.

Extending the economists' measures

Real per capita income has obvious limitations as a measure of average living standards. There are well-known problems with estimation of national income or product, such as the valuation of nonmarketed goods and services, defining the market, securing comprehensive coverage, and index number issues where time series are sought. But more fundamental are the conceptual and philosophical questions of the relationship among aggregate output, income, and consumption as recorded by national accounting conventions on the one hand and, on the other, changes in the economic or social welfare of the community. Abramovitz (1981: 1–2) succinctly expresses these concerns:

It is elementary . . . that per capita output growth and welfare growth are not the same thing. National product is not even an adequate long-term measure of net output relevant to welfare. It makes inadequate allowance for the quality and variety of goods. It excludes the household and treats all government expenditure as final product. It neglects the externalities of production and consumption and the costs of growth proper, for example, the dislocation of people. It makes dubious assumptions about people's ability to appraise and guard against the dangers carried by jobs and products. And there is much more to economic welfare than can be captured by any long-term measure of output: job stability, income scarcity, a fair distribution of opportunities and rewards.

The discussion of these problems (see for example Usher 1980) has not been confined to theoretical speculation. As a result of the debates that began in the 1960s concerning the *desirability* of economic growth, with its putative adverse consequences for environmental quality and natural resource exhaustion, attempts were made to redefine and reestimate GNP. The pioneering American study was by Nordhaus and Tobin (1973). This retained the principal strength of the GNP-based measures of economic wellbeing – namely, using market prices to value and aggregate the production or consumption of diverse goods and services into a single number. The objective was to broaden the range of economic activities that were included in the calculation, either adding to or subtracting from GDP to obtain a new "measure of economic welfare".

Gillin (1974) uses the Nordhaus–Tobin framework to construct a measure of economic welfare (MEW) for Australia for the period 1948/9 to 1972/3. Starting with private final consumption, deductions were made for purchases regarded as intermediate (for example the cost of journeys to work); the imputed annual flow of the services of household durables were included while their initial "capital" cost was excluded; leisure time was valued and included, as were nonmarketed household services; an urban disamenity adjustment was deducted; and an allowance was made for the flow of services from government capital assets.

Table 12.3. GDP and MEW 1948/9 to 1972/3

	$ million in 1966/7 prices		Annual growth rate (%)
	1948/9	1972/3	
1. GDP	10,051	30,058	4.7
2. Imputation for leisure	11,201	18,625	2.1
3. Imputation for nonmarket activity	9,335	22,623	3.8
4. All other adjustments	−3,749	−5,344	(−) 1.5
5. MEW–A (1 + 4)	6,302	24,714	5.9
6. MEW–B (1 + 2 + 4)	17,503	43,339	3.9
7. MEW–C (1 + 3 + 4)	15,637	47,337	4.7
8. MEW–D (1 + 2 + 3 + 4)	26,838	65,962	3.8

Source: Gillin 1974: 78.

Two adjustments stand out as swamping all others in importance – the imputed value of leisure activities and the imputed value of nonmarket activities, mainly the provision of household services. Each of these items was in aggregate equal to or greater in value than that of private final consumption expenditure as recorded in the national accounts. A summary of the results is shown in Table 12.3.

Adoption of the full MEW measure reduces the growth rate below that of GDP – from 4.7 to 3.8 percent per year. What is of interest to the present discussion of living standards is the differing impacts on these growth rates of the major components in Gillin's study. His estimates of both leisure and nonmarket services grow more slowly than GDP. But the other items (disamenities, etc.), which on balance are negative in their effects on the level of MEW, also grow more slowly, thus raising the rate of MEW improvement when considered alone. We are thus faced with a menu of possible adjustments to GDP that will change our measure of growth, and hence of conventionally defined improvements to living standards, according to the selection made. The rather crude estimation methods employed by Gillin suggest that little weight should be placed on the detail of his findings. They nonetheless raise the issue of whether the inclusion of leisure and household services in a broad-based measure of GDP would alter our picture of past trends in Australian living standards.

In a recent study that estimated "community income" for Australia between 1891 and 1981 by adjusting GDP to include an estimate for nonmarket household services, it was found that the long-run growth rates per capita were little changed from those obtained using GDP series

(Snooks 1983). It is too early to predict whether future research will confirm the finding that the value of household services delivered outside the market, however significant in absolute terms when compared with the value of GDP, has grown historically at rates close to those of unadjusted GDP.

The study of historical changes in leisure has also begun. Hours of work declined irregularly this century, but the evidence typically cited relates to standard hours per week. Recognition also should be given to changes in overtime, part-time work, and annual leave and public holidays and to differences between male and female working hours. After making such adjustments, Carter and Maddock (1984) suggest that the rate of reduction in working hours between 1911 and 1948 was greater than that experienced since. If the assumption is made that reduced hours of work become increased leisure hours (and not intermediate "inputs" such as longer journeys to work or increased household maintenance activities), and if it is accepted that increased productivity offers the worker a choice of increased leisure or income, then the revealed preference for relatively more leisure before 1948 and relatively more income after is significant. An aggregation of income and leisure would raise the resulting growth rate of economic wellbeing before 1948 relative to that for later years. The sharp distinction between these two periods evident in the real GDP per capita growth rates would then be muted. This possibility is, however, complicated by other uses of time and changes in life expectancy, issues to which we shall return.

To conclude this discussion on extensions to conventional measures of living standards, attention is drawn to the possible influence of changes in immigration. The higher the proportion of the foreign born in the resident population, and the greater the gap between Australia and the (presumably lower) country-of-origin real GDP per capita in the year of migration, the more will the conventional measure of Australian average income understate the rise actually experienced by the resident population to any reference year. An effort to compute this effect is reported by Withers (1985) for the period 1948 to 1981, much of which witnessed sizeable immigration. "Resident economic welfare" in 1981 relative to 1948 had risen at an average rate of 2.5 percent per annum in his calculations, in comparison with a 2.2 percent per annum rise in per capita real GDP conventionally measured. This exercise also usefully draws attention to the improved living standards afforded immigrants relative to what (counterfactually) they might have experienced had they remained in their countries of origin, as well as to an additional difficulty in comparing GDP-based measures of living standards across periods (or countries) with varying migration characteristics.

Table 12.4. *Measures of housing size and crowding 1911 to 1981*

Census year	Rooms per dwelling	Occupants per dwelling	Rooms per occupant
1911	4.93	4.53	1.09
1921	4.94	4.40	1.12
1933	4.99	4.08	1.22
1947	4.98	3.75	1.33
1954	5.04	3.55	1.42
1961	5.12	3.55	1.44
1966	5.20	3.47	1.50
1971	5.00	3.31	1.51
1976	5.34	3.12	1.71
1981	5.43	2.98	1.82

Sources and notes: The statistics are from the censuses of the Commonwealth of Australia. Note that Australia-wide estimates were not available before 1911. The dwellings figures are for occupied private dwellings.

Social indicators

One response to the inadequacies of GDP as a welfare indicator has been to eschew the aggregation goal and seek a range of partial "social indicators" of community wellbeing. This approach has found favour with development economists and with those responsible for the design of social welfare programmes and the identification of poverty in advanced societies, including Australia (Owens 1980).

The quality of housing is one important component in living standards. In Table 12.4 the average size of occupied private dwellings at each census is shown together with the number of occupants. The combined effect of slightly larger houses and a fall of one-third in the average number of occupants is a 67 percent increase in the number of rooms per occupant. There is an acceleration in this measure of improvement after 1947, although the postwar break in trend is much less dramatic than that for real incomes.

An improvement in the general health of a community would constitute an improvement in one important dimension of its standard of living. As the inputs into the health "industry" are more easily measured than the output, the ratios of doctors to population and number of hospital beds to population are often employed to capture the growth in available health services. The number of persons in New South Wales per doctor fell only slightly from 1,795 in 1901 to 1,737 by 1911. By 1939 the figure was down to 770, in 1960 to 656, and by 1980 to 304.

Table 12.5. *Education statistics*

	1901	1947	1981
1. % of population 15–19 engaged in full-time study	7.6[a]	11.3	34.7
2. No. of university students as % of 20–4 age group	0.5	4.9	12.8

[a]For 1911.
Sources: Australian Bureau of Statistics, *University Statistics*; Commonwealth *Year Book*; McLean and Pincus 1982: Table 12.4.

These data are fragile, and the production function linking the supply of doctors to the quantity and quality of health care is unclear. However, the increased availability of medical personnel between 1900 and the second world war was quite dramatic. Similarly, sharp rises occurred throughout the century in the availability of hospital beds. Again for New South Wales, the population per bed was 246 in 1901 and 141 in 1939. A slight rise occurred in the immediate postwar period but by 1980 the figure had fallen to 89.[7]

Another widely used indicator of economic wellbeing is the level of educational attainment. Literacy rates were already high by the end of the nineteenth century, and as the years of compulsory schooling were raised, so the proportion of the population over five and under fifteen at school also rose – from 64 percent in 1901 to 89 percent in 1947 to 98 percent (six to fifteen) in 1981. The retention in education beyond the minimum leaving age therefore seems relevant to an assessment of twentieth-century increases in educational levels. Table 12.5 shows two such proxy retention ratios. They indicate that stagnation in education standards was not a feature of the period between federation and the second world war, but that once again an acceleration in established trends occurred during the postwar decades.

Expectation of life at particular ages is a further common measure of a society's standard of living. Obviously life expectancy is a complex function of many social and economic variables, among them the quality and quantity of food, basic hygiene practices, public health measures, the provision of water and sewerage services to households, and the quality of medical services. The result of improvements in such areas has been a rise in life expectation this century by a remarkable 16.2 years at birth for males and 19.6 years for females (Table 12.6). About

[7] Sources are Coward (1980: 39) and the New South Wales *Year Books*.

Table 12.6. *Life expectation (years)*

Age	Sex	1901–11	1946–8	1981
1. At birth	M	55.2	66.1	71.4
	F	58.8	70.6	78.4
2. At age 1	M	60.0	67.3	71.2
	F	62.9	71.5	78.2
3. At age 60	M	14.4	15.4	17.3
	F	16.2	18.1	22.1

Source: Year Book Australia, 1983, p. 137.

two-thirds of this increase (10.9 and 11.8 years respectively) occurred in the first four decades; the fall in infant mortality was important to this outcome.

It has previously been mentioned that a decline in average hours of work occurred during the twentieth century, and that this decline appeared to be greater before 1948 than since. In particular, *standard* hours were relatively constant during the long period of postwar growth in real income per person. A different perspective on the implications for wellbeing of the reduction in hours of work and the increase in expectation of life is to view trends in *lifetime* allocation of time. Recognising changing age-specific workforce participation rates, reduction of hours of work other than through reductions in the *per week* standard, and differences in work and leisure patterns between males and females, Carter and Maddock (1984) report that for males lifetime expected "market" hours were 3 percent lower in 1947 than in 1911 but had fallen a further 20 percent by 1981, whereas leisure time had risen 41 and 25 percent respectively during the two periods. For females, by contrast, market hours increased by 20 percent and 50 percent (most of the latter increase occurring since 1961), while their leisure time also increased by 20 and 19 percent over 1911–47 and 1947–81 respectively.

12.3   Economic inequality

The study of long-run changes in economic inequality is of interest for several reasons. Ideas of social fairness or justice relate importantly to equity issues, and social progress is in part taken to mean movement towards particular distributional objectives, although these may change over time. The pursuit of a more egalitarian society, the reduction in the incidence and severity of poverty, and the discouragement via taxation of the accumulation of very large private asset holdings are objectives common to many Western democracies this century. Another reason for interest in past trends in economic inequality is to assist in the design of specific redistributive policies and in monitoring the impact of such policies after their implementation.[8]

Comprehensive statistical surveys or censuses of the distribution of income or wealth in the community have, until recently, been few in number. The first major inquiry this century was the war census of 1915, which sought information on both income and wealth (Knibbs 1918). Prior to 1976 only the 1933 census asked questions on personal income, and there has been no wealth survey since 1915. Beginning in 1968/9, official surveys were undertaken into the distribution of income. Private studies of income and wealth distribution, or of some of their components, are growing in number, but few relate to historical (in this context, pre-1967) trends, the principal interest here. All the evidence suggests some decline in both income and wealth inequality in Australia this century. Interest therefore lies in the magnitude of the decline, its timing, and its determinants.

The distribution of income

The decline in income inequality between the war census of 1915 and the first of the official surveys of recent years in 1968/9 has been examined by Jones (1975). He does not use the 1933 census information on income, and confines attention to these two sets of evidence more than half a century apart. His conclusion is that "it would require a mind peculiarly resistant to evidence to deny that over the last half century there has been a significant reduction in inequality of income distribution among men" (p. 32). Jones estimates that, after making a number of adjustments to improve the comparability of the data sets, the Gini coefficient declined from 0.420 in 1915 to 0.338 in 1968/9. He further points out that this overall trend towards greater equality was not uniform by income class, with the share of the top 1 percent of male income recipients falling from 14.6 percent of *net* income in 1914/15 to 7.9 percent of *gross* income in 1968/9, while the share of the bottom 20 percent of male income earners actually fell slightly from 6.5 to 5 percent. Differences between the two dates in the age structure of the population, in the number of pensioners, and in the tax structure complicate comparisons, but the impression is conveyed that increased equality has been

---

[8] There is a very large general literature on the economics of inequality – theoretical and empirical. For an introduction and survey see Atkinson (1983). For surveys of recent Australian writings see Piggott (1984) and Richardson (1979). Ingles (1981) and Maddock et al. (1984) provide guides to statistical sources and a bibliography respectively.

achieved more by reducing the income share of the very rich than by raising the relative position of the poor.

There have been a small number of attempts to seek additional evidence on income distribution trends during the century or to fill the long gap that follows the 1915 war census.[9] In a study based on tax information, Berry (1977) calculated before-tax income distributions for six years between 1922/3 and 1972/3 and concluded that "Australia has undergone a considerable equalization of incomes over the past fifty years" (p. 23). There is a sharp fall in the share of the top income groups – for example that of the top 5 percent declines from 42 to 16 percent – while the lowest 20 percent of income recipients increase their share from 2 to 8 percent. The most striking feature of the evidence is the timing of the movement towards greater equality: Most occurred between 1932/3 and 1942/3, with a little further movement to 1953/4. By contrast, there is no significant change in the 1922/3 to 1932/3 decade nor in the twenty years after 1952/3. However, some forms of income are excluded from taxation-based estimates of income distribution, for example, undistributed company income. Also, taxable rather than gross income may be the basis of the before-tax estimates. There may be considerable tax avoidance that is not uniform across classes of income recipients. And as the average and marginal tax rates have risen for higher proportions of the population, the incentive to evade or avoid taxes has also risen.

An attempt to draw on the income information in the 1933 census has been made by McLean and Richardson (1986). They compare several measures of income inequality in that year with measures based on the 1915 war census, on a 1979 income survey, and on the 1981 census. Where individual incomes among males are considered, inequality increases between 1915 and 1933. An effort to remove the effect of the depression on the 1933 distribution leaves the Gini coefficient close to that for 1915. All the reduction in income inequality between 1915 and 1981 has occurred since 1933. A marked fall in inequality between 1933 and 1979 is also observed where family per capita income is the basis of measurement. If supported by subsequent research, these findings suggest that the twentieth-century decline in income inequality may not have occurred steadily across the decades, and that the period between the 1930s and the 1970s may contain most of the reduction.[10]

---

[9] One study of tax returns for 1942/3 (Brown 1957) compared income distributions for the years 1938/9 to 1942/3.

[10] Further evidence on trends in income inequality is presented in N. G. Butlin (1983). He computes an estimate of the New South Wales income distribution in 1901 (no data are presented), compares this with the results of the 1968/9 income distribution survey,

The distribution of wealth

The disparity in wealth among individuals is typically greater than that of income; manifestations of great personal wealth are frequently very obvious; and the links between wealth and power – social, economic, and political – are often close. It is therefore surprising that there have been so few attempts to determine the distribution of personal wealth in Australia this century, with no official census or major survey having been conducted since 1915.

The results of two studies are brought together in Table 12.7. Intertemporal comparisons are hazardous because of the lack of comparability of the estimates, but it seems clear that the distribution of personal wealth has become more equal since 1915.[11] The different estimation methods employed may account for most of the differences in the estimates for recent years. Podder and Kakwani used a net worth definition of wealth, with the household as the economic unit, and the estimates obtained from a survey covering only 2,757 households.[12] Recalling that our present interest is in coverage or bias relative to that which may be present in the 1915 war census, the plausible inference seems to be that the Podder and Kakwani estimates of personal wealth distribution are biased towards greater equality. The Raskall procedures were more complex, involving use of estate valuations adjusted by mortality multipliers for each age group, an independent assessment of aggregate private wealth, and a matching of the two with "blow-up" ratios to offset assumed biases and incompleteness. No strong bias relative to the 1915 distribution is as likely as in the case of the Podder and Kakwani study. For this reason, as well as the more comprehensive empirical basis to the inquiry, my assessment is that the Raskall estimates for 1970 are the more reliable.

A study of Victorian probate records by Rubinstein (1979) provides six observations of the distribution of personal wealth during the twentieth century. Because consistent methods and sources were employed, intertemporal comparisons are more securely based than for the studies

and reports that the Gini coefficient is virtually unchanged (0.45 and 0.46 respectively) but that the Lorenz curves "cross in such a way as to suggest a higher proportion of individuals in receipt of low incomes in 1968/69" (p. 6).

[11] Soltow (1972) finds a similar distribution of wealth in Australia in 1915 and in the United States in 1860.

[12] This survey had a response rate of only 50 percent. Although Podder and Kakwani conduct some tests for bias resulting from the low response rate, they cannot know the bias on the wealth (net worth) questions, though like other researchers in this area they ruefully note that "wealth data are generally believed to be subject to systematic errors or bias due to understatement" (1976: 78).

Table 12.7. *Distribution of personal wealth (percentage of total)*

	1915	1966/7	1970
First quintile	0.03	0.91	1.04
Second quintile	0.43	7.81	3.83
Third quintile	2.01	15.06	7.46
Fourth quintile	7.80	22.72	15.49
Fifth quintile	89.71	53.51	72.18
Top 10%	—	—	58.50
Top 5%	66.2	24.58	45.50
Top 1%	39.46	9.26	22.00
Concentration ratio	0.86	0.52	0.70

Sources: For 1915 and 1966/7: Podder and Kakwani 1976: Table 14, p. 90. For 1970: Raskall 1977: 47.

reported in Table 12.7. Inequality fell without pause or reversal: "The Gini coefficient declined steadily and progressively at each time interval, among both men and women" (p. 34). A summary of Rubinstein's estimates, for males only, is shown in Table 12.8.[13] Other noticeable features include the extreme inequality of wealth holding in the late nineteenth century and the relative stability of the mean value of estates measured in constant prices. Of special interest are the similar wealth inequality estimates obtained by Raskall for Australia as a whole in 1970 and those by Rubinstein for Victoria in 1962/3 and 1973/4, whether the Gini coefficient or the share of the top 1 percent is the basis of comparison. This lends further support to the view that the Podder and Kakwani estimates may not be reliable. In a comment on the wide differences between their results and his own findings, Rubinstein suggests three possible causes: his inclusion of rural wealth, which tends to be more highly concentrated than urban; the greater spread of household ages; and underrepresentation of the very rich in the Podder and Kakwani survey (Rubinstein 1979: 39).

The final empirical study I shall mention is that by Gunton (1975), in which he uses probate data and the estate multiplier method to estimate personal wealth in Australia for each year from 1953 to 1969. He reports no definite trend towards greater equality during that period – the Gini coefficient declines somewhat from 0.681 in 1953 to 0.637 in 1964 before rising to 0.667 in 1969 (p. 182). These ratios are again much closer to those of Raskall and Rubinstein than the estimates of Podder and Kak-

[13] See also a study of New South Wales wealth holding by Rubinstein (1980).

Table 12.8. *Inequality measures for Victorian estates (men only, 1880 to 1973/4)*

Year	Gini	Share of top 1%	Mean value, £s	Mean value (1911 £s)
1880	0.957	0.67	473	472
1908/9	0.904	0.45	885	900
1923/4	0.871	0.35	1,412	833
1938/9	0.867	0.33	1,541	956
1953/4	0.816	0.27	3,660	789
1962/3	0.769	0.20	5,533	976
1973/4	0.746	0.20	8,804	879

Source: Rubinstein 1979: Table 2, p. 35; Table 3, p. 37.

wani, as are his estimates of the share of wealth held by the most wealthy 1 percent. Gunton, too, attempts to make the information published rom the 1915 census as comparable as possible in concept to his estimates of wealth distribution (p. 185). Using data for all wealth holders, he finds that the Gini coefficient declines from 0.826 to 0.681 in 1953, but argues that the estimates should not be compared: "It seems probable that the 1915 Census provided a better coverage of the very low end of the wealth distribution than that provided by available estate duty statistics for the period 1953 to 1969 because of latter day reluctance to process very small deceased estates with the exception of foreign domiciles" (pp. 184–5). Hence Gunton compares the Gini coefficients for the two dates on the basis of two alternative definitions of the wealth holding population. The outcome is only a very small fall in inequality between 1915 and 1953 or 1969, with most occurring between the latter two dates. Again, the problems of ensuring comparability with 1915 may be such as to render suspect any strong conclusion about the magnitude of the movement to a more equal wealth distribution in Australia.

Further dimensions of economic inequality

The nature and extent of economic inequality are only partly captured by aggregate measures of income and wealth distribution. Additional information might be sought from trends in earnings distributions and margins for skills; in workforce participation and unemployment rates; in regional differences in per capita income or related indicators; in poverty; and in the distribution of ownership of particular assets, especially housing. Here, we briefly refer to evidence relating to the first three.

The structure of wages by occupation or skill does not appear to have shown any secular trend over the very long run, although some short-run variation is evident.[14] The major study is by Hancock and Moore (1972), who report no clear evidence for a decline in the ratio of skilled to unskilled wage rates among twenty-eight occupations over the period 1914 to the late 1960s. Regrettably, there are no long-run historical series of average *earnings* by occupation; the principal source of data is the average *award rates* of pay. The relationship between the two can be influenced, cyclically or secularly, by overaward payments (earnings drift), and by the overtime worked. Hancock and Moore offer the view that for the interwar period there was little in the way of overaward rates paid, but that this was not true in the postwar decades (pp. 109–10). An additional problem with this picture of no long-term compression of the wage structure is that changes in the distribution of occupations in the workforce have to be taken into account.[15]

The study of income and (especially) wealth distribution in history often reduces to an inquiry into the experience of the rich, partly because we are able to recover more financial information about them than about the poorer classes, who left few records. One summary statistic germane to the study of the poor is, of course, the level of unemployment. In recent years it is likely that a major (if not the major) cause of poverty has been unemployment. To be a useful indicator of poverty, the unemployment rate should be disaggregated by age, marital status, and sex; some assessment should be made of average duration of unemployment among the unemployed; and the availability and level of unemployment assistance should be considered.[16] However, the overall unemployment rate conveys something of the changing importance of the problem. From 1905/6 to 1919/20, the average rate was 3.9 percent; during the 1920s it rose to 6 percent, then to 13.5 percent across the depression decade (1930/1 to 1938/9). The postwar years of "full" employment (1.9 percent from /7 to 1973/4) gave way in the 1970s to measured unemployment rates reminiscent of the 1920s – 5.6 percent

[14] See for example Lydall (1968: 191–3) and Oxnam (1950).
[15] A more recent study of very long-run trends in the ratio of unskilled to skilled workers' wage rates in New South Wales since 1828 suggested a "strongly persistent egalitarian trend broken briefly . . . by depression in the nineties and during slow economic growth and significant structural change in the twenties" (N. G. Butlin 1983: 15). It is made clear that these findings are to be interpreted as preliminary.
[16] To illustrate, unemployment among all males in September 1983 was 11.7 percent compared with 20.3 percent in the census of 1933; but the rate among females was very similar (13.8 and 13.7 percent respectively); and that among fifteen- to nineteen-year-olds in 1983, male and female, was above that in 1933. Few would claim, however, that the unemployed today face absolute levels of poverty similar to those in 1933.

on average between 1973/4 and 1981/2, with higher rates in the first half of the 1980s.

Regional economic inequalities, have not been a major political or social issue in Australia in the twentieth century. It is unclear whether that is because the conditions that might have produced such disparities have never been present or because federal government policies have successfully offset tendencies to widening differences in regional growth experiences. Given the size of the country and its economic dependence on the discovery and utilisation of natural resource supplies, the expectation might be that wide variation in regional economic growth would be a prominent characteristic of its history. One obvious index of changing economic fortunes is the regional distribution of population, yet over the eighty years during which the population has grown from four to fifteen million its distribution between the states has changed only marginally.

There is evidence that relatively small differences in average income have existed among the states. The 1915 war census reported that average income varied around the commonwealth average of $220 from a high of $250 for Western Australia to a low of $186 for South Australia. The variation in average net assets was from $1,184 in New South Wales through a commonwealth average of $1,110 to $892 in Queensland.[17] From 1938/9, estimates of gross personal income by states for the household sector are available. If the per capita figures are expressed as a percentage of the Australian average, the range between highest and lowest fluctuated around twenty points until the early 1970s, after which it rapidly narrowed, and from 1976/7 has been steady at close to twelve points. The comparable range from the 1915 income figures is twenty-nine percentage points.

12.4   Speculations

If this book had been written in the late 1960s the most likely explanation for the recorded improvements in living standards and reduced inequality since 1900 would centre on the increased economic role of government, its commitment to growth and full employment, and the extension of the welfare state to ensure the wide distribution of the benefits of economic prosperity. From the perspective of the mid 1980s this interpretation looks less plausible. There has been no retreat from

---

[17] Knibbs (1918: 24, 30). The figures are the averages for males and females, residents of Australia, and calculated over the number of returns, not the population as a whole. The comparisons shown ignore the figures for the Territories.

the goals of the early postwar era, and the importance of government in the economic life of Australians has continued to increase. In the last fifteen years, however, this has not prevented sustained high levels of unemployment, worsening structural problems in the economy, and a return to near stagnant growth in real per capita incomes. Since these features are also evident in the recent economic history of most advanced economies (just as the growth and stability of the 1950s and 1960s were widely experienced) it is clear that Australia's dependence on international economic conditions is still considerable. The ability of Australians since 1900 to secure significant improvements in their standards of living in the absence of favourable conditions in the world economy has been, and remains, heavily circumscribed.

An alternative perspective on Australia's record in delivering higher living standards in the twentieth century is by way of international comparisons. It is possible that for a period during the second half of the nineteenth century Australians had the world's highest average incomes.[18] By 1980 a dozen or more countries recorded higher GDP per capita. One response is to argue that the initial (late-nineteenth-century) levels were unsustainable once the per capita natural resource endowment was reduced through immigration and natural increases (N. G. Butlin 1965). However, possession of abundant natural resources is not necessary to the attainment of high living standards. Similarly, rapid population growth is sometimes seen as a stimulus to, sometimes a drag on, the growth of per capita GDP.

Finally, the social indicators and other nonconventional measures of living standards we have consulted suggest that on balance the measured growth rate should be augmented, not reduced. Whether similar conclusions would be arrived at with respect to living standards in other countries is unclear. The lower average hours of work and larger average size of house and garden here than in Japan, for example, suggest that Australia's standard of living might lie above that of the average Japanese even though the GNP per capita is now comparable.[19]

Turning from consideration of the levels of economic wellbeing to its distribution, a major issue concerns the contribution of government, specifically its social welfare programmes, to the observed decline in measured inequality. The issue is complex. Economic growth may have taken a form that directly reduced income and/or wealth distribution. For example, if the lower postwar levels of unemployment (at least until

---

[18] One estimate puts Australian GDP per head in 1870, 43 percent above that of the UK, the next highest, and 82 percent above that of the USA: Maddison (1982: 8).

[19] King (1974) compares social and economic indexes of development among the advanced countries.

recently) account for a significant part of the reduction in inequality compared with the interwar period, and if it is held that the postwar experience of full employment was primarily attributable to the concurrent world economic boom, then there is less scope for an explanation of the trend in inequality to be made in terms of the impact of (Australian) government policies.

The much faster growth in per capita GDP after 1940 accompanied (and permitted) the extension of the social welfare system. How redistributive was its impact? Any assessment is complicated by the possible displacement of private charity or if some substitution of state for intrafamily or within-household redistribution resulted. The more critical issue is the extent to which the progressivity of taxation and criteria for access to welfare effected a transfer of resources from rich to poor. The evidence here points to qualified success in redistribution despite massive expansion in taxation and public sector delivery of social welfare services. Before the second world war only the very needy qualified for most forms of assistance. Although only the rich paid income taxes, indirect taxes were the more important source of government revenue, and it is possible these were regressive. The "welfare all round" that accompanied the extension of income taxes to lower income brackets in the postwar period appears to have resulted in a significant net redistribution towards lower income groups.[20]

In assessing the redistributive impact of government social welfare and related policies it is pertinent to note that they can themselves "create" categories of the relatively poor. It has been observed in the United States that new groups of relatively poor individuals or households have emerged to replace those who have been assisted by the expansion of welfare programmes, the net effect being that measures of aggregate inequality show no decline since the late 1940s (Blinder 1980). If single young people who are unemployed or are students leave home and form a household, or if a woman leaves her husband and lives alone on a single mother's pension, measured household inequality may increase. Yet by the choices exercised, their "welfare" has increased (though taxpayers' welfare may have gone down). The interesting and important conclusion is that economic growth and higher living standards may have permitted the widening of access to government social welfare, which has in turn induced or permitted a wider choice of life styles and easier household formation (and dissolution), with the consequence that

[20] See N. G. Butlin, Barnard, and Pincus (1982: esp. chaps. 6–8 and pp. 334–9). Kakwani (1983) provides an analysis of income tax and transfer policies on household income inequality in recent years.

measured inequality may increase. Herein may lie one reason why inequality measures of an aggregate form do not show greater falls in
Australia since 1915.

Speculation as to the causes of the decline in wealth inequality requires
first a judgment on how extensive and how steady that has been. With
currently available evidence, that is itself necessarily speculative. Possible forces at work to reduce this form of inequality in Australia that
have been suggested include the decline of the importance of the rural
sector, the spread in the ownership of dwellings, the narrowing of award
wage differentials, and the long postwar period of low unemployment
(Podder and Kakwani 1976: 90). However, the links between these and
other determinants of the decline in wealth inequality are not yet clearly
established.

12.5   Conclusion

Whether increased "happiness" or "quality of life" has accompanied
the improved material standards and the narrowing in the dispersion of
income and wealth that has occurred since 1900 is difficult to ascertain.
Studies undertaken elsewhere have found a positive correlation between
subjective evaluations of "happiness" and objectively measurable economic factors within a single society in cross-section studies by income
or socioeconomic group, but not in time series comparisons. The explanation proffered is that

Material aspirations or tastes vary positively with the level of economic development. Moreover, these changes in tastes are caused by the process of income
growth itself (though the cause–effect relation may run both ways). As a result
of secular income growth, the socialisation experience of each generation em-
bodies a higher level of living and correspondingly generates a higher level of
consumption standards. Even within the life-cycle of a given generation, the
progressive accretion of household goods due to economic growth causes a
continuous upward pressure on consumption norms. This upward shift in standards (tastes) tends to offset the positive effect of income growth on well-being
that one would expect on the basis of economic theory.

These observations by Easterlin (1974: 116) suggest that a measure of
agnosticism is appropriate in any simple equating of rises in material
living standards as conventionally measured by economists and more
fundamental subjective welfare improvement.

There is no doubt, however, that Australians on average are better
clothed, housed, fed, and educated now than at the time of federation.
They also live longer, work less, travel more, and enjoy more leisure.
A considerable proportion of these gains have been achieved since the
second world war, but the preceding four decades also saw major im-

provements. The incidence of these improvements has not been identical for men and women; the poorest groups in society (apart from the Aborigines, until very recently) may have gained relative to the middle class; and the position of the highest-income and wealth-owning groups has also deteriorated relative to that of the rest of the community. These considerable achievements, although not unique among the developed countries, were not inevitable. One need only ask whether any observer in 1900 could confidently have foretold Australia's greater success by the 1980s in promoting material living standards than New Zealand's or Britain's, not to mention Argentina's.

References

Abramovitz, M. 1981. "Welfare quandaries and productivity concerns". *American Economic Review* 71: 1–17.

Atkinson, A. B. 1983. *The Economics of Inequality*. 2d ed. Oxford: Oxford University Press (Clarendon Press).

Bambrick, Susan. 1970. "Australian price indexes". Ph.D. thesis, Australian National University.

Berry, M. J. 1977. "Inequality", in A. F. Davies et al. (eds.), *Australian Society*, pp. 18–54. Melbourne: Longman Cheshire.

Blinder, A. S. 1980. "The level and distribution of economic well-being", in M. Feldstein (ed.), *The American Economy in Transition*, pp. 415–79. Chicago: Chicago University Press.

Boehm, E. A. 1965. "Measuring Australian economic growth, 1861 to 1938–39". *Economic Record* 41: 207–39.

1979. *Twentieth Century Economic Development in Australia*. 2d ed. Melbourne: Longman Cheshire.

Brown, H. P. 1957. "Estimation of income distribution in Australia", in M. Gilbert and R. Stone (eds.), *Income and Wealth, Series 6*, pp. 202–38. London: Bowes & Bowes.

Butlin, M. W. 1977. *A Preliminary Annual Database 1900/01 to 1973/74*. Research Discussion Paper 7701. Sydney: Reserve Bank of Australia.

Butlin, N. G. 1962. *Australian Domestic Product, Investment and Foreign Borrowing, 1861–1938/39*. Cambridge: Cambridge University Press.

1965. "Long-run trends in Australian per capita consumption", in K. Hancock (ed.), *The National Income and Social Welfare*, pp. 1–19. Melbourne: Cheshire.

1983. *Trends in Australian Income Distribution: A First Glance*. Working Paper in Economic History No. 17. Australian National University.

Butlin, N. G., A. Barnard, and J. J. Pincus. 1982. *Government and Capitalism: Public and Private Choice in Twentieth Century Australia*. Sydney: Allen & Unwin.

Carter, M., and R. Maddock. 1984. "Working hours in Australia: some issues", in R. Blandy and O. Covick (eds.), *Understanding Labour Markets,* pp. 222–45. Sydney: Allen & Unwin.

Clark, C. 1963. Review of N. G. Butlin 1962. *Economic History Review* 16: 198–200.

Coward, D. 1980. "Altruism, science and cash: notes on state regulation and the medical profession, 1838–1975". Australian National University. Mimeograph.

Easterlin, R. A. 1974. "Does economic growth improve the human lot? Some empirical evidence", in P. A. David and M. W. Reder (eds.), *Nations and Households in Economic Growth,* pp. 89–125. New York: Academic Press.

Gillin, E. F. 1974. "Social indicators and economic welfare". *Economic Papers* 46: 48–82.

Gunton, R. 1975. "Personal wealth in Australia". Ph.D. thesis, University of Queensland.

Hancock, K., and K. Moore. 1972. "The occupational wage structure in Australia since 1914". *British Journal of Industrial Relations* 10: 107–22.

Ingles, D. 1981. *Statistics on the Distribution of Income and Wealth in Australia.* Research Paper No. 14. Research and Statistics Branch, Department of Social Security, Canberra.

Jones, F. L. 1975. "The changing shape of the Australian income distribution, 1914–15 and 1968–69". *Australian Economic History Review* 15: 21–34.

Kakwani, N. 1983. "The impact of personal income taxation and government transfers on income distribution and poverty in Australia", in J. G. Head (ed.), *Taxation Issues of the 1980s,* pp. 153–80. Sydney: Australian Tax Research Foundation.

King, M. A. 1974. "Economic growth and social development: a statistical investigation". *Review of Income and Wealth* 20: 251–72.

Knibbs, G. H. 1918. *The Private Wealth of Australia and Its Growth as Ascertained by Various Methods, Together with a Report of the War Census.* Melbourne: Commonwealth Bureau of Census and Statistics.

Kuznets, S. 1955. "Economic growth and income inequality". *American Economic Review* 45: 1–28.

Lindert, P. H., and J. G. Williamson. 1985. "Growth, equality and history". *Explorations in Economic History* 22: 341–77.

Lydall, H. 1968. *The Structure of Earnings.* Oxford: Oxford University Press (Clarendon Press).

McLean, I. W., and J. J. Pincus. 1982. *Living Standards in Australia 1890–1940: Evidence and Conjectures.* Working Paper in Economic History No. 6. Australian National University.

1983. "Did Australian living standards stagnate between 1890 and 1940?" *Journal of Economic History* 43: 193–202.

McLean, I. W., and S. Richardson. 1986. "More or less equal? Australian income distribution in 1933 and 1980". *Economic Record* 62: 67–81.

Maddison, A. 1982. *Phases of Capitalist Development.* Oxford: Oxford University Press.

Maddock, R., and M. Carter. 1983. *Hours, leisure and wellbeing 1911–1981.* Working Paper in Economic History No. 19. Australian National University.

Maddock, R., et al. 1984. *The Distribution of Income and Wealth in Australia 1914–80: An Introduction and Bibliography.* Source Paper in Economic History No. 1. Australian National University.

Nordhaus, W. D., and J. Tobin. 1973. "Is economic growth obsolete?" in M. Moss (ed.), *The Measurement of Economic and Social Performance,* pp. 509–32. New York: Columbia University Press.

Owens, Helen. 1980. "Social indicators", in R. G. Scotton and Helen Ferber (eds.), *Public Expenditure and Social Policy in Australia,* vol. 2: *The First Frazer Years, 1976–1978,* pp. 261–311. Melbourne: Longman Cheshire.

Oxnam, D. W. 1950. "The relation of unskilled to skilled wage rates in Australia". *Economic Record* 26: 112–18.

Piggott, J. R. 1984. "The distribution of wealth in Australia – a survey". *Economic Record* 60: 252–65.

Podder, N., and N. C. Kakwani. 1976. "Distribution of wealth in Australia". *Review of Income and Wealth* 22: 75–92.

Raskall, P. L. 1977. "The distribution of wealth in Australia 1967–1972". Planning Research Centre, University of Sydney. Mimeograph.

Richardson, S. 1979. "Income distribution, poverty and redistributive policies", in F. H. Gruen (ed.), *Surveys of Australian Economics,* vol. 2, pp. 11–62. Sydney: Allen & Unwin.

Rubinstein, W. D. 1979. "The distribution of personal wealth in Victoria 1860–1974". *Australian Economic History Review* 19: 26–41.

1980. "The top wealth-holders of New South Wales, 1817–1939". *Australian Economic History Review* 20: 136–52.

Snooks, G. D. 1983. "Household services and national income in Australia, 1891–1981: some preliminary results". Department of Economic History, Flinders University. Mimeograph.

Soltow, L. 1972. "The censuses of wealth of men in Australia in 1915 and in the United States in 1860 and 1870". *Australian Economic History Review* 12: 125–41.

Usher, D. 1980. *The Measurement of Economic Growth.* Oxford: Blackwell Publisher.

Withers, G. A. 1985. "Real income growth measurement and immigration: Australia, 1948–1981". Australian National University. Mimeograph.

CHAPTER 13

Epilogue: A comparative perspective

RODNEY MADDOCK AND IAN W. McLEAN

Each generation of commentators has its own favourite question to ask of Australian economic development. Economists of today seem most interested in the fact that levels of growth attained by the economy in recent decades are lower than those of many other countries. Most of the chapters in this volume recognise this preoccupation in one way or other. Whereas earlier generations focused on the absolute growth rate, growth rate per capita has become the new yardstick.

Australia's success as a nation, and especially the performance of policy makers, tends to be judged by this criterion. Yet it is in many ways unfair, even ahistorical, to impose one measure of success on historical periods when the objectives of past policies were quite different. In 1950, for instance, we find the eminent economist Trevor Swan (1950) writing that the two objectives of policy were economic stability and "the rapid development of Australian resources, and to create the employment and living standards necessary for the absorption of population growth of the order of 3% per annum, if possible at rising living standards". Or we can refer to the 1963 terms of reference of the Vernon Committee of Economic Enquiry ("The objectives of the Government's economic policy are a high rate of economic and population growth with full employment, increasing productivity, rising standards of living, external viability, and stability of costs and prices") to reinforce the impression that growth was perceived as an economic priority of far greater importance than comparative economic performance.

The quest for simple expansion of the size of the economy had been the dominant concern of policy since the first half of the nineteenth century. Fear of foreign invasion had been a major motivating factor, and one reinforced as recently as the second world war, when Japanese soldiers were turned back in New Guinea. To this was added a belief that Australia could achieve a modern economic structure only if it had a population sufficient to allow domestic industry to achieve important economies of scale. After the great depression, full employment and economic stabilisation were added to the list of primary objectives of policy.

Judged by these criteria, economic development and economic policy

344

over the course of this century have been extremely successful. The remarkable expansion of the scale of the economy and the dramatic additions made to population and to the capital stock are chronicled in this volume by David Pope and Rodney Maddock. Outside events have been kind to the country in that foreign invasion now seems less likely than it has at most other times in history. As well, Michael Carter has shown in his chapter that structurally the economy now is very similar to the typical modern economy, and a range of chapters suggest that the economic stability enjoyed by the economy is no less than that of comparable countries.

These older themes in Australian development have received major treatment in earlier works. Both Butlin (1964) and Sinclair (1976) focus on the expansion of scale, and Forster (1970) seeks its major themes in scale and structure. Whereas Boehm (1979) is eclectic, the other major recent work, Butlin, Barnard, and Pincus (1982), has the more modern interest in the extent to which government should be seen as endogenous. None, however, explores the question that now seems important: Why has the Australian economy performed less well in recent years than might have been expected? The fact that each generation of scholars has its own focus of attention allows us to distinguish this book from those that have gone before.

13.1   Why did Australia do worse?

The perception that the Australian economy has performed less well than many others over recent times probably derives ultimately from the international comparisons that became popular during the growth-manship decades following the second world war. The realisation that it had had amongst the highest living standards in the world late in the nineteenth century inspired concern that this was no longer the case.[1]

Did Australia do worse?

It is difficult to compare living standards between countries or even across time within one country. Most contemporary techniques start from data on national income or product per capita, and we shall follow that example. However, it must be realised that the exclusion of leisure from such measures, as well as climate and natural amenities such as the comparative lack of congestion, may lead to some downward bias

---

[1] Of course earlier economic statisticians such as Coghlan (1969) had written extensively about comparative living standards and Australia's elevated position.

Table 13.1. *Comparisons of economic performance (annual cumulative percentage increases)*

	1900–30	1930–70	1940–70	1950–70	1960–80
Real GDP					
Australia	1.9	3.9	4.2	4.6	4.3
15-country median	2.2	3.3	3.9	4.8	4.4
Population					
Australia	1.7	1.6	1.9	2.1	1.8
15-country median	0.7	0.7	0.7	0.7	0.7
Real GDP *per capita*					
Australia	0.2	2.3	2.3	2.5	2.5
15-country median	1.2	2.5	3.1	3.5	3.5

Source: Data in Maddison 1982: App. B; OECD, *Historical Statistics 1960–1981* (Paris: OECD, 1983).

in measured relative living standards of Australians beside a fuller comparison, as is suggested by Ian McLean.

Table 13.1 compares Australian performance with that of fifteen other countries. It is based on the national accounting aggregates unadjusted for purchasing power effects and hence is likely to be biased against Australia in the earlier periods.[2] The countries included in the comparison are those of Western Europe together with Canada, Japan, and the USA. The broad impression from the table is that Australia has done as well as many other economies in terms of absolute growth but that its population has grown faster, so that its per capita growth performance is below average. Looking at the first two columns alone,

[2] Even settling on comparative living standards as our indicator does not resolve the technical problems. Each country's GDP is normally measured in terms of its own currency; to compare them we have to convert them to a common unit of account. Whereas it may seem natural to make this conversion using the exchange rates between the curriencies involved, this is known to introduce biases into the analysis. The difficulty arises because even if the exchange rate does accurately reflect the relative productivity of each economy in terms of traded goods, the same does not apply to nontraded goods. One haircut in Sri Lanka might enter the domestic product of that country at a value of one Australian dollar using exchange rate valuation, but exactly the same service performed in Australia might enter our accounts at a value of five dollars. The fact that richer countries have higher prices for nontraded goods than do poorer countries means that exchange rate conversion is likely to bias downward the measured living standards of the poorer countries. Maddison (1982) does offer purchasing power adjusted comparisons, but we believe that the method he uses in the adjustment is wrong. He (correctly) multiplies Australian GDP upward in 1970 to make it comparable with the then leading country, the USA, but (wrongly) also multiplies Australian GDP upward (instead of downward) in the nineteenth century when it was the leading country. The purchasing power adjustment is derived from Kravis (1976). For criticism of the method see Marris (1984).

Table 13.2. *Comparative growth rates 1928–70: Australia, Argentina, and Canada (U.S. dollars at 1970 purchasing power; growth rates as percentages)*

Country	GDP	Population	GDP per capita
Australia	3.8	2.0	1.8
Argentina	3.2	2.1	1.1
Canada	3.9	1.8	2.1

Sources: Diaz-Alejandro 1982; Kravis 1976; Canadian *Year Book.*

however, changes that impression. Over the period from 1930 to 1970 Australia's per capita performance was almost the same as the sample median; by contrast, it did far worse than the other countries in the thirty years up to 1930. McLean and Pincus (1983) have emphasised the extremely poor performance of the Australian economy over those first thirty years of the century; there was little net growth even up to 1914, when most other economies had continued to expand.

A second feature of the table is that the per capita growth recorded by Australia to 1970 does not change very much as we alter the base of measurement from 1930 to 1940 or 1950, in contrast with that managed by the other economies. The timing of recovery from the depression and the physical destruction of the war clearly influence the measures. The big surprise, and the one that has provoked the professional curiosity of economists, was the failure of the Australian economy to match the accelerated growth rate recorded by other economies after 1960. Interestingly, the USA and UK economies were the only ones that performed worse than Australia's between 1960 and 1980.

But should we expect Australia to grow at the same rate as Japan, Denmark, or the USA? Differences in size, products, resource base, and distance from markets may lead one to expect such diverse countries to have different growth rates. Comparison with European countries that have entered the trade sanctuary of the EEC seem particularly likely to mislead. Table 13.2 contrasts Australian performance with that of two countries with which it is more directly comparable, Canada and Argentina. And matched against them Australia does much better. All three had GDP growth rates of between 3 and 4 percent and all had substantial population increases, but the GDP growth rates of Australia and Canada were quite similar. Argentina did much worse. Its GDP per capita fell from 80 percent of Australia's in 1928 to just 60 percent by 1970.

In sum, Australia has grown as fast as any other economy this century.

At the same time, the population has grown faster, so that per capita income has grown a little more slowly than in many other economies. The major periods of relatively poor performance were before 1930 (in fact especially between 1900 and 1914) and after 1960.

The major theses

Just why should Australia have performed worse over the course of the century than many other countries? Opinion amongst the contributors has been concentrated on a small number of factors: the high rate of population growth, protective policy, rent-seeking behaviour, low levels of investment in human capital, and the long-term decline in export prices.

Two fashionable arguments are dismissed rather summarily. The growth of government per se is shown by Jonathan Pincus to have been much slower in the case of Australia than in most other countries and hence an unlikely causal factor of differential growth rates unless one argues that the economy would have grown faster if the government sector had also grown faster. And Glenn Withers argues that Australian labour markets have been no less responsive to market signals than those of economies with different institutions, so that one cannot point the finger of responsibility at the unusual arbitration system. Generally Australians have been more mobile than workers in other countries, and when one acknowledges the additional impact of high levels of migration it is hard to believe that labour market rigidities have played any significant role in the sluggish economic performance.[3] The labour market is characterised by high levels of mobility and its adjustments have been broadly in the right directions.

The argument most preferred by our contributors concerns the interrelationship of the policy of protection with population growth and rent-seeking attitudes. David Pope sets out the perspective in the first of the macroeconomic chapters. Policy makers in the twenties wanted to develop a modern economy not wholly dependent on the resource industries, and they also wanted to increase the population. They succeeded: Michael Carter demonstrates the structural similarity of the economy to that of many others, and the discussion above shows the

---

[3] Keating (1983) shows that the direction of adjustment of the labour market to the various signals has been appropriate. As well, Long and Boertlein (1978) found that more Australians (excluding migrants) change address over a five-year period than do Americans, Japanese, or Canadians; that fewer of the moves are local; and that more are for job-related reasons. Rowland (1979) finds this sort of mobility to have increased over the course of the century.

rapid population increase that has been achieved. The cost of the success of the economic strategy that has dominated the century has been the lower rates of growth achieved.

Both Kym Anderson and Jonathan Pincus analyse the important costs of the strategy. Whereas general equilibrium analyses suggest that the gains from trade liberalisation would not be substantial (see for example the pioneering study of Evans 1972 or IMPACT Project results like Powell 1977), the implication for *attitudes* may well be more important. In the mid eighties Aitkin was able to write that "even in informed circles [businessmen] are criticised for their unimaginativeness, timidity and a preference for government assistance and protection rather than the bracing climate of the free market" (*Age* newspaper, October 29, 1985), and Stretton (1985: 225) makes a similar point: "For seventy years past, Australian business and political leadership has been generally mediocre and uninventive, missing many good opportunities." And probably the net should be cast more widely. The development of a protective system has shielded union leaders as much as business people from many economic pressures, and encouraged economic actors to lobby state and federal politicians for benefits rather than compete for them on the world market.

The policy of protection initially worked in the sense that its immediate objectives were achieved. The unintended cost of the policy was that it sheltered Australian decision makers and tended to limit economic growth to the rate of expansion of the domestic market. Australia largely missed out on the explosion of world trade in manufactures that has been characteristic of the last forty years.

John Freebairn points to another factor in Australia's sluggish economic performance: Over the course of the century the terms of trade have tended to move against Australia, mainly because of the low income elasticity of demand for most of the agricultural and mineral products it exports. The growth in world trade has been concentrated in precisely those products in which Australia does not have a comparative advantage. Fogarty and Duncan (1985) show the difficulties Argentina has had dealing with the collapse of its traditional export base and contrast them with Australia's comparative success. For Freebairn this success has arisen from a change in the product mix, the development of new markets, and the adoption of new techniques. Luck in mineral discovery has also played a part. Despite this, the difficult conditions faced by the export industries is shown up in the steady decline in the resource sector's share of GDP, from around one-quarter up to 1950 to around one-seventh. Clearly this has been a drag on growth.

To exacerbate matters, Australia has invested relatively little in human capital. Enrolment in educational institutions is far lower in Australia amongst both fifteen- to nineteen-year-olds and twenty- to twenty-four-year-olds than in most OECD countries, 20 percent below the average for the younger group and 50 percent below for the older. And within the education system Australia has been loath to spend in the area of technical education. From having one of the most educated labour forces at the turn of the century, Australia now lags considerably behind the other OECD countries. Freed from the need to compete on world markets in many areas, Australians have not needed to develop their skills and abilities to the extent citizens of other countries have.

13.2   Conclusion

This volume complements much of what has been written about Australian· economic development by earlier generations of economists. Much of the ground has been tilled before, but some new interpretations have emerged.

The macroeconomic chapters point to two main features. First is that the broad pattern of Australian economic experience parallels that of the world economy – growth occurs when the world economy grows, slumps when the world economy slumps. Second is that the small open economy model of the economic textbooks generally seems the relevant model for analysis of the Australian situation. However, the Australian economy has grown faster than most others under the stimulus of the inflow of foreign capital and foreign labour. Such expansion of scale has been a major objective of policy.

Shifting to the sectoral level, we obtain a new perspective from Michael Carter's work on the structure of the economy. In contrast to earlier studies, he finds that the Australian economy now is very little different from other modern economies. Kym Anderson insists that this is a consequence of the protectionist policies adopted and maintained after other countries had abandoned theirs, and a major explanation for the poor relative growth performance. Growth would have been higher in the absence of protection. Writing about the resource sector, however, John Freebairn sounds a cautionary note. He shows that the resource sector has faced a long-term decline in its prices and has generally struggled against unfavourable market conditions. It has declined in economic importance despite being technologically innovative and relatively flexible because of the low income elasticity of demand for its output. It is not really clear that the resource sector could have been a leading contributor to growth, as Anderson suggests. On the other hand, Carter does argue that the expansion of the service sector has contributed to growth, since it is largely the consequence of economic specialisation in the area of intermediate inputs to production.

Both Glenn Withers and Matthew Butlin insist that the markets they analysed adapted appropriately to market forces. Whereas labour market rigidity has often been cited as a major impediment to growth, Withers finds little of it. And Butlin considers that capital markets have become more flexible over time in their response to the demands placed on them. Regulation has diverted some energies, but the major capital sources have been tapped and the demands of borrowers met.

Jonathan Pincus gets to the nub of the comparative growth question in his chapter on government. He argues that the pursuit of public goods like population growth, which contribute to measured GDP growth, has been progressively replaced by the pursuit of public goods like equity, which do not. The willingness of government, and ultimately voters, to cede sectional claims has led to a substantial direction of energies to the winning of advantages that limit the adaptiveness of the economy. Economic agents in their private activities have also shown a proclivity to pursue protective devices with public support – marketing schemes, occupational licensing, unionisation, etc. The net effect of these processes has been to entrench a powerful set of institutions that have hampered growth and seriously weakened popular control of the economy and society.

Ian McLean presents a far more positive view of economic development over the course of the century. Living standards have improved dramatically whether measured in narrowly economic terms or through broader measures. Australians are better fed, clothed, and educated now than they were at federation, and they live longer, work less, travel more, and enjoy more leisure. And the income of the society is more evenly distributed – the richest groups have lost ground to all others, and the poorest have made up ground against the middle classes.

References

Boehm, E. 1979. *Twentieth Century Economic Development in Australia.* 2d ed. Melbourne: Longman Cheshire.

Butlin, N. G. 1964. *Australian Domestic Product, Investment and Foreign Borrowing, 1861–1938/39.* Cambridge: Cambridge University Press.

Butlin, N. G., A. Barnard, and J. J. Pincus. 1982. *Government and Capitalism.* Sydney: Allen & Unwin.

Coghlan, T. A. 1969. *Labour and Industry in Australia* (1918). 4 vols. Melbourne: Macmillan.

Diaz-Alejandro, C. F. 1982. "No less than one hundred years of Argentine economic history, plus some comparisons". Yale University. Mimeograph.

Evans, D. 1972. *A General Equilibrium Analysis of Protection: The Effects of Protection on Australia.* Amsterdam: North-Holland.

Fogarty, J., and T. Duncan. 1985. *Australia and Argentina.* Melbourne: Melbourne University Press.

Forster, C. (ed.). 1970. *Australian Economic Development in the Twentieth Century.* London: Allen & Unwin.

Keating, M. 1983. "Relative wages and the changing industrial distribution of employment in Australia". *Economic Record* 59: 384–97.

Kravis, I. B. 1976. "A survey of international comparisons productivity". *Economic Journal* 86: 1–44.

Long, L. H., and C. G. Boertlein. 1978. *The Geographical Mobility of Americans: An International Comparison.* Current Population Report: Special Studies Series P–23, No. 64. U.S. Department of Commerce, Bureau of the Census. Washington, D.C.

McLean, I. W., and J. J. Pincus. 1983. "Did Australian living standards stagnate between 1890 and 1940?" *Journal of Economic History* 43(1) (March): 193–202.

Maddison, A. 1982. *Phases of Capitalist Development.* Oxford: Oxford University Press.

Marris, R. 1984. "Comparing the income of nations". *Journal of Economic Literature* 22: 40–57.

Powell, A. 1977. *The IMPACT Project: An Overview.* Canberra: Australian Government Publishing Service.

Rowland, D. 1979. *Internal Migration in Australia.* Census Monograph Series. Canberra: Australian Bureau of Statistics.

Sinclair, W. A. 1976. *The Process of Economic Development in Australia.* Melbourne: Longman Cheshire.

Stretton, H. 1985. "The quality of leading Australians," in *Australia: The Daedalus Symposium,* pp. 197–230. Sydney: Angus & Robertson.

Swan, T. W. 1950. "Economic policy issues". Mimeograph.

Statistical Appendix

Table 1. *Population and labour force 1900/1–1980/1*

Year: Population figures relate to years ending December 31 (i.e. 1901 = Population at December 31, 1900). Net migration figures relate to the flow of migrants over the year to December 31. Remaining figures relate to financial years ending June 30 (i.e. 1901 = 1900/1).

A = Population (000)
B = Net migration (000; i.e. excess of arrivals over departures)
C = Workforce including defence (000)
D = Civilian employment (000)
E = Defence (000)
F = Public administration (000)
G = Self-employed (000)
H = Unemployment rate (%)

Year	A	B	C	D	E	F	G	H
1901	3,765	−8.8	1,489	1,426	5	15	0	3.9
1902	3,826	4.3	1,537	1,458	5	18	0	4.8
1903	3,883	2.3	1,585	1,445	5	17	0	8.5
1904	3,927	−7.2	1,659	1,499	5	20	0	9.4
1905	3,984	−3.5	1,637	1,492	5	20	0	8.6
1906	4,052	6.6	1,635	1,523	5	22	0	6.6
1907	4,119	3.5	1,680	1,588	5	22	0	5.2
1908	4,197	13.0	1,703	1,641	5	22	0	3.4
1909	4,275	13.2	1,752	1,690	5	22	0	3.3
1910	4,324	28.9	1,829	1,763	5	22	0	3.3
1911	4,483	35.5	1,839	1,782	5	23	441	2.9
1912	4,569	69.3	1,950	1,898	5	24	462	2.4
1913	4,733	83.7	2,048	1,937	8	26	487	5.0
1914	4,872	54.8	2,095	2,017	10	28	499	3.3
1915	4,941	−17.4	2,114	1,956	32	30	487	5.9
1916	4,932	−91.1	2,128	1,929	125	33	483	3.5
1917	4,875	−133.9	2,183	1,896	215	35	480	3.3
1918	4,935	−21.9	2,183	1,893	215	37	482	3.4
1919	5,030	19.5	2,155	1,924	153	38	490	3.6
1920	5,304	27.4	2,098	1,999	27	39	506	3.4
1921	5,412	107.8	2,170	2,037	9	40	514	5.8
1922	5,511	17.3	2,249	2,104	8	39	530	6.1
1923	5,633	38.0	2,310	2,187	8	38	552	5.0

353

Table 1. *(cont.)*

Year	A	B	C	D	E	F	G	H
1924	5,750	37.5	2,348	2,230	7	38	562	4.7
1925	5,874	43.7	2,462	2,302	6	38	570	6.3
1926	5,992	37.4	2,466	2,338	7	38	572	4.9
1927	6,111	42.2	2,513	2,402	6	37	574	4.2
1928	6,235	48.9	2,562	2,398	6	38	575	6.2
1929	6,356	27.2	2,568	2,389	6	38	575	6.7
1930	6,436	9.0	2,557	2,300	6	38	569	9.8
1931	6,500	− 8.5	2,556	2,131	6	37	573	16.4
1932	6,553	− 10.8	2,605	2,086	6	36	590	19.7
1933	6,604	− 3.0	2,729	2,208	5	36	608	18.9
1934	6,656	0.2	2,761	2,313	7	39	612	16.0
1935	6,706	2.3	2,818	2,417	7	42	609	14.0
1936	6,753	− 0.3	2,822	2,504	8	44	607	11.0
1937	6,807	1.5	2,823	2,565	9	46	602	8.8
1938	6,867	5.2	2,880	2,655	10	48	602	7.5
1939	6,930	9.1	2,952	2,682	11	52	599	8.8
1940	6,997	13.9	3,001	2,677	54	56	584	9.0
1941	7,069	13.4	3,024	2,662	216	63	549	4.9
1942	7,144	5.2	3,148	2,628	461	79	505	1.9
1943	7,197	6.2	3,299	2,572	696	103	463	1.0
1944	7,266	1.3	3,354	2,600	721	124	476	1.0
1945	7,342	− 2.2	3,346	2,637	669	127	508	1.2
1946	7,430	− 2.3	3,247	2,775	402	118	566	2.2
1947	7,518	− 13.7	3,210	3,034	83	117	622	2.9
1948	7,639	10.6	3,277	3,167	46	119	635	2.0
1949	7,795	55.1	3,368	3,282	36	120	642	1.5
1950	8,045	150.0	3,473	3,379	34	125	648	1.8
1951	8,308	152.5	3,591	3,512	40	130	661	1.1
1952	8,528	111.4	3,686	3,579	60	132	667	1.4
1953	8,740	94.0	3,681	3,511	64	134	662	2.9
1954	8,903	42.9	3,723	3,584	64	129	672	2.0
1955	9,090	68.2	3,799	3,685	62	130	685	1.4
1956	9,313	97.3	3,896	3,777	61	137	691	1.5
1957	9,531	94.0	3,942	3,806	56	140	690	2.0
1958	9,744	78.7	4,001	3,848	49	141	689	2.6
1959	9,947	65.4	4,027	3,898	49	146	686	2.0
1960	10,161	76.8	4,143	3,997	48	146	689	2.4
1961	10,392	90.1	4,334	4,189	46	150	691	2.3
1962	10,643	61.5	4,382	4,196	47	153	699	3.2
1963	10,846	62.5	4,445	4,297	49	158	707	2.2
1964	11,055	71.6	4,547	4,421	51	164	714	1.7
1965	11,280	99.3	4,669	4,559	53	172	722	1.2
1966	11,505	104.9	4,820	4,691	61	182	723	1.4
1967	11,705	86.9	4,972	4,823	73	188	728	1.5
1968	11,912	91.9	5,097	4,939	79	197	720	1.6
1969	12,146	113.1	5,216	5,057	82	206	718	1.5

Year	A	B	C	D	E	F	G	H
1970	12,407	129.0	5,383	5,221	84	217	743	1.4
1971	12,663	122.9	5,532	5,369	84	230	756	1.4
1972	13,070	103.6	5,596	5,410	82.	239	752	1.9
1973	13,284	56.3	5,741	5,538	78	250	759	2.2
1974	13,491	67.5	5,873	5,702	70	264	784	1.7
1975	13,710	87.2	6,171	5,856	68	284	869	4.2
1976	13,849	13.5	6,300	5,929	69	303	928	4.9
1977	13,991	25.6	6,360	5,966	69	303	1,007	5.2
1978	14,164	54.8	6,445	5,981	70	308	1,048	6.2
1979	14,331	51.6	6,481	6,007	70	314	1,066	6.3
1980	14,517	69.0	6,621	6,151	72	N.A.	1,068	6.1
1981	14,727	93.4	6,769	6,312	73	N.A.	1,098	5.9

Sources: Population and net migration figures are taken from various issues of *Year Book, Australia* (Australian Bureau of Statistics cat. no. 1310.0).

The workforce and civilian employment are taken from *A Preliminary Annual Database 1900/01 to 1973/74*, Research Discussion Paper 7701 (Sydney: Reserve Bank of Australia, 1977), M. W. Butlin, and from *The Labour Force, Australia* (ABS cat. no. 6204.0).

Figures for the armed forces (1979/80 and 1980/1) are for December 31 and are taken from *Year Book Australia, 1981* (ABS cat. no. 1301.0).

All other figures are average employment over the year and are taken from Butlin 1977 and from *Civilain Employees, Australia, June 1966 to June 1979* (ABS cat. no. 6214.0).

The series for public administration and self-employed for the years 1974/5 to 1980/1 were formed by extending the series given in Butlin 1977 using figures derived from *The Labour Force, Australia* and from *Civilain Employees, Australia, June 1966 to June 1977*.

The unemployment rate is taken from Butlin 1977 and from various issues of *Reserve Bank of Australia, Statistical Bulletin*.

Table 2. *Prices and price indexes: deflators of the main expenditure aggregates 1900/1–1980/1 (1966/7 = 1.0000)*

Year: Year ending June 30 (i.e. 1901 = 1900/1)
A = Private consumption
B = Public consumption, including defence
C = Fixed capital formation, private dwelling
D = Fixed capital formation, private nondwelling
E = Fixed capital formation, public dwelling
F = Fixed capital formation, public nondwelling
G = Change in stocks
H = Exports
I = Imports
J = Gross domestic product

Year	A	B	C	D	E	F	G	H	I	J
1901	0.1419	0.0862	0.1021	0.1341	0.1034	0.1191	0.1330	0.1450	0.1550	0.1330
1902	0.1348	0.0886	0.1014	0.1299	0.1026	0.1124	0.1280	0.1520	0.1500	0.1280
1903	0.1362	0.0918	0.0978	0.1279	0.0989	0.1123	0.1320	0.1630	0.1470	0.1320
1904	0.1236	0.0903	0.0952	0.1256	0.0963	0.1126	0.1240	0.1660	0.1480	0.1240
1905	0.1231	0.0894	0.0913	0.1253	0.0923	0.1118	0.1250	0.1700	0.1440	0.1250
1906	0.1275	0.0922	0.0846	0.1315	0.0857	0.1131	0.1290	0.1790	0.1540	0.1290
1907	0.1224	0.0949	0.1130	0.1336	0.1144	0.1221	0.1270	0.1870	0.1630	0.1270
1908	0.1359	0.1020	0.1273	0.1356	0.1288	0.1238	0.1370	0.1810	0.1630	0.1370
1909	0.1428	0.1076	0.0971	0.1374	0.0983	0.1258	0.1410	0.1730	0.1560	0.1410
1910	0.1475	0.1104	0.0865	0.1417	0.0875	0.1261	0.1450	0.1760	0.1580	0.1450
1911	0.1502	0.1138	0.0780	0.1476	0.0789	0.1305	0.1460	0.1730	0.1620	0.1460
1912	0.1650	0.1129	0.1116	0.1579	0.1129	0.1431	0.1590	0.1760	0.1640	0.1590
1913	0.1613	0.1116	0.1346	0.1653	0.1362	0.1470	0.1580	0.1850	0.1690	0.1580
1914	0.1779	0.1116	0.1358	0.1675	0.1375	0.1484	0.1690	0.1870	0.1740	0.1690
1915	0.2049	0.0918	0.1377	0.1854	0.1394	0.1632	0.1860	0.1890	0.1740	0.1860
1916	0.2294	0.0750	0.1442	0.2251	0.1460	0.2059	0.1930	0.2310	0.2150	0.1930
1917	0.2723	0.0782	0.1507	0.2522	0.1526	0.2363	0.2100	0.2850	0.2700	0.2100
1918	0.2840	0.0868	0.1647	0.2777	0.1667	0.2583	0.2220	0.3020	0.3070	0.2220
1919	0.2900	0.0977	0.1751	0.2535	0.1772	0.2574	0.2340	0.2950	0.3490	0.2340
1920	0.2957	0.1465	0.2116	0.2923	0.2141	0.2956	0.2710	0.3270	0.3960	0.2710
1921	0.2955	0.1781	0.2184	0.2962	0.2211	0.3206	0.2630	0.3270	0.4600	0.2630
1922	0.2722	0.1865	0.2193	0.2886	0.2220	0.2692	0.2490	0.2500	0.3700	0.2490
1923	0.2821	0.1634	0.2220	0.2890	0.2247	0.2546	0.2640	0.2960	0.3040	0.2640
1924	0.2647	0.1641	0.2217	0.2888	0.2244	0.2495	0.2640	0.3610	0.2730	0.2640
1925	0.2611	0.1704	0.2275	0.2882	0.2303	0.2550	0.2720	0.4070	0.2640	0.2720
1926	0.2763	0.1753	0.2255	0.2900	0.2282	0.2624	0.2700	0.3120	0.2790	0.2700
1927	0.2752	0.1831	0.2283	0.2922	0.2311	0.2634	0.2700	0.3020	0.2690	0.2700
1928	0.2734	0.1936	0.2273	0.2919	0.2300	0.2650	0.2740	0.3240	0.2590	0.2740
1929	0.2787	0.1883	0.2279	0.2926	0.2306	0.2619	0.2750	0.2990	0.2560	0.2750
1930	0.2587	0.1909	0.2265	0.2767	0.2292	0.2307	0.2480	0.2310	0.2470	0.2480
1931	0.2436	0.1886	0.2178	0.2769	0.2204	0.2346	0.2250	0.1750	0.2470	0.2250
1932	0.2261	0.1680	0.2061	0.2699	0.2086	0.2128	0.2080	0.1730	0.2440	0.2080
1933	0.2225	0.1619	0.2079	0.2641	0.2104	0.2017	0.2050	0.1700	0.2270	0.2050

Year	A	B	C	D	E	F	G	H	I	J
1934	0.2191	0.1518	0.2045	0.2625	0.2070	0.2029	0.2120	0.2160	0.2220	0.2120
1935	0.2410	0.1462	0.2053	0.2613	0.2078	0.2021	0.2190	0.1810	0.2220	0.2190
1936	0.2413	0.1463	0.2066	0.2598	0.2091	0.2043	0.2290	0.2280	0.2250	0.2290
1937	0.2461	0.1484	0.2175	0.2750	0.2201	0.2136	0.2420	0.2750	0.2340	0.2420
1938	0.2593	0.1608	0.2228	0.2813	0.2255	0.2199	0.2460	0.2440	0.2470	0.2460
1939	0.2875	0.1520	0.2310	0.2343	0.2500	0.2238	0.2510	0.1990	0.2440	0.2510
1940	0.3074	0.1525	0.2458	0.2457	0.2445	0.2292	0.2590	0.2350	0.2780	0.2590
1941	0.3208	0.1849	0.2798	0.2682	0.2786	0.2551	0.2610	0.2490	0.3290	0.2610
1942	0.3335	0.2077	0.2906	0.3254	0.2899	0.2724	0.2650	0.2540	0.3820	0.2650
1943	0.3614	0.2344	0.3415	0.3256	0.3413	0.3191	0.2790	0.2730	0.4400	0.2790
1944	0.3605	0.2450	0.3571	0.3306	0.3571	0.3299	0.2870	0.2800	0.4690	0.2870
1945	0.3522	0.2419	0.3590	0.4906	0.3571	0.3271	0.2980	0.3110	0.4810	0.2980
1946	0.3753	0.2375	0.3704	0.3320	0.3676	0.3383	0.3210	0.3500	0.4910	0.3210
1947	0.3763	0.2517	0.3778	0.3520	0.3750	0.3504	0.3520	0.4860	0.5610	0.3520
1948	0.3998	0.2860	0.3765	0.3994	0.4000	0.3825	0.3910	0.6780	0.6580	0.3910
1949	0.4270	0.3132	0.4303	0.4411	0.4286	0.4132	0.4300	0.7950	0.6890	0.4300
1950	0.4690	0.3450	0.4774	0.4850	0.4483	0.4557	0.4690	0.8550	0.7310	0.4690
1951	0.5416	0.4195	0.5386	0.5738	0.5143	0.5145	0.5890	1.4380	0.8400	0.5890
1952	0.6679	0.5019	0.6449	0.6873	0.6348	0.6088	0.6140	1.1210	1.0440	0.6140
1953	0.6831	0.5542	0.7304	0.7486	0.7590	0.6700	0.7020	1.1340	0.9740	0.7020
1954	0.7153	0.5705	0.7384	0.7573	0.8125	0.6791	0.7220	1.1030	0.9120	0.7220
1955	0.7346	0.5943	0.7749	0.7701	0.8256	0.6993	0.7260	1.0250	0.9290	0.7260
1956	0.7585	0.6494	0.8226	0.8048	0.8316	0.7533	0.7490	0.9610	0.9660	0.7490
1957	0.7944	0.6724	0.8387	0.8377	0.8500	0.7752	0.8000	1.0750	1.0060	0.8000
1958	0.8113	0.6882	0.8525	0.8647	0.8723	0.7859	0.8010	1.0130	1.0150	0.8010
1959	0.8247	0.6929	0.8554	0.8772	0.8750	0.8008	0.8010	0.8950	1.0040	0.8010
1960	0.8436	0.7606	0.8659	0.8941	0.8810	0.8231	0.8380	0.9570	0.9600	0.8380
1961	0.8821	0.7939	0.8961	0.9063	0.8919	0.8438	0.8630	0.9150	0.9700	0.8630
1962	0.8850	0.8129	0.8960	0.9122	0.8983	0.8680	0.8740	0.9180	0.9620	0.8740
1963	0.8944	0.8354	0.8972	0.9159	0.9048	0.8660	0.8830	0.9380	0.9710	0.8830
1964	0.9097	0.8737	0.9159	0.9270	0.9167	0.8920	0.9160	1.0180	0.9620	0.9160
1965	0.9415	0.9193	0.9424	0.9526	0.9388	0.9330	0.9400	0.9820	0.9750	0.9400
1966	0.9697	0.9480	0.9702	0.9741	0.9697	0.9582	0.9680	1.0030	0.9900	0.9680
1967	1.0000	1.0000	1.0000	1.0000	1.0000	1.0000	1.0000	1.0000	1.0000	1.0000
1968	1.0318	1.0480	1.0306	1.0228	1.0294	1.0347	1.0280	0.9660	1.0010	1.0280
1969	1.0557	1.0994	1.0595	1.0622	1.0625	1.0752	1.0620	0.9850	1.0010	1.0620
1970	1.0994	1.1773	1.1013	1.1063	1.1000	1.1271	1.1100	1.0020	1.0120	1.1100
1971	1.1629	1.2995	1.1547	1.1799	1.1585	1.1935	1.1690	0.9820	1.0520	1.1690
1972	1.2378	1.4530	1.2414	1.2622	1.2381	1.2709	1.2500	1.0240	1.1000	1.2500
1973	1.3022	1.5799	1.3454	1.3205	1.3333	1.3732	1.3620	1.2140	1.0810	1.3620
1974	1.4539	1.8380	1.6170	1.4320	1.6522	1.5560	1.5590	1.4220	1.2010	1.5590
1975	1.7637	2.2573	2.0367	1.7007	2.0310	1.9702	2.0395	1.8018	1.7544	1.8553
1976	2.0388	2.5982	2.3585	2.3310	2.2539	2.2781	4.2451	1.9369	1.9474	2.1317
1977	2.2751	2.8849	2.6477	2.5986	2.5759	2.5364	2.8933	2.1550	2.2579	2.3636
1978	2.4921	3.1106	2.8086	2.9049	2.7337	2.7550	2.4032	2.2414	2.5579	2.5547

Table 2. *(cont.)*

Year	A	B	C	D	E	F	G	H	I	J
1979	2.7178	3.3093	2.8921	3.1972	2.8483	2.9503	2.8854	2.5928	2.7912	2.7681
1980	2.9788	3.6253	3.1200	3.5211	3.0960	3.3113	3.9526	2.9640	3.3035	3.0427
1981	3.2593	4.0723	3.4929	3.8627	3.4892	3.7119	2.6522	3.1928	3.5912	3.3432

Sources: Butlin 1977; *Australia National Accounts: National Income and Expenditure, 1982/83* (ABS cat. no. 5204.0).

Table 3. *National income: main expenditure aggregates, current prices, 1900/1–1980/1 (million dollars)*

Year: Financial years ending June 30 (i.e. 1901 = 1900/1)
A = Private consumption
B = Public nondefence consumption
C = Defence spending
D = Fixed capital formation, private dwelling
E = Fixed capital formation, private nondwelling
F = Fixed capital formation, public dwelling
G = Fixed capital formation, public nondwelling
H = Change in stocks
 I = Exports
 J = Imports
K = Gross domestic product

Year	A	B	C	D	E	F	G	H	I	J	K
1901	326	19	1	9	18	0	29	−1	103	85	419
1902	324	23	1	18	22	0	32	9	97	82	444
1903	335	21	1	13	21	0	31	−11	94	77	428
1904	320	22	1	11	18	0	22	22	106	74	448
1905	324	25	1	12	17	0	21	−3	121	74	444
1906	334	27	1	12	20	0	21	12	133	81	479
1907	364	31	1	19	29	0	24	17	148	95	538
1908	389	30	2	19	26	0	30	−4	145	101	536
1909	410	32	1	13	25	0	37	17	139	101	573
1910	436	31	2	13	27	0	40	29	157	112	623
1911	495	32	4	13	32	0	50	19	167	128	684
1912	556	33	5	21	37	0	63	2	164	147	734
1913	578	36	5	32	40	1	70	30	170	160	802
1914	629	42	6	34	43	1	71	18	171	151	864
1915	683	40	12	30	24	1	73	−31	142	136	838
1916	757	42	39	23	26	1	71	38	166	194	969
1917	774	53	65	19	39	0	61	−15	243	217	1,022
1918	811	54	67	19	36	0	52	1	209	187	1,062
1919	903	53	49	26	51	0	62	17	227	243	1,145
1920	953	60	12	31	69	9	97	−50	300	228	1,253
1921	1,027	68	7	28	80	15	120	121	268	352	1,382
1922	960	76	7	42	89	5	122	24	268	215	1,378
1923	1,117	85	5	60	87	4	122	39	262	271	1,510
1924	1,185	80	5	66	90	5	129	32	265	288	1,569
1925	1,214	83	5	67	86	4	145	72	341	295	1,722
1926	1,303	80	8	69	82	2	152	−28	302	311	1,659
1927	1,357	83	11	76	79	3	164	12	286	342	1,729
1928	1,325	92	10	78	75	3	168	0	293	305	1,739
1929	1,314	97	8	68	77	3	158	2	308	323	1,712
1930	1,293	88	7	49	49	2	139	18	216	295	1,566
1931	986	82	5	25	47	0	104	−13	201	150	1,287
1932	913	79	5	15	35	0	69	−2	219	123	1,210

Table 3. *(cont.)*

Year	A	B	C	D	E	F	G	H	I	J	K
1933	976	77	5	26	34	0	73	5	225	157	1,264
1934	1,010	82	6	29	48	0	77	12	259	167	1,356
1935	1,104	85	9	37	66	0	97	−7	244	203	1,432
1936	1,211	87	11	47	70	0	103	−8	287	234	1,574
1937	1,269	85	10	54	76	1	119	5	356	258	1,717
1938	1,368	90	16	61	101	1	136	53	350	319	1,857
1939	1,378	86	26	64	97	1	128	6	314	281	1,819
1940	1,388	92	98	58	114	0	116	78	376	340	1,980
1941	1,436	92	340	54	96	0	100	14	378	365	2,145
1942	1,538	100	614	34	82	0	76	32	416	395	2,497
1943	1,540	104	1,072	14	70	0	60	−53	428	377	2,858
1944	1,470	108	964	10	80	0	64	−69	593	315	2,905
1945	1,636	120	760	14	104	0	70	−77	528	313	2,842
1946	1,798	146	414	30	168	0	90	89	557	357	2,935
1947	2,158	188	82	68	220	18	164	139	656	572	3,121
1948	2,580	230	40	96	272	26	210	182	914	803	3,747
1949	2,975	271	82	145	352	33	262	45	1,138	979	4,324
1950	3,492	316	108	190	454	39	381	54	1,325	1,260	5,099
1951	4,153	386	200	272	649	54	549	125	2,111	1,726	6,773
1952	5,093	473	330	345	787	73	733	377	1,493	2,437	7,267
1953	5,095	519	406	363	780	63	731	−294	1,893	1,312	8,244
1954	5,753	474	400	381	939	78	730	109	1,750	1,601	9,013
1955	6,417	536	400	420	1,062	71	800	166	1,714	1,983	9,603
1956	6,800	663	380	436	1,204	66	861	229	1,719	1,953	10,405
1957	7,169	706	380	442	1,275	43	907	−45	2,191	1,736	11,332
1958	7,675	741	380	503	1,355	36	962	56	1,805	1,925	11,588
1959	8,018	843	380	550	1,372	43	1,057	253	1,892	1,960	12,448
1960	8,985	926	386	620	1,571	32	1,182	168	2,134	2,286	13,718
1961	9,458	1,014	396	673	1,742	30	1,226	478	2,177	2,603	14,591
1962	9,629	1,123	406	603	1,725	47	1,355	−219	2,464	2,205	14,928
1963	10,298	1,222	412	663	1,917	38	1,402	253	2,504	2,620	16,089
1964	11,106	1,342	449	773	2,146	44	1,552	126	3,169	2,873	17,834
1965	12,153	1,507	543	917	2,493	46	1,810	572	3,049	3,485	19,605
1966	12,793	1,666	724	911	2,745	64	1,993	106	3,151	3,629	20,524
1967	13,702	1,865	844	991	2,838	65	2,107	367	3,477	3,711	22,545
1968	14,911	2,073	983	1,112	3,044	70	2,298	138	3,557	4,155	24,031
1969	16,133	2,322	1,017	1,299	3,434	68	2,460	668	3,919	4,276	27,044
1970	17,870	2,655	990	1,489	3,674	88	2,652	485	4,755	4,764	29,894
1971	19,626	3,123	1,073	1,538	4,302	95	2,825	342	5,071	5,118	32,877
1972	21,940	3,649	1,108	1,759	4,530	78	3,218	−128	5,644	5,238	36,560
1973	25,049	4,236	1,169	2,119	4,376	52	3,400	−322	6,956	5,349	41,686
1974	29,964	5,435	1,338	2,626	5,373	76	3,809	1,638	7,806	7,632	50,433
1975	36,442	7,780	1,432	2,433	6,207	298	5,355	1,021	9,921	10,227	61,789
1976	43,508	9,836	1,616	3,211	7,201	356	6,339	116	11,005	10,831	72,859
1977	49,775	11,493	1,903	4,021	7,976	342	6,825	1,134	13,206	13,788	83,212

Year	A	B	C	D	E	F	G	H	I	J	K
1978	55,170	13,026	2,090	3,872	8,970	341	7,671	−468	13,979	15,008	90,329
1979	62,168	14,315	2,432	4,060	11,109	276	7,964	1,263	16,502	17,784	102,565
1980	70,108	16,095	2,613	4,862	11,415	281	8,682	691	21,502	20,918	115,667
1981	79,337	18,931	3,224	6,104	15,210	364	9,953	251	22,003	24,749	131,805

Sources: Butlin 1977: *Australian National Accounts, National Income and Eenditure, 1982/83* (ABS cat. no. 5204.0).

Table 4. *National income: main expenditure aggregates at constant 1966/7 prices, 1900/1–1980/1 (million dollars)*

Year: Financial years ending June 30 (i.e. 1901 = 1900/1)
A = Private consumption
B = Public consumption, including defence
C = Fixed capital formation, private dwelling
D = Fixed capital formation, private nondwelling
E = Fixed capital formation, public dwelling
F = Fixed capital formation, public nondwelling
G = Change in stocks
H = Exports
I = Imports
J = Gross domestic product

Year	A	B	C	D	E	F	G	H	I	J
1901	2,298	232	88	134	0	243	−8	710	548	3,150
1902	2,404	271	178	169	0	285	70	638	547	3,469
1903	2,460	240	133	164	0	276	−83	577	524	3,242
1904	2,588	255	116	143	0	195	177	639	500	3,613
1905	2,632	291	132	136	0	188	−24	712	514	3,552
1906	2,620	304	142	152	0	186	93	743	526	3,713
1907	2,975	337	168	217	0	197	134	791	583	4,236
1908	2,863	314	149	192	0	242	−29	801	620	3,912
1909	2,871	307	134	182	0	294	121	803	647	4,064
1910	2,956	299	150	190	0	317	200	892	709	4,297
1911	3,296	316	167	217	0	383	130	965	790	4,685
1912	3,369	336	188	234	0	440	13	932	896	4,616
1913	3,583	367	238	242	7	476	190	919	947	5,076
1914	3,536	430	250	257	7	479	107	914	868	5,112
1915	3,329	567	218	129	7	447	−167	757	782	4,505
1916	3,296	1,080	159	116	7	345	197	723	902	5,021
1917	2,839	1,508	126	155	0	258	−71	856	804	4,867
1918	2,856	1,394	115	130	0	201	5	692	609	4,784
1919	3,110	1,044	148	201	0	241	73	773	696	4,893
1920	3,219	491	147	236	42	328	−185	920	576	4,624
1921	3,510	421	128	270	68	374	460	789	765	5,255
1922	3,526	445	192	308	23	453	96	1,072	581	5,534
1923	3,959	551	270	301	18	479	148	885	891	5,720
1924	4,476	518	298	312	22	517	121	734	1,055	5,943
1925	4,650	516	294	298	17	569	265	838	1,117	6,331
1926	4,716	502	306	283	9	579	−104	968	1,115	6,144
1927	4,931	513	333	270	13	623	44	947	1,271	6,404
1928	4,846	527	343	257	13	634	0	904	1,178	6,347
1929	4,714	558	298	263	13	603	7	1,030	1,262	6,225
1930	4,999	498	216	177	9	603	73	935	1,194	6,315
1931	4,047	461	115	170	0	443	−58	1,149	607	5,720
1932	4,038	500	73	130	0	324	−10	1,266	504	5,817
1933	4,387	506	125	129	0	362	24	1,324	692	6,166

Year	A	B	C	D	E	F	G	H	I	J
1934	4,609	580	142	183	0	379	57	1,199	752	6,396
1935	4,581	643	180	253	0	480	−32	1,348	914	6,539
1936	5,019	670	227	269	0	504	−35	1,259	1,040	6,873
1937	5,156	640	248	276	5	557	21	1,295	1,103	7,095
1938	5,276	659	274	359	4	619	215	1,434	1,291	7,549
1939	4,793	737	277	414	4	572	24	1,578	1,152	7,247
1940	4,515	1,246	236	464	0	506	301	1,600	1,223	7,645
1941	4,476	2,337	193	358	0	392	54	1,518	1,109	8,218
1942	4,612	3,438	117	252	0	279	121	1,638	1,034	9,423
1943	4,261	5,018	41	215	0	188	−190	1,568	857	10,244
1944	4,077	4,375	28	242	0	194	−240	2,118	672	10,122
1945	4,645	3,638	39	212	0	214	−258	1,698	651	9,537
1946	4,791	2,358	81	506	0	266	277	1,591	727	9,143
1947	5,676	1,144	180	625	48	468	395	1,350	1,020	8,866
1948	6,335	1,105	255	681	65	549	465	1,348	1,220	9,583
1949	6,968	1,127	337	798	77	634	105	1,431	1,421	10,056
1950	7,445	1,229	398	936	87	836	115	1,550	1,724	10,872
1951	7,669	1,397	505	1,131	105	1,067	212	1,468	2,055	11,499
1952	7,625	1,600	535	1,145	115	1,204	614	1,332	2,334	11,836
1953	7,458	1,669	497	1,042	83	1,091	−419	1,669	1,347	11,744
1954	8,042	1,532	516	1,240	96	1,075	151	1,587	1,755	12,483
1955	8,735	1,575	542	1,379	86	1,144	229	1,672	2,135	13,227
1956	8,965	1,606	·530	1,496	79	1,143	306	1,789	2,022	13,892
1957	9,024	1,615	527	1,522	51	1,170	−56	2,038	1,726	14,165
1958	9,460	1,629	590	1,567	41	1,224	70	1,782	1,897	14,467
1959	9,722	1,765	643	1,564	49	1,320	316	2,114	1,952	15,541
1960	10,650	1,725	716	1,757	36	1,436	200	2,230	2,381	16,370
1961	10,722	1,776	751	1,922	34	1,453	554	2,379	2,684	16,907
1962	10,880	1,881	673	1,891	52	1,561	−251	2,684	2,292	17,080
1963	11,514	1,956	739	2,093	42	1,619	287	2,670	2,698	18,221
1964	12,208	2,050	844	2,315	48	1,740	138	3,113	2,986	19,469
1965	12,908	2,230	973	2,617	49	1,940	609	3,105	3,574	20,856
1966	13,193	2,521	939	2,818	66	2,080	110	3,142	3,666	21,202
1967	13,702	2,709	991	2,838	65	2,107	367	3,477	3,711	22,545
1968	14,451	2,916	1,079	2,976	68	2,221	134	3,682	4,151	23,376
1969	15,281	3,037	1,226	3,233	64	2,288	629	3,979	4,272	25,465
1970	16,255	3,096	1,352	3,321	80	2,353	437	4,746	4,708	26,932
1971	16,877	3,229	1,332	3,646	82	2,367	293	5,164	4,865	28,124
1972	17,725	3,274	1,417	3,589	63	2,532	−102	5,512	4,762	29,248
1973	19,236	3,421	1,575	3,314	39	2,476	−236	5,730	4,948	30,606
1974	20,609	3,685	1,624	3,752	46	2,448	1,051	5,489	6,355	32,350
1975	20,662	4,081	1,195	3,650	147	2,718	501	5,506	5,829	33,304
1976	21,340	4,408	1,361	3,081	158	2,783	27	5,682	5,562	34,179
1977	21,878	4,643	1,519	3,069	133	2,691	392	6,128	6,107	35,206
1978	22,138	4,860	1,379	3,088	125	2,784	−195	6,237	5,867	35,358
1979	22,874	5,061	1,404	3,475	97	2,699	438	6,365	6,371	37,052

Table 4. *(cont.)*

Year	A	B	C	D	E	F	G	H	I	J
1980	23,536	5,160	1,558	3,242	91	2,622	175	7,254	6,332	38,015
1981	24,342	5,440	1,748	3,938	104	2,681	95	6,891	6,892	39,425

Sources: Butlin 1977; *Australian National Accounts, National Income and Expenditure, 1982/83* (ABS cat. no. 5204.0).

Index

Abramovitz, M., 80*n*, 325
advantage, comparative, 7, 9, 13, 27, 33, 133,
  134, 147, 157, 168, 174, 349
agriculture: as proportion of economic activity,
  18–20, 40, 112, 127, 134, 136–7, 139, 142, 143,
  146, 160, 199, 204, 208, 275; assistance to, 15,
  16, 22, 39, 41, 49, 57, 97*n*, 98, 135, 138–40,
  151–3, 304–5; diversification of, 11–12, 39–41,
  101, 133, 137, 139; employment, 27, 40, 41, 55,
  135, 137, 138, 140, 142, 153, 156–7, 162, 163,
  183, 198, 199–200, 202, 207–9, 259–60, 263,
  275; farm units, 11, 25, 135–6, 140, 142, 153;
  income, 135–6, 138, 142–3, 148, 156, 157, 183;
  investment in, 41, 55, 87, 101, 138, 139, 149,
  151–3, 162, 230–1, 233, 236, 238, 240; policy,
  15, 33, 39, 101, 133, 135, 137, 138–40, 142,
  150–3, 157–8; prices, 15, 74, 138, 139, 142, 143,
  145, 149, 157; production, 25–6, 127, 133, 137,
  138, 139, 140, 142, 163, 199, 204, 208; protection, 55, 142, 148, 183, 187, 189; technology, 6,
  10, 25, 27, 39, 101, 135, 137, 139–40, 149–53;
  see also exports
Aitkin, D.A., 259, 349
America, *see* United States
Anderson, Karl, 182*n*
Anderson, Kym, 101, 165*n*, 172, 186*n*, 189,
  349, 350
Anderssen, W.E., 174*n*
Anstie, R.K., 120
arbitration and conciliation, 248–50, 255, 268–9,
  270–2, 274–7, 280, 283, 348; Commonwealth
  Court, 13, 54, 55–6, 72, 94*n*, 114, 252–5, 258,
  269; *see also* wages
Argentina, 6, 8, 64, 199–201, 202, 204, 258,
  341, 347, 349
Arndt, H.W., 177, 187
Atkinson, A.B., 331*n*
Auld, D.A., 90
Australian Council of Trade Unions (ACTU),
  127, 253–4
Australian Labor Party, 48, 54, 93, 95, 98, 127,
  156, 173, 175, 188, 243, 249, 253, 266, 279,
  281, 307–9
Australian Science and Technology Council, 150

Baker, D., 40
Bailey, C., 162
Bairoch, P., 203*n*
balance of payments, 11, 53, 67, 69–70, 76, 99,
  100, 101, 102, 151, 153, 306; under protection, 177, 183, 184–5, 187

Balassa, B., 187*n*
Baldwin, R.E., 181*n*
Bambrick, S., 57
Bank of New South Wales, 121, 235, 240
banking, 12–13, 45–6, 71, 93, 229–42, 307; deregulation of, 126, 243–5; legislation, 232,
  241, 243–5; policies, 232–3, 234–5, 240–1,
  244; Royal Commission (1936), 93, 240–1,
  243, 245, 246; SRDs, 243–4
banks: agricultural, 39, 230–1; central, 45, 93,
  94, 232, 241, 313; merchant, 232, 233, 244–5;
  savings, 230, 232–3, 235–39, 242, 244, 245,
  246; trading, 45–6, 49, 229–30, 232, 233, 235,
  237, 238–40, 242, 243
Barnard, A., 1, 22, 23*n*, 79*n*, 195*n*, 206, 210*n*,
  212, 259, 260, 296, 298*n*, 311, 339*n*, 345
Barry, P., 119
Bauer, P.T., 219*n*
Baumol, W.J., 219*n*
Becker, G.S., 219*n*
Benham, F.C., 180*n*, 182*n*
Berry, M.J., 332
Bland, F.A., 44
Blandy, R., 271
Blinder, A.S., 339
Boehm, E.A., 1, 4, 12*n*, 18*n*, 34, 62*n*, 68–9, 71,
  74, 79*n*, 116, 124, 166, 172, 291, 320*n*, 323*n*,
  345
Boertlein, C.G., 348*n*
boom, postwar, 20, 25–6, 38, 79, 96–102, 106,
  112–13, 283; causes, 80–4; demand and sup-
  ply, 79, 83, 84–92, 97, 101, 111, 121; invest-
  ment, 24–5, 82, 83, 86–9, 94, 96, 111–12, 124,
  129, 151, 241–5, 311–12
booms, 2, 10, 24, 35, 97, 124, 126, 129; mining,
  10–12, 20, 101, 107, 112, 123–4, 125, 134,
  140–2, 146, 165, 172, 174, 231, 242, 253; pastoral, 9–11; property, 12, 230
Borrie, W.D., 182*n*
Boschan, C., 269
Brash, D.T., 88
Bray, G., 269
Brennan, G., 299
Bretton Woods agreement (1944), 80, 97
Brigden, J.B., 54, 158, 165*n*, 180*n*, 181–3
Britain: Australia's relationship with, 5–6, 7, 11,
  13, 15, 33, 44, 46, 91, 96, 176, 263, 300–1, 309,
  310; capital market, 6, 7, 11, 12, 24, 42, 44, 51–
  3, 64, 99, 234; employment, 6, 56, 64, 97, 199–
  200, 202, 206, 256, 257, 259, 267, 273, 274,
  295–6; growth rate, 6, 7, 38, 107, 204, 209, 224,

365